REIMAGINING CHILD SOLDIERS
IN INTERNATIONAL LAW AND POLICY

Reimagining Child Soldiers in International Law and Policy

MARK A. DRUMBL

Class of 1975 Alumni Professor of Law
Director, Transnational Law Institute
Washington and Lee University

OXFORD
UNIVERSITY PRESS

Great Clarendon Street, Oxford OX2 6DP

Oxford University Press is a department of the University of Oxford.
It furthers the University's objective of excellence in research, scholarship,
and education by publishing worldwide in

Oxford New York

Auckland Cape Town Dar es Salaam Hong Kong Karachi
Kuala Lumpur Madrid Melbourne Mexico City Nairobi
New Delhi Shanghai Taipei Toronto

With offices in

Argentina Austria Brazil Chile Czech Republic France Greece
Guatemala Hungary Italy Japan Poland Portugal Singapore
South Korea Switzerland Thailand Turkey Ukraine Vietnam

Oxford is a registered trade mark of Oxford University Press
in the UK and in certain other countries

Published in the United States
by Oxford University Press Inc., New York

British Library Cataloguing in Publication Data

Data available

Library of Congress Cataloging in Publication Data

Data available

Typeset by SPI Publisher Services, Pondicherry, India
Printed in Great Britain
on acid-free paper by
Clays Ltd, St Ives plc

ISBN 978–0–19–959265–4 (Hbk)
978–0–19–959266–1 (Pbk)

1 3 5 7 9 10 8 6 4 2

*Dedicated to youth and communities forging
better futures from bitter pasts.*

Preface and Acknowledgements

The international community strives to eradicate the scourge of child soldiering. Mostly, though, these efforts replay the same narratives and circulate the same assumptions.

This book takes a second look at these efforts. It aspires to refresh law and policy so as to improve preventative, restorative, and remedial initiatives while also vivifying the dignity of youth. Along the way, this book also questions central tenets of contemporary humanitarianism, rethinks elements of international criminal justice, and hopes to embolden the rights of the child.

The organizational framework is straightforward. Chapter 1 broaches the issues, sets out dominant assumptions, and provides a quick overview of the central arguments. Chapters 2 and 3 introduce a diversity of accounts of the realities of child soldiering that, to date, have been inadequately considered by international lawyers and policymakers. These Chapters are descriptive in that they present these accounts. They also are synthetic in that they interpretively distil common themes and, thereby, build a composite. These Chapters also are analytic in that they lay a foundation for the normative arguments that ensue. Chapters 4 and 5 transition the book to international law and policy. These Chapters respectively address two themes: first, accountability *of* child soldiers and, second, accountability *for* child soldiering. These Chapters examine law and policy as they are and, much more importantly, the direction in which both are heading. Chapters 6 and 7 then suggest a variety of reforms to the content and trajectory of law and policy in light of the complex realities of child soldiering. International lawyers and policymakers are predisposed to dissemble these complexities. Although understandable, this penchant ultimately is counterproductive.

This book extensively discusses research conducted and published by a broad range of scholars and practitioners, who pursue diverse methodologies, including surveys, participant observation, and qualitative studies. Extensive citations supplement this book's discussion of this dynamic body of research. This means that some sections of this book are heavily footnoted. My purpose is for this discussion to assist readers by serving a compilation and reference function. As an international lawyer with an interest in political transitions from episodes of systematic human rights abuses, I draw from this research, which originates outside of the legal academy, to interrogate the content of law and policy. On the one hand, the fact that this book draws from and synthesizes the work of others can be taken to be a limitation. Readers will not find in these pages new on-the-ground data that I personally have collected or heterodox experiences that I personally have encountered. On the other hand, this approach offers considerable advantages. It permits this book to transcend the *micro* and energize a discussion at a cross-national, interdisciplinary, and "big picture" panoptic level. Pivoting off this "big picture," this book urges reform through a dynamic process of critique and renewal. It aims to build upon and enhance the efforts of global civil society, international lawmakers, and UN agencies.

So many people have helped and inspired me. I thank Kokouvi Luc Dodzi Akakpo, Cécile Aptel, Robert John Araujo, Ronald Atkinson, Olympia Bekou, Susan Benesch, Johanna Bond, Christopher Bruner, Naomi Cahn, Cynthia Chamberlain, Roxana Cimpeanu, Nancy Combs, David Crane, Rob Cryer, Beth Dougherty, Susan Franck, Steven Freeland, Ken Gallant, Tom Ginsburg, Larry Helfer, Tim Jost, Dan Joyner, Linda Keller, Rick Kirgis, Brandon Kohrt, Erik Luna, Tim MacDonnell, Larry May, Nesam Mcmillan, Jens Meierhenrich, Martin Mennecke, Russ Miller, David Millon, Sarah Nouwen, Mark Osiel, Di Otto, Kim Lane Scheppele, Penelope Simons, Rob Sloane, Chris Slobogin, Alette Smeulers, Barry Sullivan, Scott Sundby, Immi Tallgren, Tim Waters, Harvey Weinstein, Mike Wessells, Bert Westbrook, and three anonymous reviewers for instructive comments and encouragement. I am very appreciative to John Louth, Merel Alstein, and Beth Cousins at OUP for the enthusiasm and thought they have invested in this project.

This book grew from workshops held at a variety of universities, including Alabama, Arkansas, the Australian National University, Beloit, Bond, Cornell, Georgia, Loyola-Chicago, McGill, Melbourne, Monash, Ottawa, Queen's, Sydney, Vanderbilt, the VU Amsterdam, Washington and Lee, Windsor, and Yale. Participants in each of these workshops provided invaluable feedback. I also appreciate comments generated at two sessions of the International Studies Association Annual Meetings in New York and Montréal, as well as the University of South Carolina's Conference on Rebuilding Sierra Leone.

This book would not have been possible without the unflagging support of my home institution, Washington and Lee University, and the wonderful people with whom I have the privilege of working. Linda Newell unflappably tracked down more sources than I ever could count. Diane Cochran delivered critical administrative and moral support. Dori Hamilton admirably handled my technophobia. Through the generosity of the Frances Lewis Law Center, Michael Baudinet, Joanna Heiberg, Lisa Markman, Christine Shepard, and Scott Weingart were able to provide absolutely stellar editing and research assistance. They went well beyond the call of duty with aplomb, inventiveness, and determination. I also thank Pakapon Phinyowattanachip, Mark Sullivan, and Christopher Zona for their hard work. Any errors in the text are my own.

Much of this book was written in Australia while I was on sabbatical leave in 2010. During this precious time, I had the joy of being Visiting Scholar and Senior Fellow at the University of Melbourne, School of Law; Parsons Visitor at the University of Sydney, School of Law; and Visiting Professor at the Centre for Applied Philosophy and Public Ethics on the campus of the Australian National University in Canberra. Without the inspiration and friendship of Kevin Jon Heller, this visit would not have happened. I remain deeply in his debt. In addition, Tom Campbell, Hilary Charlesworth, Mark Findlay, David Kinley, Larry May, and Gerry Simpson—among many others—deserve great thanks for their kindness in hosting me, and my family, for such a wonderful experience.

Nothing in my life would ever be possible without the patience, support, joy, laughter, and grace of my beautiful wife Michelle and our delightfully inspiring sons Paul and Luke. I owe so much to them. I also thank my parents. They always are there for me, and now us, like sunshine.

Scattered parts of Chapters 3 and 5 herein are materially updated, with permission, from my essay *Child Soldiers: Agency, Enlistment, and the Collectivization of Innocence*, *in* COLLECTIVE VIOLENCE AND INTERNATIONAL CRIMINAL JUSTICE: AN INTERDISCIPLINARY APPROACH 207–231 (Alette Smeulers, ed., Intersentia, 2010). Adaptations reflect the evolution of my thoughts, emergence of new research, and recent developments. Seven short paragraphs in Chapter 7(i) herein are adapted from discussion at pages 187–194 of my first book, ATROCITY, PUNISHMENT, AND INTERNATIONAL LAW (Cambridge University Press, 2007).

Table of Contents

Abbreviations

AFRC	Armed Forces Revolutionary Council
AUC	Autodefensas Unidas de Colombia
CAR	Central African Republic
CDF	Civil Defence Forces
CRC	Convention on the Rights of the Child
DDR	Disarmament, demobilization, and reintegration
DRC	Democratic Republic of the Congo
ECCC	Extraordinary Chambers in the Courts of Cambodia
ELN	Ejército de Liberación Nacional
FARC	Fuerzas Armadas Revolucionarias de Colombia
FNI	Front des nationalistes et intégrationnistes
FPLC	Forces patriotiques pour la libération du Congo
FRELIMO	Mozambican Liberation Front (Frente de Libertação de Moçambique)
FRPI	Force de résistance patriotique en Ituri
ICC	International Criminal Court
ICCPR	International Covenant on Civil and Political Rights
ICTR	International Criminal Tribunal for Rwanda
ICTY	International Criminal Tribunal for the former Yugoslavia
IDDRS	Integrated Disarmament, Demobilization and Reintegration Standards
IMT	International Military Tribunal (Nuremberg)
LRA	Lord's Resistance Army
LTTE	Liberation Tigers of Tamil Eelam
NGOs	Non-governmental organizations
NPFL	National Patriotic Front of Liberia
OTP	Office of the Prosecutor (ICC)
PTSD	Post-traumatic Stress Disorder
RENAMO	Mozambican National Resistance (Resistência Nacional Moçambicana)
RPA	Rwandese Patriotic Army
RUF	Revolutionary United Front
SCSL	Special Court for Sierra Leone
SLA	Sierra Leonean Army
STL	Special Tribunal for Lebanon
SWAY	Survey for War Affected Youth
TRC	Truth and reconciliation commission
UN	United Nations
UNICEF	United Nations Children's Fund
UNITA	National Union for the Total Independence of Angola (União Nacional para a Independência Total de Angola)
UNTAET	UN Transitional Administration in East Timor
UPC	Union des patriotes congolais

1

Coming of Age in Atrocity

It is easy to see the child soldier superficially as a contradiction in terms or simply as an anachronism. Neither childhood nor youth, after all, should be about war or weapons. Nonetheless—and however jarring—militarization suffuses the lives of many children.

At the very least, worldwide, tens of thousands of persons below the age of eighteen currently are associated with armed forces or armed groups. Adults who serve in such forces or groups, moreover, may have joined while younger than eighteen. In addition, the past decade has seen the demobilization of many tens of thousands more child soldiers. Although joyful, their return journey to civilian life also is bittersweet. They come back home to the communities where they initially had been recruited—at times, forcibly—and where, in some instances, they had committed terrible atrocities. While associated with armed forces or groups, many child recruits are subject to brutalities, beatings, and rape. Drug and alcohol abuse is common.

International law and policy cover considerable ground in their efforts to eradicate child soldiering and promote the well-being of current and former child soldiers. States adopt treaties and instruments, while also endorsing principles and declarations. Experts issue reports. Organizations draft best practices and "how to" guidelines. Authorities prepare model interventions. Conscripting, enlisting, or using younger children—namely, under the age of fifteen—in hostilities is an international war crime for which adult commanders recently have been convicted. Additional verdicts are imminent, including as regards Charles Taylor, Liberia's former dictator.

Although international interventions have helped reduce specific incidents, the practice of child soldiering still persists. It may shift locally, and abate here and there, but it endures globally. Preventative measures, therefore, remain inadequate. Former child soldiers experience challenges in adjusting to civilian life. Reintegration is complex and eventful. The homecoming is only the beginning. Reconciliation within communities afflicted by violence committed by and against child soldiers is incomplete. Shortfalls linger on the restorative front.

What, then, to do? The reflexive response among international lawyers and transnational policymakers is to hone familiar tools and work them even faster. In practice, this means that humanitarian efforts ramp up the chorus of outrage regarding the plight of child soldiers. These efforts typically highlight themes of vulnerability, frailty, victimization, and incapacity.

The reflexive response is full of good intentions. It is rhetorically compelling. But it is becoming palliative. This book urges lawmakers and policymakers to transcend what passes as conventional wisdom. It encourages them to peer beyond into a more demanding space. The time is right for something new.

Meaningful reform, however, first requires the international community to *reimagine* child soldiers and the sources of child soldiering. This reimaginative exercise, in turn, calls into question habits and expectations that pervade contemporary humanitarianism, the universality of human rights, strategies for juvenile civic engagement, and post-conflict justice. Lessons learned from recent experiences with child soldiering and the improvements that can be made on this front, therefore, weave into a much broader revisionist tapestry.

This book raises a number of admittedly tough questions. Are child soldiers necessarily well served by formulaic stereotypes that no child ever can volunteer to participate in armed forces or armed groups? That all child soldiers are used and none wish to engage in martial activities? That no person under the age of eighteen can commit human rights abuses for reasons other than being cruelly forced to do so? That all conflicts that implicate children are innately senseless? That children associated with armed forces or groups see themselves as victims? As misled? The way international activists conceptualize an issue may morph into a self-fulfilling prophecy that, in turn, fails to concretize optimal programmatic interventions for the intended beneficiaries.

Remedial efforts currently undertaken for former child soldiers accentuate medicalized trauma recovery and psychotherapy. Although taken as obvious, is this emphasis the best way forward? Perhaps readers may be happily surprised to learn that the mental health of former child soldiers may be less precarious and more robust than commonly believed. Hence, programmatic interventions ought to include more in the way of economic, educational, justice, and occupational efforts. Readers also may be surprised to learn that many child soldiers exit fighting factions not by way of humanitarian rescue but, rather, entirely on their own by dint of personal initiative. They escape. Or they abandon the armed force or group once they grow weary of militarized life or begin to see the futility in the putative cause for which they are fighting. In short, rescue is less common than conventional wisdom may suppose, while escape is more common.

How to effectively sanction commanders who conscript, enlist, or use children in hostilities? For the moment, entities that finance, fund, or arm groups and forces that deploy children largely fall below the radar screen. How can this blind spot be addressed? Some child soldiers are implicated in grievous acts of atrocity. Should transitional justice mechanisms be considered for them? For reasons this book sets out, criminal trials are ill-fitting in this regard. But is there not room to be more creative about engineering justice such that it involves more than just courtrooms and jailhouses? In the case of child soldiers, it is not axiomatically wise to eschew accountability conversations. Accountability measures other than criminal trials— such as truth commissions and traditional ceremonies—may facilitate reintegration, rehabilitation, restoration, and reparation. In the long-term, shielding juveniles from law's obligations while conferring upon them law's beneficent protectiveness might not durably anchor them as rights-bearers.

If some children join armed forces or groups for social, economic, or political reasons, does treating them as passive or incompetent address their grievances? Is it helpful to downplay how the child entered militarized life, whether by abduction, voluntary enlistment, or because he or she was born into the armed group? Are policies that eliminate distinctions among the roles that child soldiers perform during conflict necessarily wise? At present, girl soldiers are consistently under-served by post-conflict programming. So, too, are children who are born into armed groups. What about the many children—and adults—who did not associate with armed groups but were aggrieved by the conduct of children who did? What does justice mean for them?

However embedded, perceptions of the victim status of child soldiers remain somewhat contingent upon the nationality of those persons injured by their conduct. Child soldiers who commit violence—for example, terrorist attacks—against Western targets are seen less like deluded children and more like menacing adults. On a related note, how does the West treat child soldiers affiliated with armed factions who, following their decommissioning, may seek refugee status within its borders? What actions by Western states may abet child soldiering? As this book unpacks, law and policy do not always apply consistently. Their forward trajectory may ebb and flow depending on state power and politics.

(i) Defining the Terms

Who, exactly, is a child soldier? A standardized—and increasingly legalized—definition has emerged, in large part through two major international conferences. The first, which was held in Cape Town in 1997, focused on the demobilization and social reintegration of child soldiers in Africa. A follow-up conference was convened in Paris in 2007. Co-hosted by the United Nations Children's Fund (UNICEF) and the French government, this event was of a larger scale and global orientation. It included representatives of fifty-eight states along with many key stakeholders.

The Cape Town and Paris conferences each led to the adoption of non-binding instruments that have since obtained widespread professional, operational, and political currency. The initial development and subsequent circulation of these influential instruments owes much to the involvement of non-governmental orga-nizations (NGOs), United Nations (UN) agencies, donors, and activists. This constellation of actors also has sensitized a global public through media outreach, film, and literature.

These instruments include as child soldiers much more than only those persons younger than eighteen who carry weapons, engage in combat, or who take (or have taken) a direct part in hostilities. Also included are children used for auxiliary activities (for example, portering, spying, and cooking) and children forced into sexual servitude. The impetus among policymakers is to discourage distinctions from being drawn between children who serve as combatants and children who do not or who do so only incidentally. One motivation in this regard is to ensure inclusiveness toward both girl and boy soldiers. Accordingly, and responsively, official nomenclature has drifted away from *child soldier* as initially set out and defined in the Cape Town Principles.[1] The move is now toward the somewhat tongue-tying *children associated with armed forces or armed groups*, defined in the Paris Principles to cover:

Any person below 18 years of age who is or who has been recruited or used by an armed force or armed group in any capacity, including but not limited to children, boys, and girls used as fighters, cooks, porters, messengers, spies or for sexual purposes. It does not only refer to a child who is taking or has taken a direct part in hostilities.[2]

Whereas *armed forces* refer to official state militaries, *armed groups* refer to non-state entities distinct from those forces (notably, rebel or protest movements, dissident factions, and insurgents).

Notwithstanding some differences between the Cape Town and Paris definitions, both still share considerable textual overlap regarding the actual persons they protect. Experts often become ensnared in debates over terms and titles.[3] Terminology matters, to be sure, but debates over it may devolve into distractions. For reasons of convenience and brevity, this book primarily uses the term *child soldiers*, but understands its definitional scope as based on the 2007 Paris Principles. This book, furthermore, understands the determination of who is considered a child soldier to arise not at the point of exit from militarized life, but at the point of entry. Hence, a *former child soldier* is a person who was initially associated with armed forces or armed groups while under the age of eighteen, even if he or she is eighteen or older at the time of release, demobilization, escape, or rescue.

At its very core, settled international law makes it unlawful to recruit or use anyone under the age of fifteen in armed forces or armed groups. Actors and activists push to discard fifteen and replace it across-the-board with eighteen.[4] This push actuates the Straight 18 advocacy position. As this book sets out,

---

[1] Cape Town Principles and Best Practices (April 27–30, 1997) (definitions), *available at* <http://www.unicef.org/emerg/files/Cape_Town_Principles(1).pdf> (a child soldier is "any person under 18 years of age who is part of any kind of regular or irregular armed force or armed group in any capacity, including but not limited to cooks, porters, messengers and anyone accompanying such groups, other than family members;" and explicitly including girls recruited for sexual purposes and forced marriage; and affirming that the definition "does not, therefore, only refer to a child who is carrying or has carried arms") [hereinafter Cape Town Principles].

[2] The Paris Principles: Principles and Guidelines on Children Associated with Armed Forces or Armed Groups (February 2007), Prin. 2.1, *available at* <http://www.child-soldiers.org/childsoldiers/Paris_Principles_March_2007.pdf> [hereinafter Paris Principles]. As of September 2010, ninety-five states have endorsed the Paris Commitments, which the Paris Principles accompany.

[3] Yet another term of art circulated by experts is "children associated with fighting forces."

[4] For example, UNICEF "joins other organizations, child rights advocates and NGOs in advocating a 'straight 18 ban' on all recruitment, compulsory or voluntary and participation of children under 18 in hostilities." UNICEF, ADULT WARS, CHILD SOLDIERS: VOICES OF CHILDREN INVOLVED IN ARMED CONFLICT IN THE EAST ASIA AND PACIFIC REGION 12 (2002); *see also* Human Rights Watch, SOLD TO BE SOLDIERS: THE RECRUITMENT AND USE OF CHILD SOLDIERS IN BURMA 14 (2007) (calling on the Burmese government to cease recruiting and to demobilize children younger than eighteen from armed forces,

international law has absorbed many of the aspirations of the Straight 18 position. Armed groups, for example, are barred from recruiting anyone younger than eighteen. International law treats state armed forces more ambiguously. This means that international law has not yet absorbed every aspiration of the Straight 18 position. However, international law's trend-line arcs toward the Straight 18 horizon. Accordingly, much of settled law has become dated, if not stale, and is becoming increasingly so. The Straight 18 position has considerable momentum and portends what will be. Its advocacy efforts have exercised even greater influence in shaping transnational policy initiatives, best practices, and persuasive authority such as the commitments and principles emerging from the Cape Town and Paris processes.[5]

As recently as 2008, it was estimated that military recruitment of children and their use in hostilities "still takes place in one form or another in at least 86 countries and territories worldwide."[6] Accordingly, this book considers evidence from an array of jurisdictions. Although many child soldiers are found within the ranks of armed groups, state actors also incorporate children into armed forces. Burma (Myanmar) is presently the largest state recruiter of child soldiers. Subject to a variety of conditions, persons under the age of eighteen may voluntarily enlist in armed forces and reserves in a number of countries, albeit a minority overall, including Australia, Bangladesh, Canada, China, Germany, India, the Netherlands, the United Kingdom, and the United States. In addition, this book examines recent and ongoing evidence of child soldiering in armed forces or armed groups in Afghanistan, Angola, Cambodia, Colombia, Democratic Republic of the Congo (DRC), Indonesia, Liberia, Libya, Mozambique, Nepal, Papua New Guinea, Philippines, Sierra Leone, Sri Lanka, Sudan, Rwanda, Timor-Leste, and Uganda.

The focus of this book tilts toward the involvement of child soldiers in atrocity-producing conflicts, particularly conflicts in which international courts and tribunals indict (and, in some instances, are able to prosecute and punish) alleged offenders. Several recent conflicts that have become internationally judicialized situate in Africa, to wit, the DRC, Uganda, Rwanda, Sudan, and Sierra Leone. A number of these jurisdictions, moreover, have undertaken ambitious programmatic initiatives to reintegrate former child soldiers. So, too, have some jurisdictions whose atrocity-producing conflicts have not formally become subject to international judicialization efforts. Liberia is a case-in-point. Consequently, this book is more about child soldiering in African states than it is about child soldiering elsewhere. In this regard, this book entwines with my own experiences with international justice which also, starting with my legal work in Rwanda over a

and also to "[d]evelop and impose effective and appropriate sanctions against individuals found to be recruiting children under 18 into the armed forces").

[5] The term "best practices" (also, "good practices") initially arose within corporate planning and has now entered the lexicon of domestic and international administrative law. Best practices are not formally binding rules. They refer to consensually agreed upon regulatory measures and processes, often informal in nature, that over time crystallize into preferential models. Because of their iterated use and replication, best practices acquire a quasi-legal character.

[6] Coalition to Stop the Use of Child Soldiers, CHILD SOLDIERS GLOBAL REPORT 2008 12 (2008).

decade ago, center on Africa. Persons who were minors at the time of allegedly committing acts of genocide were among the suspects I assisted in the Kigali prison. My choice to focus on child soldiers in Africa is not intended to dilute the reality that child soldiering truly is a global phenomenon. To be clear, only a plurality—reportedly, about 40%—of the global number of child soldiers is located on the African continent. When responding to Africa, transnational narratives often sensationalize and objectify through intemperate depictions, distorted lenses, and paternalistic hues.[7] My aim is to transcend these pernicious impulses and the half-truths that emerge from them; and to resist tiresome tendencies that Africanize a global phenomenon and pathologize African conflicts.

More boys than girls are represented in the subgroup of child soldiers who commit acts of atrocity. One of my goals is to emphasize that these children can return to civilian life and can integrate within the community. Consequently, this book comes to talk more about boy soldiers than it does about girl soldiers. This book does incorporate considerable data regarding girl soldiers, however, whose roles in communal violence are considerably more complex than may prosaically be assumed. Moreover, my recommended policy reforms would diversify post-conflict programming. They would accord greater centrality to initiatives specific to girl soldiers and implement a gender-sensitive approach.

In what remains of this first Chapter, I introduce core concepts and evidence. I also foreshadow the book's trajectory.

(ii) Images of Child Soldiers

Transnational discourse typifies child soldiers in a variety of images. These portraits communicate easily with the public, but Myriam Denov is right to point out that they also inordinately simplify the complex lives and experiences of child soldiers.[8] In this regard, I would add, these images may poorly serve their subjects.

One image is that of a very young child—a guileless naïf—hued as clueless and dependent. This image telescopes the child soldier as a helpless object manipulated locally by adult malevolence, yet at the same time to be rescued transnationally by adult humanitarianism. It portrays child soldiers as forced into service, forced to

---

[7] Referencing the Lord's Resistance Army (LRA), a notorious rebel group in Northern Uganda, Ben Mergelsberg notes: "The narrative of the LRA abducting young, innocent children, brainwashing them and forcing them to fight is common in the media. It evokes a generalized image of the child soldier as a vulnerable innocent without any agency, brutally abducted, drugged and turned into a monster." Ben Mergelsberg, *Between two worlds: former LRA soldiers in northern Uganda, in* THE LORD'S RESISTANCE ARMY: MYTH AND REALITY 156, 156 (Tim Allen and Koen Vlassenroot eds, 2010). Mergelsberg, however, adds that: "[T]he view of helpless children without agency in what has happened to them often does not correspond to their actual experiences. Passive victims on first sight, they turned out during my fieldwork to be active survivors with a good sense of why they were fighting, how they survived and what they needed most after their return." *Id.* at 156–157.

[8] Myriam Denov, CHILD SOLDIERS: SIERRA LEONE'S REVOLUTIONARY UNITED FRONT 5–14 (2010) (elegantly discussing portrayals and representations of the child soldier, which she chides for their extremism and exoticism).

fight, and forced to kill. Its visuals are of deranged militias that steal children from their families and tear them from their communities. In the hands of such militias, these children become neutered mechanical means used to fulfill nefarious ends over which they have no input. They are no more than "instruments of war" and "the weapon of choice."[9] In another influential account, that of distinguished human rights activist Roméo Dallaire, child soldiers are portrayed as an "end-to-end weapon system" and as "tools;" what is more, children "are vulnerable and easy to catch, just like minnows in a pond," with the involved adults depicted as "evil."[10] This image melds with and, in turn, disseminates a narrative—now transposed into law and policy—through which child soldiers are construed first and foremost as victims. In terms of on-the-ground practice, however, the conceptual understanding of child soldiers principally as victims tends toward operational interventions that essentialize their victimhood. This first image, therefore, typifies the child soldier as a *faultless passive victim*.

A second image, which harmonizes with the victim narrative, is that of child soldiers as *irreparable damaged goods*. Pursuant to this image, child soldiers are tormented and scarred. They form part of a "lost generation."[11] This image captures the pain of militarized life and the concomitant physical and emotional injuries. Yet it does so at the cost of overlooking the resilience of former child soldiers and children in war zones generally. This depiction defines expectations and sets parameters. Constructions of the child soldier as psychologically devastated and pilfered by conflict, for example, have spurred the preeminence of trauma recovery models in post-conflict programming.

A third image—somewhat antiquated, yet still in circulation—posits the child soldier as a *hero*, whose valor flows from fighting for a just cause that resists oppression or from demonstrating patriotism.[12] In contradistinction to the faultless passive victim image, the hero image plays up the independence, conviction, nobility, and enterprise of the child soldier. This portrayal also may venerate military service, however, and feed into pernicious norms of masculinity and hyper-aggression. It can lead to a parlous situation for the unpopular side. In Timor-Leste, for example, "children who fought on the side of independence

---

[9] Olara Otunnu, *Keynote Address: The Convention and children in situations of armed conflict, in* CHILDREN IN EXTREME SITUATIONS, Working Paper Series No. 00–05, LSE Development Studies Institute 48, 49 (Lisa Carlson, Megan Mackeson-Sandbach, and Tim Allen eds, 2000), *available at* <http://www2.lse.ac.uk/internationalDevelopment//pdf/WP05.pdf>. Otunnu, an eminent public servant, served as the UN Special Representative for Children and Armed Conflict from 1997 to 2005.

[10] Roméo Dallaire, THEY FIGHT LIKE SOLDIERS, THEY DIE LIKE CHILDREN 3, 12, 15, 150 (2010) (also referring to former child soldiers as "immature souls in small bodies"). Dallaire, now a Senator in Canada, is well known for his outspoken role as commander of the UN Assistance Mission for Rwanda during the country's 1994 genocide. He recently has oriented his efforts to eradicating child soldiering. To this end, he founded the Child Soldiers Initiative.

[11] P.W. Singer, CHILDREN AT WAR 38, 44 (2006).

[12] Denov, *supra* note 8, at 9–10 (noting also the celebrity status of some high-profile child soldiers viewed as heroically transcending from violence to redemption).

were considered heroes [while] [t]hose who fought on the opposing side were stigmatized, and some were later targeted."[13]

A final image dramatically appears in journalistic accounts, political grandstanding, and national security circles. This image stylizes the child soldier as *demon and bandit*: irredeemable, baleful, and sinister. Pursuant to this depiction, the child soldier is a ticking time-bomb, bad seed, and warped soul incorrigibly determined to kill with alacrity.[14] This flawed image comports with two alarming policy outputs. The first is the pointlessness of investing in the rehabilitation of former child soldiers. The second is the neglect of girl soldiers. The demon and bandit image, after all, tends to present child soldiers as wild boys, which clouds the reality that "[a]s many as 40 percent of child soldiers may be girls."[15] Girl soldiers already are poorly served by extant programming that underappreciates the specific gender-based reintegrative challenges they face. The demon image piles onto these challenges, many of which involve recovery from abhorrent sexual violence and forced marriage. Many girls give birth while associated with armed forces or groups. Rates of HIV, AIDS, and sexually transmitted diseases are high. Upon cessation of hostilities, it is not uncommon for local communities to marginalize these young mothers and view their children with repugnance. Insofar as the fathers of these children (at times themselves teenagers) may have been abusive fighters and unit commanders, the "bad seed" may be perceived by communities as passing down intergenerationally. Girl soldiers, assuredly, are not an indiscriminate group of interchangeable members. Girls who become "wives" of commanders exert power over girls without "husbands." This latter group, in turn, comes to suffer even greater levels of sexual abuse. Some girls commit terrible acts of atrocity against other girls, boys, women, and men. The demon and bandit image also obscures the fact that boys, too, are sexually abused.

These four images are not equals. Hierarchy and ordinality can be theorized among them with regard to their operational influence in shaping official policies and sculpting conventional wisdom.

The faultless passive victim image has achieved widespread traction within—and is avidly disseminated by—influential intergovernmental organizations and UN agencies, along with NGOs and other actors that populate global civil society.[16] It has consequently come to dominate international discourse. The faultless passive

---

[13] UNICEF Innocenti Research Centre in cooperation with the International Center for Transitional Justice, CHILDREN AND TRUTH COMMISSIONS 47 (2010) (citation omitted) [hereinafter CHILDREN AND TRUTH COMMISSIONS].

[14] Denov, *supra* note 8, at 6; *see also* Christopher Blattman and Jeannie Annan, *The Consequences of Child Soldiering*, 92(4) REVIEW OF ECONOMICS AND STATISTICS 882, 882 (2010) (reporting on and critiquing the use of this imagery); Michael Wessells, CHILD SOLDIERS: FROM VIOLENCE TO PROTECTION 45 (2006, first paperback 2009) (noting that "this portrayal contradicts much evidence and does injustice to the rich interplay between personal and situational influences on decisions to become soldiers").

[15] Wessells, CHILD SOLDIERS, *supra* note 14, at 9 (citing a 2005 Save the Children Report).

[16] *Cf.* Mats Utas, SWEET BATTLEFIELDS: YOUTH AND THE LIBERIAN CIVIL WAR 7–8 (2003) (noting that "the perspective of humanitarian aid agencies (Save the Children/UNICEF, in particular) will often describe child soldiers, and deal with them, solely as victims"); Jo Boyden and Joanna de Berry, *Introduction, in* CHILDREN AND YOUTH ON THE FRONT LINE: ETHNOGRAPHY, ARMED CONFLICT AND

victim image binds communities of conscience. Chapter 2 of this book unpacks how this image has ascended as a metaphor for the child soldier: continuously defining the child soldier at the point of entry into conflict, during conflict, at the point of exit from conflict, and also in the aftermath of conflict. Applied top-down in a wide-range of places, this image is portable. It forms part of transnational rule of law discourse and technique. Although projections of it by communities of conscience have become more refined over time, its core attributes persist and, in fact, are hardening into law and policy. This portrait scripts official conversations about child soldiers. Accordingly, these conversations become conformist and stilted.

Global civil society, advocacy groups, donors, and activists lack the formal capacity to make international law. Although some international and intergovern-mental organizations, including some UN agencies, may exercise lawmaking abi-lity, most do not (including many whose mandates touch upon child soldiering). By virtue of their activities, however, all of these actors shape the content of binding international law as traditionally made by states and, what is more, often determine the legally oriented content of best practices, rule of law blueprints, and policy guidelines.[17] I refer to this normative, aspirational, and operational mix of interna-tional law, policy, and practice—constituted as it is directly and indirectly by a broad constellation of actors—as the *international legal imagination*.[18] On the topic of child soldiers, the faultless passive victim image fills the international legal imagination. This image thereby contributes to and influences the substance of international law and policy.

Attending to the scourge of child soldiering has become a portal for transnational rights discourse and its broader reformist ambitions to enter local constituencies. In this regard, the child soldier has become a site that serves broader political purposes. One purpose is the naturalization of certain characteristics of childhood. Another purpose is the universalization of a child as anyone below the age of eighteen. This book carefully considers the relationship between internationalized legal norms regarding coming of age, which are rooted in chronology, and diverse localized understandings, which are more malleably informed by experience, activity, rela-tionship, and station in life.

DISPLACEMENT xi, xv (Jo Boyden and Joanna de Berry eds, 2004) ("[C]hildren and adolescents are portrayed as the passive recipients of adult agency, the victims of wars waged by others and of brutality that is alien and imposed. . . . Personal volition is denied and emphasis given to their vulnerability and helplessness . . ."); Eyal Ben-Ari, *Facing Child Soldiers, Moral Issues, and "Real Soldiering": Anthropolog-ical Perspectives on Professional Armed Forces*, 37(1) SCIENTIA MILITARIA: SOUTH AFRICAN JOURNAL OF MILITARY STUDIES 1, 13 (2009) ("Even a cursory review of the websites devoted to young soldiers reveals the extent to which visual representations in photographs or drawings are designed to evoke images of blamelessness and helplessness.").

[17] These actors may participate in conferences in which states negotiate and adopt major multilat-eral treaties.

[18] The term "international legal imagination" is not coined herein as a neologism, but no other scholarship appears to meaningfully address, define, or deploy it as an analytic tool. Among a tiny handful of unrelated references thereto in the published literature is Carl Landauer, *Regionalism, Geography, and the International Legal Imagination*, 11 CHI. J. INT'L L. 557 (2011) (mentioning this term in passing without definition or deployment).

One goal of the faultless passive victim image is to curb punitive policies and harsh measures that may flow from the demon caricature. At times, pressure may arise within post-conflict societies to pursue such policies against former child soldiers. Transnational actors may discursively respond to these pressures by even further underscoring the unwitting dependency and sacrificial nature of militarized youth. In so doing, transnational actors unhelpfully dichotomize conversational frames such that child soldiers become either "sinners" or "saints."[19]

Because the depiction of the demon child soldier tends to hail from the global South (notably Africa), it reinforces racial stereotypes. Nor, however, are racial overtones absent from the faultless passive victim image. This portrait may inadvertently pathologize entire social structures by presenting the children as needing to be saved from their communities, from their cultures, and from their families.

Although not the doing of global civil society, the turn to victimhood narratives to thwart punitive policies and retributive measures can be selective. Owing to state behavior, the political suitability of these narratives correlates to whom, exactly, the conduct of the child soldiers aggrieves. A center/periphery divide emerges. As this book unpacks, transnational conceptions of faultlessness do not fully reach children from the periphery who commit atrocious acts against Westerners. Whereas the child perpetrator targeting Africans tends to be held as a mindless captive of purposeless violence, the child perpetrator targeting Westerners tends to be held as an intentional author of purposeful violence.

In short, all extreme images of child soldiers run the risk, as Denov eloquently counsels, of "reflect[ing] and reproduc[ing] enduring hierarchies between the global North and South, cementing notions of race, perversity and barbarism, alongside the dehumanization of child soldiers and their societies."[20]

Within post-conflict societies guided by international judicialization and administration efforts, policy initiatives generated by the faultless passive victim imagery presuppose and designate local child soldiers as programmed to commit terrible abuses over which they have neither appreciation nor control. Child soldiers are seen as forcibly coerced into military service and, in the case of atrocity-producing conflicts, compelled to commit horrific human rights abuses.[21] As a group, and *ipso facto* as individuals, they are taken to lack any volition. Seen as "faceless," they "have not yet developed a concept of justice."[22]

---

[19] For use of such language, *see*, e.g., Bryan Lonegan, *Sinners or Saints: Child Soldiers and the Persecutor Bar to Asylum after* Negusie v. Holder, 31 B.C. Third World L.J. 71 (2011).

[20] Denov, *supra* note 8, at 14.

[21] For a typical presentation, *see* Valentina Spiga, *Indirect Victims' Participation in the* Lubanga *Trial*, 8 J. Int'l. Crim. Just. 183, 192 (2010) ("It is common knowledge that children are often forced to take up arms and have little choice on whether or not to enlist; after their recruitment, they are coerced to commit actions, of which—in most cases—they have little understanding."). The international legal imagination, however, stiffly balks at generalizing this explanatory account in cases of perpetrators aged eighteen or older. For this group, as Chapter 2 *infra* shows, "following orders" is a paltry defense.

[22] Dallaire, *supra* note 10, at 3, 138 (also describing some child soldiers as "zombies"). Noting that Dallaire's book "[p]arallel[s] [his] own childhood, in which he spun fictional worlds in the forests beyond his family's log cabin ... [and is] inspired by Antoine de Saint-Exupéry's *Le Petit Prince*," one reviewer lauded it for "perfectly captur[ing] the innocence and experience of childhood that war so

Is the projected image fully explanatory? If not, do its deficiencies or omissions matter? This book argues that, notwithstanding accuracy in many individual cases, the portrayal of the child soldier as a faultless passive victim is unduly reductive. It belies considerably more varied actual individual experiences. This image—as do all extreme images of the child soldier—occludes, flattens, and conceals details. And, yes, these details are salient. They matter. It is inadequate to generalize an over-arching understanding of child soldiering based on the more extreme cases. Extra-polating from the extremes instead of the mean sensationalizes vulnerability and trauma.[23] A proportionate and inclusive process of inductive reasoning requires even-handed consideration of the full gamut of individual experiences, not only a subset of those cases most compatible with pre-determined advocacy efforts. Child soldiers and child soldiering are not so simple.

In the end, I urge the international legal imagination to adopt a supple, empathetic, and dexterous approach to child soldiers that vivifies their dignity rather than the current *Zeitgeist* that encases their vulnerability. I hope for this book to contribute, however modestly, to that process.

(iii) Social Realities of Child Soldiering: Circumscribed Action

Accumulated knowledge about child soldiers arises from a diversity of disciplines. The richness that might flow from this diversity, unfortunately, lies fallow. These disciplines and their concomitant literatures often communicate poorly with each other. In terms of the development of law, best practices, and policy, the play of various literatures has been uneven. Child psychology and trauma studies have exerted considerable influence. So, too, have reports published by transnational pressure groups, NGOs, activists, and UN agencies. The recommendations of child rights advocates also have proven instrumental.

Other disciplines and their literatures have not resonated with the international legal imagination. In fact, the international legal imagination holds contributions from these fields at arm's length. Thus, these contributions remain untapped. This gate-keeping occasions a loss, insofar as the only way to eradicate child soldiering and promote genuine post-conflict reconciliation is to understand the phenomenon as multidimensionally as possible. Examples of undervalued contributions include ethnographic participant observation, anthropological studies, qualitative research, survey data, and feminist theory. Another is adolescent developmental neurobiology,

---

savagely steals from them." Samantha Nutt, *Arms and the child*, THE GLOBE AND MAIL (November 5, 2010).

[23] This impulse even arises in the work of Jeff McMahan, a leading moral philosopher, in his otherwise brilliantly nuanced discussion. Jeff McMahan, *Child Soldiers: The Ethical Perspective* 9–10 (working paper, cited with permission, 2007) (offering the following as an illustrative hypothetical case: an eight year-old boy, forced by a group of armed men to kill his best friend in view of his entire village, and then abducted to a camp; after several years of indoctrination, brutalization, and training, he is administered drugs, given a light automatic weapon, and sent to fight for an unjust cause at the age of eleven or twelve).

which focuses on the social category of adolescents as distinct from young children. This book canvasses these literatures so as to integrate them more robustly into conversations about child soldiering. In this regard, this book is both synthetic and creative. It aims to revisit the epistemology of child soldiering. It intends to develop a less didactic and more grounded composite.

Although not monolithic, these literatures tend to perceive child soldiers neither as crushed nor as succumbing, but rather as traversing, surviving, coping, and making what they can out of bad circumstances not of their own doing. These literatures foreground individuality and adaptation, rather than aimless collective subservience. They voice a more dynamic account of child soldiers as *social navigators* interacting with, instead of overwhelmed by, their environments— even when those environments involve the most invidious of circumstances.[24] These literatures also tend to place children, adolescents, youth, and adults along a broader continuum that is less rigidly stratified by chronological age demarcations.

Presentation of this information is meant to holistically *understand* child soldiering so as to more meaningfully *prevent* its occurrence. Although the faultless passive victim image may serve as an anodyne to distressing and delicate conversations about militarized youth, the international legal imagination needs to do better. Rote deontological denunciation can only take us so far. Within transnational discourse, the seemingly inevitable obverse to the innocence of the children is the iniquity of the adult commanders of rogue armed groups. Although serving rhetorical purposes, presenting these commanders as crazed demented evildoers also obscures the reasons why they recruit children in fighting forces. Perhaps these reasons are more conventional and strategic, and less visceral, than the portrayal diffused by the international legal imagination. In any event, unraveling these reasons would help clarify the sources of child soldiering. Such clarification is necessary for the success of dissuasive efforts and the effective sanction of adult commanders.

What might these various literatures teach us? Chapters 2 and 3 of this book tackle this question. At this early juncture, nevertheless, it might be opportune to anticipatorily highlight—albeit briskly—some central elements.

Young children certainly are associated with armed forces or armed groups. In some instances, many young children may be forcibly recruited and, in fact, may fight. Most child soldiers, however, are not young children. Most are adolescents— often aged fifteen, sixteen, or seventeen. Overall, the young, pre-pubescent child is simply not indicative of the norm. The marketing and advertising work of charity organizations, however, still inclines toward underscoring the tender age of child soldiers. One visual, for example, involves the surrealistic juxtaposition of bullets in what looks like a Crayola crayon box.[25] Although certainly eye-catching and

---

[24] I draw the concept of social navigation from Mats Utas. *See* Mats Utas, *Victimcy, Girlfriending, Soldiering: Tactic Agency in a Young Woman's Social Navigation of the Liberian War Zone*, 78(2) ANTHROPOLOGICAL QUARTERLY 403, 408, 426 (2005).

[25] *See*, e.g., <http://www.warchild.org.uk/issues/child-soldiers> (visited on June 24, 2011).

well-intended, this approach may neither resonate with nor strike at the heart of the problem of child soldiering.

In light of the centrality of *adolescents* (often older teenagers) to the phenomenon of *child* soldiering, is it not apposite to consider adolescent developmental psychology? This burgeoning field, which increasingly is turning to sophisticated neuroscientific and neurobiological methods, demonstrates that adolescents typically are more susceptible than adults to outside or peer influence. In comparison to adults, adolescents are more represented in reckless behavior; they have a gauzier ability to foresee the future; are more impulsive, impetuous, and risk-taking; and have more transitory personalities. Adolescents trust more readily and their trust can be easily misplaced. But neither is the adolescent brain child-like nor pre-logical. On many key metrics, in fact, available research indicates that older adolescents are much more like adults than children. Instead of pursuing rigid child/adult binaries, then, perhaps it would make sense for law and policy to engage with interstitial developmental categories.

Persons under the age of eighteen associated with armed forces or armed groups largely get there in one of three ways: (1) they are abducted or conscripted through force or serious threats; (2) they present themselves, whether independently or through recruitment programs and become enlisted/enrolled; or (3) they are born into forces or groups. The first two paths, which are the most common, are not always capable of firm demarcation. However, they are distinguishable and, moreover, should be distinguished.

Readers may find it surprising, but most child soldiers are neither abducted nor forcibly recruited. The international legal imagination, nevertheless, heavily emphasizes this path to militarization. Doing so exposes this horrific aspect of the phenomenon of child soldiering. This emphasis, however, also leads to the undertheorization and underexploration of *youth volunteerism*. The international legal imagination cannot just wish away the fact that significant numbers of children join armed forces or armed groups in the absence of evident coercion and, in fact, exercise some—and at times considerable—initiative in this regard. Even within the most maleficent of conflicts, children come forward and present themselves for service.

In response, the international legal imagination predetermines that no child has the capacity to volunteer or to consent to serve—whether innately or because of nightmarish circumstances, or both. Volunteering is presented as an illusion.[26] The international legal imagination is particularly skeptical of armed groups and, in their case, flatly views juvenile volunteerism as an impossibility or absurdity. For all intents and purposes, then, enlistment of volunteers becomes no different than abduction.

---

[26] Jason Hart, *Saving children: What role for anthropology?*, 22(1) ANTHROPOLOGY TODAY 5, 7 (2006) ("The authors of global accounts of 'child soldiers' . . . have little time for the idea that children may be capable of exercising any real measure of choice about recruitment. . . . [T]he very notion of voluntary recruitment is largely an illusion.")

The international legal imagination is remiss to neglect the prevalence and relevance of children who volunteer for military service. To be sure, cases arise where determinations of volunteerism would be specious. Children may be offered up—like chattel—by family members or local leaders. They may be tricked into joining. They may come forward to serve as a cook, only to be given an automatic weapon and placed on the front lines. Some children may rashly present themselves for service because of excessive impulsivity.[27] That said, as Chapter 3 will show, many children, notably older adolescents, come forward intentionally to join armed forces or groups. Environmental factors and situational constraints—which include poverty, insecurity, lack of education, socialization into violence, and broken families—certainly inform their decisions to enlist. This book argues that children's engagement with these factors can be more usefully understood as interactive and negotiated processes of negative push and affirmative pull.

In joining armed forces or groups, children may simply be pursuing paths of economic advancement, inclusion in occupational networks, pursuit of political or ideological reform, and professional development. Children—particularly, older adolescents—are not invariably lost on these paths. They traverse and cross them as best they can. However disturbing to outsiders, this may mean joining armed forces or armed groups. Moreover, at times child recruits deceive their parents and other commanders. They conceal their age, travel great distances, and persevere tenaciously in their quest to associate with armed forces or groups. They may join despite community and family exhortations to the contrary. These children, too, count as child soldiers. Although armed groups may seek to undermine legitimate governments through macabre methods, they may also serve as engines of protest against illegitimate rulers, state authoritarianism, and kleptocratic dictatorship.

What child soldiers actually say about their experiences may contrast with how international observers broadcast those experiences. In interviews, for example, former child soldiers often describe themselves as having volunteered for service. Some interviewers respond by discounting all such statements. They thereby massage complex data to fit a simple pre-existing theory. P.W. Singer—whose work on child soldiers has received considerable attention—finds the notion of voluntary recruitment "misleading," in part because children are "of an age at which they are not capable of making mature decisions."[28] Helping hands may prefer to believe that child soldiers are ignorant of the absence of choice in their lives and lack the cognitive capacity for discernment. This strategy, however well-intentioned, may demean by unduly accenting gullibility. This strategy, moreover, depletes the

---

[27] Over time, as hardships weigh on them, these children may come to regret their decision. Some of them then exit, while others are compelled to stay; others persist and remain with the group; some advance within the ranks. Longitudinally, these latter cases become considerably more ambiguous.

[28] Singer, *supra* note 11, at 62. Singer's book relies heavily on humanitarian and human rights reports, journalistic accounts, psychology scholarship, and military/security studies literature. It makes only marginal reference to ethnographic or anthropological work. *See also generally* Office of the Special Representative of the Secretary-General for Children and Armed Conflict, CHILDREN AND JUSTICE DURING AND IN THE AFTERMATH OF ARMED CONFLICT 10 (Working Paper No. 3, September 2011) ("Children . . . lack the mental maturity and judgment to express consent or to fully understand the implications of their actions.") [hereinafter CHILDREN AND JUSTICE].

informational record and leads to misguided recommendations. It risks presenting youth inanimately as objects of study rather than vibrantly as sources of information. Although assertions of volunteer service made by child soldiers should not be immunized from contextual analysis, I believe it is wrong summarily to dismiss them. Young people may understand volunteerism within the context of their lives and apply it fairly to themselves.

Dismissing what adolescents have to say owing to their putative jejunity contrasts sharply with assumptions of juvenile capacity and autonomy that animate other areas of law and policy. For example, when it comes to bioethical debates regarding consent to medical treatment and access to reproductive rights and technologies, in many jurisdictions adolescents tend to be presumed competent. International human rights law highlights that adolescents can exercise rights of freedom of association and expression. So, too, does international family law. This book argues that protective policies predicated upon children being constructed as enfeebled *before and during* conflict may counterproductively result in children persistently being treated as enfeebled *after* conflict. I remain skeptical that atrophied delineations of capacity, and the notion that adolescents categorically require infantilizing rules to protect them, actually promote the aspiration to engage them robustly as full members of society. Moreover, many persons initially recruited as children age into adulthood during conflict or before they feasibly can enroll in post-conflict programming. In these instances, infantilizing aspects may become perceived both by them and the community as particularly ill-fitting.

Once associated with armed forces or groups, what do children actually do? How are they used? Children rotate among various roles, which include combat, auxiliary support, or accompanying forces as sex slaves or compelled conjugal partners.[29] These roles expose them to great danger. In contradistinction to often graphic media representations, significant numbers of children neither fight nor carry weapons.[30] Even fewer become implicated in the systematic perpetration of acts of atrocity that potentially might fall within the scope of extraordinary international crimes (such as war crimes, crimes against humanity, and genocide) proscribed by international criminal law.

The dominant explanatory account is that those child soldiers who commit extraordinary international crimes are forced by commanders and, hence, operate under extreme duress; they are incapacitated by compelled ingestion of narcotics and alcohol; they are brainwashed and resocialized by the endemic violence that envelops them; and they are plagued with fears of brutal punishment. Hence, moral responsibility should be excused, even for grievous acts of violence. Excuse begets

---

[29] In this book, I very occasionally turn to the phrases "child combatant" or "child ex-combatant" specifically to refer to child soldiers who have materially (as opposed to incidentally) fulfilled combat roles.

[30] Wessells, CHILD SOLDIERS, *supra* note 14, at 71 ("Contrary to popular conceptions, many child soldiers never fight, and many neither carry their own weapon nor know how to use one."); Ben-Ari, *supra* note 16, at 1 (reporting that children "sometimes act as combatants who directly participate in hostilities [but] more often they are deployed as auxiliaries ... or in various support roles").

forgiveness which, *arguendo*, establishes a firm footing for the child soldier's reintegration.

This dominant account explains many acts of atrocity perpetrated by persons under the age of eighteen. Despite their frequency, however, these cases cannot be universalized. The international legal imagination tends, once again, to wish away the fact that not all child soldiers materially implicated in acts of atrocity actually conform to this explanatory account. In this regard, the international legal imagination undertheorizes the challenge at hand, perhaps selfishly insofar as:

[T]he fact that children are capable of violence clearly falls outside entrenched modernist formulations of childhood. Children who behave violently—who rape, murder and kill—pose a conundrum because they dismantle the idea of the romantic innocence and vulnerability of childhood.[31]

Considerable heterogeneity arises among child soldiers with regard to their relationship to violence that, in turn, underscores the ongoing salience of disposition, choice, and residual discretion to exceed or subvert command authority. Some child soldiers lie to and manipulate commanders to avoid killing. Others refuse to inflict gross human rights abuses upon third-party civilians or combatants. Other child soldiers, however, torture, rape, and kill to navigate volatile militarized hierarchies. Some do so gratuitously or to pursue lucre.

Accordingly, afflicted communities may perceive child soldiers in a considerably more individuated fashion. They may see them as actual persons known to them rather than as anonymously fungible "beasts of no nation."[32] These details matter. Furthermore, regardless of why they did it and the circumstances thereof, the fact remains that the acts of child soldiers do impose staggering consequences upon the lives of others, including children.[33]

Given the distortions and omissions engendered by the faultless passive victim lens (as well as the occlusions triggered by other currently circulated images), is there another way to talk about child soldiers that reflects the complexities of their experiences?

---

[31] Alcinda Honwana, *Innocent & Guilty: Child-Soldiers as Interstitial & Tactical Agents, in* MAKERS & BREAKERS: CHILDREN & YOUTH IN POSTCOLONIAL AFRICA 31, 37 (Alcinda Honwana and Filip de Boeck eds, 2005).

[32] This is the title of a prominent novel which tracks the story of Agu, a fictional child soldier. Uzodinma Iweala, BEASTS OF NO NATION: A NOVEL (2005). On this note, many documentaries, movies, novels, memoirs, and autobiographies evoke the vicissitudes of the child soldier. For a handful of examples, *see* Ahmadou Kourouma, ALLAH N'EST PAS OBLIGÉ (2000); China Keitetsi, CHILD SOLDIER: FIGHTING FOR MY LIFE (2002); Faith J. H. McDonnell and Grace Akallo, GIRL SOLDIER: A STORY OF HOPE FOR NORTHERN UGANDA'S CHILDREN (2007); *Blood Diamond* (2006, dir. Edward Zwick); *Wit Licht* (2008, recut as *The Silent Army*, dir. Jean van de Velde).

[33] Mariatu Kamara with Susan McClelland, THE BITE OF THE MANGO 40–41 (2008) (Sierra Leonean author Kamara describes how, as a child, she became a double amputee: "Two boys steadied me as my body began to sway. As the machete came down, things went silent. I closed my eyes tightly, but then they popped open and I saw everything. It took the boy two attempts to cut off my right hand. The first swipe didn't get through the bones, which I saw sticking out in all different shapes and sizes.").

This book proposes to approach individual child soldiers through a *model of circumscribed action*. A circumscribed actor has the ability to act, the ability not to act, and the ability to do otherwise than what he or she actually has done. The effective range of these abilities, however, is delimited, bounded, and confined. Yet, the abilities themselves are neither evanescent nor ephemeral. Circumscribed actors exercise some discretion in navigating and mediating the constraints around them. Circumscribed actors dispose of an enclosed space which is theirs—the acreage of which varies according to an oscillating admixture of disposition and situation—in which they exercise a margin of volition. Within this space, they make short-term decisions. Circumscribed actors scale social environments they did not create. Although acted upon, they also act upon others. Oppression, after all, does not axiomatically void the oppressed's capacity for decision-making. Nor is it normatively desirable as a matter of policymaking to adopt such an arthritic and atrophied view of the oppressed.

Circumscribed action is not a metaphor, nor a photograph, nor an ideal-type, nor an image whose reification is sought and to which all *prima facie* categorized individuals are to conform. Rather, circumscribed action is presented as a *spectrum* or *continuum* that embraces the inherent diversity among the individuals aligned along its axis.[34] Presenting circumscribed action as a spectrum, instead of a singular category, facilitates procedural inquiry regarding the specific histories and experiences of these individuals.

When law internalizes the chronological watershed of the age of eighteen, and turns to it to contrast the capable adult from the incapable child, law creates an exigent situation for young adults. After all, neuroscience teaches us that, as a matter of age, cognitive functions continue to develop well into the mid-twenties. When the law draws bright-lines, outsiders may become excessively exposed to the very vicissitudes from which law aims to insulate insiders. Abusive commanders may simply shift their focus from older children to young adults. In the end, law may simultaneously protect too much and too little. Accordingly, a turn to a model of circumscribed action would abandon the current predilection for two oppositional polarities—that is, child or adult—and thereby relieve younger adults from the weight of excessive hardship and older children from the straitjacket of excessive infantilization.

(iv) An Emergent Legal Fiction and its Effects

Where does the faultless passive victim image intend to shift international law and policy?

For starters, toward eighteen as the threshold age of permissible military service. This book argues that attainment of this goal would be facilitated were its pursuit to

---

[34] Wessells, CHILD SOLDIERS, *supra* note 14, at 74 ("The lives of child combatants exhibit significant diversity, cautioning against stereotypes of child combatants as bloodthirsty predators or innocents herded onto the killing fields.").

be paired with a less judgmental and more tempered portrayal of those persons intended for protective coverage. Another intended shift involves the vitiation of the legal relevance of distinctions among kinds of recruitment or use and, correspondingly, to annul the possibility that any child ever can volunteer to serve or to perform functions within armed forces or groups.

Considerable momentum also is afoot to exclude children (including child soldiers), whether *de jure* or *de facto*, from the jurisdiction of international or internationalized courts and tribunals that adjudge extraordinary atrocity crimes. Although prosecuting child soldiers for such crimes is certainly not unlawful, such prosecutions, as Chapter 4 elaborates, increasingly are seen as inappropriate and, even, illegitimate. The push for international institutions to abjure criminal trials for child soldiers implicated in acts of atrocity conceptually seeps into the national and local court systems of post-conflict societies. As a result, national criminal prosecutions of former child soldiers become discouraged as well.

The faultless passive victim narrative also suffuses post-conflict justice modalities other than criminal trials. For example, in the case of truth-seeking and reconciliation mechanisms, ascendant best practices advise that children can only participate therein voluntarily as witnesses or victims.[35] These best practices also advocate that all child participants—including children formerly associated with armed forces or groups—be treated equally as victims or witnesses.[36] In other words, children are not to be distinguished *inter se* in terms of their individual conduct. Nor, apparently, are child soldiers to be distinguished from other children in conflict zones. Individual participation in acts of atrocity is, therefore, not approached through a *quid pro quo* dialogue of forgiveness. The elimination of distinctions among group members helps accord legal protection to as many children as possible. Nevertheless, this book cautions against this policy preference. Child soldiers can be treated as a generally protected class while distinctions among individual class members still remain respected.

The preferred push is to void victim-perpetrator ambiguity in the case of child soldiers. When the child inflicts horrors, responsibility passes entirely to the adult abductor, enlister, recruiter, or commander. Although abjured for child soldiers, international criminal tribunals are invoked to prosecute as war criminals those adults who conscript, enlist, or use children below the age of fifteen as active participants in hostilities. Straight 18 aspirations endeavor to expand this prohibition to cover all children, that is, all persons younger than eighteen.[37]

---

[35] Paris Principles, *supra* note 2, Prins 3.8 (also adding the stipulation that child participation must be by informed consent of both the child and parent or guardian where appropriate and possible) and 8.16.

[36] *Id.* Prin. 8.15.

[37] *See*, e.g., REDRESS Trust, VICTIMS, PERPETRATORS OR HEROES? CHILD SOLDIERS BEFORE THE INTERNATIONAL CRIMINAL COURT 1 (2006) ("It is recommended that the ICC should follow suit and raise the legal age of child recruitment, enlisting or 'use' from fifteen to eighteen."); *Integrated Disarmament, Demobilization and Reintegration Standards* (IDDRS) §5.30, p. 23 (2006), *available at* <http://www.unddr.org/iddrs/05/download/IDDRS_530.pdf> ("It is a serious breach of international humanitarian law, human rights law and international criminal law to use children as soldiers under the age of 15, and in most circumstances to use children under 18.").

The international community has invested considerable resources and energy to prosecute a handful of adult militia leaders for unlawful conscription, enlistment, or use of children younger than fifteen. The Special Court for Sierra Leone (SCSL), a hybrid court created cooperatively between the UN and the Sierra Leonean government, has issued several convictions on such charges. The inaugural trial at the International Criminal Court (ICC) in The Hague—involving Thomas Lubanga Dyilo, a DRC rebel leader—is proceeding exclusively on these charges. The Rome Statute, the multilateral international treaty establishing the ICC, also permits victims to participate in the criminal proceedings against an accused. On this note, ICC judges have determined the class of persons harmed by child soldiers not to be direct or indirect victims of Lubanga's alleged conduct and, thus, have denied applications brought by class members to participate in the criminal proceedings against him.

Although the faultless passive victim image reflects the experiences of many child soldiers, I argue—borrowing a term of art from legal philosopher Lon Fuller—that its transposition into law spins a *legal fiction*.[38] According to Fuller, a fiction "is neither a truthful statement, nor a lie, nor an erroneous conclusion."[39] Fuller identifies many kinds of legal fictions. What I call the legal fiction of faultless passive victimhood most closely approximates the category of neglective or abstractive fictions.[40] For Fuller, neglective fictions constitute the "most obvious example of the process by which our minds simplify reality."[41]

Legal fictions are neither intrinsically malignant nor intrinsically benign. They are constructs that serve both ill and good. In the case of child soldiering, the legal fiction of faultless passive victimhood fulfills a number of valuable purposes. Because it offers a disambiguated and pointed message, it helps marshal resources and co-ordinate condemnation. Many of the reforms the fiction has impressed upon the architecture of law, policy, and best practices are salutary.

Along with a variety of gains, however, indulging this legal fiction also produces operational shortcomings.

One example, elaborated upon in Chapter 5, arises from the prosecution of adult recruiters and users of child soldiers. These prosecutions, to be clear, help condemn child soldiering. International lawyers and policymakers, however, exaggerate their deterrent value. Such bullishness is unwise. It distracts from the need to search well beyond the architecture of the courtroom and jailhouse in order to meaningfully dissuade and, ultimately, end child soldiering. Much more than a handful of criminal prosecutions is required to promote the well-being of children in conflict zones. When international criminal law fixates on the adult recruiter or user, it flits past the multiple sources of child soldiering—institutional, power politics,

---

[38] Lon L. Fuller, LEGAL FICTIONS 9 (1967) (a fiction is "either (1) a statement propounded with a complete or partial consciousness of its falsity, or (2) a false statement recognized as having utility").
[39] *Id.* at 5.
[40] *Id.* at 106 (citing Hans Vaihinger, DIE PHILOSOPHIE DES ALS OB 28 (4th edn, 1920)). For Vaihinger, these fictions constitute "a series of methods in which the deviation from reality manifests itself specifically as a disregard of certain elements in the fact situation." *Id.* (citing Vaihinger at 28).
[41] *Id.*

commercial, and historical. State responsibility for unlawful recruitment of children, along with other forms of collective sanction, therefore remains undertheorized and underdeveloped. This book hopes to encourage deeper reflection and more action along these lines. As part of their goal to accentuate the moral culpability of adult recruiters or users, criminal prosecutions amplify how post-traumatic stress syndrome debilitates former child soldiers. If convicting perpetrators becomes entwined with tropes of youth helplessness, however, the upshot may be incarcerating a handful of adults while simultaneously perpetuating gerontocracy by eroding tenets of juvenile autonomy and ability.

Chapter 6 identifies and expounds upon several other externalities supported or generated by the faultless passive victim image. Of greatest concern is the sidelining of *transitional justice* from post-conflict initiatives to reintegrate former child soldiers and to reconstruct their communities.[42] The phrase transitional justice designates the range of processes by which societies come to terms with histories of widespread violence, how they reckon with terrible human rights abuses, and how people within afflicted constituencies come to live together again. Transitional justice is concerned with redress, historical clarification, and reconciliation. Processes commonly associated with transitional justice include criminal trials, civil liability (for example, private tort actions, restitutionary claims, and public reparations), lustration, community service programs, truth and reconciliation commissions, endogenous mechanisms,[43] public inquiries, and restorative ceremonies. These processes vary considerably *inter se* regarding how, to whom, and to what degree they allocate responsibility for acts of atrocity. They nevertheless share the pursuit of social repair through a framework that recognizes the pain that these acts have wrought. These institutions also share the belief that there can be no durable stability if injustices and human rights abuses are left unaddressed. This does not necessarily mean that perpetrators have to confess or atone. Many endogenous ceremonies, for example, do not contemplate such methods, preferring instead to address past wrongs through future-oriented work and cultivation of relationships.

The international legal imagination's propensity is to generically ease a potential three-dimensional status of child soldiers as perpetrators, witnesses, and victims into a two-dimensional portrayal of child soldiers as victims and witnesses alone. This constriction, however, engenders some opportunity costs. In response, this book advances the normative claim that transitional justice initiatives other than

---

[42] Together with their adult counterparts, many—but certainly not all, and in some jurisdictions only a few—child soldiers may return to their communities of origin through disarmament, demobilization (release), and reintegration (DDR) programs. Disarmament involves the collection of weapons. Demobilization means the discharge of individuals from fighting forces. Reintegration is the step through which the former fighter transitions to a civilian role. For discussion of DDR and transitional justice, *see infra* Chapter 6(i).

[43] I borrow political scientist Phil Clark's unorthodox use of the term "endogenous" to describe ceremonies, rites, and rituals that arise, often informally, at the local level to promote social repair and purification following wrongful conduct. In this book, I also deploy the more conventional terms "traditional" and "customary" in this regard. I recognize the contested meaning and use of these terms, but turn to them only descriptively and purely out of convenience. I do not aim to theorize these terms.

criminal trials, in particular truth commissions and endogenous mechanisms, can help facilitate reintegration and reconciliation in cases of child soldiers implicated in acts of atrocity. Chapter 6, which explores this claim in depth, directs specific attention toward restorative justice approaches.

I do not call for former child soldiers to be criminally prosecuted for suspected violations of international criminal law before international institutions and, if found guilty, to be punished through incarceration. Nor do I recommend prosecutions or imprisonment at the national level. My reservations extend even more emphatically to proceedings before military commissions or tribunals, which are particularly susceptible to procedural irregularities and political vagaries. The outrageous situation faced at Guantánamo Bay by Omar Khadr, a Canadian child soldier who, as a minor, had associated with al-Qaeda, is painfully illustrative.[44]

As a matter of outcome, then, I concur in the international legal imagination's push to discard criminal trials for child soldiers. I disagree, however, when it comes to why. My skepticism regarding criminal trials for child soldiers implicated in acts of atrocity flows from my broader circumspection regarding the ability of the atrocity trial to attain its principally avowed penological goals, especially in the case of lower-level cadres, regardless of the age of the accused.[45] These goals include retribution, deterrence, and expressivism. Penological goals of rehabilitation and reintegration, which should be particularly salient in the context of juveniles, do not centrally figure among international criminal law's aspirations. The fact that child soldiers do not serve as conflict entrepreneurs or political leaders dulls the benefits of incapacitating them. Former child soldiers and those persons harmed by their conduct require restoration, which sequestered incarceration does not provide.

To recap, this book does not turn to criminal law as a regulatory solution. Why, then, does it devote considerable space to review the interface of the international legal imagination with the question of the potential criminal culpability of child soldiers? Why be concerned with assessing how, and for which reasons, conventional wisdom has come to eschew criminal trials for child soldiers enmeshed in the

---

[44] In October 2010, a US Military Commission convicted Khadr through a plea bargain of charges that included violating the laws of war. Khadr pleaded guilty to five charges—including throwing a grenade in a 2002 firefight that killed a US combatant, Christopher Speer, in Afghanistan—as well as various other crimes in connection with terrorist activity. He was formally sentenced by a military jury to forty years' imprisonment. Because of a diplomatic agreement, however, Khadr will likely be repatriated to Canada to serve out seven years of his sentence (which the agreement capped at eight years in total) in accordance with Canadian law. Khadr was not credited for the eight years he had spent in detention prior to his conviction. Khadr was fifteen years old at the time of his capture by US forces. In addition to his age, his lengthy pre-trial detention by the US at Guantánamo Bay (he was twenty-four years old at the time he pleaded guilty), and the problematic conditions he faced while in custody, Khadr's situation is controversial owing to evidence that confessions he allegedly made had been secured following implicit threats of gang rape. Charlie Savage, *U.S. Wary of Example Set by Tribunal Case*, N.Y. TIMES (August 27, 2010). For more discussion of the *Khadr* case, *see infra* Chapters 4 and 7.

[45] Mark A. Drumbl, ATROCITY, PUNISHMENT, AND INTERNATIONAL LAW 149–180 (2007); *see also infra* Chapters 5(iii) and 6(ii).

commission of acts of atrocity? The answer lies in the fact that what the international legal imagination says, recommends, and exhorts ultimately bears heavily upon the reconstructive journeys of inter- and post-conflict societies. Transnational interventions matter. Although excluding child soldiers from international and national criminal trials may well be appropriate as a policy *result*, the current *rationales* for so doing, and the forces that propel those rationales, have come to overshoot their mark. Fear that child soldiers may become subject to punitive criminal trials has induced a crudely fulsome protectionism that has come to insulate child soldiers from accountability processes generally, regardless of the goals or potentials of those processes. This protectionism needlessly cocoons child soldiers from the tough questions that societies must reckon with in order to come to terms with mass violence. The solution, then, is not for international criminal law to recognize the criminal culpability of children but, instead, for transnational discourse to develop a more fine-grained approach to post-conflict accountability. I have elsewhere urged the adoption of more careful approaches to victimization and perpetration as a general matter.[46] Hence, the proposals made in this book dovetail with my overarching vision of what post-conflict justice ideally ought to look like.

As Chapter 6 demonstrates, afflicted communities want their children back home. They welcome the return of former child soldiers. Transnationally motored discourses of forgiveness without reciprocal obligation may appear, at first blush, to mesh with local sentiments of forgiveness without reciprocal obligation. Impulses arise in afflicted communities to accept excuse—namely, constraint enhanced by youth—in the case of the antecedent violent acts of child soldier returnees.

Transnational discourse, however, overestimates the uniformity and flexibility of community sentiment. A careful mining of the evidentiary record reveals that communities care about conduct during conflict, that is, why and how did the child join fighting forces and, once there, what did he or she do. Communities do not take all child soldier returnees to be fungible moral equals and to require identical approaches to reintegration. It is unclear whether community members unambivalently accept that the cognizability of their injuries should hew so tightly to the age of the perpetrator. The fact that community members demonstrate variable and volatile sentiments, ranging from joy to cordiality to antipathy, is understandable. In fact, it should be obvious. Regardless of who perpetrated it and why, mass atrocity invariably engenders a broad gamut of raw emotions among survivors and targeted populations. To pretend otherwise is foolhardy. To base policy on such pretension is quixotic.

Unsurprisingly, certain subgroups of former child soldiers face reintegration hurdles. Their home communities simply do not accept the suitability of the collectivized faultless passive victim narrative as applied to them as individuals. One such subgroup is child soldiers who have served for long periods of times with armed forces or groups. Another subgroup involves child soldiers suspected of

---

[46] Drumbl, *supra* note 45.

having committed atrocities or believed to have been affiliated with units that inflicted atrocities. These subgroups are at risk for marginalization and a recrudescence of militarized life, crime, and violence.

The legal fiction, therefore, neither represents nor reaches a relevant number of child soldier returnees, for whom reinsertion is far from seamless or self-evident. For this subgroup, unconditional excuse does not resonate within afflicted communities. Instead, consideration might be given to exploring processes of forgiveness predicated upon mutual and reciprocal obligation among returnees and the community. Reintegration cannot always be assumed. The violence may be too much.

Collaterally, transitional justice measures also may relieve the child soldier's sense of injustice. The child soldier may justifiably harbor resentment toward the community that idled while forcible recruitment ensnared its youth. Transitional justice measures may enable the child soldier to tell what happened to him or her— and to identify or learn who in the community may have abetted unscrupulous warlords. Transitional justice processes create a venue to discuss much more than accountability and responsibility. They also may authenticate stories of resistance to atrocity and contestation to cruel orders.[47] In this regard, transitional justice processes may come to benefit not only subgroups of child soldiers implicated in atrocity, but all child soldiers as well. Through participation in transitional justice processes, former child soldiers even may help educate other children in the community about the perils of becoming associated with armed forces or groups.

In my work with adult atrocity perpetrators I have come to experience that many—perhaps self-servingly—view themselves as victims or tools who simply ended up on the losing side of circumstance. The international legal imagination gives short shrift to their representations of subservience and victimhood. Adults, after all, are not legally excused from choices, often exercised in times of chaos, to join armed forces or groups that commit atrocity. Their responsibility is not evacuated. Many adults are compulsorily conscripted, as well, yet this does not *ab initio* absolve them from the consequences of their conduct. Many adult soldiers are little older than eighteen and live in strikingly similar situations to child soldiers. They are thus contemporaries. Can so much differentiation realistically hinge upon a simple matter of chronological age? Jo Boyden and Joanna de Berry remain unconvinced:

[C]hildren and adolescents can be very active in defining their own allegiances during conflict, as well as their own strategies for coping and survival. This implies that the prevailing dichotomy between adult as active perpetrator and child as passive victim needs challenging.[48]

According to anthropologist Susan Shepler, writing within the context of Sierra Leone, "[c]oming to terms with the participation of child soldiers . . . is key to

---

[47] Regarding transitional justice and resistance to atrocity, *see* Bronwyn Leebaw, JUDGING STATE-SPONSORED VIOLENCE, IMAGINING POLITICAL CHANGE (2011).

[48] Boyden and de Berry, *supra* note 16, at xv.

postwar reconciliation and peace building."[49] I believe that international law and policy, however, fails to demonstrate adroitness or finesse in negotiating this quandary. One way to redress this blind spot is to trim the emphasis on criminal law binaries of guilt or innocence, corruption or purity, victim or perpetrator, and adult or child.

Adopting a baseline of circumscribed action might open the space necessary to effect meaningful conceptual shifts and, thereby, synergistically liaise with the work of those observers who believe that transitional justice matters for child soldiers.[50] For example, international lawyer Cécile Aptel recognizes the value of non-penal proceedings in acknowledging children's wrongdoing and diminishing stigma. She suggests that "more thinking is required concerning the liability of children who have participated in the commission of crimes."[51] This book hopes to respond to this need and inspire a framework for reform. Meaningful change cannot occur, however, until the presumptive imagery recedes from the tautness of passive victimhood and embraces something more dynamic, such as circumscribed action.[52] Efforts to engage with transitional justice will remain superficial unless liberated from the strictures of victimhood discourse. This discourse, and its correlative imagery, is simply too tendentious.

In short, then, this book advises that the legal fiction of faultless passive victimhood should be dismantled and, therewith, its controlling effects deflated.

Assuredly, as is the case with any reformative process, renewal may produce fresh concerns. In reimagining the child soldier, and recommending policy shifts keyed thereto, this book is anticipatorily mindful of three sets of concerns: *pragmatics* (are the suggested reforms affordable or realistic?), *fear* (is this book opening the door to harsh punishment for child soldiers, thereby leaving them worse off?), and *overreach* (instead of circumscribed action, why not just a rebuttable presumption of victimhood?). Various sections of the book address these concerns. Chapter 7 takes

---

[49] Susan Shepler, *The Rites of the Child: Global Discourses of Youth and Reintegrating Child Soldiers in Sierra Leone*, 4 J. HUM. RTS. 197, 198 (2005).

[50] CHILDREN AND TRUTH COMMISSIONS, *supra* note 13, at x–xi, 65; CHILDREN AND TRANSITIONAL JUSTICE: TRUTH-TELLING, ACCOUNTABILITY AND RECONCILIATION Annex (Key Operational Principles) (UNICEF Innocenti Research Centre and Human Rights Program at Harvard Law School, Sharanjeet Parmar, Mindy Jane Roseman, Saudamini Siegrist, and Theo Sowa eds, 2010) [hereinafter CHILDREN AND TRANSITIONAL JUSTICE]; CHILDREN AND JUSTICE, *supra* note 28, at 27, 39 (encouraging restorative, rehabilitative, and traditional justice processes).

[51] Cécile Aptel, *International Criminal Justice and Child Protection, in* CHILDREN AND TRANSITIONAL JUSTICE, *supra* note 50, at 67, 107–111.

[52] For example, Human Rights Watch's suggestion that former child soldiers "participat[e] in restorative justice processes to help the child acknowledge their actions and gain reacceptance by the community" is hampered by the very foundational images Human Rights Watch disseminates about children as choicelessly coerced into fighting and unthinkingly committing violent acts. Human Rights Watch, COERCION AND INTIMIDATION OF CHILD SOLDIERS TO PARTICIPATE IN VIOLENCE 15 (2008). The IDDRS encourages more robust connections between transitional justice and DDR programming— including for child soldiers, for whom restorative mechanisms notably are discussed. Notwithstanding their innovative nature, the IDDRS recommendations also remain cabined by the IDDRS's depiction that "[f]ormer child soldiers are victims of criminal policies for which adults are responsible." IDDRS, *supra* note 37, at §5.30, p. 9.

on the trickiest one, namely, fears that child soldiers become subject to harsh treatment and renewed abuse.

In the end, I remain persuaded that the proposals in this book are worthwhile. They also convey broader pedagogic value. In this regard, Chapter 7 adumbrates connections between reimagining child soldiers, on the one hand, and three cognate challenges, on the other. These challenges are: reforming domestic justice systems in cases of ordinary common crime committed by juveniles, rehabilitating victims of transnational crimes that fall outside the aegis of international criminal law (e.g., sex-and drug-trafficking), and revisiting the place of international criminal law within the overall framework of post-conflict justice.

(v) Conclusion

It is much easier to express outrage regarding the oxymoron of the child soldier than it is to interrogatively theorize the oxymoron so as to enhance preventative and remedial policies. It is considerably easier to pre-judge *ex ante* that children and adolescents bear no responsibility for the situations they find themselves in and what they interstitially do within those situations than to examine *ex post* why, exactly, they militarize and then why, exactly, some among them become involved in committing terrible crimes. The easier path that assuages transnational sensibilities, however, is not necessarily the best path to protect children or safeguard the public. Policy based on the convenient answer may simply be poor policy.

2

Children Who Soldier:
Practices, Politics, and Perceptions

It is tricky to ascertain the overall number of child soldiers. Figures are imprecise. Why? For starters, commanders conceal child soldiers from outsiders. Some children hide their own age. Child soldiers may serve in remote and rugged locations, where they often fulfill low-visibility auxiliary functions. The lines between mobilization, demobilization, and remobilization are porous and, hence, hinder accurate estimates. Former child soldiers may be susceptible to renewed recruitment by commanders who value their skills, knowledge, combat experience, and abilities. At times, divisions between various armed groups concurrently embroiled in hostilities are permeable. Children who fight for armed groups against the government have been known, following capture, to become pressed into military service for the government. Children may exit armed factions in order to obtain demobilization benefits, only to re-enlist soon thereafter. Finally, child soldiering can morph into a cross-border or regional phenomenon sustained through economic motivations.[1]

Several years ago, it was commonly cited that anywhere from 250,000 to 300,000 children worldwide were associated with armed forces or armed groups. This range has embedded itself into public discourse and remains a common point of reference. At the time, however, even this range was subject to contestation. Some observers posited its upper end as higher, while others maintained that it reflected only those children who were actively used in hostilities.[2]

In very recent years, the overall number of child soldiers has likely declined. In the very least, it has not increased. However, the practice still endemically persists. The number of child soldiers drops in regions where conflict attenuates. The number spikes where conflict erupts or renews. And where conflict festers, the number stagnates. Where there is armed conflict, invariably, there are child soldiers. Child soldiers also appear in places neither blighted by war nor destabilized by systemic violence.

---

[1] Coalition to Stop the Use of Child Soldiers, CHILD SOLDIERS GLOBAL REPORT 2008 117 (2008).
[2] See, e.g., Theresa Betancourt, Ivelina Borisova, Julia Rubin-Smith, Tara Gingerich, Timothy Williams, and Jessica Agnew-Blais, PSYCHOSOCIAL ADJUSTMENT AND SOCIAL REINTEGRATION OF CHILDREN ASSOCIATED WITH ARMED FORCES AND ARMED GROUPS: THE STATE OF THE FIELD AND FUTURE DIRECTIONS 1 (2008) ("[I]t is estimated that at any given time, anywhere from 300,000–500,000 children are involved with fighting forces worldwide."); P.W. Singer, CHILDREN AT WAR 30 (2006) (reporting estimates that, "in addition to the 300,000 active child combatants, another half million children serve in more than fifty state military and paramilitary forces presently at peace").

In any event, the number of *current* child soldiers is only one indication of the scope of child soldiering. The number of *former* child soldiers also is of central concern. Over the past decade, several armed conflicts that involved children as participants—such as in Northern Uganda, Sri Lanka, Liberia, and Sierra Leone—thankfully have wound down. The attenuation of these conflicts exposes the myriad of challenges of durably reintegrating former child soldiers into civilian life and promoting social repair and reconciliation. Many future-oriented lessons can be learned from these experiences. Child soldiers also exit armed forces while conflict still rages, mostly through escape or abandonment. Owing to the spontaneity of the process, the number of children who exit conflict in this fashion is difficult to gauge. Some subsequently cycle back to violence. Finally, on the most somber note, rates of child soldier casualties in or as a result of recent armed conflicts have not been accurately determined.

This Chapter begins by surveying the places where children currently are, and recently have been, associated with armed forces or armed groups. It then explores how international efforts to eradicate the practice of child soldiering overlap with broader normative understandings of modern childhood, incorporate the progress narrative of contemporary humanitarianism, and synergize with popularized perceptions of the changing nature of armed conflict. An epistemological concern—how do we know what we know about child soldiering?—lurks below the surface of these efforts. Competition has arisen among disciplines regarding the appropriate vocabularies, tools, and methodologies to conceptualize the sources and effects of child soldiering. Faultless passive victim imagery prioritizes some disciplines, neglects others, and politicizes certain lines of inquiry.[3] As a result, the analytic lexicon and tool-kit of potential policy options each has narrowed.

(i) Then, Recently, and Now

Children have participated in armed conflict throughout history. They have fought as soldiers; maintained morale as drummer boys; cooked, portered, and sustained garrison life; served as a defense of last resort; suffered indignities and abuses; and inspired through their courage. Historically, their involvement in war was not usual. Nor was it encouraged in the case of front-line participation. But neither was it repudiated as a matter of law. Responsibility for child soldiering did not trigger criminal punishment. Hence, the assertion that the contemporary presence of children in combat "violat[es] the once universal rule that they simply have no

---

[3] *Cf.* Jo Boyden, *Anthropology Under Fire: Ethics, Researchers and Children in War, in* CHILDREN AND YOUTH ON THE FRONT LINE: ETHNOGRAPHY, ARMED CONFLICT AND DISPLACEMENT 237, 248 (Jo Boyden and Joanna de Berry eds, 2004) [hereinafter CHILDREN AND YOUTH ON THE FRONT LINE] ("A focus on children's rights and protection has brought with it a concern to treat the young as especially deserving victims, as opposed to conscious agents, of political conflict. As a consequence, important topics such as children's moral development, their political consciousness and activism, and hence their motives for enlistment, are neglected in favour of research focusing on impairment to health and other negative war impacts.").

part in warfare, either as target or participant,"[4] presents an artificially sweetened version of history. The unlawfulness of the use of child soldiers and the criminalization thereof is a new dimension to an historical phenomenon.

Carl von Clausewitz, a renowned philosopher of war, reportedly entered the Prussian Army at the age of twelve.[5] Alexander the Great first became a regent at the age of sixteen. Jeanne d'Arc, who as a teenager invigorated despondent French forces in the Hundred Years' War, remains a hagiographic figure. A bronze statue of her on horseback—proud, poised, and tautly raising her *oriflamme*—adorns the plaza outside the State Library of Victoria, in Melbourne, Australia. I wrote much of this book while on sabbatical leave in Melbourne and regularly walked by this statue on my way to the university. Several blocks away, I then passed a mural on an outside wall of the Australian Red Cross building. Personifying the organization's appeal to end the military recruitment of children, this mural depicts a very young boy—in shorts and short-sleeves, knees bare, his left sock fallen down, with a mop of messy hair—eerily standing under the weight of weaponry and ammunition belts. The contrast between these two works of art is striking. Each radiates an exaggerated treatment of its subject. When juxtaposed, however, they reveal the trajectory of the child soldier in public life. What was once the possibility of martial pride now slouches toward the unavoidability of collective shame.

Children soldiered in both the Union and Confederate armies in the US Civil War.[6] Cadets of the Virginia Military Institute—many aged fifteen to eighteen—fought fiercely for the Confederacy in the 1864 Battle of New Market. They were credited with the victory. The Virginia Military Institute is located in Lexington, Virginia, the town where I live. The Stonewall Jackson Memorial Hall, situated right in the heart of its campus, displays a mural by Benjamin Clinedinst. This mural lionizes the youthful cadets' battle charge.

A century later, children participated in the US civil rights movement. Teenagers took a stand in desegregating schools and lunch-counters. Nine months before Rosa Parks' celebrated activism, fifteen year-old Claudette Colvin refused to yield her seat on a Montgomery, Alabama, bus. Colvin was arrested. Colvin's is an untold story of the civil rights movement—she was, unlike Parks, perceived as too young, too brash, and—then—too pregnant to serve as a model for a major public boycott.

In Birmingham, Alabama—ground zero for much of the civil rights struggle—the Children's March in 1963 involved large numbers of youth, some of whom ended up facing fire hoses. In Birmingham's Kelly Ingram Park, a statue sculpted by James Drake in 1992 commemorates this march. It depicts a young girl with braids and a taller boy, each standing defiantly behind jail bars. They radiate calmness, grit,

---

[4] Singer, CHILDREN AT WAR, *supra* note 2, at 7.
[5] Alice Schmidt, *Volunteer* Child *Soldiers as Reality: A Development Issue for Africa*, 2(1) NEW SCHOOL ECONOMIC REVIEW 49, 69 n. 15 (2007).
[6] David M. Rosen, ARMIES OF THE YOUNG: CHILD SOLDIERS IN WAR AND TERRORISM 5 (2005). Adopting an ethnohistorical approach, Rosen argues that the construction of the child soldier cannot be disentangled from the pursuit of a global politics of age through which childhood serves as a proxy for other political interests. *Id.* at 157.

confidence, and determination in the best tradition of the non-violent political protestor. Elsewhere in the park, another statue (from 1995, entitled "Foot Soldiers") portrays a somewhat older youth threatened by a policeman and dog. Although recoiling from the dog's bared fangs, the youth keeps his feet firmly in place. He refuses to cede any ground.

A revered monument in Warsaw—the statute of the "Little Insurgent"— commemorates Polish child resistance to the Nazi occupation. Jewish child soldiers also doggedly contested Nazi oppression in the ghettos and forests of Eastern Europe.[7] Their acts of bravery and heroism have come to be widely lauded. Jewish child resisters were hardly passive pawns of adults. In fact, they first had to thwart the more moderate Jewish ghetto leadership, which portrayed them as irresponsible.[8] Hannah Arendt has written critically of the various *Judenräte*, the local Jewish councils whose leaders "almost without exception, cooperated in one way or another, for one reason or another, with the Nazis."[9] Youth movements challenged the *Judenräte*.

The international legal imagination, however, currently gives short shrift to the possibility that juveniles may fight to achieve coherent goals. It depicts them as apolitical. That said, in modern times, children have participated, including in militarized capacities, in national liberation movements and anti-colonial campaigns. They have stood on the front lines of self-determination assertions. Youths have struggled against racism, autocracy, and governmental abuses—often energizing resistance and becoming heralded as heroes. For example, "[s]pontaneous participation of school children and students in South Africa played a leading role in the struggle against apartheid."[10] Julius Malema, a provocative figure who is currently leader of the African National Congress' youth wing, claims he had been taught to fire a gun at the age of eleven. In 2011, a lawsuit alleged that Malema fomented hate speech against the Afrikaner population. Legal counsel for the complainants raised Malema's having carried a gun "illegally" as a child during the anti-apartheid armed struggle and sardonically noted how that "seems to be typical of Africa, using children to fight wars."[11] Children strove to overcome oppression in El Salvador and Palestine and Nepal—at times crossing the line into armed conflict. The face of the protests that rocked the Arab world in 2011 was youthful.

These vignettes form part of the composite picture of child soldiering. The practice also has a bitterly reprehensible side. The picture of child soldiering includes horrid brutalities visited upon child recruits, such as abduction, torture,

---

[7] *Id.* at 19–56.

[8] *Id.* at 36.

[9] Hannah Arendt, Eichmann in Jerusalem: A Report on the Banality of Evil 125 (1977) (orig. 1963). This aspect of Arendt's work has proven controversial. Yehuda Bauer has parried it. Yehuda Bauer, Rethinking the Holocaust 77–78 (2001).

[10] Barbara Fontana, *Child Soldiers and International Law*, 6(3) African Security Review (1997), *available at* <http://www.iss.co.za/pubs/asr/6No3/Fontana.html>.

[11] Celia W. Dugger, *Separating Free Speech From Hate in South Africa*, N.Y. Times (April 30, 2011) (quoting Adv. Roelof du Plessis, who suggested that Malema was a Communist and that South Africa was heading toward genocide against Whites).

sexual abuse, murder, forced drug ingestion, and compelled participation in the commission of crimes against humanity. The international community's growing concern with human rights, and its salutary stance that children are entitled to those rights, represents another new dimension to child soldiering. Perceptions of children as rights-bearers have facilitated bringing these grotesque aspects of child soldiering out into much sharper public relief. The tireless efforts of global civil society have proven invaluable in this regard.

Today, child soldiers—as with former child soldiers—exist in each of the world's regions.

In Colombia, child soldiers were voluntarily enlisted and forcibly recruited into armed opposition groups (the FARC and the ELN), where they laid mines and undertook support tasks. The largest pro-government paramilitary group, the AUC, also recruited child soldiers. Peace negotiations in Colombia have informally demobilized many child soldiers, although 14,000 children are still reported to be associated with armed forces or armed groups. Child soldiers have been recruited into the Bolivian armed forces. Children have participated in armed violence in Guatemala and Peru.

UNICEF estimates over 6,000 cases of child recruitment between 2003 and 2008 by rebels in Sri Lanka.[12] The Liberation Tigers of Tamil Eelam (LTTE or Tamil Tigers)—a violent secessionist group which fought the Sri Lankan government—turned extensively to child soldiers. The LTTE was defeated in 2009; scattered attempts have since taken place to reconstitute it. The Sri Lankan government has declined to criminally prosecute former LTTE child soldiers for war crimes. The Khmer Rouge used youthful cadres. In fact, "[i]n Cambodia... children and adolescents fast became Pol Pot's foot soldiers, its torturers, its workers and its spies, policing family and community life and leading the relentless marches though the countryside that killed so many civilians."[13] Child agency also had an obverse side in Cambodia, insofar as "some of the children... defied the Khmer Rouge by running away from indoctrination centres and hiding in their homes... [and]... [i]n order to escape the attention of the authorities, many pretended to be deaf, mute or foolish."[14]

The Burmese government voraciously recruits children through harsh methods.[15] One quarter of its national armed forces (the Tatmadaw) is estimated to be composed of persons under the age of eighteen. Child soldiers also are found within the thirty or so non-state armed groups in Burma, although in smaller numbers.[16]

---

[12] *Retraining Tiger Cubs*, THE ECONOMIST (July 16, 2009), *available at* <http://www.economist.com/node/14052240>.

[13] Jo Boyden, *Children, War and World Disorder in the 21st Century: A Review of the Theories and the Literature on Children's Contributions to Armed Violence* 7 (Queen Elizabeth House, University of Oxford, Working Paper No. 138, 2006).

[14] Boyden, *Anthropology Under Fire*, *supra* note 3, at 256.

[15] The military leaders of Burma changed the country's name to Myanmar in 1989. The UN uses Myanmar. Some states, however, use the name Burma, which the country's democracy movement prefers. This book uses Burma.

[16] Human Rights Watch, SOLD TO BE SOLDIERS: THE RECRUITMENT AND USE OF CHILD SOLDIERS IN BURMA 6 (2007).

In Nepal, child soldiers—3,000 of whom were released in early 2010 as part of peace negotiations—participated in Maoist rebel groups. Some children joined these forces to protest the government. Others joined under false promises.[17] Child soldiers served in pro-Indonesian militia forces in Timor-Leste. *Chega!*, a truth commission report published in Timor-Leste in 2005, noted that child militia members took part in serious human rights violations. Armed groups in Indonesia also have turned to children. Children have been associated with armed forces or armed groups in Bangladesh, Laos, Pakistan, Thailand, the Philippines, and Jammu and Kashmir.

In its war with Iraq, Iran extensively deployed children. In addition to fighting, Iranian authorities used children to walk across minefields in order to clear them. Children reportedly still are militarily recruited in Iran. Iraqi children also fought in the war with Iran. Moreover, Iraqi youth (incorporated into civilian militias) participated in the 2003 conflict against the United States and its allies.[18] In post-Saddam Iraq, children have engaged in suicide bombing. Child soldiers have fought, killed, and died in Afghanistan through successive conflicts.[19] Hundreds of Taliban-supporting child fighters have been arrested in recent years in Afghanistan. Northern Alliance forces, moreover, "often commanded young boys to come with them to fight, and refusal typically led to beatings or destruction of the refusing child's home."[20] Child soldiers face serious reintegration challenges in Afghanistan today: many Taliban volunteer child recruits, for example, currently enrolled in rehabilitation programs simply wish to re-enlist and return to the battlefield. In Palestine, the face of the first *intifada* was youthful: among those arrested, the average age was seventeen.[21] Children remain militarily involved in the Occupied Territories. Internal conflict in Yemen enmeshes children as participants.

In Libya, the permissible age of recruitment under national law is eighteen. Under Muammar Qaddafi, Libya's state armed forces nevertheless recruited minors. In fact, and in the face of international judicialization efforts, the recent conflict saw an uptick in such recruitment. Rebel armed groups in Libya for their part enlisted volunteer children, mostly sixteen and seventeen year-olds, in their

---

[17] Among children thusly recruited, many ran away because of abuse while others chose to remain. Radhika Coomaraswamy, *Child Soldiers: Root Causes and UN Initiatives* 2 (February 2009) (lecture on file with the author). In Nepal, "targeted advocacy work" prompted a proposal that child soldiers be recognized "primarily as victims" in the development of draft legislation for a national truth and reconciliation commission. Cécile Aptel and Virginie Ladisch, THROUGH A NEW LENS: A CHILD-SENSITIVE APPROACH TO TRANSITIONAL JUSTICE 14 (ICTJ, August 2011).

[18] P.W. Singer, *Talk Is Cheap: Getting Serious About Preventing Child Soldiers*, 37 CORNELL INT'L. L. J. 561, 562 (2004).

[19] *Id.* at 571 (specifically discussing use of child soldiers by the Taliban). Teenagers joined the Taliban forces willingly: "Some say their parents supported the decision to take up arms. Others left home without warning, disregarding the wishes of relatives and heeding what they call a religious and moral obligation." Kevin Sieff, *Young Afghan fighters eager to rejoin Taliban*, WASH. POST (September 15, 2011) (reporting also the "disappointing results" of reintegration programs in Kabul which trace, in part, to the "intransigence of the teens") (on file with the author).

[20] Michael Wessells, *Psychosocial Issues in Reintegrating Child Soldiers*, 37 CORNELL INT'L L. J. 513, 514 (2004).

[21] Ilsa M. Glazer, *Book Review*, 79(2) ANTHROPOLOGICAL QUARTERLY 373, 382 (2006). Israel has imprisoned Palestinian children for security offenses or for being associated with an armed group.

campaign. NATO, *de facto* committed to ousting Qaddafi, expressed only limited distress regarding these rebel child recruits. Desperate for fighters, rebel militias took whomever was willing and able. But, still, teenage recruits came forward to serve. In some cases, their parents encouraged them to join; in others, they contradicted the wishes of their parents and, on their own, traveled great distances to sign up. Why? To try to oust a dictator, expiate anger, and break a cycle of indignity that they perceived their parents as having endured.[22] Fighting exposed these youths to great peril. One article, appearing in the Canadian press, warned of their lack of preparedness. Reporting from inside a rebel camp, this article floridly noted "[a] shambolic line of soldiers, many under 18 and at least three only 15" while recounting how "[t]he scene . . . looked like a teen remake of *The Dirty Dozen. . . .* [N]ot so much West Point as *Welcome Back, Kotter.*"[23] The farcical tone of this article is not particularly helpful. In places it is strikingly belittling, to wit, remarking that some recruits were "barely able to tie their boots properly." Does this tone reflect the way the rebel recruits see themselves? Does it presage a propitious way to deter child soldiering?

Virtually all of the multiple sides to systemic conflict in the DRC conscripted, enlisted, or actively used child soldiers. Children allegedly formed around 30% of the militia forces of DRC rebel leader Thomas Lubanga Dyilo, who faces trial at the ICC.[24] Officially, DRC government forces ceased enlisting children under the age of eighteen in 2003, but some children still serve in those forces (into which some rebel units have been incorporated). Although the involvement of children in armed conflict in the DRC has attenuated over time, it has not disappeared. Far from it. As of 2011, 30,000 child soldiers apparently remain in armed groups.[25] In the DRC, many children who have passed through disarmament, demobilization, and reintegration (DDR) programs subsequently become re-recruited. Abhorrent violence (notably sexual torture) inflicted by members of militia forces, including children, remains widespread. As is the case elsewhere, some former child soldiers test positive for HIV/AIDS.

Armed conflict in Angola and Mozambique—now quiescent—directly implicated thousands of children, often forcibly, but also through self-enlistment for ideological or material aspirations.[26] Angola's UNITA faction extensively invoked harsh disciplinary measures against its youthful cadres. Children actively serve as

---

[22] Kareem Fahim, *In Libya Revolt, Youth Will Serve, or at Least Try*, N.Y. TIMES (March 11, 2011); Anthony Shadid, *Veering From Peaceful Models, Libya's Youth Revolt Turns Toward Chaos*, N.Y. TIMES (March 12, 2011).

[23] Doug Saunders, *Ill-equipped teenagers members of the Libyan anti-Gadhafi rebels*, THE GLOBE AND MAIL UPDATE (July 10, 2011) (on file with the author).

[24] Luis Moreno-Ocampo, *Opening Statement*, The Case of the Prosecutor v. Lubanga, ICC-01/04-01/06, p. 16 (The Hague, January 26, 2009).

[25] Inna Lazareva, *Many DRC Children Volunteer to Fight*, IWPR ICC-Africa Update (No. 291, March 10, 2011).

[26] Alcinda Honwana, CHILD SOLDIERS IN AFRICA 7, 29, 54 (2006); Jessica Schafer, *The Use of Patriarchal Imagery in the Civil War in Mozambique and its Implications for the Reintegration of Child Soldiers*, *in* CHILDREN AND YOUTH ON THE FRONT LINE, *supra* note 3, at 87, 90.

combatants in extant conflicts in the Central African Republic (CAR), Chad, and Côte d'Ivoire. The use of child soldiers also is reported in Burundi and Zimbabwe. Evidence of child soldiering among national armed forces recently has emerged in Somalia.[27] Charles Taylor, the former Liberian head of state currently facing international prosecution, had, in his early political days, built an army around child soldiers. Estimates suggest that 21,000 child soldiers fought in Liberia.[28]

Government forces and rebel groups in the Sudan turned to child soldiers throughout internecine conflict, most extensively in the 1990s, although recourse to children still persists. UNICEF reports "that up to 6,000 child soldiers, some as young as 11, have been recruited by rebels and government forces in Darfur;" it estimates another 2,000 child soldiers in southern and eastern Sudan.[29] Elegant accounts have been rendered of the "lost boys" of Sudan—children tumultuously afflicted by conflict between the north and the south of the country—many of whom ended up resettled elsewhere as refugees.[30] In light of the very recent recrudescence of hostilities in Sudan, this time in the central Nuba region of the country, the potential implication of children as victims, perpetrators, and witnesses of atrocity once again emerges.

Children suffered terribly in the 1994 Rwandan genocide. Hutu extremists targeted Tutsi children, even infants, for elimination. Epidemiological survey research regarding the Rwandan genocide found that 95.9% of children witnessed violence, 87.5% saw dead bodies or parts of bodies, while 69.5% witnessed someone being killed or injured.[31] Minors also became perpetrators. Some manned the barricades that identified the Tutsi "cockroaches" to be eliminated. A few even were suspected of planning the genocide. Youths—many of them teenagers—also became central to the effort to oust the genocidal government. These youths staffed the ranks of the Rwandese Patriotic Army (RPA), the only military force actually to intercede to halt the genocide.[32] The RPA has been lauded for its efficiency, discipline, and determination. That said, it also has been suspected of committing systematic human rights abuses and war crimes against the Hutu population following the genocide.

In Northern Uganda, one estimate puts the number of children who had been abducted by the rebel Lord's Resistance Army (LRA) at between 25,000 and

---

[27] Jeffrey Gettleman, *Children Carry Guns for a U.S. Ally, Somalia*, N.Y. TIMES (June 13, 2010) (reporting also that rebel insurgent groups in Somalia extensively use child soldiers).

[28] Olaoluwa Olusanya, *Granting Immunity to Child Combatants Supranationally*, in SENTENCING AND SANCTIONING IN SUPRANATIONAL CRIMINAL LAW 87, 87 (Roelof Haveman and Olaoluwa Olusanya eds, 2006).

[29] Louis Charbonneau, *Interview—ICC looking at child soldier issue in Darfur*, Reuters (June 2, 2009).

[30] Dave Eggers, WHAT IS THE WHAT: THE AUTOBIOGRAPHY OF VALENTINO ACHAK DENG (2006); *War Child* (2008, documentary film, dir./prod. Karim Chrobog).

[31] Luc Chauvin, James Mugaju, and Jondoh Comlavi, *Evaluation of the psychosocial trauma recovery programme in Rwanda*, 21 EVALUATION AND PROGRAM PLANNING 385, 387 (1998).

[32] Upon a visit, Dallaire notes that "a good number seemed well under eighteen" and that he "admiringly studied these young soldiers and junior NCOs." Roméo Dallaire, THEY FIGHT LIKE SOLDIERS, THEY DIE LIKE CHILDREN 35 (2010) (noting also that some "might have been as young as fourteen when they first entered the fray").

38,000.[33] At some points, minors comprised 90% of LRA forces. The LRA has been embroiled in a decades-long conflict with the Ugandan National Army. This conflict has far-reaching consequences for Northern Uganda's ethnic Acholi population. The LRA was named as such in 1993. Its precursor was known as the Holy Spirit Mobile Forces. In the mid-1980s, under the leadership of Alice Lakwena, these Forces initially attracted support from young Acholi men and women.[34] Although now massively weakened, with nearly all abductees having escaped, the LRA remains active. It continues patterns of looting, violence, and abduction. Its activities have migrated from Uganda to the DRC, South Sudan, and CAR. Notwithstanding having been indicted by the ICC, LRA leader Joseph Kony remains at large. Children also serve in the ranks of the Ugandan army and, previously, within Ugandan President Museveni's National Resistance Movement.[35]

Thousands of children were associated with all sides of the conflict that raged in Sierra Leone from 1991 to 2002, whether the Revolutionary United Front (RUF), the Armed Forces Revolutionary Council (AFRC), the pro-government Civil Defence Forces (CDF), or the Sierra Leonean Army (SLA).[36] Although children were recruited by force, significant numbers willingly joined. Nonetheless, "the majority of [Sierra Leonean] youth, including those in desperately poor situations, did not join the military or rebel movements."[37] Among child soldiers, commission of atrocities (including amputations of the hands and feet of civilian populations), resocialization into violence, and drug use all were widespread. Most child soldiers remained low-level auxiliaries, but some over the age of fifteen became generals.[38] Reasonably free and fair elections occurred in Sierra Leone in 2007. Despite facing significant challenges, the country has stabilized.

Children also have served as fighters in recent European conflicts, that is, in Chechnya, Croatia, Bosnia and Herzegovina, and Serbia. Many states—including the United Kingdom, the United States, China, India, the Netherlands, Canada, France, New Zealand, Germany, and Australia—permit voluntary recruitment of

---

[33] Phuong N. Pham, Patrick Vinck, and Eric Stover, *The Lord's Resistance Army and Forced Conscription in Northern Uganda*, 30 HUM. RTS. Q. 404, 404 (2008) (reporting on the period from 1986 to 2006).

[34] Sverker Finnström, LIVING WITH BAD SURROUNDINGS: WAR, HISTORY, AND EVERYDAY MOMENTS IN NORTHERN UGANDA 75–76 (2008).

[35] REDRESS Trust, VICTIMS, PERPETRATORS OR HEROES? CHILD SOLDIERS BEFORE THE INTERNATIONAL CRIMINAL COURT 9 (2006).

[36] Theresa S. Betancourt, Stephanie Simmons, Ivelina Borisova, Stephanie E. Brewer, Uzo Iweala, and Marie de la Soudière, *High Hopes, Grim Reality: Reintegration and the Education of Former Child Soldiers in Sierra Leone*, 52(4) COMP. EDUC. REV. 565, 565 (2008) (citation omitted) (estimating that 15,000 to 22,000 children were "taken from their families and forced to serve the military groups in a number of ways").

[37] Susan Shepler, *The Social and Cultural Context of Child Soldiering in Sierra Leone* 8 (2004) (manuscript on file with the author) (citing the work of Yusuf Bangura).

[38] Pacifique Manirakiza, *Les enfants face au système international de justice: à la recherche d'un modèle de justice pénale internationale pour les délinquants mineurs*, 34 QUEEN'S L.J. 719, 761 (2009) (footnote omitted).

minors into national armed forces, albeit largely under strict conditions.[39] Michael Wessells argues that "[t]his normalization and legitimation of child soldiering by countries such as the United States and the United Kingdom, which claim to protect children and to have children's best interests at heart, creates an international climate conducive to children's exploitation as soldiers by rogue groups such as the LRA."[40] P. W. Singer, on the other hand, upbraids the Coalition to Stop the Use of Child Soldiers for "wast[ing] ... political capital by engaging in a long drawn out public relations war with the U.S. and British governments."[41] He skeptically notes that a Coalition report listed US policy and LRA abductions "as equivalent abuses under the same heading."[42]

The contrasting positions of Wessells and Singer illuminate a broader theme. International efforts, which largely track Wessells' approach, treat all armed forces or armed groups as equals, regardless of their actual nature or structure. Although certainly recognizing that the situation of some child soldiers is more urgent, the international legal imagination tries not to render protection contingent upon inquiries about the internal workings of the armed forces or groups. This approach has much to say for it, not the least of which is its predictability, clarity, and consistency. The fact remains, however, that armed forces and armed groups that involve children are not all alike. They differ widely. Some have rules that preclude child volunteers from going anywhere near conflict zones. Some armed forces that have such rules, however, may not always be willing or able to enforce them. Some armed forces offer enlistees solid benefits, training, and career prospects. Other armed forces or groups abuse child recruits. Rape of girls may be chronic. Others deliberately place ill-equipped children on the front lines.

In any event, it is important not to make too much hay out of a simple birthday. Many US volunteer soldiers actually fighting in Iraq and Afghanistan are barely over the age of eighteen. Their reasons for enlisting include pursuit of economic opportunity and training, martial pride, patriotism, furthering family legacies, and the lure of adventure. Some are there because they are caught up in a maze of successive rotations. They are not child soldiers and, hence, are not a protected class. But, still, when tragedy strikes they often are referred to as "just kids."[43]

(ii) Helping Hands, Humanitarian Handiwork, and Victim Purity

Global civil society has engaged the scourge of child soldiering. Several leading organizations (including Human Rights Watch, Defence for Children International,

---

[39] Chapter 5(i) examines this topic in greater detail. Reportedly, 26,755 recruits joined the US armed forces at the age of seventeen between January 1 and September 30, 2002. Michael Wessells, CHILD SOLDIERS: FROM VIOLENCE TO PROTECTION 17 (2006, first paperback 2009).

[40] *Id.*

[41] Singer, *Talk Is Cheap*, *supra* note 18, at 574.

[42] *Id.*

[43] Greg Jaffe, *Lt. Gen. John Kelly, who lost son to war, says U.S. largely unaware of sacrifice*, WASH. POST (March 2, 2011).

International Save the Children Alliance, and World Vision International) began in 1998 to unite as the Coalition to Stop the Use of Child Soldiers. Many other NGOs also are committed to the cause, along with UNICEF and diverse UN organs. The integrated efforts of these actors, activists, and advocates have catalyzed a vibrant movement. This movement informs the public of the harms occasioned by child soldiering, galvanizes opposition to this pernicious practice, and also advances a much broader child rights framework. This constellation of actors has undertaken yeoman's work and has effected tremendous strides.

The portrayal of child soldiers as faultless passive victims has proven central to the campaign to end child soldiering.[44] This portrayal telegraphs a compelling visual and cues a clear message. It mobilizes. Notwithstanding strategic advantages, deployment of this imagery also runs certain risks. Mindfulness regarding these risks is all the more important given that the intended beneficiaries, children in armed forces or groups, have very little control over or say in the content of the messages disseminated on their behalf.

Although this portrayal has become more sublime over time, its core essentialisms have sunk in. What is more, international law and policy are absorbing them. Accordingly, it is worthwhile to take a second, and slightly more interrogative, look at how advocacy networks conceive of the child soldier. Their approaches may—perhaps unsuspectingly—present a number of shadow sides. I would like to sound four cautionary notes: (a) victimhood may lead to victimcy;[45] (b) "it's not your fault" can only go so far; (c) the framed image coddles stereotypes of contemporary conflicts in the developing world as "new wars;" and (d) the focus on children associated with armed forces or armed groups may at once be too broad and too narrow.

(a) From Victimhood to Victimcy

A chorus of observers has remarked how global civil society and UN agencies describe, project, and approach former child soldiers as vulnerable victims bereft of agency.[46] Transnational networks concerned with child soldiers can, thereby, be found to rely upon and nourish a sanitized approach that, according to political

---

[44] This campaign mimics the dynamics of innocent victims, abnormal oppressors, and noble humanitarians that David Kennedy and Makau Mutua artfully expose as motoring international human rights law generally. Makau Mutua, *Savages, Victims, and Saviors: The Metaphor of Human Rights*, 42 HARV. INT'L L. J. 201, 201–202, 227 (2001); David Kennedy, THE DARK SIDES OF VIRTUE: REASSESSING INTERNATIONAL HUMANITARIANISM 14 (2004).

[45] The term victimcy is Mats Utas'. *See infra* notes 51–52.

[46] Angela Veale, *The Criminal Responsibility of Former Child Soldiers: Contributions from Psychology*, *in* INTERNATIONAL CRIMINAL ACCOUNTABILITY AND THE RIGHTS OF CHILDREN 97, 102 (Karin Arts and Vesselin Popovski eds, 2006); Jason Hart, *The Politics of "Child Soldiers"*, XIII(1) BROWN JOURNAL OF WORLD AFFAIRS 217, 220 (2006). *See also* Schmidt, *supra* note 5, at 49, 64 (noting also that "presenting weak and vulnerable 'children' can help to mobilize resources"); Ben Mergelsberg, *Between two worlds: former LRA soldiers in northern Uganda*, *in* THE LORD'S RESISTANCE ARMY: MYTH AND REALITY 156, 171 (Tim Allen and Koen Vlassenroot eds, 2010) (cautioning against "the discourse of the innocent and victimized child soldier without agency [that is] reflected in many child soldier testimonies quoted in NGO campaigns or the media").

scientist Charli Carpenter, "parse[s] complex events into a simplistic frame that will capture the attention of a Western audience often ignorant of and apathetic to world affairs."[47] Carpenter posits that this approach is intended to generate sympathy, funding, and even the political will for multilateral intervention. She then incisively adds that:

An important requirement for eliciting sympathy is the construction of a victim who is "spontaneously acceptable to Western viewers in his or her own right." Acceptability is dictated foremost by '100% victim status'—the symbolic victim must be seen as entirely lacking agency; s/he must be both unable to help her/himself and an unequivocal non-participant in the political events from which his/her misery results....[48]

In the case of the child soldier, operational reliance on presumptions of vulnerability and victimhood does not cease once concerns have been identified and funds procured. These presumptions extend into the actual content of programmatic interventions. Jessica Schafer, drawing from her work in Mozambique, points out how "[t]he idea that most fighters were unwilling, coerced and often uncomprehending children persisted and was implicit in the design of reintegration programmes."[49] In contrast, Schafer's own research prompts her to remark that these fighters had a much broader range of motives. They did not see themselves "overwhelmingly as innocent children, co-opted into a war without knowledge or understanding."[50]

Child soldiers may initially perceive the programs as irrelevant or unsuitable for them. Eventually, however, the incentives offered by victimhood status may come to suffuse how former child soldiers see themselves. In this regard, former child soldiers can develop "victimcy." Cultural anthropologist Mats Utas uses this term to denote child soldiers' displaying "individual agency by representing themselves as powerless victims"[51] and thereby "hiding ... actions in passive victimhood and reaping the benefit of other people's pity."[52] Over time, victimcy hobbles energized citizenship and youth autonomy. It regenerates dependency. It curries incapacity.

(b) It's Not Your Fault

What to do about child soldiers suspected of implication in the commission of acts of atrocity? How to approach their homecoming? In Sierra Leone, according to

---

[47] R. Charli Carpenter, *"Women, Children and Other Vulnerable Groups": Gender, Strategic Frames and the Protection of Civilians as a Transnational Issue*, 49 INT'L STUD. Q. 295, 316 (2005).

[48] *Id.* (citing R. Braumann, citation in original).

[49] Schafer, *supra* note 26, at 90.

[50] *Id.*

[51] Mats Utas, *Fluid Research Fields: Studying Excombatant Youth in the Aftermath of the Liberian Civil War, in* CHILDREN AND YOUTH ON THE FRONT LINE, *supra* note 3, at 209 (citation omitted). For Utas, "victimcy is also a political response to real security threats, as well as an economic strategy in relation to humanitarian aid projects, and as such is an obstacle to research." *Id.*

[52] Mats Utas, *Agency of Victims: Young Women in the Liberian Civil War, in* MAKERS & BREAKERS: CHILDREN & YOUTH IN POSTCOLONIAL AFRICA 53, 75 (Alcinda Honwana and Filip de Boeck eds, 2005). *Cf.* Honwana, CHILD SOLDIERS IN AFRICA, *supra* note 26, at 15 ("My observations in the field show that populations affected by war are likely to enhance their victim status in the presence of NGOs.").

Susan Shepler, "NGO workers explained to communities that their children were not responsible for their crimes because of their age."[53] Communities accepted these explanations, but not seamlessly. Shepler remarks that the notion that "anyone under 18 years is to be considered a child and therefore not to be held accountable" is a "newly imported idea" for Sierra Leoneans, who share a much more "pliable and contingent" vision of youthful innocence.[54] Some distance arose between the local vision and that of the international legal imagination. In response, NGO personnel organized sensitization and reintegration workshops for local communities. Workshops were intended to "calm the residents and to explain they had to accept the former child soldiers 'into their hearts'."[55] These workshops were pedagogic. During them, attendees received instruction on a variety of topics, including the international rights of the child and trauma. And, indeed, local constituencies listened. After all, what NGOs and international organizations believe, and what they do, matters considerably to inter- and post-conflict communities. The fact remains that, "[i]n West Africa and in other so-called weak states, NGOs are clearly better funded and more present than the state in many cases."[56] In such jurisdictions, socio-legal spaces become infused with foreign expertise and technocracy.

International expectations as embodied in formal treaties, best practices, and how-to manuals concerning the rights of the child are intended to shift the tenor of national and local policies. Assuredly, at times international expectations do not occasion substantive shifts since they mesh with local values. When they do occur, moreover, many of these shifts are salutary. However, it should not be taken as axiomatic that portable international technique about child soldiers as a group is in all cases superior to local intuition about child soldiers as individuals. Do community members lack understanding of the violence that may have roiled their lives? Is it not somewhat sophomoric for internationals to claim they grasp the etiology of child violence so much better than locals? Regardless of why some Sierra Leonean child soldiers did what they did, some of their acts were terribly sadistic.[57] This fact cannot be swept away so blithely.

In Sierra Leone, in any event, official responses included telling former child soldiers that, whatever had happened, "it wasn't their fault." This pedagogy matches an advocacy position of general application, which fills the international

---

[53] Susan Shepler, *The Rites of the Child: Global Discourses of Youth and Reintegrating Child Soldiers in Sierra Leone*, 4 J. Hum. Rts. 197, 200 (2005). Explanations also emphasized that the children had a right to family reunification. *Id.* at 200–201.

[54] *Id.* at 205, 209 n. 15. *Cf.* Tim Kelsall, Culture Under Cross-Examination: International Justice and the Special Court for Sierra Leone 158 (2009) (remarking that "conceptions of children in rural Sierra Leone differ greatly to those preferred by the international community").

[55] Shepler, *The Rites of the Child, supra* note 53, at 202. Shepler, who provides an ethnographic description of a reintegration meeting she attended in a village she calls Essex, penetratingly observes: "[This event] was supposed to be about children, but there were no children present. It was supposed to be about community involvement, but the answers seemed to come from the top down." *Id.* at 204.

[56] *Id.* at 207.

[57] *Cf. Bringing the wicked to the dock*, The Economist (March 9, 2006) ("Child soldiers, some not yet in their teens, would rip open pregnant women's stomachs after taking bets on the sex of the fetus. Women's vaginas were sewn up with fishing line. Mouths were clamped shut with padlocks.").

legal imagination and which exhorts that "[c]hild perpetrators are ... victims of criminal policies for which adults are primarily responsible."[58] Ishmael Beah—a former child soldier in Sierra Leone and currently a leading advocate to end the practice—attests to this phenomenon in his courageous and widely read memoir.[59] In this work, Beah candidly describes the grievous violence that he and his unit perpetrated.[60] Following his decommissioning by "four beaming men in ... UNICEF shirts," Beah relates how he was told, and eventually came to believe, that none of what happened was his fault:

In the morning I would feel one of the staff members wrap a blanket around me saying, 'This isn't your fault, you know. It really isn't ... '
   'None of what happened was your fault. You were just a little boy ... '
   'None of these things are your fault,' she would always say sternly at the end of every conversation. Even though I had always heard that phrase from every staff member—and frankly I had always hated it—I began that day to believe it.[61]

Shepler similarly identifies "discourses of abdicated responsibility," a phrase she coins to describe the refrain on the part of some former child soldiers that: "I didn't choose to fight, I was forced, I was drugged, I was too young to know any better."[62] According to Shepler, the dénouement of conflict is such that "some child excombatants exercise agency, paradoxically, through their claims of war-time *nonagency*."[63] She thereby evokes similar themes to Utas' victimcy.

   The "it's not your fault" pedagogy also pervaded Northern Uganda. Noting that many reception centers in Northern Uganda are run by NGOs, Ben Mergelsberg reports that his informants were told in these reception centers "that to have been part of the LRA was not their fault, since they were innocent victims, abducted and made to do things they had never wanted to do."[64] Andrew Mawson also examines this subtext to social reconciliation in Northern Uganda. Mawson argues that the

---

[58] No Peace Without Justice and UNICEF Innocenti Research Centre, INTERNATIONAL CRIMINAL JUSTICE AND CHILDREN 34 (2002) [hereinafter INTERNATIONAL CRIMINAL JUSTICE AND CHILDREN].

[59] Ishmael Beah, A LONG WAY GONE: MEMOIRS OF A BOY SOLDIER (2007). Fearful of once again becoming a child soldier, Beah fled Sierra Leone. His voyage was ingenious and intrepid. In the US, Beah pursued his education. Although deeply influential and widely popular—having sold over 700,000 copies—his book has attracted controversy regarding alleged inaccuracies in reporting details of his conflict experiences (these controversies do not relate to the "it's not your fault" aspects of post-conflict programming). *See*, e.g., Graham Rayman, *Boy Soldier of Fortune: A celebrated memoir threatens to blow into a million little pieces*, VILLAGE VOICE (March 18, 2008), *available at* <http://www.villagevoice.com/2008-03-18/news/boy-soldier/full>. Beah refutes these allegations.

[60] Beah, *supra* note 59, at 143–144, 159.

[61] *Id.* at 131, 151, 160, 165–166. For other examples, *see* Tom Masland, *Voices of the Children*, NEWSWEEK 24, 28 (May 13, 2002) (reporting on Abbas, a youthful fighter for the RUF, who describes his involvement in acts of mutilation and burning other combatants to death with plastic and tires, only to add: "God must forgive boys like us. It was not our fault."); *Cry Freetown* (2000, dir./prod. Ron McCullagh, narrated by Sorious Samura) (interviews with former boy soldiers, one of whom states: "[W]e started killing, but I know it's not my fault. This is why I believe God won't blame me—it's not my fault" (subtitled English translation)).

[62] Shepler, *The Rites of the Child, supra* note 53, at 199.

[63] *Id.* at 200 (emphasis in original).

[64] Mergelsberg, *supra* note 46, at 165; *see also* Joanne N. Corbin, *Returning home: resettlement of formerly abducted children in Northern Uganda*, 32(2) DISASTERS 316, 331 (2008) ("Educational

Acholi definition of a child was "augmented and adapted to the circumstances of war to enable the adoption of a non-punitive approach to justice and allow for wide-spread social reconciliation."[65] He remarks how this process occurred though modern NGOs instead of traditional Acholi institutions. According to Mawson, the "main focus of child rights organisations and child protection organisations has been on the children themselves, who are seen as victims."[66] Three other researchers corroborate these observations by reporting from Northern Uganda that "[d]ifferent high-ranking officials ma[de] speeches about the ex-combatants, largely portraying them as vulnerable innocent victims who need all the support, encouragement and help they can get to become part of the community again."[67]

Shepler adroitly examines the effects of discourses of abdicated responsibility. These discourses and attendant assertions of innocence generally helped ease the reintegration of child soldier returnees.[68] In this regard, they served beneficial ends. At first blush, then, they seemed to work. In Northern Uganda, too, abductees who came home faced a largely positive reception and were warmly accepted.

However, particularized evidence from disparate sources warns that discourses of innocence, non-responsibility, and excuse are of limited utility in the reintegration of minoritarian—albeit key—at-risk subgroups of child soldiers, including children suspected of implication in acts of atrocity or children who remained for a long time with fighting forces.[69] Skepticism on the part of community members regarding the generic suitability of faultless victimhood imagery in the specific case of certain individual returnees did not prompt the proponents of that imagery to revisit their own assumptions. Instead, it just seemed to harden them to try even more to change local minds. Hence, the official response tended to repeat the narrative instead of rethink it, thereby whittling down an opportunity for dialogic refinement. Yet, re-sensitizing communities even more ardently in these discourses did not attenuate specific reintegration challenges. The operational effectiveness of re-sensitization therefore remains debatable.

What is the broader takeaway? I contend that transnational demands for unconditional forgiveness may exceed local capacity or expectations. Declaring non-responsibility may come to be seen as legitimating irresponsibility. A delicate situation arises, including the ominous specter of impunity.

---

programmes for community members about how the children were forced to commit violence will need to continue as this may reduce the community's anger and fear towards them.").

[65] Andrew Mawson, *Children, Impunity and Justice: Some Dilemmas from Northern Uganda*, in CHILDREN AND YOUTH ON THE FRONT LINE, *supra* note 3, at 130, 131.

[66] *Id.*

[67] Grace Akello, Annemiek Richters, and Ria Reis, *Reintegration of former child soldiers in northern Uganda: coming to terms with children's agency and accountability*, 4(3) INTERVENTION 229, 232 (2006).

[68] Shepler does note that this "model of innocent child is in conflict with an earlier model of youth as hardworking and humble." Shepler, *The Rites of the Child*, *supra* note 53, at 197.

[69] For detailed discussion in Sierra Leone and Northern Uganda, *see infra* Chapter 6(v). *Cf.* Mawson, *supra* note 65, at 135, 141 (cautioning that "pretending atrocities have not been committed is also not an option" in Northern Uganda and nimbly asking: "Can a convenient fiction about what is a child carry the weight of so much violence?").

(c) New Wars

According to Mary Kaldor, today's "new wars" (or "dirty wars") depart from "old wars," that is, inter-state conflict leading to final victory and definitive surrender.[70] The new wars literature is diverse—and controversial—but shares certain themes.

New wars are seen as anarchic.[71] They arise from the political failure of the state and the disintegration of state institutional structures. Hence, new wars often occur within states as opposed to between states; their transnational dimensions are not inter-state dimensions *per se*. Fighting factions in new wars, nonetheless, derive support from the globalization of access to resources, weapons, publicity, and personnel. New wars involve splintering of warring parties, deployment of violence by non-state actors, the emergence of militias and other paramilitary syndicates, mutual and frequent infliction of international humanitarian law violations, and the proliferation of small arms among the general population. The lines between combatants and civilians become porous. Militia forces are volatile and irregularly staffed. Ideology putatively plays less of a role in fueling conflict.

The initial new wars literature was somewhat analytic in tone. Activists and advocates have come to seize upon it for hortatory purposes, however, emphasizing how civilians (especially vulnerable groups such as women and children) are the primary victims of new wars and, consequently, that international humanitarian law and international criminal law ought to shift to deter the unprecedented scale of these tragedies. The ground-breaking 1996 Report on the Impact of Armed Conflict on Children—commonly referred to as the Machel Report, after its eminent author Graça Machel of Mozambique—estimates that, "[i]n recent decades, the proportion of war victims who are civilians has leaped dramatically from 5 per cent to over 90 per cent."[72] The 90% statistic recurs in the often alarmist discussion of new wars, especially when juxtaposed with the 5% of yore. Is it really plausible, however, that our old wars of the twentieth century limited the proportion of civilian war victims only to 5%? Are civilians in new wars that much more susceptible to disease, famine, and direct attacks than civilians in old wars? If the comparison is between percentages of direct civilian deaths from war-related violence (5%), on the one hand, and percentages of civilian deaths totaling from war-related violence, disease, displacement, and famine (90%), on the other hand, then the resultant contrast—albeit rhetorically captivating—is really between apples and oranges. Were participants in old wars more respectful of international humanitarian law than participants in new wars? It goes without saying that

---

[70] Mary Kaldor, New & Old Wars: Organized Violence in a Global Era (1998); *cf.* Erica Bouris, Complex Political Victims 5 (2007).

[71] Robert D. Kaplan, The Coming Anarchy (2000).

[72] Report of the Expert of the Secretary-General, *Impact of Armed Conflict on Children*, U.N. Doc. A/51/306 ¶ 24 (August 26, 1996), *available at* <http://www.unicef.org/graca/a51-306_en.pdf>; *see also* International Criminal Justice and Children, *supra* note 58, at 29 ("[C]ivilian fatalities during armed conflicts have risen from 5 per cent at the beginning of the 20th century to an estimated 90 per cent during the 1990s."). For further discussion of the Machel Report, *see* Chapters 4 and 5, *infra*.

egregious violations of international humanitarian and criminal law occurred within traditional inter-state armed conflicts such as the Second World War and the Iran-Iraq war. Although outside the ambit of the Machel Report's discussion, much older wars (such as expansionist colonial campaigns throughout the Americas, Asia, and Africa) saw wide-scale atrocities, sexual violence, and fatalities among civilian populations.

Global civil society specifically posits the senselessness of new wars. The child soldier, in particular, has no conceivable interest in violence and nothing to gain through conflict. Hence, it is an absurdity that any minor could rationally or volitionally engage in conflict or ever want to participate therein. Synergies thus arise between activist interpretations of the new wars literature and, conversely, conceptualizations of the child soldier as faultless passive victim.

Dr. Elisabeth Schauer, the expert who testified for the judges on the psychological impact of child soldiering at the ICC's high-profile *Lubanga* trial, explicitly began her report (and testimony) by referencing the new wars paradigm.[73] The coziness of the new wars literature with the international legal imagination belies the push-back against this literature that emerges from other quarters.[74] In this vein: Christopher Blattman and Jeannie Annan, drawing from their research on the LRA in Northern Uganda, sharply fault the new wars scholarship for the thinness of the evidence upon which it hangs its claims of criminal, depoliticized, and unintelligible conflict.[75] Might the new wars paradigm typify warring groups, in particular rebel organizations, as predatory and cultish, thereby downplaying their political agendas and their at times strategic and conventional actions?[76] If so, then the turn to this paradigm falls short of the clear-eyed appraisal that is actually needed to curb or eradicate the association of children with armed groups. Finally, although inadvertent, intemperate treatment of new wars can unproductively disseminate sensationalist sound-bites of atavistic tribalism.

---

[73] Elisabeth Schauer, *The Psychological Impact of Child Soldiering*, Prosecutor v. Lubanga, Case No. ICC-01/04-01/06, Public Document (ICC Trial Chamber I, February 25, 2009), p. 2. Dr. Schauer serves as a director of Vivo International, an NGO whose main activities she describes as "research[ing] evidence-based method of psychological rehabilitation after trauma ... concentrat[ing] on posttraumatic stress disorder, depression, suicidality." ICC Case No. 01/04-01/06, English language Transcript (April 7, 2009) lines 11–12 and 14–15 on p. 81 [hereinafter Schauer Testimony]. She attended the ICC "at the express invitation of the Judges." *Id.* line 19 on p. 97.

[74] Myriam Denov, Child Soldiers: Sierra Leone's Revolutionary United Front 37 (2010).

[75] Christopher Blattman and Jeannie Annan, *On the nature and causes of LRA abduction: what the abductees say, in* The Lord's Resistance Army: Myth and Reality 132, 154 (Tim Allen and Koen Vlassenroot eds, 2010).

[76] Although certainly not bleaching the extensive violence the LRA inflicted upon abductees, Blattman and Annan conclude that abduction is on average "less grotesquely violent than often imagined." *Id.* at 133. The RUF, also popularly held to be a senseless new wars organization, may initially have articulated something approximating a political agenda. *See*, e.g., Danny Hoffman, *Disagreement: Dissent Politics and the War in Sierra Leone*, 52(3) Africa Today 3, 9 (2006); *but see contra* Ibrahim Abdullah, *Bush path to destruction: the origin and character of the Revolutionary United Front/Sierra Leone*, 36(2) Journal of Modern African Studies 203, 224 (1998) (arguing that no revolutionary theory guided the RUF).

(d) Too Much, Yet Too Little

The capaciousness of the Paris Principles guards against the undesirable prospect that children who do not carry weapons—disproportionately, girl soldiers—fall outside the scope of protection. The antecedent Cape Town Principles also explicitly understand the term child soldiers to cover many more than just those children who carry weapons.

Notwithstanding its numerous advantages, this capaciousness also presents some drawbacks. When such a broad range of activities are included within one unitary protected category, a risk arises that the very different experiences and conduct of each individual child soldier become confusingly analogized. Is it unequivocally wise to shy away from distinguishing group members *inter se*? How comparable are children who materially porter to those who commit atrocities? To those who are forced conjugal partners? Although it would determine all children associated with armed forces or armed groups to be a generally protected class, a more fine-grained approach would encourage internal segmentation. One outcome of such segmentation would be to tailor policies toward the specific needs of subgroups and, within those subgroups, toward exploration of what is best for at-risk individuals.

The Paris Principles' push toward the terminology of children associated with armed forces or armed groups redresses perceived gaps in the Cape Town Principles. This terminology offers a broader emphasis. Yet, it also creates a new definitional concern, namely, what is and what is not an armed group? The answers to these questions determine to whom the enumerated protections apply. The Paris Principles do not cover children associated with entities—such as organized gangs, sex trafficking rings, and drug cartels—that fall short of the capacity to engage in armed conflict.[77] These entities, however, may inflict systematic violence and criminal behavior against group members and the public at large.[78] In Mexico, for example, children have served as assassins for drug cartels. A hazy line is often all that separates militarized armed groups from criminal syndicates. Recruitment into such syndicates and gangs may compare to recruitment into armed groups. So, too, might the reasons why some children join them. The overwhelming focus on *militarized* children thereby diverts attention from the needs of *criminalized* children.

On a related note, if the focus on children formerly associated with armed forces or armed groups becomes perceived as inordinate, tensions may emerge. Other critical constituencies also require support. Adults associated with armed forces or groups also return home. Children and adults in war zones who do not associate

---

[77] Paris Principle 2.3 defines armed groups as referring to "groups distinct from armed forces as defined by Article 4 of the Optional Protocol to the Convention on the Rights of the Child on the involvement of children in armed conflict." Art. 4 does not provide a definition, however. Ostensibly, the fact that the Optional Protocol relates to the involvement of children in *armed conflict* intimates that armed groups are able to engage in such conflict.
[78] I thank Cynthia Chamberlain for this insight.

with armed forces or groups also suffer from military conflict. Experiences of wartime violence are certainly not limited to combatants alone.

(iii) Universal Childhood

Chronology legally determines childhood and, hence, defines a person's classification as a child soldier. Radhika Coomaraswamy, the Special Representative of the UN Secretary-General on Children and Armed Conflict, succinctly affirms the transnational consensus: "The line between lawful recruitment and unlawful recruitment is drawn based solely on age . . . not on any act of the child."[79] The Integrated Disarmament, Demobilization and Reintegration Standards (IDDRS)—referencing the age of eighteen—maintain that "the age of a person must be the key factor in deciding whether he/she is considered to be a child or not, rather than what is considered to be the customary understanding of childhood or adulthood in his/her culture."[80]

A chronological approach offers advantages. Although some persons may be unaware when they were born, calculating age in years generally is manageable. This approach consequently provides economy, transparency, and predictability. A firm chronological rule can readily be enforced through a standardized system of birth registration, so long as that system is adequately resourced. Age in years serves as a general proxy for capacity, typically correlating with discernible social and psychological maturation.[81]

The UN Convention on the Rights of the Child (CRC) establishes an ecumenical baseline definition of a child as anyone "below the age of eighteen years unless under the law applicable to the child, majority is attained earlier."[82] The CRC "defines a child simply in terms of age."[83] It is the first treaty that "codified the 18th year as the generally accepted transition point to adulthood."[84] Even if persons have attained majority under national law, CRC protections continue to apply to them until they reach the age of eighteen.

The CRC is among the most broadly ratified multilateral treaties. Only the United States and Somalia are non-parties. The CRC protects children and accords

---

[79] *Written Submissions*, Prosecutor v. Lubanga, Document ICC-01/04-01/06-1229-AnxA ¶ 10 (March 18, 2008) (citing the Paris Principles and additionally submitting that: "All 'voluntary' acts or statements or other indications or interpretations of consent by children under the legal age for recruitment are legally irrelevant.").

[80] *Integrated Disarmament, Demobilization and Reintegration Standards* (IDDRS) §5.30, p. 24 (2006), *available at* <http://www.unddr.org/iddrs/05/download/IDDRS_530.pdf>.

[81] *But see contra* Veale, *supra* note 46, at 105 ("The simple equation of age with a particular developmental level, a level of knowledge, competencies, cognitive understanding or emotional maturity is not supported in developmental research.") (footnote omitted).

[82] United Nations Convention on the Rights of the Child, G.A. Res. 44/25, Art. 1, Annex, U.N. Doc. A/RES/44/25 (November 20, 1989) (entered into force September 2, 1990) [hereinafter CRC].

[83] Steven Freeland, *Mere Children or Weapons of War—Child Soldiers and International Law*, 29 U. OF LA VERNE L. REV. 19, 28 (2008).

[84] Beth A. Simmons, MOBILIZING FOR HUMAN RIGHTS: INTERNATIONAL LAW IN DOMESTIC POLITICS 311 (2009).

them a broad series of rights—civil, political, economic, social, associational, and expressive—which it assumes them capable of discharging. It is a comprehensive document oriented toward the promotion of the "best interests of the child."[85] The phrase "best interests of the child" initially emerged in the context of domestic family relations law in cases of adoption and parental separation. In theory, this concept means that decisions have to take into account what is best for the child, not what is best for parents, or a particular care-giver, or what most closely conforms to settled social norms. This concept, however, has frequently been criticized for vagueness and for lacking in a typology of precise factors or characteristics. Colloquially, however, it persists as shorthand to refer to the child's well-being, welfare, maximal survival and development, freedom from discrimination, and external respect for his or her views.

NGOs, advocates, and activists turn to the legal bright-line of eighteen as a proxy for when incapacity ends and capacity begins in militarized contexts. Schauer's testimony at the *Lubanga* trial is illustrative. In her examination by counsel for the Prosecution, the following tautological exchange occurred:

Question: [B]ased on your professional opinion—

Answer: Mm-hmm.

Question: —can a child ever be considered psychologically to have voluntarily joined an armed group? Are there any circumstances in which that might be the case?

Answer: No. Otherwise, we wouldn't have a law that makes you 18 to become an adult.[86]

According to Utas, "[h]umanitarian aid agencies tend to make a fetish of childhood as a closed, age-bound category of agency-free individuals."[87] Childhood becomes presented as a halcyon, pristine time characterized by innocence. Naïri Arzoumanian and Francesca Pizzutelli illustratively report a letter from the director of an NGO in Liberia. This letter underscores that the decision not to hold child soldiers accountable for their part in atrocities was made "in pursuance of," *inter alia*, the CRC—in turn described as "perceiv[ing] children as being innocent."[88] Unsurprisingly, then, once children become participants in conflict, discussion gravitates to themes of "innocents lost" and "innocence lost."[89]

---

[85] CRC, *supra* note 82, Art. 3(1).

[86] Schauer Testimony, *supra* note 73, lines 20–25 on p. 47 and line 1 on p. 48. Schauer adopts the definition of the child soldier as a person below the age of eighteen. *Id.* lines 19–21 on p. 40. Schauer subsequently testified that "anything under [the age of] 21 isn't really an informed consent joining an army, but that's from the idea of really understanding implications for life." *Id.* lines 11–12 on p. 90.

[87] Utas, *Fluid Research Fields*, *supra* note 51, at 211.

[88] Naïri Arzoumanian and Francesca Pizzutelli, *Victimes et bourreaux: questions de responsabilité liées à la problématique des enfants-soldats en Afrique*, 85 RICR 827, 846 (2003); *see also* Shepler, *The Social and Cultural Context*, *supra* note 37, at 2 (noting that "beliefs about childhood [are] built on a modern ideology that sees children as innocent and separates childhood as a special time").

[89] *See*, e.g., Jimmie Briggs, INNOCENTS LOST: WHEN CHILD SOLDIERS GO TO WAR (2005); Steven Freeland, *Innocence Lost as Recruitment of Child Soldiers Continues*, SYDNEY MORNING HERALD (February 15, 2010).

Notwithstanding international aspirations to universalize childhood (and formal support of such efforts by governments, states, and officials), multiple childhoods residually abound within and among societies and localities. The question of who is a child does not have a settled answer. This ambiguity should not be cause either for surprise or disappointment. After all, the characteristics of childhood (as well as its duration) inescapably hinge upon culture, history, context, as well as the specific activity in question.[90] Even within the West—often essentialized as the font for transnational approaches to the subject[91]—attitudes about the categorization and characteristics of childhood vacillate considerably. Whether in literary fiction, faith, or law, Western perceptions of childhood are desultory, ambivalent, and frequently depart from tropes of innocence.[92] Some anecdotal references are illuminating. William Golding's *Lord of the Flies* depicts children shorn from adult supervision as brutes who can only be saved from themselves once the adults return, even though those adults themselves are at war with others. Stanley Kubrick's *A Clockwork Orange* screens the sadistic "old ultra-violence" of a youth gang in a dystopian London to the tune of Beethoven and "Singin' in the Rain." Christianity requires life-long moral struggle to overcome original sin. Western jurisdictions, moreover, demonstrate erratic approaches to children who perpetrate violent crime. Hardly any Western states adhere to eighteen as the minimum age for basic penal responsibility for ordinary common crimes. This begs the question whether exogenously fueled discourses of abdicated responsibility would play more smoothly among Western populations than they do in Sierra Leone or Northern Uganda. Or would they, perhaps, provoke greater irascibility?

In sum, international consensus belies on-the-ground complexities regarding when childhood ends and adulthood begins, particularly in the context of militarization and violence. International efforts seek to overcome these complexities. In so doing they rely on a normative construct of childhood. This construct is uniform. It associates childhood with certain attributes and expectations. This construct also determines classification as a child according to a simple metric that is fixed, formal, categorical, and collective. Childhood thereby becomes rigid. This simple metric supersedes other indicators that also may serve to signal the start of adulthood.

---

[90] For discussion of childhood as an institution constructed around and informed by socio-economic phenomena, *see* Philippe Ariès, CENTURIES OF CHILDHOOD: A SOCIAL HISTORY OF FAMILY LIFE (Robert Baldick trans., 1962).

[91] Schafer, *supra* note 26, at 87; *see also* David J. Francis, *International Conventions and the Limitations for Protecting Child Soldiers in Post-conflict Societies in Africa, in* CHILDREN AND WAR: IMPACT, PROTECTION AND REHABILITATION, PHASE II: PROTECTION 8, 10 (2006) [hereinafter CHILDREN AND WAR], *available at* <http://www.arts.ualberta.ca/childrenandwar/papers/Children_and_War_Phase_II_Report.pdf> (tracing contemporary transnationalized beliefs about childhood to a "rather restrictive, western-centric perception").

[92] Western states overall settle on eighteen as the general age of majority. Many benefits and burdens of majority status, however, do not correlate with attainment of this specific age. National laws in Western states present as checkerboards where adulthood arrives more rapidly in cases of certain opportunities and responsibilities, but later in others. Thousands of minors join armed forces in Western states. Lorraine Macmillan, *The Child Soldier in North-South Relations*, 3 INT'L POL. SOC. 36, 47 (2009).

These other indicators reflect a messier calculus, that is, a more malleable, experiential, individuated, and incremental determination of coming of age.

Inelastic antipodean constructs of childhood and adulthood can appear artificial to survivors in war-torn communities. For survivors, perceptions of who is a child, who can soldier, who can be an atrocity perpetrator, what responsibility means, and how someone becomes an adult all may remain vividly contextual. Conflict-stricken communities value chronological approaches to childhood, to be sure, but not necessarily to the exclusion of more nuanced (and less technical) approaches to assessing individual transitions from childhood to adulthood.[93] If internationally exhorted abstractions of childhood become too unyielding, they may turn into shibboleths. Local communities may turn away from them.

Naturalizing age markers of eighteen—or even fifteen—as the edge of childhood may interface awkwardly with demographic realities. In most developing countries, children comprise approximately half of the population.[94] In conflict societies the demographic concentration may be even younger. Based on data from 2005, a report calculated that 47.1% of the DRC's population and 50.4% of Uganda's population was under the age of fifteen.[95] In 2001, life expectancy in Sierra Leone was reported as thirty-three years for men and thirty-five years for women.[96] It may be unwieldy in such situations to designate such a broad swath of the population as needing special protection owing to minority status. Alternately, ascribing special status to so many people may strip that status of actual meaning.

International norms assume children's lives to differ from adult lives. In conflict and post-conflict societies, however, differences may be illusory. Insecurity, poverty, and crisis displace responsibilities inter-generationally. Hence, within such contexts adulthood may not be reducible to a technical matter of chronology. Rather, it may be derivative of the stations a person is called upon to occupy in life. These stations include serving in the labor force, becoming the head of a household, completing ceremonial rites of passage,[97] or participating in warfare.[98] On this

---

[93] Freeland, *Mere Children or Weapons of War, supra* note 83, at 28–29; Wessells, *Psychosocial Issues, supra* note 20, at 513–514. *See also* Christine Tokar, *Indigenous Protections of Children in Armed Conflict: Observations from Sierra Leone and Liberia, in* CHILDREN AND WAR, *supra* note 91, at 19, 20 (noting that in parts of Africa the words "child" and "youth" are "not necessarily age-based stages as we have come to know them in the Western world").

[94] In the United States, by contrast, approximately 24% of the population is under eighteen.

[95] REDRESS Trust, *supra* note 35, at 7; *see also* Schmidt, *supra* note 5, at 50 (citing data that children under the age of eighteen account for 54% and 57% of the population in the DRC and Uganda respectively).

[96] Rachel Brett and Irma Specht, YOUNG SOLDIERS: WHY THEY CHOOSE TO FIGHT 173 (2004) (reporting 2.3 million out of a total population of 4.6 million as under the age of eighteen).

[97] David J. Francis, *'Paper protection' mechanisms: child soldiers and the international protection of children in Africa's conflict zones*, 45(2) JOURNAL OF MODERN AFRICAN STUDIES 207, 223 (2007) ("[T]raditional sodality institutions such as *Poro* and *Sande, rites de passage* across much of Africa,... confer on children as young as 14 the status and obligation of adulthood.").

[98] Wessells, CHILD SOLDIERS, *supra* note 39, at 5 ("[A] 15-year-old boy carrying an automatic rifle and traveling with a military group might be viewed as a child by international human rights observers, but... as a young adult by people in a rural African village."); *see also* Freeland, *Mere Children or Weapons of War, supra* note 83, at 29 ("[T]he very act of playing a role in warfare or armed conflict will of itself deem that person *not* to be a child in the eyes of his/her community.").

latter note, Eyal Ben-Ari generally remarks that "becoming a soldier is a means for achieving adult status."[99]

In looking at the child soldier, the international legal imagination should not overlook CRC Article 5, which recognizes the "evolving capacities" of children. Article 5's language is cumbersome. It elliptically states that evolving capacities are to inform the responsibilities, rights, and duties of parents, members of extended family, legal guardians, or the community to provide appropriate direction and guidance in the exercise by the child of his or her rights. At its core, however, the evolving capacities canon is about progressively according children greater autonomy as they get older. Although "evolving capacities" is a general interpretive aid for the treaty as a whole, CRC Article 14(2) specifically mentions it in the context of the child's right to freedom of thought, conscience, and religion. Relatedly, CRC Article 12(1) requires that the child who is "capable of forming his or her own views" shall be assured "the right to express those views freely in all matters affecting [him or her];" these views, in turn, are to be "given due weight in accordance with the age and maturity of the child."

In contrast, the international legal imagination largely resists plasticity, along with the relevance of interstitial categories (such as adolescent, apprentice, or initiate), in the specific context of child soldiering.[100] It does so despite the fact that porousness among child, adolescent, initiate, youth, and adult as social categories may be particularly salient during periods of armed conflict. The international legal imagination's preference is for the binary parsimony of the child, on the one hand, and the adult, on the other. The seventeen year-old commander is a child soldier, as is the nine year-old porter.

In this sense, the international legal imagination is even more firmly chronological in its understanding of who is a child soldier than who is a child.

One effect of this hardening of the chronological approach is that international law comes down harshly on fighters who sit just over the watershed divide: for example, the twenty year-old. International law does so despite evidence that cognitive capacity, neurobiological function, and discernment skills continue to develop well past the age of eighteen.[101] Although the young adult may claim youth as a mitigating factor in international criminal sentencing, youth *per se* bears no relationship to findings of culpability or criminal responsibility.

The case of Drazen Erdemović, a young ethnic Croat foot soldier, is illustrative. Erdemović had enlisted in a non-combat Bosnian Serb unit. His unit ended up on Branjevo farm near Srebrenica. Erdemović was ordered to kill Muslim civilians.

---

[99] Eyal Ben-Ari, *Facing Child Soldiers, Moral Issues, and "Real Soldiering": Anthropological Perspectives on Professional Armed Forces*, 37(1) SCIENTIA MILITARIA: SOUTH AFRICAN JOURNAL OF MILITARY STUDIES 1, 6 (2009) (citations omitted).

[100] In the West, the emergence of adolescence as a separate and distinct socio-developmental category has been conventionally linked to a 1904 study by American psychologist G. Stanley Hall. Adoption of child labor laws and the popularization of advanced education resulted in the incremental extension of minors' period of dependence.

[101] Robin Marantz Henig, *What Is It About 20-Somethings?*, N.Y. TIMES MAGAZINE (August 22, 2010) at MM28 (discussing evidence from Western societies that brain development continues into the twenties). Communities in post-conflict societies may perceive fighters aged eighteen or older as sharing certain child-like characteristics. Schafer, *supra* note 26, at 101–102; Mawson, *supra* note 65, at 136.

He refused his commander's orders. He was then told that if he did not comply, he himself would be shot. Erdemović later turned himself in. He confessed to reluctantly killing one hundred civilians.[102] His mental and emotional states were fragile. Erdemović, who had joined armed forces at the age of eighteen in the context of mandatory military service and committed atrocities while in his early twenties, was—on the basis of his confession—convicted by the International Criminal Tribunal for the former Yugoslavia (ICTY) and, ultimately, sentenced to five years' imprisonment. In his case, a majority of the ICTY Appeals Chamber ruled that, when it comes to killing innocent civilians, duress may never be raised as a defense.[103] Judges McDonald and Vorhah separately issued an opinion trumpeting the inappositeness of duress to the overarching normative framework and goals of international justice. They did so "give notice in no uncertain terms that those who kill innocent persons will not be able to take advantage of duress as a defence and thus get away with impunity for their criminal acts in the taking of innocent lives."[104]

In sum, childhood inflates to cover all fighters under the age of eighteen, at which point the full weight of adult expectations abruptly begins. A more refined appreciation of interstitial developmental categories would enhance the dexterity of international law in addressing young adults.

Alcohol abuse—commonly cited as voiding the capacity and discernment of child soldiers—also was widespread among adult atrocity perpetrators in Rwanda and throughout the Balkans. The defense of intoxication, however, has to date played not even a nominal role in international criminal prosecutions. To suggest that it should occupy a more vigorous place in the case of adults would, I believe, invoke great consternation among human rights activists and international lawyers (other than, perhaps, members of the defense bar). Under the ICC's Rome Statute, adult foot soldiers cannot exculpate themselves from culpability through claims that they were merely following orders to commit genocide or crimes against humanity.[105] Such claims could mitigate their punishment, but would go no way to relieve their criminal responsibility for these specific acts of atrocity.

Overriding the contested nature of who is a child may be especially unproductive in the context of children and armed conflict insofar as most child soldiers are between the ages of fourteen and eighteen, with significant numbers clustering in the older echelons of this cohort.[106] Younger children do participate in armed

---

[102] Judith Armatta, Twilight of Impunity 294 (2010).

[103] Prosecutor v. Erdemović, Case No. IT-96-22-A, Appeals Judgment (ICTY Appeals Chamber, October 7, 1997) ¶ 19.

[104] *Id.* Joint Separate Opinion ¶ 80. Textually, the approach of the ICC's Rome Statute to duress is more permissive than *Erdemović*'s deontological denunciation. Rome Statute of the International Criminal Court, Art. 31(1)(d), 2187 U.N.T.S. 90 (July 17, 1998, entered into force July 1, 2002) [hereinafter Rome Statute]. The ICC, however, has not yet ruled on the scope of duress as a defense.

[105] Rome Statute, *supra* note 104, Art. 33 (precluding the defense of superior orders for crimes determined to be manifestly unlawful and classing genocide and crimes against humanity as such).

[106] Coalition to Stop the Use of Child Soldiers, *Frequently asked questions, available at* <http://www.child-soldiers.org/childsoldiers/questions-and-answers> (visited on June 23, 2011). For observers who say most child soldiers fall in the fifteen to eighteen age bracket, *see* Steven Hick, *The Political Economy of War-Affected Children*, 575 Annals of the American Academy of Political and Social Science 106, 110 (2001); Save the Children, When Children Affected by War Go Home: Lessons Learned from Liberia 9 (2003).

forces or groups; depending on the conflict there may actually be quite a few younger fighters. In atrocity-producing conflicts, the age of recruitment may drop—albeit not axiomatically so—as factions become more desperate for members. All things considered, however, the average child soldier is not a young, pre-pubescent child of tender years. Overall, child soldiers are adolescents.[107] Proportionally, the common child soldier is a teenager. Although, over time, transnationalized discourse has become somewhat more sublime on this aspect, the faultless passive victim image still inclines toward the archetype of child soldiers as very young and barely able to carry their AK-47s.

Employing the qualifier *child* soldier or *children* associated with armed forces or groups shapes public conversations. Nonetheless, adolescents occupy meaningfully different social spaces than children. Hence, the conflation of the child with the adolescent may come to be viewed skeptically. Drawing from her work in Northern Uganda, Prudence Acirokop addresses this perplexing situation:

> People interviewed . . . were quick to point out that traditional justice mechanisms should not apply to children accused of crimes because they are not considered to be responsible for their actions. Further questioning revealed that adolescents are not necessarily considered children in Acholi culture.[108]

Persons who have come of age risk being infantilized when cast as chronologically underage. This outcome is not in their best interests.

(iv) Too Few Perspectives?

Certain disciplines and professions exercise outsize influence in shaping how the international community thinks about child soldiers. As alluded to earlier in this Chapter, psychologists—in particular, child psychologists and experts in trauma studies—have been instrumental. Human rights and humanitarian organizations, along with child welfare advocates and activist authors, also have played a formative role through the evidence they gather, the reports and books they publish, and the remedial efforts they undertake.[109]

---

[107] Wessells, CHILD SOLDIERS, *supra* note 39, at 7 (citations omitted). *See also* Betancourt et al., PSYCHOSOCIAL ADJUSTMENT, *supra* note 2, at 10 ("Teenagers (age 13–18) are most often targets of recruitment because of their relative size and strength, their advanced mental and cognitive development, and their role in many societies (particularly those facing the difficulties of conflict) as being much like adults with responsibilities for helping to care for their families."); Brett and Specht, *supra* note 96, at 2–3 ("The focus on adolescents must be stressed. This age group accounts for the vast majority of the world's 'child soldiers'"); Schmidt, *supra* note 5, at 54 (concluding that "adolescents make up the vast majority of child soldiers worldwide, yet they are neglected in research and programming") (citations omitted).

[108] Prudence Acirokop, *The Potential and Limits of* Mato Oput *as a Tool for Reconciliation and Justice, in* CHILDREN AND TRANSITIONAL JUSTICE: TRUTH-TELLING, ACCOUNTABILITY AND RECONCILIATION 267, 276 (UNICEF Innocenti Research Centre and Human Rights Program at Harvard Law School, Sharanjeet Parmar, Mindy Jane Roseman, Saudamini Siegrist, and Theo Sowa eds, 2010).

[109] Before proceeding to examine these contributions in greater detail, a word about nomenclature is in order. Whereas humanitarian organizations concern themselves more with delivering food, shelter,

(a) Humanitarian, Human Rights, and Child Welfare Reports

Reports and publications conducted under the aegis of international organizations, UN agencies, and NGOs have generated a trove of information about child soldiering. Some of these documents are of exemplary rigor. They carefully and neutrally compile an evidentiary record, while ensuring that advocacy efforts remain separate from data gathering and information presentation. In other instances, however, reports fail to separate their investigatory undertakings from their reformist ambitions. Aspirations shape exposition. Evidence becomes culled. Distortions thereby arise. These reports recurrently employ a drafting style that textually downplays dissident facts and demonstrates an affinity for an impersonal passive voice. Victims of the acts of child soldiers receive comparatively little attention, especially if they themselves are not children. Human rights violations committed by child soldiers, when presented, observably pair with near-rote repetition of the fact the children always were forced to do what they did. Typical recourse to the passive voice anonymizes the authors of the impugned force. Although the term volunteer may appear in discussions of child enlistment, it invariably ends up placed within quotation marks. The implication is clear. The term is not to be taken literally. If anything, its use is begrudged.

Even those reports that strive to avoid drafting and data presentation distortions, however, face a variety of other challenges, notably structural bias. Quantitative fieldwork undertaken by humanitarian or human rights organizations through short-term encounters with respondents that are limited to one or few recorded interviews may be particularly susceptible to such bias. Utas posits that such fieldwork "normally yield[s] responses in victim modes and tend[s] to conceal many important aspects of lived experience."[110] A variety of exogenous pressures may affect the information obtained from former child soldiers. No different than adult respondents, child soldier respondents may tend to tell the interviewer what they believe the interviewer wishes to hear. Interviewees may seek to validate the sensibilities and expertise of transnational organizations, to conform to conventional wisdom, or to obtain benefits. It may simply be more comfortable for interviewees to take cues from interviewers. In light of the brevity of the interviewer-interviewee encounter (assuming an encounter even exists, insofar as survey data also is obtained through written questionnaires), limited opportunity—if any—arises to establish

and infrastructure to devastated regions, human rights organizations concern themselves more with promoting rights, equality, and justice. On the ground, tensions may arise between both sets of helpers. On the subject of child soldiering, however, humanitarian and human rights organizations adopt similar assumptions and precepts, as do child rights advocates. Accordingly, for the purposes of this book, I semantically merge these organizations and advocates, along with their impulses and reports, while also recognizing that this merger obscures attitudinal differences. I distinguish international humanitarian law from international human rights law.

[110] Utas, *Fluid Research Fields*, *supra* note 51, at 209 (citations omitted); *see also* Honwana, CHILD SOLDIERS IN AFRICA, *supra* note 26, at 15 ("The relationship between caregiving agencies and researchers especially affects conversations with children, who may believe they must present themselves as helpless and dependent in order to be seen as deserving of assistance.")

the kind of personal interaction or comfort level that may filter out or discourage strategic responses.

Despite these caveats, throughout this book I still refer to survey data on questions of why children end up in armed forces or armed groups and what they do while associated therewith. One example in this regard is the Survey for War Affected Youth (SWAY) from Northern Uganda, focusing on youth abduction into the LRA. The initial phase of SWAY findings were published in report form in 2006 for UNICEF Uganda (which also provided partial support).[111] SWAY's two principal researchers, Jeannie Annan and Christopher Blattman, have since updated and added to these initial findings and the interpretation thereof in several published academic articles. Although entirely not immune from the structural concerns that affect quantitative survey data generally, SWAY tempered these concerns through multiple strategies. It included in-depth qualitative interviews and cross-checked all reported youth abductions into the LRA so as to identify inconsistencies. It routinely informed all interviewed youth that participation in the survey would not be linked to any assistance. And it asked multiple questions so as to make misrepresentation—whether inadvertent or deliberate— significantly more challenging.[112]

Anthropological and ethnographic research offers an alternate source of information about child soldiering. Ethnographic method focuses on long-term fieldwork, first-hand participant observation, dialectic interpretation, in-depth case-studies and interviews, establishment of trust and understanding with respondents through ongoing interaction, a focus on the *micro* and *meso* levels, and a search for individual and local meanings instead of universal common denominators.[113] Its purpose is to "answer[] a question rather than test[] a hypothesis" and is it "not based on prior assumptions or models."[114] Ethnography often articulates its information in the language of the respondent. To be sure, anthropology's "deep hanging out"—namely, its "localized, long term, close-in, vernacular field research"—must remain subject to sober assessment, rigorous review, and critical reflection.[115]

---

[111] Jeannie Annan, Christopher Blattman, and Roger Horton, THE STATE OF YOUTH AND YOUTH PROTECTION IN NORTHERN UGANDA: FINDINGS FROM THE SURVEY FOR WAR AFFECTED YOUTH (September 2006) [hereinafter SWAY]. How did SWAY understand the term youth? SWAY drew from a sample of males, which included an oversampling of abductees, between the ages of fourteen and thirty at the time of the survey. According to the SWAY report, LRA abductions targeted adolescent boys; 65% of LRA abductions were of children or adolescents; and of males abducted before age thirty, two-thirds were under eighteen.

[112] Blattman and Annan, *On the nature and causes of LRA abduction*, supra note 75, at 135 (noting that, because of these precautions, abductions—if at all overstated—are no more so than by 5%).

[113] Galit A. Sarfaty, *Why Culture Matters in International Institutions: The Marginality of Human Rights at the World Bank*, 103 AM. J. INT'L L. 647, 651–652 (2009); Kimberly Theidon, *Transitional Subjects: The Disarmament, Demobilization and Reintegration of Former Combatants in Colombia*, 1 INT'L J. TRANSITIONAL JUST. 66, 74 (2007). For Daniel Miller, ethnography is more than "mere methodology." It commits ethnographers to be in the presence of the people they study, to evaluate what these people actually do, to pursue a long-term investigation, and to engage in holistic analysis. Daniel Miller, CAPITALISM: AN ETHNOGRAPHIC APPROACH 16–17 (1997).

[114] Sarfaty, *supra* note 113, at 651.

[115] Clifford Geertz, AVAILABLE LIGHT: ANTHROPOLOGICAL REFLECTIONS ON PHILOSOPHICAL TOPICS 110 (2001).

Overall, information gathered through ethnographic method yields a less wooden account of child soldiering that contrasts with the tenets of faultless passive victimhood or any of the extreme images currently in circulation. Accordingly, ethnographic method forms a valuable complement—perhaps even an antidote—to conventional wisdom.

(b) Child Psychology and Trauma Models

Developmental psychology assesses life-span changes in physical, intellectual, emotional, perceptual, and social development. Among life stages, childhood receives considerable academic and clinical attention. Child development is a robust subfield within the general developmental psychology literature.[116] As a subfield it has many facets, one of which is that "child development is governed by universal psychological and biological structures and marked by fixed stages."[117] Child development research, according to Jo Boyden, emphasizes early childhood, which is:

Identified as a critical period of accelerated growth and change and as central to successful adaptation in later life. The emphasis on the first years of life has reinforced notions about children as vulnerable, immature and dependent and has also resulted in a shortage of systematic information on development during middle and late childhood.[118]

Can findings derived from research on young children be extended into the context of adolescence? Boyden is skeptical. She warns that "to generalize about middle childhood and adolescence from the uncontroversial facts of dependence and immaturity in the first years of life is to ignore the resourcefulness of many children in all age groups and the social competencies of those beyond early childhood in particular."[119] Child development psychology also has been chided for its inattentiveness to cultural, environmental, class, and social differences and expectations.

The conventional wisdom is that former child soldiers suffer from high rates of post-traumatic stress disorder (PTSD) and related afflictions because of their experiences of extreme violence, their immaturity, their fragility, and the effects of drug ingestion. The influence of child development psychology in framing how the international community thinks about child soldiers has come to influence what the international community prefers to do for child soldiers. Insofar as "NGOs and NGO workers tend to view former abductees through a psychological trauma lens,"[120] it follows that interventions for former child soldiers often repose

---

[116] However dated, cognitive work such as that of Jean Piaget remains influential. Jean Piaget, LA PSYCHOLOGIE DE L'INTELLIGENCE (1947).

[117] Jo Boyden, *Children under Fire: Challenging Assumptions about Children's Resilience*, 13(1) CHILDREN, YOUTH AND ENVIRONMENTS (2003), *available at* <http://www.colorado.edu/journals/cye/13_1/Vol13_1Articles/CYE_CurrentIssue_Article_ChildrenUnderFire_Boyden.htm> (footnote omitted).

[118] *Id.*

[119] *Id.*; *see also* Hart, *The Politics of "Child Soldiers"*, *supra* note 46, at 224.

[120] Christopher Blattman and Jeannie Annan, *Child combatants in northern Uganda: Reintegration myths and realities*, *in* SECURITY AND POST-CONFLICT RECONSTRUCTION: DEALING WITH FIGHTERS IN THE AFTERMATH OF WAR 103, 109 (Robert Muggah ed., 2009).

upon psychotherapy, counseling for PTSD, diagnostic interventions, and mental health recovery. These methodologies have been criticized for drawing too heavily from biomedical assumptions as actualized domestically in Western societies.[121]

Schauer's findings among children in Northern Ugandan internally displaced persons' camps who had never been abducted were that 8.4% presented with PTSD symptoms; among children who had been abducted, the rate was 33%; and among those who had been abducted for over a month the rate rose to 48%.[122] Other data also attest to the prevalence of PTSD among child soldiers.[123] Theresa Betancourt, writing with several other researchers, has noted a "number of small and large research studies with former child soldiers in Angola, Mozambique, Sierra Leone, and Uganda [that] have documented high prevalence of psychological trauma, post-traumatic stress disorder... symptomatology, and social dislocation."[124] A study of former child soldiers in Nepal revealed that they displayed greater severity of mental health problems than children who did not soldier; after adjusting for traumatic exposures and other covariates, soldier status was significantly associated with depression (2.41 odds ratio) and PTSD among girls (6.8 odds ratio), and PTSD among boys (3.81 odds ratio), but was not associated with general psychological difficulties, anxiety, or function impairment.[125] The Timor-Leste Commission for Reception, Truth and Reconciliation reported a high incidence of trauma among child militia members implicated in the violence that plagued the country in the late 1990s.

Activists may present the neurobiological effects of conflict on some child soldiers quite emphatically, noting "permanent physical damage to circuits in their heads."[126] It has been asserted that "[c]hildren who participate in conflict must be viewed as victims of institutionalized child abuse who have suffered human rights violations and psychosocial harm."[127]

---

[121] Derek Summerfield, *Childhood, War, Refugeedom and 'Trauma': Three Core Questions for Mental Health Professionals*, 37(3) TRANSCULTURAL PSYCHIATRY 417, 424 (2000); *see also* Honwana, CHILD SOLDIERS IN AFRICA, *supra* note 26, at 150 ("Dominant paradigms shaping aid policies and international interventions during and after conflicts in Africa have been informed by Western biomedical notions of health and illness. But Western understandings of distress and trauma and Western approaches to diagnosis and treatment cannot properly or effectively be applied to societies that have different ontologies of health and illness.").

[122] Schauer, *supra* note 73, at 11.

[123] *Id.* at 10 *et seq.* Specifically, *see* Christophe Pierre Bayer, Fionna Klasen, and Hubertus Adam, *Association of Trauma and PTSD Symptoms With Openness to Reconciliation and Feelings of Revenge Among Former Ugandan and Congolese Child Soldiers*, 298(5) JOURNAL OF THE AMERICAN MEDICAL ASSOCIATION 555 (2007) (finding in a study of 169 Ugandan and Congolese former child soldiers that 34.9% met symptom criteria for PTSD).

[124] Betancourt et al., *High Hopes, Grim Reality*, *supra* note 36, at 571.

[125] Brandon A. Kohrt, Mark J. D. Jordans, Wietse A. Tol, Rebecca A. Speckman, Sujen M. Maharjan, Carol M. Worthman, and Ivan H. Komproe, *Comparison of Mental Health Between Former Child Soldiers and Children Never Conscripted by Armed Groups in Nepal*, 300(6) JOURNAL OF THE AMERICAN MEDICAL ASSOCIATION 691 (2008).

[126] Dallaire, *supra* note 32, at 138.

[127] Carrie E. Kimmel and Jini L. Roby, *Institutionalized Child Abuse: The Use of Child Soldiers*, 50(6) INTERNATIONAL SOCIAL WORK 740, 750 (2007).

Other research regarding the psychological well-being of former child soldiers is less downbeat, suggesting that the mental health of former child soldiers is not as precarious as commonly imagined. Wessells attests to being buoyed by their resilience.[128] Tracking former Mozambican child soldiers, three other researchers remark that, as a group, they fared as well as, and often better than, national averages on key socio-economic and child welfare indicators.[129] Although recognizing that the "abducted experience the most violence overall, [and that] the violence experienced by the non-abducted is still tremendously grave," the SWAY report describes the psychosocial health of its overall sample population in Northern Uganda as "remarkably robust."[130] While sensitively recognizing the existence of distress among abductees, Blattman and Annan also conclude that "[t]he survey and interview evidence suggest that on average formerly abducted youth appear similar in their mental health to youth in the area who have not been abducted."[131] The aggregate psychological consequences of LRA abduction tend to be overestimated and economic and educational consequences underestimated.[132] On this latter note, when it comes to the measurable effects of abduction upon education and wages, there is limited significant difference between child and adult abductees.[133] Angela Veale and Aki Stavrou report research that formerly abducted girl mothers in Gulu, in Northern Uganda, simply did not identify themselves as disempowered victims: "On the contrary, compared with girls who never were abducted, they considered themselves equal to men; they could sow, harvest, and construct a granary, they felt their moral values to be stronger, they were more hard working and enduring."[134]

Brandon Kohrt—the first author of the Nepalese study summarized earlier—punchily posits in a subsequent (and separately co-authored) publication that:

The Hollywood image and those that some organizations employ to raise funds to support intervention programs for former child soldiers depict rogue armed groups violently tearing children away from idyllic family settings. The story continues that these haphazard militias shatter children's lives through the dehumanizing experiences of war, drugs, and crime, leading to severe psychological trauma and disability. . . . Although such portrayals are accurate in some cases, the experience of child soldiers is a far more varied and complex picture.[135]

---

[128] Wessells, *Psychosocial Issues, supra* note 20, at 515.

[129] Neil Boothby, Jennifer Crawford, and Jason Halperin, *Mozambique child soldier life outcome study: Lessons learned in rehabilitation and reintegration efforts,* 1(1) GLOBAL PUBLIC HEALTH 87, 100 (2006).

[130] SWAY, *supra* note 111, at iv, 51 (noting also that "two thirds of youth report low to medium amounts of emotional distress—remarkable in a population with an average of 9 traumatic experiences"). The Schauer report mentions SWAY only briefly. Schauer, *supra* note 73, at 12, 32.

[131] Blattman and Annan, *Child combatants in northern Uganda, supra* note 120, at 113.

[132] Blattman and Annan, *On the nature and causes of LRA abduction, supra* note 75, at 153–154.

[133] Christopher Blattman and Jeannie Annan, *The Consequences of Child Soldiering,* 92(4) REVIEW OF ECONOMICS AND STATISTICS 882, 891–892 (2010).

[134] Angela Veale and Aki Stavrou, *Former Lord's Resistance Army Child Soldier Abductees: Explorations of Identity in Reintegration and Reconciliation,* 13(3) PEACE AND CONFLICT: JOURNAL OF PEACE PSYCHOLOGY 273, 288 (2007) (citing research by Onyango, Atyam, Arwai, and Acan).

[135] Brandon A. Kohrt, Wietse A. Tol, Judith Pettigrew, and Rohit Karki, *Children and Revolution: Mental Health and Psychosocial Well-Being of Child Soldiers in Nepal, in* THE WAR MACHINE AND GLOBAL HEALTH 89, 91 (Merrill Singer and G. Derrick Hodge eds, 2010) (citations omitted).

Notwithstanding these variations and complexities, the programmatic focus on psychopathology endures, sustained as it is by faultless passive victim imagery. In turn, this imagery germinates an expectation that former child soldiers are scarred, even demolished, by their conflict experiences. In this vein, Schauer's expert report prepared for the *Lubanga* trial paints a grim picture of the mental health of former child soldiers. Schauer connects PTSD to an array of other impairments, including poor performance in school and on cognitive tests, depression, dissociation, derealisation, and suicide. She underlines the need for therapy to target brain dysfunction. She implores that more attention be accorded to mental health. Her testimony accentuates the need to apply "evidence-based knowledge in psychiatry and psychology," while dismissing customary and traditional approaches:

I think it's a pretty colonial attitude of people to think that they should deal with their own thing traditionally. . . . I think traditional things are highly overrated, at the same time not capable of providing the service.[136]

Although PTSD therapy should form part of post-conflict programming for child soldiers, overstating its relevance may yield interventions that align neither with their needs nor with those of the community. A mismatch ensues. Furthermore, community welfare is not necessarily fostered by individualized psychotherapeutic approaches, especially when pursued to the detriment of traditional reintegration mechanisms. These mechanisms often root in an understanding of repairing war trauma as a collective journey rather than personal endeavor and involve reparative works, cleansing ceremonies, and reunification rituals. More pluralized approaches to programming could emphasize individual and communal resilience, adaptability, and agility, while also enlivening measures that touch on educational, occupational, physical recuperation, conflict resolution, and justice aspects.

   Children abducted into armed groups do not axiomatically suffer greater psychosocial harm than similarly abducted young adults. Among populations not associated with armed forces or groups living in war-torn regions, young adults do not necessarily suffer less than children either. Should the dichotomization of adult and child, then, be interrogated?

   On this note, according to the SWAY report, "[r]epresentatives of some local NGOs admitted that it was far easier to obtain funds for war-affected children."[137] Aid providers may well have attended too much to children and not enough to young adults, a tendency the SWAY report attributes in part to the "international focus on children."[138] The SWAY report then adds:

This child-centred approach is problematic because . . . along most dimensions young adults are doing no better than children and, in some instances, such as literacy and education levels, young adults are doing much worse. . . . [T]hose abducted as young adults have actually struggled more in economic terms than those taken as children. . . . The emphasis

[136] Schauer Testimony, *supra* note 73, lines 10–12 and 18–19 on p. 67.
[137] SWAY, *supra* note 111, at 73 (noting also that these representatives indicated they would somewhat surreptitiously extend funds to young adults).
[138] *Id.* at 72.

on children has meant that some young adults are treated as children, which was apparent from the language used by some social workers working with youth. They often referred to them as 'formerly abducted children' and talked about them as dependent and helpless, when many of them are in fact parents themselves and taking care of their families.[139]

Activists and policymakers should not draw global attention to the plight of child soldier returnees at the cost of downplaying the myriad of challenges faced by adult returnees, whether younger or older.

Significant numbers of child soldiers worldwide are adolescents. In light of the centrality of *adolescents* to the phenomenon of *child* soldiering, would it not seem sensible—while remaining within the psychological literature—to consider what adolescent developmental psychology generally has to say? Adolescent developmental psychology is a burgeoning field. It is filling critical knowledge gaps, in part through sophisticated neuroscientific and neurobiological research. To date, law's recourse to this research largely has gravitated to measuring culpability and capacity for the purposes of criminal law adjudication, sculpting appropriate levels of due process, and determining punishment for acts of ordinary common criminality committed by juveniles in peace-time.[140] I neither recommend criminal law adjudication for former child soldiers nor focus on ordinary common crimes committed in peace-time. Hence, much of the adolescent development research, whether in form or application, remains beside the immediate purpose at hand. Nonetheless, the core findings that emerge from this research comport with the reimaginative exercise I envision.

When compared to typical adults, adolescents typically are more susceptible to outside or peer influence; are more represented in reckless behavior; have a gauzier ability to foresee the future; are more impulsive, impetuous, and risk-taking; and have more transitory personalities. In the context of criminal law adjudication, therefore, extant research supports the view that adolescents as a group have diminished culpability. Typically having less guilt than adults,[141] they do not fall among the "worst" criminal offenders as measured by deliberation, intent, or premeditation. But neither is the adolescent brain child-like nor pre-logical.[142] According to juvenile justice scholar Terry Maroney, the teenager "is not (like a child) so compromised as to be fully excused, but neither is she fully

---

[139] *Id.* at 73.

[140] The pertinence of this research to the development, interpretation, or application of law and policy is not yet unreservedly accepted. Moreover, because developmental neuroscience "supports only probabilistic generalizations about youth as a class, it is unhelpful in making highly individualized determinations." Terry Maroney, *The False Promise of Adolescent Brain Science in Juvenile Justice*, 85 NOTRE DAME L. REV. 89, 94 (2009).

[141] Laurence Steinberg and Elizabeth S. Scott, *Less Guilty by Reason of Adolescence: Developmental Immaturity, Diminished Responsibility, and the Juvenile Death Penalty*, 58 AM. PSYCHOLOGIST 1009, 1013 (2003).

[142] Christopher Slobogin and Mark R. Fondacaro, *Juvenile Justice: The Fourth Option*, 95 IOWA L. REV. 1, 20 (2009) ("[T]he research on adolescent psychology does not suggest that adolescents lack capacity to formulate intent or are seriously compromised in their ability to recognize the wrongfulness of criminal behavior."); *see also id.* at 6 ("Fifteen-, sixteen-, and seventeen-year-olds, the age groups that commit most juvenile crime, are much closer to adults than pre-adolescents on the traditional measures of criminal desert.") (footnote omitted).

responsible."[143] Available research emphasizes *less* responsibility, not *lack* of responsibility; it stresses *limited* responsibility, not *non*-responsibility.

Hence, at a minimum, adolescents' typical level of responsibility would support their participation in justice processes, other than prosecution and incarceration, geared toward restoration, rehabilitation, reconciliation, and risk management. Adolescents who have committed serious acts of violence are not as a whole so fragile to be incapable of participating in such processes, nor so lacking in cognizance to be unable to grasp the consequences of their conduct, nor so bereft of the wherewithal to make amends after the fact.

That said, might child soldiers be too compromised as a group to participate in transitional justice processes eventuating away from courtrooms and jailhouses? Child soldiers mainly are adolescents, to be sure, but as adolescents many also face routine exposure to violence, abuse, abduction, torture, rape, and narcotics. This exposure affects cognitive development and may, in individual cases, prompt replication of hyper-aggressive behavior. Many adolescents who commit serious common crimes have suffered similar exposure, as well, whether at home or in gangs. But the cataclysm of endemic armed conflict offers a particularly onerous set of situational pressures. Many child soldiers share the limitations of the adolescent's diminished responsibility and, in addition, many endure the resocialization effects of armed conflict, violence, and drug dependency. Owing to the intersectionality between these two sets of factors, *arguendo*, former child soldiers should be collectively excluded from all transitional justice processes, regardless of form, with narrow exceptions only in cases where they come forth on their own free will as witnesses or victims. Their reintegration and reconciliation, even in cases of grievous violence, could thereby simply proceed upon the excuse of non-responsibility alone.

Although much is to be said in favor of this position, I believe it is too limiting and too inhibiting. When it comes to why children associate with armed forces or groups and, once there, why some commit systematic acts of atrocity, child soldiers are not entirely the products of their immediate environment. As Chapter 3 will demonstrate, disposition matters even in the most noxious of circumstances. Typifying the most acute cases of resocialization and abuse sensationalizes the extremes. Essentializing victimhood and non-responsibility, moreover, fails to serve the best interests of former child soldiers implicated in acts of atrocity, the individuals they harmed, and survivors in the community. Girls formerly associated with armed forces or groups and their children born during captivity also are underserved and face some of the steepest reintegration challenges (including homelessness and segregation).

---

[143] Maroney, *supra* note 140, at 111; *see also* Nuno Ferreira, *Putting the Age of Criminal and Tort Liability into Context: A Dialogue Between Law and Psychology*, 16 INT'L J. CHILD. RTS. 29, 35 (2008) (noting that by the age of ten or eleven children have the basic capacity to make moral judgments); Barry C. Feld, *Juvenile and Criminal Justice Systems' Responses to Youth Violence*, 24 CRIME & JUST. 189, 245 (1998) (noting that "younger offenders may be less criminally responsible than more mature violators . . . ").

Maroney offers a valuable insight. She contends that "[u]ndue emphasis on the immature brain also might alter our social commitment to allow teens incrementally greater control over important aspects of their lives."[144] In support of this concern, Maroney evokes US Supreme Court Justice Antonin Scalia, who "excoriated the American Psychological Association for taking what he saw as inconsistent stances on teen maturity in death penalty and abortion cases."[145] In a 2005 dissent, Justice Scalia noted that, for the purposes of obtaining an abortion without parental consent, the American Psychological Association concluded that "by middle adolescence (age 14–15) young people develop abilities similar to adults in reasoning about moral dilemmas, understanding social rules and laws, [and] reasoning about interpersonal relationships and interpersonal problems."[146] National laws also presume some adolescent capacity and voluntariness in the bioethical context of access to medical treatment and informed consent. International family law also speaks to this situation. The Hague Convention on the Civil Aspects of International Child Abduction—which ceases to apply once a child reaches the age of sixteen—permits courts to refuse to order a child's return following a wrongful removal if the child objects to the return and has attained an age and degree of maturity at which it is appropriate to take account of his or her views.[147]

Maroney's work draws from her experiences with domestic juvenile justice cases in the United States. Her point, however, extends far beyond any one jurisdiction. Policymakers, lawyers, and experts who protect juveniles through arguments rooted in immaturity must remain mindful of the consequences of these arguments. These arguments may unintentionally foster perceptions that juveniles are fragile, capricious, and unreliable leading, in turn, to a weak foundation upon which to base their status as rights-holders.

In a similar vein, the line between protecting juveniles and controlling juveniles indeed may be fuzzy. So, too, may the line between protecting juveniles and inflating parental or state authority over them. By way of example, in June 2011 the US Supreme Court ruled that a California ban on the sale or rental of violent video games to persons under the age of eighteen ran afoul of the child's constitutionally protected free speech rights. "No doubt a State possesses legitimate power to protect children from harm," Justice Scalia wrote for the majority, "but that does not include a free-floating power to restrict the ideas to which children may be exposed."[148] Justice Thomas dissented. He ruled that the ban was not unconstitutional. Why? For Justice Thomas, "'the freedom of speech,' as originally understood, does not include a right to speak to minors (or a right of minors to access speech) without going through the minors' parents or guardians."[149]

---

[144] Maroney, *supra* note 140, at 159.
[145] *Id.*
[146] Roper v. Simmons, 543 U.S. 551, 617–618 (2005) (citation omitted).
[147] Hague Convention on the Civil Aspects of International Child Abduction, Art. 13 (October 25, 1980), T.I.A.S. No. 11670.
[148] Brown v. Entertainment Merchants Assn., 564 U.S. __ (2011) (slip op. p. 7).
[149] *Id.* (Thomas, J., dissenting, p. 1)

Different understandings of voluntariness and capacity can and should apply to different settings. However, regardless of the setting, excessive disparity between the capacity to receive entitlements and be taken seriously, on the one hand, and the capacity to owe obligations to others, on the other hand, risks undermining juvenile empowerment while also needlessly handing a sword to its skeptics.

(v) Conclusion

One publication critically noted in its recommendations that "[a]n industry is emerging around child soldiers, generated by what is 'sexy' such that a real disjuncture exists between donor agencies (responding to 'fashionable funding' in project design) and on-the-ground needs as determined locally."[150] Although this publication is slightly dated, its admonition remains relevant. International expertise brings many benefits. However, these benefits can be undermined if local perspectives and voices, especially those of the former child soldiers themselves, become lost in the process of program design and content development.[151]

What passes as common knowledge about child soldiers is actually only partial knowledge. The way the international legal imagination currently thinks and talks about child soldiers is incomplete. Unsurprisingly, then, current efforts to eradicate the practice, reintegrate returnees, foster rehabilitation, and heal communities also are incomplete. The international legal imagination can do better. As a starting point, it must take a second—and more even-handed—look at the realities of child soldiering.

---

[150] Lisa Ruth Shulman, *The Role of Early Childhood Development Programs in Conflict and Post-Conflict Settings, in* CHILDREN AND WAR, *supra* note 91, at 24, 25.

[151] Paris Principles 7.46 to 7.49, which call for the involvement of local voices, should be robustly actualized.

3

Not So Simple

How do children come to be associated with armed forces or armed groups? Once there, which roles do they serve? What do they do and how are they used? What is known about why some child soldiers become implicated in acts of extraordinary international criminality?

This Chapter addresses these questions by bringing into sharper relief a variety of accounts that, to date, the international legal imagination has tended to neglect. Although drawing from the experiences of child soldiers in many of the world's regions, this Chapter focuses on atrocity-producing conflicts that have become internationally judicialized and in whose aftermath considerable efforts have been undertaken to reintegrate demobilized or released child soldiers.

These accounts mainly concern persons under the age of eighteen at the time of their association with armed forces or armed groups. In light of the legal and policy push to establish eighteen as the minimum age of association with armed forces, it would be unduly limiting to consider research that relates only to the subset of child soldiers younger than fifteen. In any event, when it comes to armed groups (which comprise an important part of the ensuing discussion), that minimum age already has been established as eighteen under international law.[1]

Much more remains to be learned about the intersections among children, militarization, and armed conflict. Systematized knowledge on the subject is incomplete. Country- and locality-specific studies (whether qualitative, participant observation, or quantitative) provide richness and depth. Insofar as their focus is on the *micro*, however, they do not by definition, design, or purpose self-evidently lend themselves to serve as bases upon which to postulate cross-national or *macro* generalities. Hence, there is a need for modesty and caution in aggregating their results. While I recognize these limitations, caveats, and lacunae, I nonetheless hope to distil some overarching themes from the information that these methodologically and regionally diverse studies provide. I encourage international lawyers and policymakers actively to consider these themes in the formulation and reformulation of their craft.

Much of the available research casts doubt upon the explanatory value and operational utility of the faultless passive victim metaphor or any of the other extreme portraits of child soldiering currently in circulation.

---

[1] Optional Protocol to the CRC on the involvement of children in armed conflict, Art. 4(1), G.A. Res. 54/263, U.N. Doc. A/RES/54/263 (May 25, 2000) (entered into force February 12, 2002). For extensive discussion of the legal aspects regarding recruitment or use, *see infra* Chapter 5.

(i) The Association of Children with Armed
Forces or Armed Groups

Children who become associated with armed forces or armed groups get there in one of three ways: (1) they are abducted, or conscripted through coercion or severe threats;[2] (2) they come forward, whether independently or through recruitment programs, and are, in turn, enlisted by commanders; or (3) they are born into forces or groups.

Comparatively fewer children enter military life through birth than through the first two paths. In cases where conflict drags on for decades, however, some children truly come of age in militarized contexts. Not infrequently, their mothers themselves are children, having been abducted into sexual slavery. In some cases, their fathers (and possibly even mothers) are notorious human rights abusers. Once conflict ends, children born into armed forces or groups often come to face considerable stigma.

The first two paths to militarization—which are the most common—are permeable. On the ground, "[a] very fuzzy line is often all that separates voluntary from coerced participation."[3] The international legal imagination is predisposed to erase this line. Its impulse is to treat voluntary participation as tantamount to coerced participation and, accordingly, to fold the former into the latter. This approach leads to the undertheorization and underappreciation of the fact that significant numbers of children exercise initiative in coming forward to join armed forces or armed groups on their own without evident coercion.[4]

The international legal imagination disclaims the possibility that children, including older adolescents, can be found to exercise initiative or actually volunteer to join armed groups and, increasingly, even armed forces. In support of this position, the international legal imagination evokes the combined effects of innate developmental limitations and overwhelming environmental circumstances. Commonly cited environmental circumstances include the instinct to survive, poverty, stunted occupational opportunities, youth demographic bulges, domestic violence, and broken families. Frequent reference also is made to the omnipresence of lightweight AK-47s—which Singer casually calls "new toys for tots"[5]—that are cheap and easy to use.

---

[2] Although some delineation might be effected between abduction and being forced to join by serious threats, little value arises in exploring these shades of difference.

[3] Guy Goodwin-Gill and Ilene Cohn, CHILD SOLDIERS: THE ROLE OF CHILDREN IN ARMED CONFLICTS 23–24 (1994).

[4] P.W. Singer, CHILDREN AT WAR 61 (2006) ("[R]oughly two of every three child soldiers have some sort of initiative in their own recruitment."); Michael Wessells, *Psychosocial Issues in Reintegrating Child Soldiers*, 37 CORNELL INT'L L. J. 513, 514 (2004) ("The best evidence available indicates that significant numbers of children join armed groups without explicit coercion ..."); David Rosen, *Child Soldiers, International Humanitarian Law, and the Globalization of Childhood*, 109(2) AMERICAN ANTHROPOLOGIST 296, 298–299 (2007) ("[T]he vast majority of child soldiers are not forcibly recruited or abducted into armed forces and groups.").

[5] Singer, CHILDREN AT WAR, *supra* note 4, at 45–46.

Situational pressures and environmental factors unequivocally influence children who come forward to associate with armed forces or armed groups. The overall explanatory yield of these factors, however, remains more apparent than real. Poverty is a common characteristic among child soldiers. Nearly all child soldiers are poor. Rachel Brett notes, however, that "[e]ven in war zones, there are many more poor children who do *not* become child soldiers than those who do."[6] A study of intrastate African conflicts between 1975 and 2003 found that neither poverty nor orphan rates could explain the significant variation among child soldier rates across conflicts and countries.[7] Nor does child soldiering invariably present as an element of those conflicts that occur within or among the many jurisdictions characterized by large youth demographic cohorts. Easily obtainable light-weight automatic weaponry augments the power of all soldiers. In the case of children, access to such weaponry certainly consolidates the power of elites for whom the children fight. Conversely, such access also affords youthful fighters an opportunity to challenge—and, even, invert—spited gerontocratic hierarchies and to secure immediate economic gains.[8] An adolescent holding an AK-47 can quickly become a big man. In any event, children participate in conflict without automatic weaponry. In the Rwandan genocide, for example, many victims were murdered by use of *panga* (machete) and *masu* (club studded with nails). In Sierra Leone, child soldiers used cutlasses, fire, and knives. In sum, child soldiering connects to these conventionally cited environmental and situational forces. It is, however, much more than merely epiphenomenal to these forces.

The presentation of volunteering as indistinguishable from forcible conscription helps channel public indignation toward the scourge of child soldiering. This homogenization, however, fails to reflect the lives of significant numbers of children who end up in armed forces or armed groups. Jason Hart laments the complexities that are lost "by authors who readily shuffle quotes from children in one setting with those from somewhere entirely different to build up a generic picture of child recruitment in which the worst stands for all."[9] Didactically presenting the worst as standing for all accents abduction and forcible conscription as *the* path to child

---

[6] Rachel Brett, *Adolescents volunteering for armed forces or armed groups*, 85 INTERNATIONAL REVIEW OF THE RED CROSS 857, 860 (2003) (emphasis in original).

[7] Simon Reich and Vera Achvarina, *Why Do Children 'Fight'? Explaining Child Soldier Ratios in African Intrastate Conflicts* 2 (University of Pittsburgh, Ford Institute for Human Security: Policy Brief 04–3 (2005)).

[8] David J. Francis, *International Conventions and the Limitations for Protecting Child Soldiers in Post-conflict Societies in Africa*, in CHILDREN AND WAR: IMPACT, PROTECTION AND REHABILITATION, PHASE II: PROTECTION 8, 11 (2006) [hereinafter CHILDREN AND WAR], *available at* <http://www.arts.ualberta.ca/childrenandwar/papers/Children_and_War_Phase_II_Report.pdf> ("Access to AK47 rifles and being part of an armed group provides economic opportunities through looting and pillage at the war front. . . . Boys are converted into commanders, with power and influence.").

[9] Jason Hart, *The Politics of "Child Soldiers"*, XIII(1) BROWN JOURNAL OF WORLD AFFAIRS 217, 218 (2006); *see also* Michael Wessells, CHILD SOLDIERS: FROM VIOLENCE TO PROTECTION 3 (2006, first paperback 2009) ("Too often, children have been portrayed as passive innocents whom adults have forced and intimidated into soldiering. . . . [T]his one-dimensional portrayal misses an important part of the picture of child soldiering.").

recruitment when, in actuality, it is only *a* path to recruitment. And it is a path that significant numbers of children do not follow.

Extrinsic constraints invariably shape decisions by persons under the age of eighteen to join armed forces or armed groups. Yet these children—notably, older adolescents—are not pathetic. Many resourcefully shape their own choices and their own lot in life. Some children briskly decide to join, while other cases concern children who "had thought about the possibility of joining for years."[10] Sometimes, as I have written elsewhere, raw survival concerns motivate their decisions.[11] In other situations, motivations are more textured, to wit, "[m]any children view joining an armed group as entering an opportunity space in which they can obtain things they could not have obtained otherwise—including a family, power, revenge, wealth, education, and a means of achieving a cause."[12] The fact that some children reciprocally interact with their environment rather than being entirely suppressed by it simply cannot be wished away. The relationship between children and militarization is characterized by erratic and unstable patterns of push and pull.

Whereas certain conflicts are characterized by a preponderance of abduction and forcible conscription, other conflicts involve large numbers of participants who exercise some degree of personal initiative in coming forward to serve. Conflict in Northern Uganda, for example, involved greater levels of forcible recruitment than the situation in the DRC, especially given the LRA's rapaciousness in pursuing widespread abduction. One survey of former DRC child soldiers indicated that 9% were abducted or joined out of fear, 34% joined for material reasons, 21% joined because of belief in the group's ideology, 10% for revenge, and 11% because they wanted to leave their home.[13] Conflict remains ongoing in the DRC, where out of nearly two thousand child recruitment cases in armed groups in 2009, 47% (928 cases) were considered voluntary, 587 cases forced, and the remaining 473 cases neither voluntary nor forced.[14]

Competing armed groups embroiled in the same conflict may pursue different methods of recruiting children. In Sierra Leone, the rebel RUF and AFRC favored abduction, while many children joined the CDF on their own out of patriotism to support the democratically-elected Sierra Leonean government, protect their families and communities, or punish the rebels. The RUF was notably brutal in its kidnapping practices and, together with the AFRC, not infrequently turned to tattooing and scarification of abductees' bodies so as to inhibit their escape. The incidence of abduction in the DRC also correlated (and continues to correlate) with

---

[10] Rachel Brett and Irma Specht, YOUNG SOLDIERS: WHY THEY CHOOSE TO FIGHT 65 (2004).

[11] Mark A. Drumbl, ATROCITY, PUNISHMENT, AND INTERNATIONAL LAW 172 (2007).

[12] Wessells, CHILD SOLDIERS, *supra* note 9, at 46; Alice Schmidt, *Volunteer* Child *Soldiers as Reality: A Development Issue for Africa*, 2(1) NEW SCHOOL ECONOMIC REVIEW 49, 50 (2007) (arguing that "a substantial part of volunteerism is 'real' rather than 'structurally forced' as is often suggested").

[13] Radhika Coomaraswamy, *Child Soldiers: Root Causes and UN Initiatives* 4 (February 2009) (lecture on file with the author) (reporting a 2007 survey by the International Labour Organization).

[14] Inna Lazareva, *Many DRC Children Volunteer to Fight*, IWPR ICC-Africa Update (No. 291, March 10, 2011) (referencing empirical data from the UN).

the specific armed faction in question. In certain war-torn regions of the DRC, local militias and communities share strong links.[15] Without such militias, villages may wholly lack security owing to the collapsed nature of the state. Although militia groups selfishly exploit insecurity in the region, the fact remains that families may send children to these groups and, moreover, children may join them to defend their village.

Volunteers and abductees may fight alongside each other within the ranks of the same armed force or group. The CDF, after all, also abducted children; and some, albeit few, children independently joined the RUF. It has been reported that "[e]ven in the LRA, research shows that many of the children did join willingly for different reasons."[16] In Sri Lanka, the LTTE pursued policies of forcible recruitment, but some children independently (and in the absence of any coercion) traveled to areas controlled by the LTTE in order to enlist because of family problems, frustration with life in the community, and poverty.[17] In addition to forced recruitment, "[i]n Angola, the reasons given for enlistment included political commitment, ethnic loyalties, peer pressure, food and the opportunity to engage in looting."[18]

In certain hotspots within conflict zones, a high percentage of children may become militarily associated—perhaps up to 50%. These rates include abductions as brief as an hour to carry loads and material.[19] That said, the majority—often an overwhelming majority—of children in conflict zones do not end up in armed forces or armed groups.[20] Significant numbers of children endure terrible harms in such zones, to be sure, but often as civilians unassociated with any fighting faction. In this regard, Michael Wessells identifies as among the "great fallacies" on the subject of child soldiers that they are the worst off among children in conflict zones. Notwithstanding the perils they face, child soldiers "often have better access to food and protection than do other children, who are subject to scourges such as attack, displacement, and HIV/AIDS, and who have no means of defending themselves."[21]

The remainder of the recruitment discussion proceeds through three subsections. The first subsection presents a case-study of Northern Uganda, where brutal abduction was the recruitment norm. The second subsection considers Sierra Leone, a case-study that presents an admixture of abduction and degrees of

---

[15] *Id.*

[16] Coomaraswamy, *supra* note 13, at 5 (citation omitted).

[17] Jo Boyden, Jo de Berry, Thomas Feeny, and Jason Hart, *Children Affected by Armed Conflict in South Asia: A review of trends and issues identified through secondary research* 53 (Refugee Studies Centre, Oxford University, Working Paper No. 7, 2002).

[18] Jo Boyden, *Anthropology Under Fire: Ethics, Researchers and Children in War, in* CHILDREN AND YOUTH ON THE FRONT LINE: ETHNOGRAPHY, ARMED CONFLICT AND DISPLACEMENT 237, 250 (Jo Boyden and Joanna de Berry eds, 2004) [hereinafter CHILDREN AND YOUTH ON THE FRONT LINE].

[19] *See* ICC Case No. 01/04–01/06, English language Transcript (April 7, 2009) lines 11–17 on p. 86.

[20] Wessells, CHILD SOLDIERS, *supra* note 9, at 43 ("In war zones, most children, typically over 90 percent, do not enter armed groups.").

[21] *Id.* at 23 (noting that "[c]hild soldiers may also be better off because their groups meet their basic needs by looting and robbing villages").

volitional enlistment. The third subsection offers some vignettes of recruitment practices globally, including conflicts in which youths exercised considerable initiative in associating with fighting forces.

(a) Abduction and Escape in Northern Uganda

The initial phase of SWAY included a survey of 1,018 households and 741 young men and boys in Northern Uganda.[22] Former abductees were oversampled.

In its heyday (from the mid-1990s to the mid-2000s), the LRA was overwhelmingly responsible for the prevalence of abduction throughout Northern Uganda. Although some recruits joined voluntarily, abducted children consistently have comprised the vast majority of LRA fighters.[23] Presently, the LRA is in a depleted state. Military campaigns waged against it by the Ugandan army have taken their toll. The LRA has migrated outside of Uganda, yet the Ugandan army remains active against it in the DRC, South Sudan, and CAR. The LRA still continues to perpetrate human rights abuses, however, including child abduction and forcible conscription. In recent years, nonetheless, it has not been able to replenish its membership.

SWAY's researchers obtained detailed information regarding the experiences of LRA captives and have since updated these initial findings. SWAY drew from a sample of males, which included abductees, between the ages of fourteen and thirty at the time of the survey (2005 to 2006). Accordingly, initial SWAY findings derived from a sample that was not limited to persons under the age of eighteen at the time of the survey, nor to persons abducted by the LRA, nor (among those who were abducted) to persons under the age of eighteen at the time of abduction.[24] According to the SWAY report, however, 65% of LRA abductions implicated children or adolescents (with by far the most heavily targeted group being adolescent boys) and "[o]f those males abducted before the age of 30, two-thirds were under 18."[25] The LRA often deliberately avoided younger children or released them.[26] Transnational interventions tend to overlook the one-third of LRA fighters

---

[22] Jeannie Annan, Christopher Blattman, and Roger Horton, THE STATE OF YOUTH AND YOUTH PROTECTION IN NORTHERN UGANDA: FINDINGS FROM THE SURVEY FOR WAR AFFECTED YOUTH 6 (September 2006) [hereinafter SWAY].

[23] Andrew Mawson, *Children, Impunity and Justice: Some Dilemmas from Northern Uganda*, in CHILDREN AND YOUTH ON THE FRONT LINE, *supra* note 18, at 130, 133 ("Although some people undoubtedly join voluntarily—many more than would ever be prepared to admit it if and when they return from the LRA—since 1994 possibly as many as 80 percent of fighters have been abducted.").

[24] In Northern Uganda, childhood and youth are perceived as separate life stages. "[C]hildren are defined as those between the ages of five and twelve . . . ." Phuong N. Pham, Patrick Vinck, and Eric Stover, *The Lord's Resistance Army and Forced Conscription in Northern Uganda*, 30 HUM. RTS. Q. 404, 405 n. 1 (2008). Youth follows childhood and continues up to the age of thirty or so.

[25] SWAY, *supra* note 22, at vi, 51, 59.

[26] Christopher Blattman and Jeannie Annan, *On the nature and causes of LRA abduction: what the abductees say*, in THE LORD'S RESISTANCE ARMY: MYTH AND REALITY 132, 134 (Tim Allen and Koen Vlassenroot eds, 2010).

abducted as young adults. This inclination is problematic. It is, after all, abhorrent to abduct persons of any age and compel them to fight.

Without understating the exposure to violence among male youth in Northern Uganda generally, the SWAY report points out "the disproportionate degree to which the formerly abducted have been witness to, and in some cases committed, acts of violence."[27] While with the LRA, abductees endured beatings, assault, and compelled labor. Abductees who failed in their escape attempts came to face renewed brutalities.

Typically, youth were abducted by "roving groups of ten to twenty rebels during night raids on rural homes."[28] SWAY's researchers estimate the scale of abduction to have been immense, with more than a third of all male youth and a sixth of all females being abducted for at least a day.[29] Nearly 11% of male abductions and 26% of female abductions lasted for one or two days, while 28% of male abductions lasted for less than two weeks.[30] Approximately 62% of the female abductees and 41% of the male abductees remained with the LRA for under two months; 18.4% of abducted males and 13.9% of abducted females remained over twelve months.[31] Five percent remained for over three years.[32]

A different study conducted in Northern Uganda found that, among returnees (adults and children) reporting to eight designated reception centers, the average length of abduction was 342 days and the median number of days of abduction was ninety-two.[33] According to this study, 16% were abducted for a week or less, 35% for a month or less, 52% for three months or less, and 20% for over a year. Girls and women were abducted for significantly longer periods of time than men and boys. A survey of sampled adults in Northern Uganda found that 37% of respondents reported having been abducted by the LRA, with 21% saying they had been abducted by the LRA for over a week and 2% for over a year.[34]

Returning to the initial SWAY findings, among returnees (it is estimated that 20% of male abductees never return) "the vast majority have escaped (rather than been rescued or released)."[35] In terms of timing, "[s]ome report attempting to

---

[27] SWAY, *supra* note 22, at 54.

[28] Christopher Blattman and Jeannie Annan, *The Consequences of Child Soldiering*, 92(4) REVIEW OF ECONOMICS AND STATISTICS 882, 883 (2010).

[29] SWAY, *supra* note 22, at 51.

[30] *Id.* at 53.

[31] *Id.* at 54, Figures 26 and 27.

[32] Christopher Blattman and Jeannie Annan, *Child combatants in northern Uganda: Reintegration myths and realities, in* SECURITY AND POST-CONFLICT RECONSTRUCTION: DEALING WITH FIGHTERS IN THE AFTERMATH OF WAR 103, 108 (Robert Muggah ed., 2009).

[33] Pham, Vinck, and Stover, *supra* note 24, at 406–407 (among returnees, 37% were aged thirteen to eighteen and 24% nineteen to thirty).

[34] Phuong Pham, Patrick Vinck, Eric Stover, Andrew Moss, Marieke Wierda, and Richard Bailey, WHEN THE WAR ENDS: A POPULATION-BASED SURVEY ON ATTITUDES ABOUT PEACE, JUSTICE, AND SOCIAL RECONSTRUCTION IN NORTHERN UGANDA 3 (2007).

[35] SWAY, *supra* note 22, at vii, 53; *see also* Jeannie Annan, Moriah Brier, and Filder Aryemo, *From "Rebel" to "Returnee": Daily Life and Reintegration for Young Soldiers in Northern Uganda*, 24 JOURNAL OF ADOLESCENT RESEARCH 639, 642 (2009) (reporting that 80% of abductees from northern Acholi districts exited the LRA by escape, with the remainder being rescued or released).

escape right away, but many report a moment of 'awakening' when they suddenly decided staying was no longer worthwhile."[36] In terms of logistics:

Of those that escape, nearly a third do so at night, sneaking away while their captors were sleeping. Roughly a third also report sneaking away while being left alone. Many of these youth report being sent to loot goods, dig up cassava, or fetch water, and walking off into the bush when they realized they were unsupervised. Finally, nearly a third report that they escape in the confusion of a battle or ambush.[37]

Escape has been linked to abductees' becoming aware that they would not actually obtain any future gains or rewards from remaining with the LRA and that the LRA would not succeed in overthrowing the government—this "gradual realization" among abductees "[led] many to abandon the group."[38] Mergelsberg similarly notes that a "common motif in most accounts" of escape was that the abductee "felt tired of the war that seemed all too meaningless."[39]

Mawson also highlights the prevalence of escape, reporting that "[i]n the mid to late 1990s it was relatively common for LRA units that crossed into Uganda from Sudan to lose as many as 50 percent of their soldiers through desertion."[40] Most girls and women forced into conjugal relationships also departed the LRA through escape.[41]

Many children in Northern Uganda went to incredible lengths anticipatorily to reduce exposure to situations that exposed them to the risk of abduction. Children known as the "night commuters" tenaciously walked for hours—often every day— from rural areas to larger provincial towns, where they spent the night sleeping in groups so as to shield themselves from LRA kidnappers.[42]

According to the SWAY report, "a large proportion of abductees say there was a time when they felt like staying with the LRA, felt loyalty to LRA leader Joseph Kony, or felt like an important member of the group."[43] Notwithstanding the burdens of captivity and the endemic nature of the surrounding violence, abductee experiences were not uniform. For example:

---

[36] SWAY, *supra* note 22, at 51.

[37] *Id.* at 62.

[38] Blattman and Annan, *On the nature and causes of LRA abduction, supra* note 26, at 140.

[39] Ben Mergelsberg, *Between two worlds: former LRA soldiers in northern Uganda, in* THE LORD'S RESISTANCE ARMY: MYTH AND REALITY 156, 163 (Tim Allen and Koen Vlassenroot eds, 2010).

[40] Mawson, *supra* note 23, at 133.

[41] Khristopher Carlson and Dyan Mazurana, *Accountability for Sexual and Gender-Based Crimes by the Lord's Resistance Army, in* CHILDREN AND TRANSITIONAL JUSTICE: TRUTH-TELLING, ACCOUNTABILITY AND RECONCILIATION 235, 245 (UNICEF Innocenti Research Centre and Human Rights Program at Harvard Law School, Sharanjeet Parmar, Mindy Jane Roseman, Saudamini Siegrist, and Theo Sowa eds, 2010) [hereinafter CHILDREN AND TRANSITIONAL JUSTICE].

[42] Phuong Pham, Patrick Vinck, Marieke Wierda, Eric Stover, and Adrian di Giovanni, FORGOT-TEN VOICES: A POPULATION-BASED SURVEY OF ATTITUDES ABOUT PEACE AND JUSTICE IN NORTHERN UGANDA 16 (2005).

[43] SWAY, *supra* note 22, at vi; *see also id.* at 60 ("[L]oyalty and dependability is at first a protective mechanism, but as time passes the goals and objectives of the LRA can be internalized.").

[S]ome of these forcible recruits become willing fighters. By no means all do so, however, and even those that become soldiers are not necessarily ever made to kill.... More than simply seeking to survive, some report that life in the bush was not all violence and misery.[44]

SWAY's researchers conclude that their findings appear to support the view that "however forcible the recruitment, some agency remains with the child or young adult."[45] Agency can be mapped out longitudinally, to wit, "while joining the rebel group is almost always involuntary, those who remain with the group for a long time do exercise some agency, perhaps a great degree."[46] A correlation arises between length of stay in the LRA and individual implication in the commission of acts of violence, including atrocities.

The initial SWAY findings (and subsequent work updating and adding thereto) can be read to depict a picture that is framed by resilience as well as oppression. These findings are at variance with popularized perceptions of child soldiers in the LRA—assuredly one of the most hideous promoters of child abduction and forcible recruitment—as incapable, unwitting, or psychologically devastated by their experiences. Nor do these findings lend credence to other essentialized images of child soldiering. They certainly do not support the demon image of child soldiers as sinister bandits all subject to the wrath or disdain of the community upon their return. The SWAY findings can be read to illuminate the coercive nature of LRA abduction and also variation in terms of individual experiences within captivity.

Some abductees—including many children—fled immediately. Others remained somewhat longer as captives and then escaped. Some persisted with the LRA well into adulthood. A few initially abducted child soldiers became LRA leaders and assumed positions of considerable influence.

Is there a broader takeaway? I advance the claim that, although abductees begin in a similarly desolate place, their paths refract over time. Abductees remain neither static nor uniform. Why? Serendipity undoubtedly plays a role. So, too, does the deportment of specific commanders. Situational and ecological factors also are influential. I believe, however, that these variables can only go so far in accounting for the diversity of experiences. The individual disposition of the child soldier also is relevant. Personal reaction to circumstance, exercise of judgment, choice, and discretionary conduct each matters even within the most painfully abject of circumstances.

My point is not to suggest that child soldiers bear moral responsibility if they dispense no effort to resist abduction or to contest their captivity. My point, rather, is to emphasize that many child soldiers do undertake such efforts—often successfully. Their stories should be foregrounded.

---

[44] *Id.* at 57, 60.
[45] *Id.* at 60.
[46] Blattman and Annan, *Child combatants in northern Uganda, supra* note 32, at 113.

(b) Militarization in Sierra Leone

In the 1990s, juveniles in Sierra Leone entered armed forces or armed groups through diverse paths, including ones demonstrative of the exercise of personal initiative.[47]

Susan Shepler links the provenance of child soldiering in Sierra Leone to four factors that fall outside the scope of conventional explanations proffered by the international legal imagination.

The first factor Shepler identifies is the prevalence of children in the work force. Insofar as "[c]hild labor almost defines childhood in Sierra Leone," Shepler reports that "[i]t did not seem unusual to Sierra Leoneans that child labor would be essential to fighting forces."[48] Put bluntly, "the use of children as workers in the pursuit of war is not surprising."[49] The point of this discussion is not to condone child labor, nor gesture away from the abuses it occasions. The point, rather, is to suggest that the involvement of children in cooking, portering, undertaking domestic chores, and serving as messengers for armies in times of conflict is not *per se* preternatural. Rather, it reflects an extension of what many children otherwise would have been doing for other groups in times of peace. Within militarized contexts, children and adolescents may undertake such labor for the same reasons that people labor generally: to make money, pursue a livelihood, and support themselves, dependents, family, and loved ones.

Although cautioning against ascribing too much in the way of volunteerism to the actions of child soldiers, William Murphy suggests that child soldiering in Sierra Leone (and Liberia) can be seen through the prism of patron-client relationships. By this, Murphy means that "big men" commanders provided protection, food, and means for survival in exchange for youth combat and labor services.[50] Authority, age, and status, however, were far from static within fluid conflict situations. Tim Kelsall, commenting on the testimony of a child soldier before the Special Court for Sierra Leone, nimbly identifies the multiple identities in play: "In the

---

[47] Schmidt, *supra* note 12, at 52 ("Richards (2002) found that while most ... RUF fighters were abductees, nearly all other combatants ... were volunteers. Another study from Sierra Leone revealed that close to half of child soldiers interviewed described their participation as voluntary ... (Aning and McIntyre 2005). A study on Sierra Leone and Liberia by Sesay (2003) found that almost three quarters of children joined voluntarily, especially on the side of pro-government forces.") (footnotes omitted).

[48] Susan Shepler, *The Social and Cultural Context of Child Soldiering in Sierra Leone* 12–13 (2004) (manuscript on file with the author). In the DRC, similarly, "children are generally required to contribute to the family livelihood by undertaking responsibilities such as herding cattle, gathering wood, carrying water, harvesting crops, cooking or going to the market." REDRESS Trust, Victims, Perpetrators or Heroes? Child Soldiers Before the International Criminal Court 7 (2006).

[49] Shepler, *The Social and Cultural Context*, *supra* note 48, at 14.

[50] William P. Murphy, *Military Patrimonialism and Child Soldier Clientalism in the Liberian and Sierra Leonean Civil Wars*, 46(2) African Studies Review 61, 69, 70, 73–74 (2003). Although circumspect about the ability of children to be able to volunteer for armed service, Murphy's anthropological work presents child soldiers more dynamically than the passive faultless victim image. *See id.* at 61, 64, 73–74 (critiquing the "model" of child soldiers as "passive victims," a dimension which "[h]uman rights organizations in particular stress;" and observing that older teenage boys could serve as patrons to younger boys, though also noting that "in some instances a younger child's reputation for special fierceness gave him authority over older children").

context of CDF initiation, then, [the witness] is a small boy; in a meeting with the President, he is a 'very small boy'; whereas in a context where the CDF has just stormed a rebel held town, he is 'a CDF man'."[51] Persons aggrieved by acts of atrocity in the town may recall that child soldier not as an innocent victim, but as a fighter who has come of age. That child may have wielded considerable authority over civilians. Kelsall interprets other testimony by this witness as depicting the initiation into fighting forces as arduous, but also "as an attractive, empowering experience" after which "the witness appears fairly free to decide his own fate."[52]

Child fosterage, apprenticeship, and secret society initiation comprise the three other entwined factors Shepler etiologically associates with child soldiering in Sierra Leone. Shepler views these aspects of youth in Sierra Leone as continuous with children's recruitment and participation in fighting factions. Shepler observes that "apprenticeship is a vital institution for the training of young people into adulthood and often involves fosterage to a master."[53] Fosterage refers to a not uncommon family situation in West Africa in which a child's primary caregiver is someone other than his or her biological parents.[54] Shepler characterizes fosterage as an ongoing exchange system. Poorer parents send their children to be raised by others, mostly extended family members, who may be wealthier. Although a fostered child may be susceptible to exploitation, the fosterage system is not inherently designed to exploit. Ideally, fosterage advances the child's education while also cementing social bonds.[55]

Shepler recounts perceptions among children that joining fighting forces would provide them with education and training. She locates apprenticeship or patronage models in each of the RUF, CDF, and SLA. It is unhelpful to downplay the genuineness of the children's perceptions by romanticizing what their lives would have been like were they not to have been associated with armed forces or groups. In 1990, just before internecine conflict began in full force in Sierra Leone, only 55% of children of primary school-age were enrolled in school.[56] Hence, although rhetorically compelling, it is not generically accurate to say that, but for their

[51] Tim Kelsall, CULTURE UNDER CROSS-EXAMINATION: INTERNATIONAL JUSTICE AND THE SPECIAL COURT FOR SIERRA LEONE 164 (2009).

[52] *Id.* at 165. Kelsall concludes that this testimony "suggests some of the complexity of the child soldiering phenomenon, then, a moral ambivalence ignored by the international community's chorus of outrage." *Id.* at 168.

[53] Shepler, *The Social and Cultural Context, supra* note 48, at 18.

[54] *Id.* at 14, 18. In a 2000 survey, 10% of Sierra Leonean children were found not to stay with their living parents. WITNESS TO TRUTH: REPORT OF THE SIERRA LEONE TRUTH & RECONCILIATION COMMISSION, Volume 3B, Chapter 4 (Children and the Armed Conflict in Sierra Leone) (2004) ¶ 334, *available at* <http://www.sierra-leone.org/Other-Conflict/TRCVolume3B.pdf> [hereinafter SLTRC, VOL. 3B, CH. 4]. For discussion of fosterage in Liberia, *see* Save the Children, WHEN CHILDREN AFFECTED BY WAR GO HOME: LESSONS LEARNED FROM LIBERIA 51–52 (2003).

[55] Shepler, *The Social and Cultural Context, supra* note 48, at 15.

[56] Theresa S. Betancourt, Stephanie Simmons, Ivelina Borisova, Stephanie E. Brewer, Uzo Iweala, and Marie de la Soudière, *High Hopes, Grim Reality: Reintegration and the Education of Former Child Soldiers in Sierra Leone,* 52(4) COMP. EDUC. REV. 565, 567 (2008) (citation omitted). Enrollment has increased following the conflict, albeit only to 69% of primary school age children. *Id.* at 569.

recruitment into armed forces or groups, the children otherwise would be taking lessons in a classroom.

Conversely, it also is problematic to drift too far toward the other extreme and cynically posit that child soldiering occasions no educational disadvantage. Evidence from Northern Uganda reveals that the abduction of children into armed groups leads to measurable loss in education—0.75 fewer years of schooling in the case of abducted male youth—reflecting a 10% reduction in total years of education as compared to non-abducted youth.[57] Moreover, enrolling a former child soldier into the general school population post-conflict may formally involve restarting education at the grade level at which he or she had left off. In practice, this may mean that a sixteen year-old takes classes with thirteen year-olds. A potentially embarrassing situation arises which, in turn, may dissuade former child soldiers from persevering with traditional classes.

Shepler also connects the participation of Sierra Leonean children in armed conflict to initiation into sodality or secret societies. Initiations into secret societies serve an important role in transitions from childhood to adulthood. According to Shepler, "[n]o one can be fully considered an adult without being initiated, and especially in rural settings, everyone is initiated."[58] She observes that the CDF recruited child soldiers "*through* secret society connections" and also notes that even "RUF abduction was like secret society initiation."[59] Ellis, writing within the context of Liberia, similarly underscores how militia initiation resembled "traditional initiation schools used to manage the transformation of children into adults at the time of puberty."[60]

Aspects of child soldiering that the international legal imagination takes as proof of incapacity and immaturity—for example, the belief of some child soldiers that they are bullet-proof if they wear certain amulets, clothing, or hats—actually may derive from processes of communication with the spirit world that accompany their initiation into traditional societies. Undoubtedly, commanders selfishly manipulate these beliefs to suit militarized ends. Yet, when outsiders seize upon these beliefs as proof of the gullibility of child soldiers, they do so in a manner that underestimates the broader "social roots" of secret societies and how children come of age within them.[61] Ellis offers the example of adolescent boys in Liberia in the 1990s, who committed terrible atrocities while wearing women's clothes. This phenomenon links to the tradition that, when boys pass through secret societies into adulthood, they go through an intermediate process of suspending gender identity, often reflected in transvestite dressing, until they become firmly rooted in male

---

[57] Blattman and Annan, *The Consequences of Child Soldiering*, supra note 28, at 889.
[58] Shepler, *The Social and Cultural Context*, supra note 48, at 20–21.
[59] *Id.* at 22 (italics in original).
[60] Stephen Ellis, *Young Soldiers and the Significance of Initiation: Some Notes from Liberia* 2, *available at* <http://www.ascleiden.nl/pdf/conference24042003-ellis.pdf> (cited with permission). Ellis specifically considers the *Poro* (for men) and *Sande* (for women), which also are present in Sierra Leone. He also draws connections between traditional initiation societies and militia violence in Senegal, Côte d'Ivoire, and Nigeria.
[61] *Id.* at 5.

adulthood.[62] To the outsider, what appears as haplessly neutered boys forced to wear women's clothes to terrorize the public at the crazed whim of their commanders is actually a more complex pattern of navigated interaction between the child and a social institution, albeit one that has been fundamentally perverted by conflict entrepreneurs.

In Sierra Leone, the recruitment of youth into political violence did not start suddenly in the 1990s. To different degrees, such recruitment occurred throughout the country's history—beginning pre-colonially, but also entangling both with colonialism and, responsively, with resistance thereto. These historical dimensions of the relationships between youth and violence, however, tend to be overlooked by contemporary international humanitarianism.

Presentation of this evidence neither endorses nor countenances child soldiering. It does not offer an *apologia* for an illicit practice. It does not whitewash the involvement of adult commanders and recruiters who enlist children or use them in hostilities. These enlisters act out of self-interest. Their conduct calls out for legal sanction and denunciation. Notwithstanding the fact that recruitment patterns favor older adolescents, commanders have enlisted young children because they consume fewer resources, are more obedient, and provide strategic advantages against the enemy in battle.[63] Nor is it my intention to absolve political officials and local leaders who, seeking to gin up their own credibility in the eyes of military commanders, abet child soldiering by strong-arming young people to enlist.

Youth, nonetheless, are neither apolitical nor clueless about material necessities. They, too, have economic and political motivations. Peters and Richards report that "many [Sierra Leonean] under-age combatants choose to fight with their eyes open, and defend their choice, sometimes proudly," which leads these researchers to conclude that child soldiers should be seen as "rational human actors, [who] have an at times quite surprisingly mature understanding of their predicament."[64] Peters and Richards report being struck by how their interviewees (notably those who had fought the RUF) rejected interpretations of the conflict as "barbarously purposeless" or as resulting from "ethnic and religious tensions." Instead, they "preferr[ed] to interpret it primarily in terms of an intergenerational struggle for a fairer society...."[65] According to Peters and Richards:

[M]any under-age combatants joined up voluntarily..., some looking for revenge,...others to survive.... Joining a militia group is both meal ticket and substitute education.... The pay may be derisory..., but weapon training pays quicker dividends than school ever did; soon the AK47 brings food, money, a warm bath and instant adult respect.[66]

---

[62] *Id.* at 9.

[63] Ishmael Beah, A Long Way Gone: Memoirs of a Boy Soldier 143 (2007) ("[O]ur size gave us an advantage, because we could hide under the tiniest bushes and kill men who wondered where the bullets were coming from.").

[64] Krijn Peters and Paul Richards, '*Why We Fight*': *Voices of Youth Combatants in Sierra Leone*, 68(2) Africa 183, 183–184 (1998).

[65] *Id.* at 187.

[66] *Id.*

Notwithstanding its horrors, conflict presents opportunities, benefits, and second chances. Children, in particular older adolescents, may dislodge what they can from available nooks and crannies.

In Sierra Leone, children who exercised initiative in coming forth to associate with armed forces or groups did not invariably face a set of illusory choices. Many interactively pursued paths of economic advancement, inclusion in occupational networks, and professional development that were continuous with, but also had morphed from, pre-conflict social topographies. They were not necessarily lost on these paths. They traversed them as best they could.

(c) Recruitment Elsewhere: Some Vignettes

A 2003 study of child soldiers in Burundi, Congo-Brazzaville, the DRC, and Rwanda reports that "[t]wo out of three present or former child soldiers surveyed said that they took the initiative of enrolling themselves 'voluntarily'—they were not kidnapped nor obliged to do so under threat."[67] In a drafting style characteristic of many of these reports, however, it is then immediately added that "one cannot consider this to be a real choice on their part because the large majority of them were desperately searching for a means of subsistence and, in the context of war, this was the most plausible solution for survival." This study, however, also recounts a number of facts that, in turn, can be interpreted to show how the phenomenon of child soldiering is not so simple. For example, for many of the child volunteer enlistees, joining an armed group allowed them to escape from marginalization at home or in school. They were the only ones in their family who decided to enroll. Many reported that the armed group offered them an opportunity for social integration and, in the end, they generally felt positively about the ambience in the armed group. According to this report, kidnapped child soldiers were treated much more harshly than those who had volunteered. Regarding exit, "[m]ore than half of the former child soldiers surveyed left the armed group of their own accord—most had to escape."[68]

In 2002, UNICEF published a report entitled *Adult Wars, Child Soldiers: Voices of Children Involved in Armed Conflict in the East Asia and Pacific Region*. Among the interviewed children, 57% said they volunteered for service while 24% said they were forced or coerced to join.[69] Despite reporting these statistics, *Adult Wars, Child Soldiers* still concludes that "most children in [East Asia and the Pacific] who join armed forces or groups are forcibly recruited."[70] *Adult Wars, Child Soldiers* warns that children who say they joined "voluntarily" have "to be understood in a

---

[67] International Labour Office, WOUNDED CHILDHOOD: THE USE OF CHILDREN IN ARMED CONFLICT IN CENTRAL AFRICA viii (2003). *Cf.* Schmidt, *supra* note 12, at 49 ("A number of recent studies from Sub-Saharan Africa show that the majority of children and young people join armed groups voluntarily for a number of reasons.").

[68] International Labour Office, *supra* note 67, at viii.

[69] UNICEF, ADULT WARS, CHILD SOLDIERS: VOICES OF CHILDREN INVOLVED IN ARMED CONFLICT IN THE EAST ASIA AND PACIFIC REGION 19 (2002) [hereinafter ADULT WARS, CHILD SOLDIERS].

[70] *Id.* at 23.

context where [they] are not exercising free choice but are, instead, responding to economic, cultural, social and political pressures."[71] This recurrent interpretive and drafting approach substitutes the normative conclusions of adult report-writers, who may simply believe they know better, for the lived experiences as described by the former child soldiers themselves.

This report identifies among its child soldier interviewees:

[S]everal voices of affirmation and gratitude for what seemed to them positive military experiences. These young fighters, both former and current, talked of learning discipline, feeling cared for, being respected or treated better than at home and having developed greater respect and love for their country or homeland.[72]

Although recognizing this information, *Adult Wars, Child Soldiers* then incorporates it in convoluted and contradictory fashion which, in turn, gives rise to other drafting anomalies:

[S]ome children speak positively about their experiences. Presenting their perspective could be seen as an approval of children as soldiers. Child soldiering is damaging to all children. It is important to recognize that not all children want to be demobilized.[73]

Might this passage's staccato cadence derive from ideological pressures? From authorial discomfort with some of the information that the investigation actually unearthed? Regardless, is it productive to highlight statements by child soldiers that conform to dominant orthodoxies, but nudge away dissident statements on the pretext of the children's incapacity?

However well-intended, this strategy creates a risk that youth perspectives become discarded as uninformed or unreliable. This strategy needlessly depletes the informational record insofar as "children are often more aware and active politically, and more developed morally and socially, than adults generally assume . . . and have many valuable insights into the causes and means of ameliorating their suffering."[74]

An alternate approach would be to listen, not override, and then meaningfully integrate that information into a broader composite.

Active service in armed forces or groups poses great dangers for children. Their mortality rates are high. The health risks are staggering. Depending on the context, however counterintuitively, youth association with armed forces or armed groups also has been identified with enhancing self-confidence, skills, and leadership qualities. Victoria Bernal (focusing on the Eritrean People's Liberation Front, which fought for Eritrea's independence), Angela Veale (focusing on the Tigray peoples' liberation in Ethiopia), and Harry West (focusing on the FRELIMO

---

[71] *Id.* at 74. Ah-Jung Lee offers a critical read of this report. Ah-Jung Lee, *Understanding and Addressing the Phenomenon of 'Child Soldiers'* (Refugee Studies Center, Working Paper Series No. 52, Oxford University, 2009) (Master's Thesis). She observes how alternative voices, although reported, are "ultimately lost" textually in the report, which is "craft[ed] . . . to support the theme of victimisation in the face of counter-evidence." *Id.* at 10.

[72] ADULT WARS, CHILD SOLDIERS, *supra* note 69, at 56; *see also id.* at 74 ("Some found a sense of power by association with armed struggle.").

[73] *Id.* at 35.

[74] Boyden, *Anthropology Under Fire, supra* note 18, at 250.

armed group, which struggled for Mozambique's independence from Portugal) each relate that girl soldiers found their involvement in the armed group to be empowering.[75] The international legal imagination unequivocally posits that military "[r]ecruitment is per se against the best interests of the child."[76] This impulse is understandable. All children do not necessarily see things the same way, nevertheless, nor necessarily in as categorical a sense. International lawyers and policymakers are remiss when they overlook these subtleties—however surprising, disconcerting, or unanticipated.

Mozambique constitutes an insightful case-study on multiple fronts. Armed conflict in Mozambique implicated a rebel group (RENAMO, the Mozambican National Resistance) and government forces (FRELIMO, the Mozambican Liberation Front). In 1964, FRELIMO initiated an insurgency movement against Portuguese colonial authorities. Portugal relented in 1975. Mozambique declared itself independent. Neighboring Rhodesia (today, Zimbabwe) and South Africa began to train and support anti-FRELIMO groups. These groups became RENAMO, which endeavored to destroy FRELIMO's capacity to rule the country. Both FRELIMO and RENAMO recruited child soldiers. RENAMO's human rights abuses were more pointed than FRELIMO's. RENAMO turned to extensive forced recruitment of children and harsh disciplinary methods. Whereas FRELIMO adopted the policy goal of equality between the sexes, RENAMO did not. Conflict in Mozambique lasted nearly three decades. FRELIMO remains as the country's ruling political party.

West interviewed former girl soldiers in the *Destacamento Feminino* (Female Detachment) of FRELIMO. His interviewees "most often told not of traumatic events that *happened to them* but, rather, of purposive acts and of epic events to *which they contributed* in defining ways."[77] They cited Mozambique's independence and political ideology as motivations for their engagement in armed conflict. According to West:

Participation in the armed struggle broadened horizons for these young women, just as it did for young men.... Many of the women who... occupy influential positions in the FRELIMO party hierarchy at national, provincial, district and local levels owe their power to their wartime careers [in the *Destacamento Feminino*].[78]

---

[75] Victoria Bernal, *Equality to Die For?: Women Guerrilla Fighters and Eritrea's Cultural Revolution*, 23 POLITICAL AND LEGAL ANTHROPOLOGY REVIEW 61 (2000) (discussing youth fighters generally, although a great number had joined when they were younger than eighteen); Angela Veale, FROM CHILD SOLDIER TO EX-FIGHTER: FEMALE FIGHTERS, DEMOBILISATION AND REINTEGRATION IN ETHIOPIA 51, 64 (2003) (showing girl ex-combatants to be more self-confident than those who did not serve, and reporting that none regarded themselves as having been victimized or as having been rendered powerless); Harry G. West, *Girls with Guns: Narrating the Experience of War of FRELIMO's 'Female Detachment'*, *in* CHILDREN AND YOUTH ON THE FRONT LINE, *supra* note 18, at 105.

[76] *Written Submissions of the United Nations Special Representative of the Secretary-General on Children and Armed Conflict*, Prosecutor v. Lubanga, Document ICC-01/04-01/06-1229-AnxA ¶ 11 (March 18, 2008).

[77] West, *supra* note 75, at 114 (emphases in original).

[78] *Id.* at 118, 119–120.

Jessica Schafer's field research in Mozambique untangles knotty questions regarding the malleability of age and transition.[79] Her study sample indicates that almost half of the fighters of both RENAMO and FRELIMO were below the age of eighteen at the time of recruitment. According to Schafer, "the concept of 'child' soldier in the sense in which it is commonly understood, with the implications of childhood vulnerability and innocence, is not useful or accurate in this particular context."[80] She notes that the Shona, the main ethnic group in her study sample, distinguish children from adolescents. Labor migration, which begins as early as the age of twelve, informs the process of entering manhood. Insofar as a majority of RENAMO's young rural recruits had spent time living away from their families, having even crossed international borders to work, they were "not really considered children by their communities in the sense in which the term is understood in the West."[81] Schafer adds that "[t]he fact that young men are involved in economic processes makes them, in the eyes of that society, potentially legitimate perpetrators of violence even though they are not yet 18 years of age."[82]

In El Salvador, notwithstanding the presence of forced recruitment on all sides of the internecine conflict, some youths willingly turned to guerrilla violence as offering what they believed to be among the few ways in which to pursue ideological social change.[83] Ah-Jung Lee examines research on Bhutan and concludes that "far from being coerced and brainwashed to fight in a barbaric war, many Bhutanese refugee children and adolescents consciously think about how they can empower their communities and seem to regard political and military engagement as a legitimate means to address their grievances."[84] It has been estimated that 60% of child soldiers in the FARC group in Colombia "joined of their own volition."[85] Kimberly Theidon's ethnographic research in Colombia prompts her to describe combatants in both the guerrilla and governmental forces (65% of her sample joined as minors) as overall having entered fighting forces "[i]n search of respect."[86] Adolescents may mobilize into armed factions to protect family members. For example, the stepfather of Sonia, a Filipina interviewee,

---

[79] Jessica Schafer, *The Use of Patriarchal Imagery in the Civil War in Mozambique and its Implications for the Reintegration of Child Soldiers*, in CHILDREN AND YOUTH ON THE FRONT LINE, *supra* note 18, at 87, 87.

[80] *Id.*

[81] *Id.* at 87–88.

[82] *Id.* at 88.

[83] Lee, *supra* note 71, at 20. Anecdotally, Ananda Millard mentions Eva, a fourteen year-old girl soldier who fought for El Salvador's Frente Farabundo Martí para la Liberación Nacional. Millard places Eva among those child soldiers who "believe that what they do is right and necessary and engage voluntarily," and reports that being "regarded as a good sniper gave [Eva] a sense of pride and accomplishment." Ananda S. Millard, *Children in Armed Conflicts: Transcending Legal Responses*, 32 (2) SECURITY DIALOGUE 187, 187 (2001) (footnote omitted).

[84] Lee, *supra* note 71, at 21.

[85] Singer, CHILDREN AT WAR, *supra* note 4, at 61 (citation omitted).

[86] Kimberly Theidon, *Transitional Subjects: The Disarmament, Demobilization and Reintegration of Former Combatants in Colombia*, 1 INT'L J. TRANSITIONAL J. 66, 75 (2007). Theidon suggests that "many of these ex-combatants do blur the line between victim and perpetrator" and "are not within those groups that are the true beneficiaries of . . . war." *Id.* at 76.

"only stopped beating her mother when [Sonia] joined the New People's Army (NPA) and threatened to come back and kill him if he continued."[87]

Minors join armed forces in Western states. Parental consent generally is required in such cases, to be sure, but many Sierra Leonean parents also consented when their children joined the CDF and even paid for their initiation. Minors and young adults proudly decide to enlist in the US army—an entirely volunteer armed force. Their decisions are not shorn of situational pressures. Many enlistees are from poorer regions of the country. They face limited occupational prospects. The fact remains, however, that US youth who enlist do so to traverse their own trajectories of social advancement, obtain economic independence, and provide for loved ones. They enlist in the name of honor, duty, patriotism, pride in family histories, and pursuit of apprenticeship. Pitying their choices flirts with demeaning their decisions.

Utas concludes that, despite the presence of forced conscription in Liberia, "most young combatants joined out of 'free' will."[88] At the outset of Liberia's internal conflict, many participants "saw it as a youth revolution, a chance to get rid of an elitist urban leadership of autocrats that showed little concern for the young of Liberia . . . [and] . . . as the only opportunity to move from the margin into the centre of politics and economy."[89] Over time the conflict changed in form. The violence increasingly lost its political purpose. It became directed against the very civilians whose interests it had purportedly been initiated to protect. The rate of forced conscription increased. That said, even at this pernicious juncture, Utas' research suggests motivational interactivity to boys' decisions to join fighting forces:

Many young excombatants state that it was the benefits that drew them to join up, both the direct gains and also escaping the disadvantages of being a civilian. Direct advantages include loot from raids; bribes during security assignments; and payoffs from protecting locals and the acquisition of power in local communities. The leap from being a powerless young boy, under the authority of parents and elders, to being a commander with a gun is momentous.[90]

Utas also lists as among the benefits "having girlfriends," "preventing other rebel soldiers from harassing oneself and one's family," and, to a lesser degree, "vengeance motives."[91] His work with Liberian girl soldiers locates motivations, albeit more

---

[87] Brett and Specht, *supra* note 10, at 90.

[88] Mats Utas, *Fluid Research Fields: Studying Excombatant Youth in the Aftermath of the Liberian Civil War*, in CHILDREN AND YOUTH ON THE FRONT LINE, *supra* note 18, at 209, 214 (footnote omitted).

[89] *Id.*

[90] *Id.* at 215. *Cf.* Save the Children, *supra* note 54, at 118 ("In some cases the young people themselves, armed with guns, had humiliated civilians whom they would have viewed with fear and respect before the war. They discovered that the power and authority of the village chief and elders was nothing compared to the power of people with guns in their hands."). For discussion in the context of young men in Darfur, *see* Julie Flint and Alex de Waal, DARFUR: A SHORT HISTORY OF A LONG WAR 48–49 (2005).

[91] Utas, *Fluid Research Fields, supra* note 88, at 215.

subdued, related to the acquisition of goods, pursuit of power, and overcoming marginalization.[92]

The international legal imagination typifies child soldiers as powerless during conflict. Paradoxically, some boy soldiers come to describe themselves as powerless *after* conflict ends. Perceived influence during periods of violence disintegrates into perceived impotence during periods of stability and security. Knowledge about fighting becomes obsolete. This sudden powerlessness prompts an adjustment challenge, of which post-conflict programming must remain mindful.[93]

(d) Summary

Child soldiers do not present a unitary narrative. Many become associated with armed forces or groups through brutal abduction. Others are conscripted through threats. Significant numbers of child soldiers, however, actively join armed forces or groups in an attempt to achieve various ends. In some cases, children are enlisted under false pretenses, through deception, or because of an impulsive snap-decision. In other cases, children—particularly older adolescents—consciously decide to join. Their reasons for coming forward, which are multiple and deeply personal, include: to defend the state, avenge, pillage, labor, acquire training, earn rations and shelter, pursue fosterage and secret society initiation, attenuate boredom and *anomie*, give voice to political viewpoints, pursue the vocation of being a soldier, struggle for political liberation and revolutionary emancipation, fight oppression, articulate collective self-determination, engage in *jihad*, and (in the case of some girls) seek gender equality and avoid arranged marriages. Some children enlist simply because they find armed action exciting. Others join because they crave stability and structure in their lives. In some cases, although few in number, children come forward because they locate meaning in cruelty. To generalize all child soldiers as visceral sadists on the basis of these few cases, however, is deeply problematic.

So long as the discourse about child soldiers retains its proclivity for parsimony rather than nuance, however, the risk persists that the discursive field becomes flooded with essentialized imagery that, whatever its content, masks the reality that child soldiering is not so simple.

Juveniles scale their surroundings and adapt to circumstances that are not of their own making. In some instances, however discomfiting to outsiders, this means

[92] Mats Utas, *Agency of Victims: Young Women in the Liberian Civil War*, *in* MAKERS & BREAKERS: CHILDREN & YOUTH IN POSTCOLONIAL AFRICA 53, 76 (Alcinda Honwana and Filip de Boeck eds, 2005) ("Many poor girls used the power of military fatigues and the barrel of a gun to lay hands on commodities of modern society that they would never have been able to obtain under normal circumstances. Their power put them in a position to rule communities and command individuals who had previously looked down on or ignored them.").

[93] Roméo Dallaire, THEY FIGHT LIKE SOLDIERS, THEY DIE LIKE CHILDREN 10 (2010) ("These were fourteen-year-olds who were going on twenty-five, who were still very much in charge and who were not going to buy into any simplistic Dick-and-Jane rehab programme delivered by adults...They could influence and they could command, and they demanded recognition of the power, the potential and the respect they had earned over years in the bush.")

joining armed forces or groups. Instead of being immobilized by militarization, some youth ingeniously mobilize around it. Concealing these complexities may offer some comfort, but this comfort is anodyne. Concealment, moreover, may trigger a disappointing side-effect, namely, a fragile basis upon which to construct a vigorous framework of defensible juvenile civic rights.

As a matter of semantics, the Straight 18 position defines volunteerism so as to render the term inapplicable to militarized youth. Can a real-world challenge, however, simply be defined out of existence? Is this productive? Facing up to the tangibility of volunteerism does not mean endorsing the militarization of children. Quite the opposite. Acknowledging this reality is a condition precedent to the genuine eradication of the practice of child soldiering. This reimagined approach does not make for lofty rhetoric. Nor is it emotively electric. Still, I believe that it leads to more effective on-the-ground dissuasive and remedial measures.

(ii) Child Soldiers and Acts of Atrocity

Some, but not most, child soldiers become implicated in the perpetration of acts of atrocity. Among this subgroup, many are forced to do so and, thus, operate under extreme duress. Commanders may "harden[] children to killing and achiev[e] unquestioning obedience."[94] Vicious punishment—including whipping, caning, and beating—maintains order.[95] Many children associated with armed forces or armed groups are desperate. They turn to violence to survive. Depending on the conflict, children may undertake acts of atrocity while high on hallucinatory drugs or alcohol. In Sierra Leone, for example, commonly used drugs included cannabis, cocaine, amphetamines, and barbiturates. At times, powdered cocaine or heroin was mixed with gunpowder, resulting in a concoction known as *brown-brown*. Some of the worst amputations, mutilations, disembowelments, and thrashings of babies and fetuses in Sierra Leone were occasioned by juveniles bewildered by narcotics.[96] Like lower-level adult cadres, some children are relentlessly brain-washed. Reoriented by propaganda, they come to despise the designated enemy. Juveniles are, on the whole, more susceptible than adults to such resocialization.

Children have been forced to commit atrocities against community members and close relatives as part of their initiation process. Singer notes a survey of child soldiers in Africa that found that 2% "had to kill a family member."[97] In other extreme instances, cannibalism may be practiced. The most abominable cases,

---

[94] Wessells, CHILD SOLDIERS, *supra* note 9, at 65.

[95] Human Rights Watch, COERCION AND INTIMIDATION OF CHILD SOLDIERS TO PARTICIPATE IN VIOLENCE 1 (2008).

[96] Drumbl, *supra* note 11, at 27 (noting that, in Sierra Leone, "many perpetrators were ordinary children, often—but not always—kidnapped and drugged, who began killing and maiming in the most grotesque fashion amid the company of their new families of killers").

[97] Singer, CHILDREN AT WAR, *supra* note 4, at 113 (footnote omitted); *see also* Scott Johnson, *Hard Target: The Hunt for Africa's Last Warlord*, NEWSWEEK 61 (May 16, 2009) (reporting that Joseph Kony "has forced new male [LRA] recruits to rape their mothers and kill their parents").

however, receive popular attention disproportionate to their actual incidence.[98] This outsize emphasis may ensure that children implicated in these horrid situations receive the care they require and that the world learns of the sheer brutalities that inhere in child soldiering. Conversely, this emphasis also dramatically sensationalizes the nettlesome problem of child soldiering by typifying the outlying extremes. It also inhibits dispassionate appraisals of the actual level of violence that prevails within various armed forces or groups. Once again, to return to Jason Hart's language, the worst comes to stand for all.

The international legal imagination largely presents all child soldiers who commit acts of atrocity in one of two ways: either as lacking the capacity or maturity to comprehend what they are doing or, secondly, as lacking the wherewithal to do other than collectively surrender to the impossible situation before them and submit to becoming programmed into the weapon of choice of evil adult commanders.[99] These two portraits are not mutually exclusive. In practice, they remain compatible.

Can these explanations, however, properly be universalized? Do all child perpetrators kill, mutilate, or rape solely because they are prerational? Immature? Overwhelmed by constraint? Drugged? Can reintegration and reconciliation be truly viable if based solely on these explanations? Perhaps the construction of all child soldiers as vicariously used by others dissembles the possibility that some child soldiers choose to do things for themselves. Does it matter if the experiences of some individual child soldiers are at variance with transnationalized imagery and expectations?

Although scattered and incomplete, accounts of the conduct of child soldiers during atrocity-producing conflicts offer corrective counterweights to the dominant assumption of faultless passive victimhood. These counterweights, in turn, should motivate international lawyers and policymakers to be less comfortable with the formulaic applicability of this assumption and, also, less sanguine about its parsimony. One inspirational thread that emerges is how significant numbers of child soldiers demonstrate resistance, courage, empathy, and mercy *not* to commit acts of violence even in situations of abject depravity.

Wessells identifies several psychological processes as bearing upon why some child soldiers become repeat perpetrators of terrible human rights abuses, including killings. These processes are: the will to survive, obedience, the normalization of violence, the satisfaction derived from killing, and ideology.[100] Similarly to the

---

[98] Regarding Northern Uganda, *see* SWAY, *supra* note 22, at 54 ("It is tragically common to hear a story of a former abductee being forced to kill a family member or friend to 'bind them to the group'. Yet we have had little sense so far whether such experiences are the norm or the exception. Our survey suggests that the truth is somewhat closer to the latter.").

[99] *Cf.* David M. Rosen, ARMIES OF THE YOUNG: CHILD SOLDIERS IN WAR AND TERRORISM 134 (2005) ("Most humanitarian accounts of child soldiers suggest that their behavior on the battlefield flows from their victimization; children fight because they have been kidnapped, brainwashed, physically and sexually abused, forced to take drugs. They kill because they are irrational or prerational or because their rationality has been stripped away by adults who have forced them to ingest alcohol or drugs.").

[100] Wessells, CHILD SOLDIERS, *supra* note 9, at 79–80.

push and pull that animates youth association with armed forces or armed groups, the relationship of the child soldier to these processes can more productively be viewed as interactive rather than stifled or smothered.[101] I believe that recognizing the interactivity between the individual and the environment suggests placing child perpetrators of acts of atrocity on a contextual continuum. Many would cluster at one end of this continuum. This end is characterized by an absence of assignable moral responsibility owing to overwhelming structural coercion and exogenous control. Other perpetrators, however, commit acts of atrocity because of how they dispositionally elect to respond to circumstances not of their creation. Others, still, demonstrate considerable volition.[102] The circumstances may not be of their own creation, but within them these perpetrators act of their own choice. Human nature vacillates. Some children undertake atrocious acts one day but refuse to do so on another day. These details matter. They should not be glossed over. Coming to terms with these details is crucial to reintegrating former child perpetrators, restoring persons harmed by their conduct, and durably reconstructing communities in the aftermath of systematic human rights abuses.

International lawyers and policymakers should remain mindful of six characteristics when it comes to formulating legal policy and assessing the propitiousness of the current trajectory thereof. I identify these characteristics as: (1) significant numbers of child soldiers are not implicated in committing acts of violence, while even fewer are implicated in perpetrating acts of atrocity; (2) juveniles grasp the laws and morals of war and human rights; (3) child soldiers retain a residual ability to exercise discretion and their exercise thereof has immense repercussions upon the lives of others; (4) although initially compromised, over time, some child soldiers become active perpetrators; (5) delinquency in peace may transition into atrocity in conflict only to, once again, possibly retransition into delinquency post-conflict; and (6) child soldiers, as individuals, are neither fungible nor moral equals. The remainder of this section organizes itself around these six characteristics.

(a) Not Many Child Perpetrators

SWAY obtained information about what abducted youth did in the LRA. Notably, "[o]nce with the LRA, not all abductees become fighters, and relatively few are forced to kill."[103] Among youth ever abducted, 87% were forced to carry heavy loads or do other forced labor, 23% were forced to step on or otherwise abuse the bodies of dead persons, 13% were forced to kill an opposing soldier in battle, 2%

---

[101] *Id.* at 73 ("Role evolution, however, is not invariably forced by outside pressures. Even in highly coercive and difficult circumstances, children continue to be actors and make choices. In some cases they manage to say no to lower-level commanders.... [N]ot all child soldiers, even following their subjugation, robotically obey all orders.").

[102] Amnesty International, *Child Soldiers: Criminals or Victims?* 2 (AI Index: IOR 50/02/00 (2000)).

[103] SWAY, *supra* note 22, at vi. "[O]nly a minority of abductees is forced to actually commit violence." *Id.* at 54.

were forced to have sex with a woman, 20% were forced to beat or cut a civilian who was not a family member or friend, 18% were forced to kill a civilian who was not a family member or friend, 12% were forced to beat or cut someone who was a family member or friend, and 8% were forced to kill a family member or friend.[104] Insofar as SWAY's inquiries regarding acts of atrocity predicated themselves upon these acts being "forced," they did not appear to afford an opening to examine whether respondents who committed such acts exercised initiative or volition. In any event, and more to the point, the SWAY findings rebut the stereotype that, in the case of the LRA, all abducted child soldiers were dragooned into committing vicious acts of atrocity which they then collectively undertook with either eager alacrity or robotic automation.

SWAY's two principal researchers interpret the relevant data as indicating that the forced commission of violence within the LRA was "less common than often feared."[105] Involvement in violence increased with length of stay in the LRA. That said, in none of the temporal categories (under two weeks, two weeks to three months, three months to one year, and over one year) did a majority of respondents report committing any specific act of violence. Among those abductees who remained in the LRA for over a year (23% of the overall abductees in the sample), 42% "ever killed at all" while lower percentages were forced to commit other crimes.[106]

According to the SWAY report, "several long-term abductees for the most part avoided extreme violence...not all long-term abductees were given a gun."[107] Moreover, "[t]he number of battles experienced is also lower than expected—3 on average for those gone 3 to 12 months, and 10 for those gone more than a year. Only a third of youth gone longer than a year report being forced to kill."[108]

In a different study, 36% of the interviewed Ugandan child soldiers and 64% of the interviewed DRC child soldiers reported having personally killed someone.[109] One hundred percent of the interviewed Northern Ugandan child soldiers were recruited by force, compared to nearly 46% of DRC interviewees. All suffered high rates of personal violence (serious beatings).

---

[104] *Id.* at 52 (other than for carrying heavy loads, 0% of never abducted youth indicated they had been forced to commit any of these acts). Schauer found *inter alia* that, among former abductees in internally displaced persons' camps in Northern Uganda, 36% were forced to kill someone and 30% were forced to abduct other children. Elisabeth Schauer, *The Psychological Impact of Child Soldiering*, Prosecutor v. Lubanga, Case No. ICC-01/04–01/06, Public Document (ICC Trial Chamber I, February 25, 2009), p. 11.

[105] Blattman and Annan, *On the nature and causes of LRA abduction, supra* note 26, at 154.

[106] *Id.* at 136 (reporting also that 29% of this group were forced to abuse dead bodies, 18% forced to beat/cut a family member or friend, 34% forced to beat/cut another civilian, 12% forced to kill a family member or friend, 32% forced to kill another civilian, and 25% forced to kill a soldier).

[107] SWAY, *supra* note 22, at 54. "Half of all male youths who stayed at least two weeks with the group received a gun, usually after only two months." Blattman and Annan, *On the nature and causes of LRA abduction, supra* note 26, at 142.

[108] SWAY, *supra* note 22, at 54.

[109] Christophe Pierre Bayer, Fionna Klasen, and Hubertus Adam, *Association of Trauma and PTSD Symptoms With Openness to Reconciliation and Feelings of Revenge Among Former Ugandan and Congolese Child Soldiers*, 298(5) JOURNAL OF THE AMERICAN MEDICAL ASSOCIATION 555, 558 (2007).

In Liberia, the weapon-to-soldier ratio was estimated as low as one to ten, such that "[m]any boys were used as porters, cooks, personal servants, and bodyguards and were stationed at checkpoints in groups with only one or two weapons between them."[110] In Sierra Leone, similarly, "[t]he majority of the population of 'child soldiers' were children who did average daily tasks: fetched water, cooked, cleaned, carried things on their heads."[111] That said, in the RUF, children who demonstrated ruthless fighting ability and who were "more criminally minded" were elevated from ordinary rank to that of child commander.[112] A study conducted in Angola from 1996 to 1998 indicates a young age of recruitment for boy soldiers (thirteen to fourteen years), a lengthy average stay with armed groups (3.8 years), and that 77.5% of consulted boy soldiers had "shot someone."[113] One survey from Mozambique found that 64% of interviewed children (aged fifteen and under) had been abducted from their families by armed groups; among these abductees, 75% were forced to serve as porters or cargo carriers and 28% (all boys) were trained for combat.[114]

A 2000 UNICEF study from northwest Cambodia revealed that, among child soldier interviewees, 35% functioned as cooks or cleaners, 21% as guards, 6% as porters, 16% as active combatants, 16% as bodyguards, and 5% as spies.[115] More than a third of former Colombian child soldiers interviewed in one survey stated that they directly participated in killings *hors de combat*.[116] Among the sixty-nine current and former child soldiers in the East Asia and Pacific region interviewed in the *Adult Wars, Child Soldiers* report, forty-six had been involved in some form of armed combat and eighteen were certain they killed at least one person.[117] This report (like others from different regions) does not suggest which of these killings (if any) constituted extraordinary international crimes, to wit, genocide, crimes against humanity, or war crimes. The definitions of these extraordinary atrocity crimes are intricate. At their core, crimes against humanity include a number of violent acts—for example, murder, enslavement, extermination, persecution, rape, torture, and sexual slavery—"when committed as part of a widespread or systematic attack directed against any civilian population, with knowledge of the attack."[118]

---

[110] Save the Children, *supra* note 54, at 144.

[111] Shepler, *The Social and Cultural Context, supra* note 48, at 13; *see also* Betancourt et al., *High Hopes, Grim Reality, supra* note 56, at 574.

[112] SLTRC, VOL. 3B, CH. 4, *supra* n. 54, ¶ 257 (reporting comments of a former RUF member).

[113] Wessells, CHILD SOLDIERS, *supra* note 9, at 131 (citing research by Christian Children's Fund/Angola).

[114] Neil Boothby, Jennifer Crawford, and Jason Halperin, *Mozambique child soldier life outcome study: Lessons learned in rehabilitation and reintegration efforts*, 1(1) GLOBAL PUBLIC HEALTH 87, 90 (2006).

[115] Cited in International Institute for Educational Planning, GUIDEBOOK FOR PLANNING EDUCATION IN EMERGENCIES AND RECONSTRUCTION, Chapter 2.5, at 106, *available at* <http://unesdoc.unesco.org/images/0019/001902/190223e.pdf> (noting also that 57% reported exposure to front-line situations).

[116] Human Rights Watch, "YOU'LL LEARN NOT TO CRY": CHILD COMBATANTS IN COLOMBIA 88 (2003).

[117] ADULT WARS, CHILD SOLDIERS, *supra* note 69, at 19, 35.

[118] Rome Statute of the International Criminal Court (ICC), Art. 7, 2187 U.N.T.S. 90 (July 17, 1998, entered into force July 1, 2002) [hereinafter Rome Statute].

Genocide is defined to include a number of acts (including killing and causing serious bodily or mental harm) committed with intent to destroy, in whole or in part, a national, ethnical, racial, or religious group, as such.[119] Certain conduct that transcends the ordinary scope of activities undertaken by soldiers during armed conflict can be prosecutable as war crimes.[120] Examples include torture, inhumane treatment, or willful murder of civilians.

In sum, notwithstanding the limitations of this research and the need for caution in interpreting the results, available information suggests that significant numbers of child soldiers do not perpetrate acts of serious violence. In some instances, only a minority—even a small minority—becomes implicated in such acts. Moreover, some of these violent acts (for example, killing an enemy soldier in battle) may theoretically conform to the laws of war and, hence, would not *per se* classify as an act of atrocity. In sum, then, it seems fundamentally unfounded to stereotype all child soldiers as depersonalized tools of atrocity or as weapons systems industrially committing crimes against humanity.

(b) Juveniles Can Understand the Laws and Morals of War

Adult Wars, Child Soldiers specifically asked interviewees about their knowledge of the laws of war and of human rights. Although the drafters of this report found that "[s]urprisingly, quite a number of recruits had been exposed to such issues," they hastily added that "from the statements [the respondents] made it appears that most had been able to absorb or retain very little of substance on these subjects."[121] However, the drafters then acknowledged that "there were child soldiers who seemed to have understood some of the basic concepts of human rights."[122]

It is not a given that children are incapable of fighting in accordance with the laws of war. Some child soldiers derive pride from their martial activities. They act with dignity, nobility, and restraint in fundamentally difficult situations. Others are cognizant of when they chose to act cruelly and accept that, as a result, they will face spiritual or moral challenges. Based on their ethnographic work in Northern Uganda, for example, Akello, Richters, and Reis report:

In focus group discussions and in-depth interviews with ex-combatants, it was commonly disclosed that they did not feel like innocent victims. They even recognized that there were various incidents where it had been possible to let a captive free, but that they chose nevertheless to kill him or her. . . . In instances where the former child soldiers had decided to commit the horrendous acts themselves, it was clear to them and to others, what they had done. They would then discuss among themselves the 'feeling of acting independently' and how the cen [*n.b.* bad or revenging spirit] of the people killed keeps disturbing them.[123]

---

[119] *Id.* Art. 6.

[120] *Id.* Art. 8 (including international and non-international armed conflict, although approaching them somewhat differently).

[121] ADULT WARS, CHILD SOLDIERS, *supra* note 69, at 39.

[122] *Id.*

[123] Grace Akello, Annemiek Richters, and Ria Reis, *Reintegration of former child soldiers in northern Uganda: coming to terms with children's agency and accountability*, 4(3) INTERVENTION 229, 236 (2006).

Child soldiers have been reputed to implicitly or explicitly threaten additional violence to cover up their crimes or intimidate victims into silence. Jeanne, a victim of sexual violence from the DRC, relates her experience:

There were about 4 of them. They were only 13 or 14 years old. They had guns and threatened to kill me if I did not have peaceful sexual relations with them; and they raped me. I knew one of them, but I couldn't say anything at the time because they would have killed me to avoid having witnesses. I know another woman who is about 30 years old who was raped by about 5 child soldiers from a Mai-Mai group. This kind of thing happened a lot in our rural areas.[124]

(c) Resistance, Refusal, Zeal: The Exercise of Residual Discretion

Even within the most invidious of circumstances, child soldiers deliberately act in ways to avoid harming others, to reduce suffering, and to protect themselves. They resist orders they find objectionable. Generally, child soldiers actualize their resistance through the means available to them, namely, subterfuge, sabotage, transgression, deception, and by discretely altering their assignments. These means are limited, but discharging them still entails choices, prescience, judgment, foresight, and volition.[125] Choices by child soldiers to exercise discretion one way or the other have immense repercussions to persons whose fates cross their paths. For example, Akello, Richters, and Reis highlight from their interviews with former LRA members the case of "[o]ne 15-year-old . . . [who] often gossiped with his friends in the neighbourhood, telling them how wise he had been by regularly deceiving the commanders by saying that he had shot the captives dead, while in reality he had let them escape."[126] At times, child soldier resistance is open and leads to terrible consequences. Hawa Dumbuya, kidnapped at the age of eight and coerced into serving as a sex slave to now convicted RUF leader Issa Sesay, refused orders to kill a pregnant woman and, in turn, her captors shot her in the leg.[127]

The most comprehensive ethnographic treatment of child soldiers in the RUF is Myriam Denov's. In *Child Soldiers: Sierra Leone's Revolutionary United Front*, Denov adopts a participatory methodology in which former child soldiers serve as researchers, interviewers, and interviewees. All of Denov's interviewees reported that they had been abducted into the RUF. Yet, even within the acutely oppressive context of the RUF, Denov identifies acts of resistance and transgression. These acts included escape, refusal to kill, avoiding drug use, and deliberately protecting

---

[124] REDRESS Trust, *supra* note 48, at 22.

[125] *Cf.* Brett and Specht, *supra* note 10, at 83 ("[F]aced with difficult or unbearable circumstances, they do exercise choices and often display qualities of extraordinary responsibility, courage, persistence, independence, determination, and resilience.")

[126] Akello, Richters, and Reis, *supra* note 123, at 237; *see also* Erin K. Baines, *Complex political perpetrators: reflections on Dominic Ongwen*, 47(2) JOURNAL OF MODERN AFRICAN STUDIES 163, 172 (2009) (reporting acts of resistance, including the release of civilians, among LRA fighters).

[127] Hannah Strange, *Inside the RUF: at last the child soldiers of Sierra Leone have their say*, LONDON TIMES (June 16, 2008).

civilians.[128] Although sporadic, and often unsuccessful, for Denov these acts reveal how child soldiers "developed ingenious and creative strategies to navigate, traverse and cope with insecure situations, and, in some cases, attempted to subvert the culture of violence," thereby demonstrating their "capacity for independent action under dire circumstances, as well as their resourcefulness and resilience."[129] While recognizing that the RUF's culture of violence transformed the lives of child abductees, Denov also artfully unpacks how their perspectives and stories "reveal a spirit of volition and a capacity for independence of action that counters a deterministic and commonly held depiction of children as having no capacity to resist or modify the circumstances and forces imposed upon them."[130]

Juveniles may subvert cruel orders, but juveniles also may take existing orders and make them even crueler. The exercise of discretion cuts both ways. Child soldiers may go beyond what is asked of them.[131] The same adolescent respondent who informed Akello, Richters, and Reis how he deceived his commanders, thereby permitting captives to escape, reported that other ex-combatants frequently carried out horrendous acts by themselves.[132] Child soldiers may turn to subterfuge to commit more crimes and conceal them from commanders.[133] Among civilian populations in conflict zones, child soldiers often are greatly feared because of their unpredictability, erraticism, and desultory capacity for gratuitous violence. Although the conventional wisdom is that child soldiers operate under the immediate thumb of adult commanders, evidence from the field suggests that subordinate/superior structures are not necessarily taut. Peters and Richards found that "[g]roups of youngsters in bush wars operate on their own initiative for long periods in remote terrain, sometimes without even radio to convey commands."[134] Kelsall underscores that armed groups in Sierra Leone were decentralized. Units acted on their own initiative and control over them was limited and rudimentary.[135] One former child soldier in Sierra Leone revealingly likened his time in armed forces with freedom as opposed to restriction:

---

[128] Myriam Denov, Child Soldiers: Sierra Leone's Revolutionary United Front 136 (2010) (some participants "reported risking their well-being and their lives to protect civilians from the violence of the RUF"); *see also id.* at 141 ("[S]everal girls reported secretly refusing to kill during battle. These children often shot their weapons in such a way that human targets were able to escape without being hurt[].").

[129] *Id.* at 130.

[130] *Id.* at 182.

[131] Alcinda Honwana, Child Soldiers in Africa 71 (2006) ("A few [boy soldiers] even exceeded the demands of their military assignments. Some acted out of vengeance, greed, immaturity, impulsiveness, or jealousy, while others did so with the expectation of being rewarded by their commanders. . . . Although few would admit to it, some soldiers undoubtedly found a thrill in killing, in wielding weapons and exercising life-and-death power over others more powerless than themselves.").

[132] Akello, Richters, and Reis, *supra* note 123, at 237.

[133] Honwana, Child Soldiers in Africa, *supra* note 131, at 68 (referencing the looting of goods).

[134] Peters and Richards, *'Why We Fight'*, *supra* note 64, at 183.

[135] Kelsall, *supra* note 51, at 79, 80.

I liked it in the army because we could do anything we liked to do. When some civilian had something I liked, I just took it without him doing anything to me. We used to rape women. Anything I wanted to do [I did]. I was free.[136]

Child soldiers are not invariably in thrall to their commanders. Some child soldiers deploy their residual discretion to commit additional crimes, while many exercise it so as to commit fewer crimes or none at all. What is more, the same child soldier may exercise his or her interstitial discretion one way one day and the other way the next day. One of my most provocative learning lessons from my work in Rwanda was that some adults who killed Tutsi by day also sheltered, at enormous personal risk and for a variety of motivations (both dignified and insalubrious), a Tutsi by night. Atrocity perpetrators—adults, youth, adolescents, or children—are complex actors operating in constrained circumstances. Unsurprisingly, then, researchers such as Erin Baines locate variable, conflicting, and diffuse individual behavior patterns even within contexts of endemic structural subjugation, such as that faced by child recruits in the LRA, where:

[C]hildren may 'play stupid' to avoid being forced to kill, or 'play smart'—including demonstrating a willingness to kill—in order to secure a better life, such as access to better food or security. Other motivations arise: some chose to adopt the 'bush mentality' to survive; others have reported mutilating civilians out of curiosity. Children and youth have found empowerment in joining militias and militaries, including protection from violence, access to goods, and decision-making. Some report killing unpopular soldiers to bring them respect and prestige among the group.[137]

Children and adolescents typically are more impressionable than adults. They are more prone to resocialization through extrinsic forces. One of the realities of mass atrocity is that adults readily can be transformed into systematic killers through exposure to authority and displacement of personal responsibility within the murkiness of a violent collective. The susceptibility of juveniles to such pressures is greater. That said, and however fragile, the persistence of residual discretion even in oppressive contexts flags an important limitation to exclusive reliance on situational explanations for acts of atrocity.

How does resocialization proceed? For starters, the armed group may come to constitute a foster family. Child fighters are unremittingly indoctrinated by political propaganda and dizzied by misinformation. Children who suffer prolonged exposure to violence have a higher propensity to become perpetrators themselves. They are more likely to detach from their peers and dissociate from their past. Child recruits may be reborn, that is, given new names and forbidden to use their previous ones. They may come, however, to earn these nicknames. In Liberia, "based ominously on what [the child soldiers] did to captured civilians and opponents," they became known as Ball Crusher, Castrator, or Nut Bag Machine.[138] In Sierra

---

[136] Peters and Richards, *'Why We Fight'*, *supra* note 64, at 194.
[137] Baines, *supra* note 126, at 179.
[138] Wessells, CHILD SOLDIERS, *supra* note 9, at 83.

Leone, individual child soldiers were given monikers such as General Share Blood, Major Cut Throat, and Queen Cut Hands.[139]

The RUF controlled children through physical violence and positive inducements.[140] Notwithstanding the subjugation child soldiers faced within the RUF, Denov explores how their responses to abduction, coercion, and militarized values were wide-ranging.[141] Individual children affiliated in various ways and to varying degrees with group values. Similarly, within the LRA "some abducted children resisted identifying with the rebels even in circumstances of extreme powerlessness, where they are forced to perpetrate brutalizing acts of violence."[142] In some instances, child soldiers come full circle when confronted with aspects of their prior life. Christine Tokar reports the case of Abdullai (a fictitious name):

Abdullai climbed the ranks from being a boy spy, a boy fighter, to being a small boy unit commander. His bush name was 'molest'.

The beginning of his turning point and his desire to leave the forces was when he recognized that his grandfather was one of the captives. Abdullai gave no signal that he recognized his grandfather. If he showed any weakness he might be forced to perpetrate tortuous acts upon him. He silently constructed a plan later that evening to link up with his grandfather. However, that opportunity never came. His grandfather was humiliated, tortured and killed by others in the same unit.[143]

Following his decommissioning, Abdullai participated in several forgiveness rituals.

In short, Dallaire's assertion that the "nascent sense of values of children caught in these civil wars often becomes...devoid of any respect for human life and conventions of any sort" is excessively stylized.[144] It overlooks the humanity of the implicated children. Child soldiers act differently under comparable extrinsic circumstances. Entirely situational accounts of their violent acts are incomplete. So, too, are entirely dispositional accounts.

(d) Diachronic Changes

Wessells notes that "depictions of child soldiers as innocents contrast sharply with the reality that some children, like some adults, learn to enjoy

---

[139] Rosen, Armies of the Young, *supra* note 99, at 60–61.

[140] Paul Richards, Fighting for the Rainforest: War, Youth & Resources in Sierra Leone 28 (1996).

[141] Denov, *supra* note 128, at 143, 182 ("Some children were highly obedient and publicly acquiesced to RUF commands for their own survival and safety, yet privately rejected or resisted the culture of violence. Others became highly integrated with the values and culture of the RUF and actively engaged and participated in brutal and excessive forms of violence.... In some cases, children's actions assumed an increasingly voluntarist nature, with some developing a sense of attachment, commitment and dedication to the RUF and its values.").

[142] Angela Veale and Aki Stavrou, *Former Lord's Resistance Army Child Soldier Abductees: Explorations of Identity in Reintegration and Reconciliation*, 13(3) Peace and Conflict: Journal of Peace Psychology 273, 285 (2007).

[143] Christine Tokar, *Indigenous Protections of Children in Armed Conflict: Observations from Sierra Leone and Liberia*, in Children and War, *supra* note 8, at 19, 23.

[144] Dallaire, *supra* note 93, at 138.

killing."[145] Other children—generally older adolescents—strategically commit systematic atrocity for instrumental gain, that is, to obtain lucre, status, or power. Kelsall observes that "children often rose to the status of patrons themselves, lording themselves over other children and adult civilians."[146] To persist in labeling these subsets of child soldiers as exclusively or primarily victims strains credulity.

Dutch criminologist Alette Smeulers has developed a typology of perpetrators of extraordinary international crimes. She places perpetrators into a variety of classifications: the mastermind, the fanatic, the criminal/sadist, the careerist, the follower/conformist, the devoted warrior, the compromised perpetrator, the professional, and the profiteer.[147] Smeulers does not view a specific classification as totalizing. She recognizes the possibility that multiple motivations guide perpetrators. Thus, she bases her classification upon determination of a predominant motivational factor. As Smeulers herself notes, many child soldiers who commit acts of atrocity—notably, those who began as abductees—can be classed as compromised perpetrators. Smeulers posits that compromised perpetrators initially become implicated in international crimes owing to the explicit or implicit use of coercion, force, or threats. She rejects, however, that the identities of compromised perpetrators remain immutable. According to Smeulers, "an initially compromised perpetrator can sadly enough be transformed into a far less reluctant participant."[148] Compromised perpetrators alter their predominant motivational impulse because of the influence of others, because of their environments, and also because of their internal responses and ambitions. Some compromised perpetrators turn into a type of perpetrator whose immorality, repugnance, and dangerousness exceed that which had been discernible at the point of entry into the armed force or group. Returning to Smeulers' taxonomy, in this regard these perpetrators may become re-classifiable as sadists, profiteers, or even masterminds. And, indeed, some child soldiers conduct themselves sadistically. The existence of these transformative processes implies longitudinal variations among individual group members, whether children, adolescents, youth, or adults.

Dominic Ongwen had initially been abducted into the LRA at the age of ten.[149] He progressively advanced to the level of brigade commander to serve—as an

---

[145] Wessells, CHILD SOLDIERS, *supra* note 9, at 83. *Cf. id.* at 74 ("Some child combatants fight reluctantly, kill only when necessary, and constantly look for escape opportunities, whereas others learn to enjoy combat and redefine their identities as soldiers. A small minority become hardened perpetrators who relish the sight and smell of blood and initiate or participate willingly in atrocities that no one ordered them to commit.").

[146] Kelsall, *supra* note 51, at 154; *see also* Pacifique Manirakiza, *Les enfants face au système international de justice: à la recherche d'un modèle de justice pénale internationale pour les délinquants mineurs*, 34 QUEEN'S L. J. 719, 737–738 (2009) ("Au départ, ils sont des victimes. Avec le temps, certains jeunes se dévouent davantage et dictent la conduite de leurs pairs. Le processus les transforme souvent en bourreaux et ils y acquièrent une certaine capacité d'action.").

[147] Alette Smeulers, *Perpetrators of International Crimes: Towards a Typology*, in SUPRANATIONAL CRIMINOLOGY: TOWARDS A CRIMINOLOGY OF INTERNATIONAL CRIMES 233, 242–260 (Alette Smeulers and Roelof Haveman eds, 2008).

[148] *Id.* at 258. What is more, "[s]omeone who is compromised in co-operating can start to derive pleasure from his position." *Id.* at 264.

[149] Baines, *supra* note 126, at 163.

adult—as a mastermind of the organization. Baines describes Ongwen as a "complex political perpetrator." She reports that, even as a child soldier, Ongwen was capable of disobeying orders, demonstrating compassion, and also engaging in serial acts of unfathomable cruelty. Ongwen fluidly adopted these multiple roles as part of his "navigat[ing] the complex terrain of the LRA to exercise agency in a given set of circumstances not of his choosing. . . ."[150]

Upon application by Chief Prosecutor Luis Moreno-Ocampo, Pre-trial Chamber II of the ICC issued an arrest warrant for Ongwen in 2005. Ongwen is being sought on charges of crimes against humanity and war crimes. He remains a fugitive. Were Ongwen, currently estimated to be in his early thirties, eventually brought into ICC custody, his prosecution would expose a number of fissures occasioned by the Rome Statute's categorically chronological and binary approach to childhood and adulthood. The ICC lacks jurisdiction over persons under the age of eighteen at the time of the alleged offense.[151] Might the ICC's jurisdictional exclusion of minors mean that it cannot hear evidence of the crimes that Ongwen had committed while a minor? If so, the historical narrative related by Ongwen's prosecution would be incomplete. Moreover, if the conduct of the child soldier is entirely attributable to the malevolent adult recruiter—in Ongwen's case, his now deceased former co-defendant Vincent Otti (another LRA leader)[152]—then why should this attribution entirely cease once the abductee reaches the age of eighteen? The international legal imagination freezes child soldiers as faultless passive victims. But how can it then simultaneously affirm that a ten year-old who had been kidnapped into the LRA—and who grew up in the LRA—deserves as an adult to stand trial as *hostis humani generis* for the most serious crimes of concern to the international community as a whole? Were it to adhere to its own logic, prevailing conventional wisdom—at the very least—should afford Ongwen a robust opportunity to plead a duress defense or to relieve his culpability by asserting some sort of developmental impairment. Alternately, conventional wisdom might suggest to the ICC Chief Prosecutor that he decline to proceed further since, in light of the circumstances, it would not be in the interests of justice to do so. But the international legal imagination demonstrates no affinity for either of these two options.

Unsurprisingly, Ongwen's family has accentuated his victim status: "'He is a lost child,' said Akot Madelena, Ongwen's aunt, who looked after him when his mother died."[153] Gauging both from its tone and its characterization of Ongwen as being among those persons bearing the greatest responsibility for LRA crimes, the ICC's

---

[150] *Id.* at 173. Committing atrocities was a vehicle for promotion within the LRA. *Id.* at 175.

[151] Rome Statute, *supra* note 118, Art. 26. For details on the ICC, including this specific provision, *see infra* Chapters 4(ii)(b) and 5(ii)(b).

[152] Baines, *supra* note 126, at 169–170. The LRA leadership executed Otti, who had become Kony's second in command, in October 2007 owing to his perceived support of the Juba peace process. Speculation has arisen that Ongwen had a hand in Otti's execution.

[153] Lucy Hannan, *Uganda's boy soldier turned rebel chief is a victim, not a criminal, says his family*, THE INDEPENDENT (June 27, 2007); *cf.* information presented at <http://ongwen.blogspot.com>; *The Dilemma of the White Ant* (2008, dir. Caroline Pare).

arrest warrant emphatically rejects this victim narrative. Ongwen elicits no pity. A bright line separates child purposelessness from adult purposefulness.

Uganda's Parliament passed the International Criminal Court Act on March 9, 2010. It did so as part of Uganda's ratification of the Rome Statute. This Act gives the newly established Ugandan High Court (International Crimes Division) jurisdiction over Rome Statute crimes. The Division, ostensibly, would not prosecute soldiers who were children at the time of their exit from conflict, but would prosecute adult commanders for offenses committed as adults even if they had initially entered the LRA as minors. The first case before the Division is that of Colonel Thomas Kwoyelo. Captured in 2009 and currently detained in Gulu, Kwoyelo had been abducted into the LRA in 1987 at the age of fifteen. Proceedings against him began on July 11, 2011. Amnesties loom as an issue. Reportedly the LRA's fourth-in-command, Kwoyelo is the highest ranked LRA official in custody. Still, he invokes a narrative of helpless subservience. He told a Ugandan newspaper that his "situation in the bush was like that of a dog and his master. When you tell a dog to do something, it will act as instructed. All orders came from Kony."[154]

(e) Delinquency in Peace, Atrocity in Conflict

At its core, extraordinary international crime is materially distinguishable from ordinary common crime, to wit, routine infringements of national penal law in peace-time. Whereas extraordinary international crime is inherently collective in nature, ordinary common crime—with limited exception—is not.[155] Differences are most evident when discriminatory motives animate extraordinary international crime. Perpetrators active in such contexts tend to be neither delinquent nor contrarian. Instead, they tend to be conformist, motivated by ideological and political goals. These goals may include disabling the "other" in order to protect the perpetrators' own group from perceived existential threats.

Nevertheless, evidence suggests that some atrocity perpetrators—adults as well as children—do have ordinary criminal backgrounds, proclivities, and propensities. Such perpetrators are neither ideologically nor collectively motivated. Ibrahim Abdullah, for example, advances the *lumpen* or *rarray* hypothesis to posit RUF youth membership as criminally disposed. Abdullah describes *lumpen* as "largely unemployed and unemployable youths, mostly male," who "are prone to criminal behaviour, petty theft, drugs, drunkenness and gross indiscipline."[156] He also extends his hypothesis to RENAMO.

---

[154] Chris Ocowun, *LRA's Kwoyelo charged with kidnap*, NEW VISION (June 4, 2009) (on file with author)

[155] For additional discussion, *see* Drumbl, *supra* note 11, at 23–45. Ordinary common crime and extraordinary international crime are not discontinuous, but situate at different ends of a continuum. Examples of criminal conduct proscribed at the level of ordinary common crime that shares some collective characteristics include gang activity, hate crime, and complex fraud.

[156] Ibrahim Abdullah, *Bush path to destruction: the origin and character of the Revolutionary United Front/Sierra Leone*, 36(2) JOURNAL OF MODERN AFRICAN STUDIES 203, 207–208, 222 (1998).

Apolitical perpetrators seize upon collective cataclysm to undertake criminal acts for personal or private gain, hoping that communal chaos affords them anonymity, cover, and impunity. They are not coerced nor necessarily motivated by survivalism. In the case of child soldiers, it is unclear why this subgroup reflexively ought to benefit from legal fictions of non-responsibility. Youth who exhibit delinquent tendencies prior to conflict and then commit atrocious acts during conflict, may also retain delinquent tendencies post-conflict. To perfunctorily release such individuals into the general public without any measure of accountability, risk assessment, or additional inquiry invites recidivism. Former child soldiers who commit acts of ordinary common criminality subsequent to their decommissioning might come to challenge personal responsibility for those acts on the basis that they had previously been exonerated for their implication in grave acts of extraordinary international criminality. Excuse may linger, only to provide misplaced cover for unrelated categories of offenses.

(f) Individual Child Soldiers Are Not Interchangeable Equals

In journalistic reporting from Sierra Leone, Jan Goodwin anecdotally discusses three child soldiers.[157] First is M.G., who no longer remembers how many people he has killed and who is tormented by regret. Second is I., a girl soldier who was frequently raped and who, following her release, wilts under severe depression. And third is M.M., a boy soldier since the age of eleven and, at the time, still on active duty for the CDF at the age of thirteen. M.M. explains: "I like to kill. It makes me happy. The rebels killed my father. I joined to avenge him. I like to watch the enemy fall down and die."[158] Goodwin reacts to M.M.:

His swagger and belligerent, I'm-in-charge tone of voice give this skinny runt of a kid the air of a dictator. The casual ease with which he wields his AK-47 conveys his menace. And his words confirm the image[.][159]

M.M. believes that a deer horn worn in his cap is a "magic control" to fend off the enemy. He earnestly attributes an injury he suffered during combat to the fact that the control had fallen out of his cap and the bullet struck him just as he bent down to pick it up. One way to make sense of M.M. is to take his belief as evidence of his immaturity and lack of discernment. But there also are other ways, at once complementary and contrarian, to understand M.M. His belief in the protection offered by his deer horn may trace (drawing from the earlier discussion of Ellis' work) to spiritual faith born from initiation rites. In this regard, M.M.'s statements may attest not to his immaturity but, rather, to his quest for maturity.

Goodwin presents each of M.G., I., and M.M. as victims of conflict. But they are not moral equals. Nor have they experienced conflict in equivalent fashion. M.G.,

---

[157] Jan Goodwin, *Sierra Leone Is No Place To Be Young*, NEW YORK TIMES MAGAZINE 48 (February 14, 1999).

[158] *Id.* at 51.

[159] *Id.*

I, and M.M. would be well-served by rehabilitative and reintegrative interventions calibrated to their individual needs, acts, and aspirations. Victims and survivors of M.G. and M.M.'s acts also might better actualize a sense of justice were these two child soldiers to be approached in a more grounded manner. When policy initiatives discourage fine-grained assessments rendered in a supportive context, those who resist the most are unheralded, those who inflict the least harm are unrecognized, and those who hurt others the most are awarded an unearned reprieve.

It would be preferable to appreciate heterogeneity within the protected group rather than assume bland homogeneity and prosaic uniformity. This heterogeneity derives from an admixture of situational constraints and individual motivation. Looking beyond each of M.G., I., and M.M., children born into armed groups—a neglected constituency—would likely benefit if child soldiers were not *ipso facto* all fungibly taken as moral equals. Indiscriminately evacuating the responsibility of all child soldiers, moreover, disadvantages those least responsible for harming third-parties. Members of this particular subset may be the least responsible because of deliberate acts of courage, dignity, and nobility that they undertook. Foregrounding stories of resistance may require some contrast with the stories of others who failed to resist or who crushed the resistance of others. Is this truly something to fear?

(g) Summary

It is wrong to typecast all children associated with armed forces implicated in acts of atrocity as faultless passive victims or to collectivize them as demons and irredeemable thugs. These images are myths.

(iii) Alternatives to Victimhood Discourse

In light of the occlusions engendered by the faultless passive victim lens, which alternatives might more helpfully capture the complexity of the child soldier experience?

I take as a starting point for this discussion the predicate that oppression does not inexorably void the oppressed's capacity for decision-making. Nor are the oppressed shorn of all ability to exercise discretion or judgment. Nor is it normatively desirable as a matter of law or policy to adopt such an arthritic and atrophied view of the oppressed.

Debates within feminist legal theory are instructive. Feminist scholars have noted how gender essentialization of women's role in conflict—which accelerate the flow of funds to support women as victims and have been central to successful sexual violence prosecutions at the international level—inadvertently spill into post-conflict phases where they may perpetuate stereotypes of women's weak and passive civic roles.[160] Valuable insights also can be extrapolated from the work of Kathryn Abrams, who examines advocacy efforts undertaken on behalf of battered women in the domestic context. Noting the centrality of dominance feminism to these efforts, Abrams assesses the potentially unanticipated consequences that arise when women are cast as constructions of male aggression.[161] Notwithstanding the success of dominance feminism in sensitizing awareness of structural gender inequity, Abrams worries that the resultant output is a female subject that seems "inhumanly passive, or acted-upon."[162] She discusses the work of Angela Harris, who identifies as a flaw of dominance feminism "a tendency to find women's essence, or at least their commonality, in their shared victimization."[163] Referencing the specific context of gender-based domestic violence, and turning to the ground-breaking contributions of Martha Mahoney, Abrams posits:

> The dominance-informed theory of "learned helplessness" has educated the public about battering and facilitated the defense of battered women who kill their spouses. Yet... these contributions have come at a cost: battered women's self-defense work utilizing the theory of "learned helplessness" has fed on and reinforced a view of battered women as pathologically passive. This view has led to denial and confusion among battered women who do not recognize themselves in the unitary images of victimization and to legal detriment when they seek custody of their children.[164]

Uncritical deployment of dominance theory as a legal strategy leads to "a female subject wholly incapable of self-direction, whom the law must rescue from her plight or relieve of responsibility for her actions."[165] Through rescue, however, the law may unconsciously renew stigma. By relieving responsibility, the law risks further disabling the putative beneficiaries of its interventions.

This vivid dialogue within feminist legal theory exemplifies the conversational pitch that hopefully could emerge within the community of scholars, policymakers, and lawyers concerned with the scourge of child soldiering. Abrams' goal is "to depict women as possessing a constrained but nonetheless salient capacity for

---

[160] Karen Engle, *Feminism and Its (Dis)contents: Criminalizing Wartime Rape in Bosnia and Herzegovina*, 99(4) AM. J. INT'L L. 778 (2005); R. Charli Carpenter, *"Women, Children and Other Vulnerable Groups": Gender, Strategic Frames and the Protection of Civilians as a Transnational Issue*, 49 INT'L STUD. Q. 295 (2005).

[161] Kathryn Abrams, *Sex Wars Redux: Agency and Coercion in Feminist Legal Theory*, 95 COLUM. L. REV. 304, 304 (1995). Dominance feminism "locates gender oppression in the sexualized domination of women by men and the eroticization of that dominance through pornography and other elements of popular culture." *Id.* at 304 n.1.

[162] *Id.* at 326. In response, Abrams situates the analytic tool of "partial agency," which provides an "account that... more concretely juxtapos[es] women's capacity for self-direction and resistance, on the one hand, with often-internalized patriarchal constraint, on the other." *Id.* at 346.

[163] *Id.* at 336.

[164] *Id.* at 345 (footnotes omitted).

[165] *Id.* at 351–352. "The pragmatic interest of feminist lawyers in securing positive outcomes for their clients has often made them complicit in this dichotomizing tendency. They have stressed the extent of their clients' subordination and constraint in ways that have muted any capacity for self-direction or agency." *Id.* at 352.

self-direction, while addressing the underlying conditions of women's oppression."[166] I share a similar goal in the case of militarized youth.

Alcinda Honwana—an anthropologist who has written with great sensitivity about child soldiers in Angola and Mozambique—discourages their presentation as passive victims. According to Honwana, "[y]oung people respond to the exigencies of war with resourcefulness and—for better and for worse—a substantial degree of adaptability."[167] She turns to agency theory as an analytic lens, arguing that "children affected by conflict—both girls and boys—do not constitute a homogeneous group of helpless victims but exercise an agency of their own."[168] Honwana understands agency to mean the scope of discretion and influence available to a person in a subordinated social situation.

More specifically, Honwana posits that, within the interstitial positions they occupy, child soldiers exert tactical agency or agency of the weak. According to Honwana, "[t]actics are complex actions that involve calculation of advantage but arise from vulnerability."[169] She distinguishes tactics from strategies. In this regard, she draws from the somewhat opaque work of Michel de Certeau.[170] De Certeau's scholarship is not about child soldiers, so Honwana novelly extends it into this context. Honwana also is influenced by structuration theory, which relates agency to an individual's ability to intervene and to have acted differently than he or she actually did.

The bottom line for Honwana is that child soldiers display tactical agency "devised to cope with and maximize the concrete, immediate circumstances of the military environment in which they have to operate."[171] According to Honwana, child soldiers are neither in a "position of power" nor necessarily "fully conscious of the ultimate goals of their actions." It is quite unclear whether they anticipate gains or benefits over the long-term. They are, however, "fully conscious of the immediate returns and they act, within certain constraints, to seize opportunities that are available to them."[172] Honwana recognizes that most of her boy respondents were forced to enter military life, but she rejects characterizing them as "empty vessels into whom violence was poured or from whom violent behavior was coerced."[173] She finds girl soldiers to be tactical agents as well,

---

[166] *Id.* at 355.
[167] Honwana, CHILD SOLDIERS IN AFRICA, *supra* note 131, at 162.
[168] *Id.* at 4.
[169] *Id.* at 73.
[170] According to Honwana, de Certeau defines strategy "as the calculation or manipulation of force-relationships that becomes possible as soon as a subject of will and power . . . can be isolated from its environment." *Id.* at 70. "A tactic, on the other hand, is a calculated action that is determined by the absence of the proper (a spatial or institutional locus that is under the subject's control) and takes place on a territory that is not autonomous." *Id.* For original source, *see* Michel de Certeau, THE PRACTICE OF EVERYDAY LIFE (Steven Rendall trans., 1984) (1980).
[171] Honwana, CHILD SOLDIERS IN AFRICA, *supra* note 131, at 51.
[172] *Id.* Honwana recognizes the limitations that inhere in the fact she can only interview survivors. *Id.* at 50.
[173] *Id.* at 73.

although the range of their tactical agency typically is narrower than that available to boys.[174]

In short, the acts that flow from exercises of tactical agency are not so readily assimilable into an absolutist "it's not your fault" narrative that purges responsibility.

Although Honwana's conceptualization of child soldiers as tactical agents has influenced the anthropological literature, it has not acquired traction within the international legal imagination. This outcome is disappointing in that tactical agency is helpful as a conversational frame to conceptualize how child soldiers navigate their roles within armed forces or groups. Notwithstanding its utility, however, Honwana's tactical agency lens brushes up against four limitations for the purpose of my analysis.

Honwana herself establishes the first limitation. Her project, and her development of the notion of tactical agency, is descriptive. It emanates from an examination of the conditions under which her respondent child soldiers actually lived. Honwana expressly disclaims "conducting a philosophical inquiry into the degrees of guilt that can be attributed to children who are coerced into active participation in civil wars."[175] She does not believe that tactical agents should bear legal responsibility for their actions.[176] Although Honwana does not explicitly state what she understands legal responsibility to signify or how such responsibility ought to be assessed, it does appear that she means criminal proceedings. Honwana's diffidence toward criminal trials for child soldiers contrasts with her recommendation of traditional purification and reintegration rituals. Yet, she does not posit such rituals as fulfilling a transitional justice function. In this regard, it would seem problematic to tilt her descriptive tactical agency lens in an analytic direction that she does not evidently intend for it to pursue.

Second, Honwana's differentiation of tactics from strategies may be a bit too abrupt. Her concomitant dismissal of strategic agency, therefore, may be somewhat premature. For a few child soldiers, tactics ultimately become strategies. These child soldiers initially enlist and then serially commit international crimes as a conscious advancement strategy. In the wake of conflict, they represent an at-risk subgroup that tends to reintegrate poorly and remains susceptible to re-recruitment.

---

[174] *Id.* at 95–97. Utas also suggests a "need for a far more complex understanding of women's experience in African and other wars than prevailing depictions that deduce from women's accounts of victimization that they have no agency." Mats Utas, *Victimcy, Girlfriending, Soldiering: Tactic Agency in a Young Woman's Social Navigation of the Liberian War Zone*, 78(2) ANTHROPOLOGICAL QUARTERLY 403, 409 (2005). *Cf.* Chris Coulter, BUSH WIVES AND GIRL SOLDIERS: WOMEN'S LIVES THROUGH WAR AND PEACE IN SIERRA LEONE (2009) (offering a sophisticated account of girl soldiering related through over one hundred interviews).

[175] Honwana, CHILD SOLDIERS IN AFRICA, *supra* note 131, at 50. That said, she recognizes that "[a]lthough the moral responsibility of individual soldiers may be severely limited by the constraints under which they fought, it is not entirely absent." *Id.*

[176] *Id.* at 162 (noting in one sentence, without any further discussion, that child soldiers do not "exercise the autonomy that legal responsibility for their own actions would require").

Third, characterizing child soldiers as tactical agents may arguably induce the emergence of another—albeit new—unitary label and, thereby, replicate short-comings similar to those that currently plague dominant reductive imagery. In this sense, the construct of tactical agency might be chided for generating its own form of categorism.

The final impediment to the analytic value of transposing tactical agency into my project concerns variation between Honwana's understanding of agency and the classic legal understanding thereof. As a matter of formal law, an agent is a natural person or instrumentality through which power is exerted or an end is achieved. The agent acts on behalf of and represents the interests of a principal.[177] The agent's authority to act may be actual, apparent, or mandated by law. Although an agent-principal agreement generally is consensual, agency relationships can arise out of coercion, oppression, or fear. Under this classic legal definition, child soldiers surely can be construed as agents of their commanders and of the states or armed groups on whose behalf they fight. However, construing child soldiers in this fashion may be just one step removed from dehumanizing characterizations that present them as impersonal tools of war or mechanized weapons systems.

Honwana, however, essentially takes agency to mean the residual scope of authority, discretion, and judgment available to the oppressed, including whatever ability the oppressed may retain to influence their oppressors.[178] In this regard, it seems that Honwana really is endeavoring to ascertain the scope of *action* demonstrated by child soldiers and the kind of status they have as *actors*. Why, then, not simply invoke this language directly?

I propose approaching the individual child soldier through a *model of circumscribed action*. A circumscribed actor has the ability to act, the ability not to act, and the ability to do other than what he or she actually had done. The effective range of these abilities, however, is delimited, bounded, and confined. Circumscribed actors exercise some discretion in navigating and mediating the constraints around them. They dispose of an enclosed space which is theirs and in which they exercise a margin of volition. The acreage of this space varies according to an ever fluctuating admixture of disposition and situation. Although encircled, circumscribed actors are not flattened. Affected by conflict, they also affect others. Threatened and harmed, they may, in turn, threaten and harm others.

---

[177] Although agency implies a relationship in which the principal directs the agent, in practice this may not always be the case. Sometimes an agent may wield considerable influence over the principal. The agent may have greater knowledge, for example, and hence effectively direct the principal instead of receiving directions. In fact, this greater knowledge or expertise may be a reason to engage the agent in the first place.

[178] Other scholars also turn to agency theory. *See*, e.g., Helen Brocklehurst, *Childhood in Conflict: Can the Real Child Soldier Please Stand Up?*, *in* ETHICS, LAW AND SOCIETY, VOLUME IV, 259, 263 (Jennifer Gunning, Søren Holm, and Ian Kenway, eds, 2009) (noting that "we still downplay or deny the political and military agency that children themselves have been shown to accept") (citation omitted); Wessells, CHILD SOLDIERS, *supra* note 9, at 73–74, 144 (underscoring that "[t]he fact that many child soldiers either attempt to escape or actually flee from armed groups testifies to the strength of their moral concerns," but also remarking that "[c]hildren's agency is a double-edged sword ... as some children deliberately seek combat and find meaning through wielding the power of the gun").

Circumscribed action is not a metaphor, nor a photograph, nor an ideal-type, nor an image whose reification is sought and to which all *prima facie* categorized individuals are to conform. Rather, circumscribed action is a *spectrum* or *continuum* that embraces the inherent diversity among the individuals who populate its axis. Presenting circumscribed action in this dynamic fashion encourages procedural inquiry into the specific histories and experiences of the individuals located within its contours, while also prompting community involvement on questions of reintegration and restoration. Procedural inquiries, in turn, reflect the core ambitions of transitional justice as undertaken outside of courtrooms and jailhouses.[179]

Consequently, individual circumscribed actors may be found to fall short of appreciable levels of cognizance. Drug ingestion, brutal coercion, inchoate developmental processes, misplaced trust, and resocialization each may be found to unduly crimp—even eviscerate—capacity. In such cases, excuse may ground forgiveness and establish a firm footing for reintegration. The actions of other circumscribed actors, however, may have been pursued with sufficient initiative such that forgiveness and reintegration would proceed most obtainably through reciprocal obligation, acknowledgement, and dialogue among the circumscribed actors, others responsible for the violence, and the community. Not all child soldiers, after all, are entirely at the behest of commanders, drugged, or infantile. Militarized youth vacillate even within tenuously interstitial positions, where they may come to exert considerable say over the life and death of others. Regardless of the outcomes of individual cases, shifting the analytic baseline from the faultless passive victim to the circumscribed actor—and restyling that baseline as an open spectrum instead of a conformist image—frees up consideration of a broad array of policy alternatives that the tutelage of extant discourse unproductively thins.

The model of circumscribed action appreciates what distinguished moral philosopher Jeff McMahan describes as seemingly "most reasonable," that is, to "view child soldiers, in general, as people who have a diminished capacity for morally responsible agency and who act in conditions that further diminish their personal responsibility for their action in war."[180] Nonetheless, this model also retains the flexibility to recognize the awareness that some child soldiers, in particular older adolescents, exercise in navigating social pathways that lead to their enlistment in armies, fighting factions, and militias. This model recognizes that they are "constrained but not choiceless."[181] It is thus conversant with child soldiers' making "the best of a bad situation."[182] What an individual determines to be "best" in any

---

[179] For extensive discussion of this and other proposed reforms, *see infra* Chapter 6.

[180] Jeff McMahan, *Child Soldiers: The Ethical Perspective* 12 (working paper, cited with permission, 2007). Elsewhere, McMahan resists characterizing child soldiers as non-responsible threats. Jeff McMahan, KILLING IN WAR 199 (2009).

[181] Bård Mæland, *Constrained but not Choiceless: On Moral Agency among Child Soldiers*, in CULTURE, RELIGION, AND THE REINTEGRATION OF FEMALE CHILD SOLDIERS IN NORTHERN UGANDA 59, 59 (Bård Mæland ed., 2010). *Cf.* Manirakiza, *supra* note 146, at 719 (arguing that minors who have committed extraordinary international crimes are "indeed victims, but most of them are also morally responsible actors").

[182] Beth A. Simmons, MOBILIZING FOR HUMAN RIGHTS: INTERNATIONAL LAW IN DOMESTIC POLITICS 336 (2009).

given situation is informed by some subjective determination. This model, by abstaining from parsimony, permits the multiple sources of child soldiering to be exposed while also comporting more faithfully with the actual adolescent development science of diminished capacity. By eschewing totalizing and conformist imagery, the model of circumscribed action vivifies child soldiers as persons.

I have presented the model of circumscribed action to diverse audiences. Reaction has been positive and encouraging. The timing seems right for this reimaginative exercise. I also have heard reservations, though, notably regarding whether the model overreaches. Some thoughtful interlocutors have expressed doubts whether it is at all possible to ascribe tangible content to the discretion that child soldiers actually may possess. Consequently, why not just replace the adjectival qualifiers—in other words, move from faultless passive victim to different language, such as partial victim, engaged victim, or rebuttable victim? Is it really necessary to cede the terrain of victimhood so as to ameliorate the reintegrative and restorative prospects of former child soldiers and other aggrieved parties? A closely related concern inquires whether a turn to circumscribed action might introduce a "blame the victim" cudgel into the conversation about child soldiers.

I would not be averse to modifying the qualifiers so as to lance some of the negative externalities that flow from fulsome presumptions of victimhood. This modification is compatible with the intended direction of the circumscribed action model. I remain skeptical, however, that simply switching the qualifying adjectives would engender meaningful reform. The metaphor of the child soldier as faultless passive victim is so robust that surpassing it entails more than just tinkering. What is required is uprooting the presumption and replacing it with a more empathetic, dynamic, and active vision. Inordinate focus on children's deficits and vulnerabilities stymies engagement with their assets and skills. According to Wessells, "[w]hen children—or adults, for that matter—see themselves as victims, they tend to act in a passive, hopeless manner that impedes their recovery."[183] Too often, the international humanitarian impulse hinges upon excessively pristine, even pious, depictions of the victims in question. This dynamic marginalizes tragedies other than those that are the most idealizable. A less demanding expectation of victims would make it easier for more people to become more effectively assisted and assist themselves in the aftermath of mass atrocity.

The prospect of misappropriation by ulterior agendas arises each time a hard-won orthodoxy is revisited. Reimagining the child soldier may spark fears of the unknown. Assumptions of childhood passivity and victim purity indeed may guard against politics of punishing child soldiers as irredeemable outlaws. Yet these assumptions are crude. Their supporting metaphors occasion weighty externalities. Other more fine-grained mechanisms—explored in Chapter 7—can inhibit the

---

[183] Wessells, CHILD SOLDIERS, *supra* note 9, at 134. For acrid critique of uses and abuses of victimhood discourse in domestic US policy-making, *see* Alyson M. Cole, THE CULT OF TRUE VICTIMHOOD: FROM THE WAR ON WELFARE TO THE WAR ON TERROR (2007). I would retain the victim nomenclature for third-party civilians attacked, maimed, raped, or killed by child soldiers—and for combatants aggrieved by widespread conduct that falls outside the laws of war—although I recommend development of a less disabling victimology for them.

rapaciousness of retributivist politics while also circumventing the problematic externalization of incapacity and jejunity on youth formerly associated with armed forces or armed groups.

The baseline of circumscribed action would neither naturalize child soldiering nor normalize children as soldiers. It would not endorse or morally justify the practice. Rather, this baseline would better support efforts to eradicate the practice of child soldiering. After all:

> While the humanitarian response can be informed by the imperative to provide rights for children purely as victims of conflict, the political response, particularly as it forms a part of the peace-building and post-conflict reconfiguration processes, demands a deeper knowledge of the origins and means of warfare and the extent to which warring parties are supported, actively, passively or through pure coercion, by their populations, including youth.[184]

Circumscribed action does not lie beyond the remit of imputation to an adult recruiter or commander. As Chapter 5 explores, a baseline of circumscribed action in fact opens the door to a much wider-ranging justice conversation. Adoption of this baseline would help allocate responsibility for the practice of child soldiering among the many individual, state, organizational, commercial, and institutional elements that conspire to germinate and sustain it throughout the world's regions. As a case-in-point, the role of NATO in Libya's internal conflict, in which rebel forces had recruited child soldiers, bears closer scrutiny.

(iv) Conclusion

On the one hand, the study of child soldiers is becoming more sophisticated, grounded, and contextualized. On the other hand, however, significant disconnects linger between what child soldiers say about their lives and how transnationalized wisdom projects their lives. Induction from the extremes persists as the norm. International law, post-conflict best practices, rule of law projects, and human rights policy are not assimilating the full breadth of available knowledge about the child soldiering experience. Instead, they still glom onto—in some instances even more obstinately—the parsimony vested in the controlling tutelage of faultless passive victim imagery. Chapters 4 and 5 examine the nesting of this imagery and its evolution into a legal fiction.

---

[184] Angela McIntyre, Emmanuel Kwesi Aning, and Prosper Nii Nortey Addo, *Politics, War and Youth Culture in Sierra Leone: An Alternative Interpretation*, 11(3) AFRICAN SECURITY REVIEW (2002), *available at* <http://www.iss.co.za/Pubs/ASR/11No3/McIntyre.html>.

4

Child Soldiers and Accountability

Insofar as no single or discrete instrument encapsulates how the international legal imagination conceptualizes the accountability of child soldiers implicated in the commission of extraordinary international crimes, it becomes necessary to canvas an array of hard law and soft law sources.[1] The international legal imagination's treatment of the personal accountability of militarized youth arises as fragments amid instruments otherwise concerned with more general topics such as the human rights of children, the prosecution of adult atrocity perpetrators, and the place of juveniles within national criminal justice systems tasked with routine management of ordinary common crimes. The enabling instruments and activities of international criminal courts and tribunals also are germane to the development of transnational legal norms. Owing to this fragmentation, best practices and policy guidelines—such as the Paris Principles—that specifically contemplate the welfare of child soldiers assume a level of importance that well exceeds their formally non-binding nature.

This Chapter considers each of international *lex lata*, *lex ferenda*, and *lex desiderata*. *Lex lata* refers to current law which is settled. *Lex ferenda* means future law, aspirationally as it should be, which is in the process of crystallizing and coalescing. *Lex desiderata* refers to law which is fancied, in this case, by global civil society and UN agencies whose efforts often determine the legally oriented content of best practices, rule of law blueprints, and policy guidelines. By considering law in these sequential forms, this Chapter—like the next one, which examines the separate question of accountability for child soldiering—pursues a "longitudinal approach to ... legal development."[2] Both Chapters look at where law, policy, and best practices are heading. Ideally, for activists, *lex desiderata* would

---

[1] I adopt an understanding of international law as straddling a continuum from hard to soft. Whereas hard law ranks highly on the dimensions of "obligation, precision, and delegation," soft law ranks more weakly thereupon. Kenneth W. Abbott and Duncan Snidal, *Hard and Soft Law in International Governance*, 54(3) INT'L ORG. 421, 422 (2000). Soft law includes instruments that are not formally binding, as well as instruments that are binding but whose content is vague or discretionary or that do not delegate monitoring or enforcement to third-parties. Gregory C. Shaffer and Mark A. Pollack, *Hard vs. Soft Law: Alternatives, Complements, and Antagonists in International Governance*, 94 MINN. L. REV. 706, 715 (2010). Some soft law instruments nevertheless contain detailed language and embody unconditional commitments, which states may reference within the context of their formal legal claims.

[2] Jens Meierhenrich, LAWFARE 5 (draft monograph, 2012). Meierhenrich draws from Paul Pierson's observation that: "There is often a strong case to be made for shifting from snapshots to moving pictures. Placing politics in time—systematically situating particular moments (including the present) in a temporal sequence of events and processes—can greatly enrich our understanding of complex

become *lex ferenda* which then would concretize into *lex lata* once many traditional actors with international legal personality adopt it as such.

Although criminally prosecuting child soldiers for their alleged involvement in acts of atrocity is permissible under international law, it increasingly is viewed as inappropriate and undesirable. As a result, its viability as a policy option sharply constricts. This constriction, in turn, thins the application of other accountability mechanisms regardless of their form or nature. The international legal imagination does not much wish to confront the quandary of the child soldier as atrocity perpetrator. The prospect of so doing induces a level of unease which prompts the international legal imagination to exhibit a rather stiff posture. Why? For one, the task is delicate. Developing careful and constructive responses is a challenge. Although understandable, the international legal imagination's diffidence also is careless, if not complacent. Discomfort with the question of accountability induces a simplistic operational preference for non-responsibility, reintegration summarily premised on excuse, and a sidelining of conflict resolution.

(i) International Human Rights Law and Humanitarian Law

International human rights law delineates positive rights of general application. International humanitarian law, which is also referred to as the laws of war, regulates what is permissible or impermissible in times of either international or non-international armed conflict. Despite some commonalities in application, international humanitarian law treats international armed conflict differently than it treats non-international armed conflict.

(a) Hard Law

The CRC is a leading multilateral human rights treaty. It addresses the intersection of children and criminal justice. It permits the "arrest, detention or imprisonment of a child," but requires that these measures "shall be used only as a...last resort and for the shortest appropriate period of time."[3] The CRC precludes the death penalty and life imprisonment without parole as sentences for children who are convicted of offenses. The CRC requires that "every child deprived of liberty shall be separated from adults unless it is considered in the child's best interest not to do so."[4] It specifies a minimum (and uncontroversial) level of due process protection for children subject to criminal proceedings, but also encourages the development of enhanced frameworks attuned

---

social dynamics." Paul Pierson, *Not Just What, but* When: *Timing and Sequence in Political Processes*, 14 (1) STUDIES IN AMERICAN POLITICAL DEVELOPMENT 72, 72 (2000).

[3] United Nations Convention on the Rights of the Child, G.A. Res. 44/25, Art. 37(b), Annex, U.N. Doc. A/RES/44/25 (November 20, 1989) (entered into force September 2, 1990) [hereinafter CRC] (also requiring that "[n]o child shall be deprived of his or her liberty unlawfully or arbitrarily").

[4] *Id.* Art. 37(c).

to their specific needs. The CRC does not favor incarceration. It prefers rehabilitation and reintegration. That said, the CRC does not bar incarceration. Article 40(3)(a) of the CRC requires parties to seek to promote the establishment of "a minimum age below which children shall be presumed not to have the capacity to infringe the penal law," but sets no such age. That said, the Committee on the Rights of the Child has considered fourteen as a low age for criminal responsibility and "has welcomed . . . proposals to set the age of criminal responsibility at eighteen."[5]

Some CRC provisions are novel, while others draw from antecedent instruments, such as the 1966 International Covenant on Civil and Political Rights (ICCPR). In Article 6(5), for example, the ICCPR precludes the imposition of the death penalty on persons under the age of eighteen at the time of committing a crime. The ICCPR also requires accused juveniles to be "separated from adults and brought as speedily as possible for adjudication" and that juvenile offenders "be segregated from adults and be accorded treatment appropriate to their age and legal status."[6]

What is the general practice within national jurisdictions when it comes to minors who commit ordinary common crimes? A sampling of baseline ages of criminal responsibility over the past decade include: seven (Switzerland, Nigeria, South Africa); ten (Australia, New Zealand); twelve (Canada, Netherlands, Uganda); thirteen (France, Afghanistan); fourteen (Japan, Germany, Austria, Italy, Russian Federation, Sierra Leone); fifteen (Sweden, Norway, Denmark); sixteen (Spain, Portugal), and eighteen (Belgium, Brazil, Peru).[7] It is not uncommon for states to modify these ages; hence, these ages remain variable. For example, in 2007, Sierra Leone raised its baseline age of criminal responsibility from ten to fourteen.[8]

Furthermore, national ages of criminal responsibility may be gradated. This means that jurisdictions establish an age of criminal responsibility and a separate age of adult criminal responsibility. This latter age may be fixed at eighteen, though not necessarily so.[9] States may lower the age of adult criminal responsibility if the

---

[5]   Amnesty International, *Child Soldiers: Criminals or Victims?* 15 (AI Index: IOR 50/02/00 (2000)). This Committee helps monitor state compliance with the CRC.

[6]   International Covenant on Civil and Political Rights, Arts 10(2)(b), 10(3), U.N. Doc. A/6316 (1966), 999 U.N.T.S. 171 (entered into force March 23, 1976) [hereinafter ICCPR]; *see also id.* Art. 14(4) (requiring in the case of juvenile persons that trial procedure takes into account their age and the desirability of promoting their rehabilitation).

[7]   Information compiled in part from the following: Olaoluwa Olusanya, *Granting Immunity to Child Combatants Supranationally, in* SENTENCING AND SANCTIONING IN SUPRANATIONAL CRIMINAL LAW 87, 94, n. 25 (Roelof Haveman and Olaoluwa Olusanya eds, 2006); Steven Freeland, *Mere Children or Weapons of War—Child Soldiers and International Law*, 29 U. OF LA VERNE L. REV. 19, 50 n. 148 (2008); Mark Hughes, *The Big Question: Should 12, rather than 10, be the age of criminal responsibility?*, THE INDEP. (March 16, 2010); BBC News, *Thousands of crimes by under-10s* (September 2, 2007), *available at* <http://news.bbc.co.uk/2/hi/uk_news/6974587.stm>.

[8]   Sierra Leone Child Rights Act 2007, Art. 70, Supplement to the Sierra Leone Gazette Extraordinary Vol. CXXXVIII, No. 43 (September 3, 2007) (Art. 2 defines a child as any person below eighteen). This legislation also repealed an earlier enactment that had permitted boys to receive sentences of corporal punishment. *Id.* Art. 33(3).

[9]   Several US states recently have increased the age of adult criminal responsibility to eighteen, although all permit persons younger than eighteen to be prosecuted as adults for especially violent crimes. As of early 2011, in eleven US states the age of adult criminal responsibility for all crimes is seventeen, while in two—New York and North Carolina—it is sixteen. Mosi Secret, *States Prosecute Fewer Teenagers in Adult Courts*, N.Y. TIMES (March 5, 2011).

specific offense is more serious. States also may turn to age—once again, generally (but not always) eighteen—to determine an individual's eligibility for juvenile, instead of adult, justice systems. Juvenile justice systems tend to focus more on treatment than on punishment, but do not necessarily exclude retributive or deterrent penologies.

Depending on the jurisdiction, minors can be prosecuted as adults or in adult venues for particularly serious violent crimes. Although such situations are infrequent, they are by no means unprecedented. In England, Robert Thompson and Jon Venables (two boys aged ten at the time of committing the crime and eleven at the time of their trial and conviction) were subject "to the full rigours of an adult public trial" for the abduction and murder of a toddler (James Bulger, aged two) by protracted battery in 1993.[10] Their trial at Preston Crown Court lasted for seventeen days. Neither served sentence in adult prison. Thompson and Venables jointly challenged their situation before the European Court of Human Rights. The resultant litigation led to a holding that the age of criminal responsibility in England and Wales (ten years) did not breach the European Convention on Human Rights.[11] To subject a person as young as eleven to a criminal trial, as such, did not infringe the Convention's fair trial guarantee. The European Court of Human Rights rejected Thompson and Venables' claims that they had been subject to inhuman and degrading treatment, and that imposing a lengthy sentence on persons of their age would automatically offend the Convention. The Court did specifically rule, however, that they had neither received a fair trial nor were able to participate fully or effectively in the process. It also ruled that the Home Secretary had violated their human rights by intervening to raise their sentences.

The intersection of adolescence and the criminal justice system has been a hot topic recently in the United States. This intersection revolves around the sentencing ramifications of developmental science's findings that adolescents have diminished culpability. The United States is a jurisdiction characterized by onerous sentencing provisions, so these findings have come to play some role in precluding the imposition of extremely harsh punishment upon juveniles. The US Supreme Court ruled in *Roper* v. *Simmons*, for example, that application of the death penalty to individuals under the age of eighteen at the time of the offense (in that specific case, for a homicide crime committed by a seventeen year-old) violated the Eighth Amendment of the US Constitution's prohibition on the infliction of cruel and unusual punishments.[12] In addition to developmental science, the US Supreme Court in *Roper* turned to international norms, which included international human rights law, to confirm the domestic consensus against the juvenile death penalty. In *Graham* v. *Florida*, decided in 2010, the US Supreme Court ruled that imposing the sentence of life imprisonment without the possibility of parole on juveniles

---

[10] Olusanya, *supra* note 7, at 99–100 (noting that Western countries "make exceptions for special cases where children have committed particularly shocking crimes").
[11] T v. UK; V. v. UK, 30 EHRR 121 (2000) (five judges dissented on this issue).
[12] 543 U.S. 551 (2005).

for non-homicide crimes also infringed the Eighth Amendment.[13] Attempts in lower courts to extend the *Graham* logic so as to void sentences of life imprisonment without parole for juveniles convicted of murder have thus far proven unsuccessful, although the US Supreme Court might ultimately weigh in on that question as well.

In sum, extant international human rights law does not preclude persons under the age of eighteen from bearing criminal responsibility; nor does it say that they typically lack the capacity to be found culpable; nor does it banish any punishment for them other than the death penalty and life imprisonment without parole. Prosecutions are discouraged, but remain lawful so long as they comport with particularized due process standards. Although these legal frameworks largely exist for children accused of ordinary common crimes,[14] they do not disclaim applicability to children, including child soldiers, suspected of committing extraordinary international crimes.

Turning to international humanitarian law, the 1949 Fourth Geneva Convention precludes imposing the death penalty on "a protected person who was under eighteen years of age at the time of the offence."[15] Two Additional Protocols to the Geneva Conventions (adopted in 1977) reinforce this prohibition.[16] Additional Protocol I covers international armed conflicts while Additional Protocol II covers non-international armed conflicts. Article 77(5) of Additional Protocol I and Article 6(4) of Additional Protocol II preclude the imposition of the death penalty for an offense related to the armed conflict on persons who were under the age of eighteen at the time of committing the offense. Consequently, the Fourth Geneva Convention and both Additional Protocols contemplate that minors can incur responsibility for war crimes. These instruments bar only the harshest punishments.

That said, Sonja Grover argues that international humanitarian law presents a basis to regard persons under the age of eighteen (including child soldiers) as protected civilians or non-combatants, prompting her to contend that they are to be absolved of all culpability for international crimes.[17] According to Grover,

---

[13] 560 U.S. ___ (2010) (slip op.), 130 S. Ct. 2011.

[14] Leena Grover, *Trial of the Child Soldier: Protecting the Rights of the Accused*, *in* 65 ZEITSCHRIFT FÜR AUSLÄNDISCHES ÖFFENTLICHES RECHT UND VÖLKERRECHT 217, 219 (2005) ("It is likely that the drafters of the CRC and similar legal instruments only contemplated the prosecution of children for domestic crimes.").

[15] Geneva Convention (IV) relative to the Protection of Civilian Persons in Time of War, Art. 68, 75 U.N.T.S. 287 (August 12, 1949).

[16] Protocol Additional to the Geneva Conventions of 12 August 1949, and relating to the Protection of Victims of International Armed Conflicts (Protocol I), 1125 U.N.T.S. 3 (June 8, 1977) [hereinafter Additional Protocol I]; Protocol Additional to the Geneva Conventions of 12 August 1949, and relating to the Protection of Victims of Non-International Armed Conflicts (Protocol II), 1125 U.N.T.S. 609 (June 8, 1977) [hereinafter Additional Protocol II]. Additional Protocol I has 171 state parties. Additional Protocol II has 166 state parties.

[17] Sonja Grover, '*Child Soldiers' as 'Non-Combatants': The Inapplicability of the Refugee Convention Exclusion Clause*, 12 INT'L J. OF HUM. RTS. 53, 61 (2008). Grover surveys general international law on the subject, which she posits "leaves open the question as to whether child soldiers, as opposed to adult soldiers, are properly accused and convicted in any circumstance of having committed an international crime." *Id.* at 56.

"[s]hould the child soldier commit an international crime, he or she cannot legitimately be held responsible under domestic or international law as: a) the child is as a non-combatant not bound by the rules of war or other armed conflict and b) the State, being responsible for the direct (or indirect) use in hostilities of these child non-combatants, must be held criminally liable for the conduct of these children in the course of their soldiering."[18] Grover's argument is iconoclastic. International law widely accepts that civilians can commit war crimes. This settled principle traces back to decisions implicating Nazi atrocity rendered over sixty years ago in *Zyklon B* and *Essen Lynching* (British Military Courts) and *Hadamar* (United States Military Commission).[19] Furthermore, state criminality (as distinguished from state civil responsibility) is deeply contested, and largely eschewed, as an element of public international law. Hence, for the moment, recourse to state criminality offers no recourse at all.[20] Many child soldiers are used by armed groups that fight against the state. How can the state realistically be held criminally responsible for the unlawful use of children by such armed groups?

Tensions may arise between promulgating policies that favor short-term protection, on the one hand, and long-term welfare, on the other. Suggesting that non-combatants cannot commit war crimes would, if adopted, inject a layer of impunity into contexts where extraordinary international crimes are committed (including against children) by both combatants and civilians. Is it not counterproductive to protect children by promoting understandings of international law that, in turn, evacuate civilian obligations to respect the law? Absolutism in insisting that child soldiers are non-combatants may fuel the risk that, depending on the politics of their captors, they not become treated as civilians but, instead, as terrorists, outlaws, or insurgents bereft of appropriate legal protection while stuck in long-term detention.[21] US modalities at Guantánamo Bay come to mind as just such a potentiality, however unattractive, of which law and policymakers must remain mindful.

(b) Soft Law, Policy, and Best Practices

The CRC's language concerning the general criminal responsibility of minors traces to a slightly earlier instrument, the 1985 UN Standard Minimum Rules for the Administration of Juvenile Justice (commonly referred to as the Beijing Rules).[22] The Beijing Rules require states to make efforts to "establish . . . a set of laws, rules and provisions specifically applicable to juvenile offenders and institutions and

---

[18] *Id.* at 61–62.
[19] United Nations War Crimes Commission, LAW REPORTS OF TRIALS OF WAR CRIMINALS, Vol. I, 46–54, 88–92, 93–103 (1947).
[20] State responsibility does not expunge individual criminal liability for overlapping conduct (or *vice versa*).
[21] In Burundi, children associated with rebel groups faced harsh treatment when captured by the government. In Nepal, Iraq, and Afghanistan, children suspected of association with armed or terrorist groups have been administratively detained and subject to human rights abuses.
[22] G.A. Res. 40/33, U.N. Doc. A/RES/40/33 (November 29, 1985).

bodies entrusted with the functions of the administration of juvenile justice."[23] The Beijing Rules do not establish a minimum age of criminal responsibility, but encourage states, when they fix such an age nationally, not to do so "at too low an age level, bearing in mind the facts of emotional, mental and intellectual maturity."[24] The Beijing Rules do not negate the capacity of juvenile offenders to commit offenses nor do they remove the state's ability to prosecute them. The Beijing Rules favor diversion to community and other services and deem strictly punitive approaches to be inappropriate, but ban only capital and corporal punishment.[25] Institutionalization is not precluded, but is described in Rule 19.1 as "a disposition of last resort and for the minimum necessary period." According to Rule 17.1(c), "[d]eprivation of personal liberty shall not be imposed unless the juvenile is adjudicated of a serious act involving violence against another person or of persistence in committing other serious offences and unless there is no other appropriate response."

Other soft law instruments also address the intersection of children and the ordinary criminal justice system. For example, the UN Guidelines for the Prevention of Juvenile Delinquency aim to help youth engage in lawful activities and thereby develop non-criminogenic attitudes.[26] Article 54 thereof provides that "[n]o child or young person should be subjected to harsh or degrading correction or punishment measures." Relatedly, the UN Rules for the Protection of Juveniles Deprived of their Liberty offer specific guidance on how to approach juveniles under arrest or awaiting trial and how to manage juvenile justice systems, in particular facilities.[27] Although these Rules permit imprisonment, they cast it as a last resort and aim instead to countervail the detrimental effects of all types of detention and collaterally foster integration. These Rules define a juvenile as any person under the age of eighteen, but leave it to individual states to determine the age limit below which a child should not be deprived of his or her liberty. Cruel, inhuman, or degrading treatment is strictly prohibited. These Rules also specify that "[a]ll juveniles should benefit from arrangements designed to assist them in returning to society, family life, education or employment after release."[28] The UN Economic and Social Council has elaborated guidelines to protect child victims and witnesses of crimes, including their rights to be informed, to be heard, to express views and concerns, and to reparation.[29]

Moving from the general to the specific, a number of documents address child soldiers. While these documents exhort compliance with extant international law,

---

[23] *Id.* Rule 2.3; *see also id.* Rule 2.2 (defining juvenile).
[24] *Id.* Rule 4.1. Commentary to Rule 2 notes that "age limits will depend on, and are explicitly made dependent on, each respective legal system.... This makes for a wide variety of ages coming under the definition of 'juvenile', ranging from 7 years to 18 years or above."
[25] *Id.* Rules 11, 17.2, 17.3, and Commentary to Rule 17.
[26] G.A. Res. 45/112, Annex, U.N. Doc. A/RES/45/112 (December 14, 1990).
[27] G.A. Res. 45/113, Annex, U.N. Doc. A/RES/45/113 (December 14, 1990).
[28] *Id.* Art. 79.
[29] Economic and Social Council Res. No. 2005/20 (July 22, 2005).

they also aim to shift the content of international law and policy closer to the Straight 18 position.

In 1996, pursuant to a UN General Assembly resolution, Graça Machel of Mozambique submitted a ground-breaking report entitled *Impact of Armed Conflict on Children* (widely known as the Machel Report).[30] The Machel Report has been a front-runner in sensitizing the international community to the hazardous effects of violent conflict on children, including child soldiers. It has had tremendous social constructivist influence. Positing that "more and more of the world is being sucked into a desolate moral vacuum," it identifies its "most fundamental demand" that "children simply have no part in warfare."[31] Aiming to "eradicat[e] the use of children under the age of 18 years in ... armed forces," the Machel Report advocates that the "media ... should be encouraged to expose the use of child soldiers and the need for demobilization."[32] In light of the Machel Report's recommendation, the Office of the Special Representative on Children and Armed Conflict was established within the UN system.

The Machel Report identifies child soldiers as victims and targets, and also "even" as perpetrators.[33] That said, it didactically presents acts of atrocity perpetrated by child soldiers as the product of coercion or manipulation by adults. The Machel Report recognizes the complexities of "balancing culpability, a community's sense of justice and the 'best interests of the child'."[34] It does not explicitly disclaim the penal responsibility of child soldiers, but neither does it encourage child soldiers to become subjects of criminal prosecutions. The Machel Report mandates the need to safeguard the procedural rights of any accused minor and specifically faults Rwanda for not having done so in the wake of the 1994 genocide. It favorably references the Committee on the Rights of the Child's position that chronological approaches ought to be the baseline for assessing criminal responsibility instead of "subjective or imprecise criteria, such as the attainment of puberty, age of discernment or the child's personality."[35] The Machel Report favorably references traditional cleansing and healing rituals.[36] Activists have turned to the Machel Report to justify portraying the victimization, faultlessness, and passivity of child soldiers in a manner that exceeds the language and tone that Machel herself had adopted. In this regard, the Machel Report's goal that "[y]oung people must not be seen as problems or victims, but as key contributors in the planning and implementation of long-term solutions"[37] may ultimately become frustrated.

---

[30] Report of the Expert of the Secretary-General, *Impact of Armed Conflict on Children*, U.N. Doc. A/51/306 (August 26, 1996), *available at* <http://www.unicef.org/graca/a51-306_en.pdf> [hereinafter Machel Report]. The UN Secretary-General appointed Machel as expert in 1994. Earlier in her life Machel had been involved with FRELIMO. David M. Rosen, ARMIES OF THE YOUNG: CHILD SOLDIERS IN WAR AND TERRORISM 12 (2005). Machel is married to Nelson Mandela.

[31] Machel Report, *supra* note 30, at ¶¶ 3–5.

[32] *Id.* ¶ 62(a).

[33] *Id.* ¶ 24.

[34] *Id.* ¶ 250.

[35] *Id.* ¶ 251.

[36] *Id.* ¶ 55.

[37] *Id.* ¶ 242.

A Strategic Review of the Machel Report was presented to the United Nations General Assembly in August 2007.[38] This Strategic Review notes advances in terms of the implementation of certain Machel Report recommendations, but also concludes that much work remains to be done. In particular, the focus of the Strategic Review is to address all impacts on all children in all situations affected by conflict: in other words, to look beyond child soldiers in terms of meeting the needs of children generally impacted by armed conflict.[39] Recommendation 5 thereof, entitled "Promote justice for children," counsels member states to "establish child-friendly mechanisms to promote the participation and protection of children in all justice systems, including transitional justice processes."[40] No explicit mention is made, however, about the child as a potential subject of these processes.

In 2010, Machel opened a study of children and transitional justice by noting:

[T]he participation of . . . children in transitional justice mechanisms must be primarily as victims and witnesses. This does not minimize the importance of accountability for children who become perpetrators. However, it does mean finding ways, within the context of child and human rights instruments, to redress the wrongs these children have suffered while they also make their redress to their communities.[41]

Elsewhere in this text, however, Machel returns to more conventional thinking.[42] Truly ameliorative reform will remain elusive until the presumptive imagery shifts to something more dynamic and less controlling, such as circumscribed action.

In 1997, the NGO Working Group on the CRC and UNICEF convened a major symposium in Cape Town. This symposium adopted the Cape Town Principles and Best Practices.[43] This hortatory document advocates for the establishment of a minimum age of eighteen years for any person participating in hostilities and for recruitment in all forms into armed forces or armed groups; and exhorts the demobilization of all persons under the age of eighteen from any kind of armed force or group.[44] The Cape Town Principles view "[f]amily reunification [as] the principal factor in effective social reintegration."[45] The

---

[38]   *Report of the Special Representative of the Secretary-General for Children and Armed Conflict,* delivered to the UN General Assembly, U.N. Doc. A/62/228 (August 13, 2007).

[39]   Executive Summary of the Strategic Review Report to the General Assembly, A/62/228 (summarizing the 10-year Strategic Review of the Machel Study: Children and Conflict in a Changing World).

[40]   *Report of the Special Representative, supra* note 38, at Part two, ¶ 107(c).

[41]   Graça Machel, *Foreword, in* CHILDREN AND TRANSITIONAL JUSTICE: TRUTH-TELLING, ACCOUNTABILITY AND RECONCILIATION ix, xii (UNICEF Innocenti Research Centre and Human Rights Program at Harvard Law School, Sharanjeet Parmar, Mindy Jane Roseman, Saudamini Siegrist, and Theo Sowa eds, 2010) [hereinafter CHILDREN AND TRANSITIONAL JUSTICE].

[42]   *Id.* at x ("Having been witnesses and victims of the crimes of war, children have a key role in addressing those crimes and in reconciliation and peace-building processes in their communities."); *id.* at xi (identifying "supporting children's right to choose whether or not to participate and to decide how they wish to be involved, with whom they wish to engage and when" as part of the "policies, procedures and practices in all transitional justice activities").

[43]   Cape Town Principles and Best Practices (April 27–30, 1997), *available at* <http://www.unicef.org/emerg/files/Cape_Town_Principles(1).pdf>.

[44]   *Id.* at 1, 4.

[45]   *Id.* at 8.

Cape Town Principles go into considerable detail regarding demobilization and reintegration programming for former child soldiers. They make no reference to the possibility of transitional justice for child soldier returnees, other than one woolly allusion that "[i]n order to be successful, reintegration of the child within the community should be carried out within the framework of efforts towards national reconciliation."[46] The Cape Town Principles recognize that "[t]raditional resources and practices in the community, which can support the psychosocial integration of children affected by war, should be identified and supported," while also calling for "[d]ialogue with communities . . . to clarify their main concerns for the children and the community's perception of their own roles and responsibilities with regard to the children."[47]

It remains unclear, however, whether the community can effectively address its own roles and responsibilities—as it must—in the absence of reciprocal dialogue regarding the roles and responsibilities of the children themselves, especially adolescents implicated in the commission of acts of atrocity.

Fifty-eight states, together with other stakeholders (donors, heads of UN agencies, and non-governmental organizations), attended an international conference co-hosted by the French government and UNICEF in Paris in February 2007. Organizers convened this conference, entitled "Free children from War," to update the Cape Town Principles. All participating states endorsed the Paris Commitments to Protect Children from Unlawful Recruitment or Use by Armed Forces or Armed Groups, which reference the significantly more elaborative Paris Principles and Guidelines on Children Associated with Armed Forces or Armed Groups.[48] As of September 27, 2010, the number of states endorsing the Paris Commitments has increased to ninety-five.[49] The Paris Commitments and Principles "are also designed to assist States and donors in meeting their obligations and taking funding decisions."[50]

The Paris Commitments address the status of children who allegedly perpetrate atrocity crimes:

Commitment 11. To ensure that children under 18 years of age who are or who have been unlawfully recruited or used by armed forces or groups and are accused of crimes against

---

[46] *Id.* at 11.

[47] *Id.* at 9–10.

[48] The Paris Commitments to Protect Children from Unlawful Recruitment or Use by Armed Forces or Armed Groups (February 2007) [hereinafter Paris Commitments], *available at* <http://www.child-soldiers.org/childsoldiers/Paris_Commitments_March_2007.pdf>; The Paris Principles: Principles and Guidelines on Children Associated with Armed Forces or Armed Groups (February 2007) [hereinafter Paris Principles], *available at* <http://www.child-soldiers.org/childsoldiers/Paris_Principles_March_2007.pdf>.

[49] Endorsees include Afghanistan, Cambodia, Central African Republic, Chad, Colombia, DRC, France, Germany, Liberia, Nepal, Niger, Paraguay, Peru, Russian Federation, Serbia, Sierra Leone, Somalia, South Africa, Sri Lanka, Sudan, Switzerland, Timor-Leste, Uganda, and the United Kingdom. Paris Commitment 2 obliges endorsees to "make every effort to uphold and apply the Paris [P]rinciples . . . wherever possible."

[50] Paris Principles, *supra* note 48, Prin. 1.14; *see also Report of the Special Representative, supra* note 38, at Part two, ¶ 55 (noting that "[p]olicies and guidelines adopted in the last decade form essential complements to progress on international legal norms," and specifically referencing the Paris Commitments).

international law are considered primarily as victims of violations against international law and not only as alleged perpetrators. They should be treated in accordance with international standards for juvenile justice, such as in a framework of restorative justice and social rehabilitation.

Commitment 12. In line with the [CRC] and other international standards for juvenile justice, to seek alternatives to judicial proceedings wherever appropriate and desirable, and to ensure that, where truth-seeking and reconciliation mechanisms are established, the involvement of children is supported and promoted, that measures are taken to protect the rights of children throughout the process, and in particular that children's participation is voluntary.

The Coalition to Stop the Use of Child Soldiers propounds that child soldiers who have committed human rights abuses should be treated "first and foremost as victims of adult crimes."[51] This approach resembles that of the Paris Principles, namely, to view such child soldiers primarily as victims. The Coalition recognizes that there will be cases where some of these child soldiers were clearly in control of their actions. For these children, the Coalition's position is nuanced, insofar as it contends that not holding them accountable "may deny justice to the victims."[52] Nor do the Paris Commitments ban criminal trials,[53] though they certainly do not encourage them. Although the Paris Commitments support truth-seeking and reconciliation mechanisms, they envision children to be involved in these initiatives only voluntarily.

The Paris Principles expound considerably on the skeletal frame of the Paris Commitments. The Paris Principles understand children associated with armed forces or armed groups as persons younger than eighteen, thereby adopting the age categorization applied by the Cape Town Principles to child soldiers. Paris Principle 1.5 affirms that the Paris Principles "tak[e] a child rights-based approach to the problem of children associated with armed forces or armed groups, [and] underscore the humanitarian imperative to seek the unconditional release of children from armed forces or armed groups at all times." Principle 3.6 exhorts that "[c]hildren who are accused of crimes under international law allegedly committed while they were associated with armed forces or armed groups should be considered primarily as victims of offences against international law; not only as perpetrators."

---

[51] *Frequently asked questions, available at* <http://www.child-soldiers.org/childsoldiers/questions-and-answers> (visited on June 18, 2011).

[52] *Id.* Acknowledgement or atonement is encouraged. Mention is also made of the possibility of prosecution under international standards of juvenile justice in some instances. In this regard, the Coalition's position is more explicitly open to the prospect of accountability than that offered by the Paris Commitments or Paris Principles. That said, in light of the first and foremost nature of victim status, together with the explicit prioritization of prosecuting persons who unlawfully recruited or used children, the actual operational push for accountability of child soldiers clearly in control of their actions would be slight at best. Moreover, as Chapter 6 *infra* posits, it is not only former child soldiers who were clearly in control of their actions who would benefit from non-penal accountability processes.

[53] Paris Commitments, *supra* note 48, commitment 10; *cf.* Paris Principles, *supra* note 48, Prins 3.9 (prohibiting only capital punishment or imprisonment for life without possibility of release) and 7.6 (on due process).

Wherever possible, Principle 3.7 mandates alternatives to judicial proceedings. Principle 3.8 emphasizes, but also adds to, the Paris Commitments:

> Where truth-seeking and reconciliation mechanisms are established, children's involvement should be promoted and supported and their rights protected throughout the process. Their participation must be voluntary and by informed consent by both the child and her or his parent or guardian where appropriate and possible. Special procedures should be permitted to minimize greater susceptibility to distress.[54]

Unless contrary to their best interests, violence against children associated with armed forces or armed groups is to be "promptly, thoroughly, and independently investigated and prosecuted,"[55] although no comparable exhortation arises in cases where these children have inflicted violence upon others, including civilians, the elderly, infants, or other children.

Section 7 of the Paris Principles lists eighty-four principles pertaining to the release and reintegration of children associated with armed forces or armed groups.[56] Section 7 is detailed. It includes guidelines regarding the psychosocial needs of children formerly associated with armed forces or armed groups. It recognizes the resilience of these children. Although justice concerns arise elsewhere in the Paris Principles (Section 8), not one among the principles in Section 7 devoted to release and reintegration explicitly mentions justice aspects. The implication, then, is that justice is to operate separately from release and reintegration. Chapter 6 of this book revisits this distancing.

Section 7 does contain a handful of principles that hint at justice concerns. For example, Paris Principle 7.53 notes that "[i]n some communities, children are viewed and view themselves as carrying bad spirits from their experiences with armed forces or armed groups;" in such instances, "[a]ppropriate cultural practices, as long as they are not harmful to children, can be essential to a child's reintegration and should be supported." Principle 7.31 guardedly encourages reintegration to be carried out in ways that facilitate local and national reconciliation.[57] Principle 7.41 supports non-violent ways of conflict management and the provision of mediation and support following the children's return. Principle 7.48 mentions engaging children in community service as a way to break stigma.[58] Each of these principles germinates a crucial process. Nonetheless, the linkages between these scattered

---

[54] *See also* UNICEF Innocenti Research Centre in cooperation with the International Center for Transitional Justice, CHILDREN AND TRUTH COMMISSIONS 10 (2010) ("Children's participation in a truth commission should always be voluntary, based on the informed consent of the child and the parent or legal guardian, when appropriate.").

[55] Paris Principles, *supra* note 48, Prin. 7.6.6.

[56] Section 7 thoroughly addresses the distinctive situation of girls, along with children with physical disabilities and wounds.

[57] Principle 7.31 cautions that such reintegration "should always be preceded by a risk assessment including a cultural and gender analysis addressing issues of discrimination and should be based on the child's best interests irrespective of national considerations or priorities."

[58] Principle 7.49 recommends that "[r]eintegration and reconciliation activities should recognise the need to redirect the potential of children and young people in developing leadership and conflict resolution skills and taking responsibility for their actions including through participation in the rebuilding of their communities and in peace building activities."

references, on the one hand, and justice, on the other, are oblique at best and, what is more, remain underdeveloped and undertheorized.

Overall, Section 7 constructs children formerly associated with armed forces or armed groups as being owed many obligations, but posits them as owing very few. Strict limits are placed on how they might be interviewed and for what purposes. Principle 7.39, which addresses stigma, return, and reintegration, notes that:

...Children are frequently perceived initially as troublemakers prone to aggressive behaviour or criminal activities. The preparation of communities and on-going support to communities needs to address these perceptions and to help communities understand that the children are primarily victims.

Mention is not herein made of transitional justice as a methodology through which to expiate these potential tensions. The way forward, rather, lies in sensitizing the community to overcome its negative feelings which, thereby, become impliedly cast as inappropriate or uninformed. Principle 7.42 propounds risk assessments to indicate "where it is likely that children will be feared, become targets of hostility for having been in enemy groups or be ostracised or neglected." In such situations, Principle 7.42 calls for "intensive community sensitisation" to be "undertaken before children return." Paris Principle 7.44 deals with the different situation where child returnees are regarded as freedom fighters or heroes. Here, the need is for "actors" to "encourage families and communities to remember that the children are primarily children."

In short, within the ongoing process of release and reintegration, the position of the Paris Principles is not to meaningfully inquire whether transitional justice mechanisms might dissipate residual enmity. Rather, it is basically to instruct the public to internalize any such feelings. The intention is to excuse acts of atrocity in conformity with the faultless passive victim image, instead of propounding a *quid pro quo* dialectic of forgiveness through reciprocal moral dialogue.

As mentioned previously, the Paris Principles do address justice, albeit separately from the release and reintegration process. The first part of Paris Principles Section 8 mandates ending the culture of "impunity for those responsible for unlawfully recruiting or using children in armed conflict." This part notes the "powerful deterrent" effect of mechanisms that would hold such individuals accountable.[59] The second part of Section 8 involves the place of children within justice mechanisms. This part begins with Principle 8.6, which states that "[c]hildren should not be prosecuted by an international court or tribunal." At the national level, children cannot be prosecuted or punished, or threatened with either, "solely for their membership" in armed forces or armed groups.[60] Principle 8.8 affirms that any proceedings that do implicate children nationally or locally are to be consistent with international standards for juvenile justice. Alternatives to judicial proceedings "should be sought for children at the national level;" in the event judicial

---

[59] Paris Principles, *supra* note 48, Prin. 8.1.   [60] *Id.* Prin. 8.7.

proceedings occur "every effort should be made to seek alternatives to placing the child in institutions."[61]

The Paris Principles remain terse about the rights of persons harmed by the conduct of child soldiers to a remedy or to redress. Textually, the Paris Principles dance around their justice concerns.

Paris Principle 8.11 states that "[c]hildren associated with armed forces or armed groups who return to communities without undergoing any judicial or other proceedings should be closely monitored to ensure that they are not treated as scapegoats or subjected to any processes or mechanisms that contravene their rights." Principles 8.12 and 8.13 protect the child in information gathering processes.

Section 8 also addresses truth-seeking and reconciliation mechanisms:

8.15 All children who take part in these mechanisms, including those who have been associated with armed forces or armed groups should be treated equally as witnesses or as victims.[62]

8.16 Children's participation in these mechanisms must be voluntary. No provision of services or support should be dependent on their participation in these mechanisms.

The approach of the Paris Principles to preclude international criminal trials and dissuade national criminal trials is to be welcomed. So, too, is the Paris Principles' commendation of truth-seeking and reconciliation mechanisms and support (albeit quite cursory) of traditional rituals. That said, the Paris Principles tamp down the ability of such mechanisms fully to explore the multidimensionality of child soldier returnees, notably their roles as perpetrators. Accordingly, the application of such mechanisms thins and becomes superficial. The Paris Principles approach all children—including children formerly associated with armed forces or armed groups—equally as victims or witnesses. This means that the children are not to be distinguished *inter se* in terms of their individual conduct. The child soldier presented primarily as victim morphs into the operational reality of the child soldier treated entirely as victim.[63] Susan Shepler adroitly captures the imbalance: "One does not want to run the risk of downplaying the violence many children experience, but a

---

[61] *Id.* Prins 8.9.0–8.9.1. For a firmer dissuasive stance, *see* Office of the Special Representative of the Secretary-General for Children and Armed Conflict, CHILDREN AND JUSTICE DURING AND IN THE AFTERMATH OF ARMED CONFLICT 27 (Working Paper No. 3, September 2011) ("The United Nations, as well as many NGOs and child protection actors share the view that children associated with armed groups should not be detained or prosecuted, but should be primarily treated as victims by virtue of their age and the forced nature of their association.") [hereinafter CHILDREN AND JUSTICE].

[62] *Cf.* Executive Summary of the Strategic Review Report to the General Assembly, *supra* note 39 ("States need to . . . support and protect the rights of children who become involved in justice processes as victims and witnesses.").

[63] *Cf.* Kokouvi Luc Dodzi Akakpo, *Procureur c. X: les leçons à tirer de la poursuite d'un enfant soldat pour crimes contre l'humanité* 6 (manuscript on file with the author, with permission, forthcoming REVUE GÉNÉRALE DE DROIT (2012)) ("[L]'ensemble de la législation internationale applicable soutient l'attribution de la qualité de victime aux enfants soldats."); Jason Hart, *Saving children: What role for anthropology?*, 22(1) ANTHROPOLOGY TODAY 5, 8 (2006) (noting as a "basic premise[]" of child-focused humanitarianism" that "the young in situations of war are to be approached solely as victims").

corrective is necessary to child protection discourses that almost completely remove any sense of agency in childhood."[64]

The Paris Commitments and Paris Principles reflect and clarify best practices that are implemented, often top-down and transnationally, in post-conflict societies grappling with the reinsertion of former child soldiers into community life. State governments may endorse these instruments for a variety of reasons, including reputational concerns and the need to appear welcoming to donors. Local communities, including the child soldiers themselves, tend to be distant from the process of establishing best policy practices and, in turn, international law and domestic incorporation thereof. Given the influence of transnational norm entrepreneurs within post-conflict societies, it is of little surprise that the voices of those who contest narratives of non-responsibility offer limited counterweight.[65] Accordingly, one way to equalize the discursive playing field—or, at least, create a more kinetic marketplace of ideas—would be to democratize the conversation by draining the tendentiousness of controlling imagery. An alternate baseline of child soldiers as circumscribed actors might facilitate this outcome by encouraging a more diversified, inclusive, and heterogeneous approach to their reintegration as individuals.

(c) Summary

Transnational activists are able to justify their approaches by gesturing to international legal frameworks while at the same time elastically stretching the content of those frameworks. In the end, and notwithstanding the details of the actual evidentiary record, the direction of both international human rights law and international humanitarian law is not oriented toward contemplating individual child soldiers as occupying interstitial positions on a spectrum of circumscribed action.

(ii) International Criminal Law

International criminal law involves the substantive and procedural frameworks that proscribe core crimes of concern to the global community within international

---

[64] Susan Shepler, *Book Review*, 17(3) CHILDREN, YOUTH AND ENVIRONMENTS (2007) (on file with the author). The position of the Office of the Special Representative of the UN Secretary-General for Children and Armed Conflict is indicative: "Any TRC [truth and reconciliation commission] needs to consider the prevailing view that child soldiers are victims rather than perpetrators... TRCs operate at their best for children where the purpose is to establish the truth, rather than make a finding of guilt or responsibility on the part of the child." CHILDREN AND JUSTICE, *supra* note 61, at 44.

[65] Legal scholar Harold Hongju Koh has undertaken seminal work on transnational norm entrepreneurs, identified as individuals or, mainly, non-governmental entities that help domesticate internationalized norms. Transnational norm entrepreneurs do so in part by mobilizing popular opinion and encouraging like-minded organizations within targeted states. Transnational norm entrepreneurs also tend to promote their cause as a universal right or obligation instead of derivative of a particular state or contingent upon a particular culture.

courts and tribunals. Although "the last word on the age of responsibility in international criminal law has not yet been said,"[66] a determined push has emerged to—*de facto* or *de jure*—exclude persons under the age of eighteen at the time of the alleged offense from the criminal jurisdiction of international or internationalized institutions prosecuting extraordinary international crimes. This push has acquired considerable traction among states, UN agencies, and global civil society, as well as those lawyers who operate and staff these institutions.

Contemporary international criminal procedure may afford certain protective measures to children when they participate in proceedings as witnesses or victims, including the possibility of *in camera* hearings, assignment of support personnel, use of screens or shielding devices, and exemptions from solemn declaration requirements. Judges balance these measures with the accused's right to a fair and public hearing. International criminal tribunals are to generally operate in a manner that is sensitive to children. Preferentially, staff members ought to have experience in dealing with juvenile victimization and justice. International criminal law considers the youth of an adult offender as a mitigating factor in sentencing. These aspects mostly are uncontroversial.

(a) From Nuremberg and Tokyo to the *Ad Hoc* Tribunals

In the aftermath of the Second World War, the International Military Tribunal (IMT) and a variety of other institutions, including the Nuremberg Military Tribunals (NMTs), concerned themselves with the crimes of Nazi Germany. No mention was made in the Nuremberg Statute, Control Council Law No. 10, or Control Council Ordinance No. 7 of the age at which criminal responsibility began; in any event, "no one under the age of 18 was charged with any crime under any of these three jurisdictional provisions."[67] Although the IMT prosecuted Baldur von Schirach for *inter alia* his use of the Hitler Youth, it did not address crimes committed by the youth themselves. The International Military Tribunal for the Far East (Tokyo Tribunal) conducted trials of the Japanese leadership. The Tokyo Tribunal did not prosecute any minors.

Other adjudicative bodies did on rare occasion prosecute minors.[68] For example, in *Bommer*, a 1947 French case adjudged by the Permanent Military Tribunal at Metz, two sisters aged between sixteen and eighteen were sentenced as war criminals to terms of four months' imprisonment each, while a third sister under the age of sixteen was discretionarily "free[d] . . . from responsibility on account of her age," of the war crime of receiving stolen goods belonging to French citizens

---

[66] Roger S. Clark and Otto Triffterer, *Article 26: Exclusion of jurisdiction over persons under eighteen,* in COMMENTARY ON THE ROME STATUTE OF THE INTERNATIONAL CRIMINAL COURT: OBSERVERS' NOTES, ARTICLE BY ARTICLE 771, 774 (Otto Triffterer ed., 2nd edn, 2008).

[67] *Id.* at 771 (citation omitted).

[68] Peter Finn, *The boy from the battlefield: Youngest Guantanamo detainee awaits military trial on war crimes charges,* WASH. POST (February 10, 2010) at A01, A08 (noting, according to a US official, "that the United States and Britain prosecuted Nazi minors in military tribunals after World War II, and that some were imprisoned").

(the acts under French municipal law were treated as tantamount to war crimes).[69] Their parents were convicted and sentenced to eighteen months' imprisonment on charges of theft of, and receiving, stolen goods. This Military Tribunal's approach to the three minors based itself in French municipal law.

For several decades following the Second World War, international criminal law largely remained silent on the question of the penal responsibility of minors for extraordinary international crimes.[70] Eminent commentators Roger Clark and Otto Triffterer note that "the 1948 Genocide Convention, the 1950 Nuremberg principles, the 1951 and 1954 ILC Draft Codes, the 1951 and 1953 ILC Draft Statutes as well as the 1949 Geneva Conventions, their 1977 Additional Protocols, and the 1972 Bellagio-Wingspread Drafts did not even mention this aspect."[71] The constitutive statutes of the International Criminal Tribunal for the former Yugoslavia (ICTY, 1993) and the International Criminal Tribunal for Rwanda (ICTR, 1994) similarly offer no guidance regarding the age of criminal responsibility. The ICTY and ICTR were established on an *ad hoc* basis by UN Security Council resolutions. The ICTY proceeds against persons responsible for serious violations of international humanitarian law committed in the territory of the former Yugoslavia since 1991; the ICTR against persons responsible for violations committed in 1994 in Rwanda and neighboring countries. Neither the ICTY nor the ICTR has prosecuted anyone under the age of eighteen at the time of the alleged offense. The ICTR Prosecutor decided "that children aged 14 to 18 would not be tried by the ICTR or called as witnesses to testify."[72] The work of the *ad hoc* tribunals now is drawing to a close. National institutions in Rwanda have tried persons under the age of eighteen at the time of the genocide for their involvement therein.

(b) International Criminal Court

The Rome Conference adopted the Rome Statute on July 17, 1998. The Rome Statute, which came into effect on July 1, 2002, establishes the ICC. The Rome Statute now claims 114 states parties. The ICC is a permanent institution. It has jurisdiction over genocide, crimes against humanity, war crimes, and aggression. The Rome Statute defines the first three crimes, but not the crime of aggression. In 2010, however, the Review Conference by consensus adopted a proposed amendment to the Rome Statute that includes a definition of the crime of aggression and conditions under which the ICC could exercise jurisdiction with respect thereto. Eventual exercise of jurisdiction, however, remains contingent upon a number of future developments.

---

[69] United Nations War Crimes Commission, *supra* note 19, at Vol. IX, 62, 66 (1949).

[70] One scholar has interpreted this silence as suggesting that "[t]raditionnellement, il semble que la justice pénale internationale considère que les enfants ne sont pas justiciables...." Jean-Baptiste Jeangène Vilmer, Réparer L'irréparable: Les Réparations Aux Victimes Devant la Cour Pénale Internationale 37–38 (2009).

[71] Clark and Triffterer, *supra* note 66, at 771.

[72] Children and Truth Commissions, *supra* note 54, at 17 (citation omitted).

In Article 26, the Rome Statute straightforwardly provides that: "The Court [ICC] shall have no jurisdiction over any person who was under the age of 18 at the time of the alleged commission of a crime."[73] Article 26 appears in Part 3 ("General Principles of Criminal Law") of the Rome Statute. It applies to persons who have not completed the eighteenth year of life at the time of commission of an alleged offense.[74] Article 26 represents a purely chronological, and entirely irrefutable, jurisdictional exclusion. The accused's actual maturity, capacity, knowledge, or intent is irrelevant. This jurisdictional exclusion applies to all minors, regardless of whether they were a child soldier or allegedly committed the act in the context of armed conflict. Article 26 blocks not only prosecution, but also investigation.

In contrast, as Chapter 5 will explore in greater detail, children (including former child soldiers) have the opportunity actively to serve as witnesses at the ICC. They may participate as victims in the proceedings against an adult accused. They may receive reparations.

At its core, Article 26 is a procedural provision; it does not constitute general substantive international law.[75] It excludes only the ICC's jurisdiction. Article 26 does not deem persons under the age of eighteen as lacking in responsibility for atrocity crimes generally under international law nor under governing national law. Article 26 was arrived at as a "jurisdictional solution,"[76] not as a jurisprudential solution. It elicited only brief discussion at the Rome Conference, where delegates were reluctant to engage with the conundrum of children as atrocity perpetrators. Delegates did not wish to invest energy in such a discussion, especially given the differences among national jurisdictions as to respective ages of criminal

---

[73] Rome Statute of the International Criminal Court, 2187 U.N.T.S. 90 (July 17, 1998, entered into force July 1, 2002). Regarding childhood being defined as below the age of eighteen, *see also* ICC Elements of the Crimes, U.N. Doc. PCNICC/2000/1/Add.2 (2000), Art. 6(e) (crime of genocide by forcibly transferring children). For a detailed treatment of the negotiation history of Art. 26, *see* Clark and Triffterer, *supra* note 66, at 772–775.

[74] Clark and Triffterer, *supra* note 66, at 776. "When the perpetrator needs more than one act to fulfill all material and mental elements of the crime, the last one is decisive for triggering or not triggering ... jurisdiction ...." *Id.*

[75] *Id.* at 775 (but also noting that Art. 26 "regulates an aspect of substantive criminal law from its procedural side ... thus showing the close connection between these two fields") (citation omitted). An ICTY Trial Chamber interpreted Art. 26 as being jurisdictional in nature and held that the proposition that minors lack criminal responsibility under conventional or customary international law was "completely unfounded." Prosecutor v. Orić, Case No. IT-03-68-T (ICTY Trial Chamber, June 30, 2006) ¶ 400. The case against Orić, an adult, involved the principle of superior command responsibility. Among a number of acts for which Orić purportedly was responsible was the conduct of an unidentified youth "between 16 and 20 years of age" who, on an unspecified date in early February 1993, had murdered a detainee. *Id.* at ¶ 398. The evidence did not establish the youth to be under eighteen at the relevant time. The defense submitted that there could be no criminal liability for a war crime committed by an individual under the age of eighteen. This submission was rejected. The *Orić* case, however, involved proof of the criminal act as an element of the charges against an adult defendant on grounds of superior responsibility. The youth was neither charged nor prosecuted. The Trial Chamber noted: "What is relevant for this case is not the age of the perpetrator, but the alleged acts or omissions of the Srebrenica military police to prevent this incident." *Id.* at ¶ 400. The Trial Chamber convictions ultimately were overturned on different grounds by the Appeals Chamber, which acquitted Orić in 2008. Prosecutor v. Orić, Case No. IT-03-68-A (ICTY Appeals Chamber, July 3, 2008).

[76] William A. Schabas, AN INTRODUCTION TO THE INTERNATIONAL CRIMINAL COURT 72 (3rd edn, 2007) (citing the Working Group on General Principles).

responsibility. In addition, Rome Conference delegates evoked concerns about resource constraints, curial competence regarding juvenile justice, sentencing issues, and the ability to provide specialized detention facilities for juveniles and properly trained staff.

Rome Conference delegates also felt that children never could meet gravity requirements. That said, the admissibility framework of the Rome Statute already serves to exclude cases of insufficient gravity. Hence, the value-added of Article 26 on this particular aspect seems uncertain. Determining the gravity of acts of extraordinary international crimes remains profoundly undertheorized. For some victims, egregious violence committed at the local level by trusted neighbors may be as grave as administrative massacre orchestrated by distant high-level political operatives.

When its provenance is deracinated, then, Article 26 reveals a much more disappointing—albeit generalizable—orientation, to wit, disinterest in or queasy discomfort among international lawmakers with the reality that children do undertake acts of atrocity. As legal scholar Steven Freeland aptly observes: "It is almost as if the drafters of the Rome Statute would prefer that a consideration of this important aspect of the shameful problem of [c]hild [s]oldiers be delegated elsewhere."[77] Assumptions regarding child soldiers as faultless passive victims legitimize this somewhat otiose avoidance of a thorny issue.

International lobbying efforts to protect children influenced the Rome Conference. Matthew Happold reports that "[t]he NGO Caucus on Children's Rights in the ICC had called for the [Rome] Statute to specify a minimum age at which individuals could be held criminally responsible for crimes within the Court's jurisdiction, which they argued should be eighteen."[78] Max du Plessis also locates "lobbying by child rights advocates" in the development of Article 26.[79] The American Non Governmental Organizations Coalition for the International Criminal Court directly identifies Article 26 as instantiating several aspects of the CRC, including primary consideration of the best interests of the child.[80] The ICC's jurisdictional exclusion framework therefore bridges to substantive elements of international human rights law.[81]

---

[77] Freeland, *supra* note 7, at 51.

[78] Matthew Happold, *The Age of Criminal Responsibility for International Crimes under International Law*, *in* INTERNATIONAL CRIMINAL ACCOUNTABILITY AND THE RIGHTS OF CHILDREN 69, 77 (Karin Arts and Vesselin Popovski eds, 2006) (footnote omitted).

[79] Max du Plessis, *Children under International Criminal Law*, 13(2) AFRICAN SECURITY REVIEW 103, 110 (2004); *see also* No Peace Without Justice and UNICEF Innocenti Research Centre, INTERNATIONAL CRIMINAL JUSTICE AND CHILDREN 54 (2002) [hereinafter INTERNATIONAL CRIMINAL JUSTICE AND CHILDREN].

[80] The American Non Governmental Organizations Coalition for the International Criminal Court, *The International Criminal Court and Children's Rights* 1, *available at* <http://www.iccnow .org/documents/FS-AMICC-ICCnChildRights.pdf> (also positing "participation in the ICC [as] a concrete step in the fulfillment of many obligations incorporated into the [CRC] and its Protocols").

[81] *Cf.* Clark and Triffterer, *supra* note 66, at 773 (noting discussion in the ICC Preparatory Committee of the ICCPR, European Convention on Human Rights, Inter-American Convention on Human Rights, and CRC).

Clark and Triffterer suggest that it remains open for national jurisdictions to prosecute alleged child perpetrators in cases of crimes proscribed by the Rome Statute and, relatedly, that for these jurisdictions to do so meshes with the ICC's complementarity principle. This principle, anchored in Article 17 of the Rome Statute, provides that national jurisdictions shall have the first opportunity to investigate and prosecute allegations of Rome Statute crimes. It is only if national jurisdictions are unable or unwilling genuinely to investigate or prosecute that the ICC itself would assume jurisdiction. Even in situations where the facts might so justify, however, it is doubtful that states whose atrocities have become subject to ICC investigation or prosecution actually would deploy national criminal justice institutions to criminally investigate or prosecute current or former child soldiers. This is so for a variety of reasons. States that are keen to retain jurisdiction in the face of ICC interventions have the incentive to mimic internationally accepted approaches in order to minimize the chances that ICC judges will find their domestic institutions wanting. For those states that self-refer internal situations to the ICC, it still remains rational to emulate the approaches of the Rome Statute in domestic law so as to look attractive to donors. Rome Statute approaches, whether procedural or substantive, have centrifugal pull as a template. The Rome Statute plays a powerful trendsetting role.[82] The ICC is the flagship institution in the field. A state that prosecutes children nationally for acts of atrocity undeniably would ruffle enlightened international sensibilities. Hence, the fact that Article 26 does not formally prohibit other institutions, whether national or local, from prosecuting children for international crimes does not mean that other institutions ever would prosecute them. Such initiatives would find no support among transnational norm entrepreneurs; ostensibly, these initiatives would be condemned. This outcome is not disappointing, to be sure, given the problematic upshot of criminally prosecuting former child soldiers on atrocity-related charges.

It is facile to surmise that Article 26 is a vapid provision to be consigned to the dust-bin of political compromises and, hence, unworthy of study or devoid of longitudinal effect. The political compromises of today can become tomorrow's substantive international law. In this vein, Paris Principle 8.6, which instructs that "[c]hildren should not be prosecuted by an international court or tribunal," begins by explicitly noting that "[t]he Rome Statute ... states that the [ICC] shall have no jurisdiction over any person who was under 18 at the time of the alleged commission of a crime." Article 26 has been described as "affirm[ing] an emerging consensus that international courts and tribunals should not prosecute children under 18 for international crimes."[83] This consensus, in turn, trickles into national

---

[82] *See generally* Marieke Wierda, STOCKTAKING: COMPLEMENTARITY 1, ICTJ Briefing, The Rome Statute Review Conference (June 2010, Kampala) ("The [Rome] Statute has inspired changes to more than 55 domestic legal systems (with legislation pending in 40 more).") (citation omitted); Géraldine Mattioli and Anneke van Woudenberg, *Global Catalyst for National Prosecutions? The ICC in the Democratic Republic of Congo, in* COURTING CONFLICT? JUSTICE, PEACE AND THE ICC IN AFRICA 55, 59–60 (Nicholas Waddell and Phil Clark eds, 2008) ("In recent war crimes cases before military courts [in the DRC], judges made explicit references to the Rome Statute in their decisions. ... [T]hese instances show an interest in incorporating concepts of international criminal law into domestic jurisprudence.").

[83] CHILDREN AND TRUTH COMMISSIONS, *supra* note 54, at 18.

and local jurisdictions. Paris Principle 8.3 provides that "[a]dvocacy should be directed at states to ratify the Rome Statute...and to adopt its provisions in national law." This exhortation does not limit itself to legislation that incorporates the Rome Statute domestically as part of the treaty ratification process. It also concerns national initiatives to redress atrocity over which the ICC would lack jurisdiction. The value of Rome Statute provisions as guidelines of how optimally to do things is thereby revealed. For example, in a 2009 intervention in Bangladesh regarding national attempts to bring perpetrators of war crimes from the country's 1971 conflict to justice, Human Rights Watch—noting *inter alia* Article 26— recommended that "[a] similar provision should be added to the International Crimes (Tribunals) Act."[84]

In sum, Article 26 indicates, is consonant with, and contributes to transnationalized imagery of faultlessness, passivity, and victimhood that animates the intersection between children and penal responsibility for atrocity crimes.

(c) Special Court for Sierra Leone

The express mandate of the SCSL is to prosecute persons who bear the greatest responsibility for serious violations of international humanitarian law and Sierra Leonean law committed in Sierra Leone since November 30, 1996. The SCSL Statute limits the SCSL's jurisdiction to defendants who were fifteen years of age or older at the time of the alleged offense.[85] The SCSL Statute accords special considerations to "juvenile offenders," to wit, defendants under the age of eighteen at the time of the alleged offense. Pursuant to SCSL Statute Article 7(1), should any juvenile offender "come before the [SCSL], he or she shall be treated with dignity and a sense of worth, taking into account his or her young age and the desirability of promoting his or her rehabilitation, reintegration into and assumption of a constructive role in society, and in accordance with international human rights standards, in particular the rights of the child."[86] The SCSL Statute exempts juvenile offenders from incarceration.[87] Instead, the SCSL "shall order any of the following: care guidance and supervision orders, community service orders, counselling, foster care, correctional, educational and vocational training programmes, approved schools and, as appropriate, any programmes of disarmament, demobilization and reintegration or programmes of child protection agencies."[88] When it comes to the overall

---

[84] Letter to Prime Minister Sheikh Hasina Re: International Crimes (Tribunals) Act, *available at* <http://www.hrw.org/en/news/2009/07/08/letter-prime-minister-sheikh-hasina-re-international-crimes-tribunals-act> (noting also that: "The Rome statute and the ICC's corresponding jurisprudence reflect international norms, which Bangladesh, as a signatory to the Rome statute, should follow.").

[85] Statute of the Special Court for Sierra Leone, U.N-Sierra Leone (January 16, 2002), Art. 7(1), 2178 U.N.T.S. 145 [hereinafter SCSL Statute].

[86] The establishment of a separate "juvenile chamber" initially had been proposed, but was removed from the final SCSL Statute. INTERNATIONAL CRIMINAL JUSTICE AND CHILDREN, *supra* note 79, at 58 (noting also that this removal "underscor[ed] the fact that it is unlikely that anyone below the age of 18 at the time of the alleged commission of the crime will be indicted by the [SCSL]").

[87] SCSL Statute, *supra* note 85, Arts 7(2), 19(1).

[88] *Id.* Art. 7(2); *see also id.* Art. 15(5).

composition of judicial appointments and prosecutorial (and investigatory) staff, the SCSL Statute requires that consideration be given to experience in juvenile justice.

The government of Sierra Leone and the UN jointly established the SCSL in 2000. The Sierra Leonean government had initially pushed for children under the age of eighteen not to be collectively excluded from criminal prosecutions.[89] In Sierra Leone, after all, "[m]any of the worst mutilations were committed by aggressive and violent 16- and 17-year olds, and the populace demanded that they be punished."[90] At the time, domestic criminal law in Sierra Leone excluded only children below the age of ten from criminal responsibility (since superseded by the 2007 Child Rights Act). In the end, Olusanya describes the SCSL approach as a "compromise between two competing interests:"

On the one hand were the Government of Sierra Leone and representatives of Sierra Leone civil society who wished to see a process of judicial accountability for child combatants presumed responsible for the crimes falling within the jurisdiction of the Court, whilst on the other hand were international and national non-governmental organisations responsible for child-care and rehabilitation programmes in Sierra Leone, who objected to any kind of judicial accountability for children below 18 years of age for fear that such a process would place at risk the entire rehabilitation programme so painstakingly achieved.[91]

In debates that occurred in the UN Security Council at the time, states did not surrender to global civil society lobbying and advocacy efforts to relieve persons under the age of eighteen from the SCSL's jurisdiction. Neither did UN officials who, in fact, brokered a compromise. The SCSL's law-in-practice, however, fails to reflect this compromise. The SCSL's first Chief Prosecutor, distinguished American military lawyer David Crane, promptly and unequivocally stated that he never would prosecute children under the age of eighteen, including child soldiers, *inter alia* because they do not bear the greatest responsibility.[92] Indeed, none have been prosecuted. In no positivistic sense does the exercise of independent policymaking discretion by international prosecutors make international law. States and international organizations with lawmaking capacity, however, did not resist Chief Prosecutor Crane's position regarding the unacceptability of prosecuting an individual who was below the age of eighteen at the time of the alleged offense. Global civil society welcomed it. To this end, despite treaty contemplation of the prosecution of juvenile offenders, and fractious debate leading up to the inclusion of those textual compromises, the actual *de facto* practice of the SCSL converges with the formal law of the ICC with regard to alleged perpetrators under the age of eighteen. In the end, poignant questions regarding the role of children in the commission of

---

[89] Barbara Crossette, *Sierra Leone to Try Juveniles Separately in U.N. Tribunal Plan*, N.Y. TIMES (October 6, 2000).

[90] du Plessis, *supra* note 79, at 109–110.

[91] Olusanya, *supra* note 7, at 93–94; *see also* David M. Rosen, *Who Is a Child? The Legal Conundrum of Child Soldiers*, 25 CONN. J. INT'L L. 81, 114 (2009) (reporting that "Sierra Leone's UN Ambassador, Ibrahim Kamara, rejected the idea that all child soldiers were traumatized victims...") (citation omitted).

[92] Press Release, Special Court for Sierra Leone, Public Affairs Office, *Special Court Prosecutor Says He Will Not Prosecute Children* (November 2, 2002).

atrocity thereby have become banished from the international judicial sphere despite evident national desire to retain such conversations within that sphere.[93]

(d) Other Internationalized Tribunals

The Special Panels for Serious Crimes (District Court, Dili, Timor-Leste)—a hybrid international/national tribunal—operated from 2002 until funding ran out in 2005. At that point, the Special Panels had prosecuted eighty-seven defendants (eighty-four convictions and three acquittals). This number represents only one-quarter of all indictees (the other three-quarters still remain at large, overwhelmingly in Indonesia). The Special Panels were mandated to prosecute crimes that had occurred in the wake of a 1999 pro-independence plebiscite in Timor-Leste, when Indonesian-backed militia forces had committed widespread attacks against civilian populations. The Special Panels had jurisdiction over both ordinary common crimes and extraordinary international crimes.

Section 45 of UN Transitional Administration in East Timor (UNTAET) Regulation 2000/30 on Transitional Rules of Criminal Procedure, applicable to courts in Timor-Leste with jurisdiction to decide cases pursuant to UNTAET regulations, defines a minor as any person below eighteen years of age.[94] Section 45, however, adds that only a minor under the age of twelve years "shall be deemed incapable of committing a crime and shall not be subjected to criminal proceedings." In fact, minors "between 12 and 16 years of age may be prosecuted . . . for any offence which under applicable law constitutes murder, rape, or a crime of violence in which serious injury is inflicted upon a victim." According to Section 45.4, a minor over sixteen years of age may be prosecuted following ordinary rules of criminal procedure. Section 45.2 stipulates that the relevant time for determining the age of a potential defendant was "the time at which the suspected crime was committed." Given its contemplation of prosecutions against minors over the age of twelve for crimes against humanity, Section 45 is a most unusual provision.[95]

To this end, *de jure*, the Special Panels had jurisdiction over minors. Unlike the situation with the SCSL, one minor initially was brought forward in the case of *Prosecutor v. X*.[96] X, aged fourteen at the time of committing the impugned acts (the killing of three young men in the Passabe massacre), was charged with crimes

---

[93] Diane Marie Amann, *Calling Children to Account: The Proposal for a Juvenile Chamber in the Special Court for Sierra Leone*, 29 PEPP. L. REV. 167, 179 (2001) ("Sierra Leoneans live in a society in which childhood cannot exist, in which responsibility must be assumed at an early age. The crimes at issue defy imagination. In this context, it is not difficult to understand why the people of Sierra Leone would want to hold war criminals accountable without regard to age.") (citation omitted).

[94] United Nations Transitional Administration in East Timor (UNTAET) Regulation No. 2000/30 on Transitional Rules of Criminal Procedure (September 25, 2000), ss. 1(q), 45.1, *available at* <http://www.eastimorlawjournal.org/UNTAETLaw/Regulations/Reg2000-30.pdf>.

[95] Section 45.3 provides that detention or imprisonment of minors should be used only as a measure of last resort and for the shortest appropriate period of time. Overall, s. 45 grants extensive due process protections to juvenile defendants.

[96] Judicial System Monitoring Programme, *The Case of X: A Child Prosecuted for Crimes against Humanity* (Dili, Timor-Leste, 2005).

against humanity (extermination and attempted extermination) and, in the alternative, murder under Article 338 of the Indonesian Penal Code. Murder in this alternative regard is a serious criminal offense, but is not a crime against humanity. X's case was resolved through a plea bargain on the first day of trial in 2002. The Prosecutor amended the indictment to state only the ordinary murder charge to which X pleaded guilty. X, who had already served eleven months in pre-trial detention, was sentenced to twelve months' imprisonment. Consequently, even though the Special Panels had jurisdiction over persons over the age of twelve for extraordinary international crimes, the one instance where a minor was indicted for crimes against humanity resolved itself through a guilty plea that placed the minor outside the formal framework of international criminal law. No trial, sentence, or confession to an extraordinary international crime took place.

The case of *Prosecutor* v. *X* has elicited negative commentary by observers and transnational advocates over fair trial concerns, the nature of X's guilty plea, and X's status as a minor.[97] It is the only case of a minor actually charged before an international or internationalized tribunal. However, both Prosecutor and defense agreed to drop the crimes against humanity charge and the Special Panels, by accepting the admission of guilt, affirmed this agreement. To this end, the practice of the Special Panels is not one in which minors actually were tried (or convicted) for extraordinary international crimes; in the single instance where this could have happened, such an outcome was averted. Why? Judicial economy and the drive to secure a conviction certainly played a role. This aversion, however, also comports with the *de facto* reluctance, even when there is *de jure* competence, to actually try minors on charges of extraordinary international crimes.

The War Crimes Chamber in the Court of Bosnia and Herzegovina has jurisdiction over persons starting at the age of fourteen.[98] This institution, although involving international experts, roots in domestic law. Article 8 of Bosnia and Herzegovina's national criminal code precludes criminal accountability for any person under the age of fourteen. For perpetrators between the ages of fourteen and sixteen at the time of the offense, only educational measures may be imposed; for perpetrators aged between sixteen and eighteen at the time of the offense, educational measures may be imposed along with, exceptionally, a punishment of juvenile imprisonment. Long-term imprisonment only is available for persons over the age of twenty-one at the time of committing the offense. To date, the War Crimes Chamber has not invoked its jurisdiction over persons under the age of eighteen.[99]

---

[97] *Id.*; Akakpo, *supra* note 63. X claimed to have been forced to join the militia and to have been assaulted by senior militia members.

[98] Cécile Aptel, *International Criminal Justice and Child Protection*, *in* CHILDREN AND TRANSITIONAL JUSTICE, *supra* note 41, at 67, 102.

[99] *Id.* at 102–103; *see also* E-mail from David Schwendiman, former Deputy Chief Prosecutor and Head of Special Department for War Crimes Prosecutor's Office of Bosnia and Herzegovina (May 28, 2010) (on file with the author).

The enabling instruments of neither the Extraordinary Chambers in the Courts of Cambodia (ECCC)[100] nor the Special Tribunal for Lebanon (STL)[101] mention minority in the context of jurisdiction. The STL has a narrow mandate that focuses on the assassination of Rafik Hariri in which no minors remotely appear to have been implicated. The Khmer Rouge used child soldiers and systematically inflicted human rights violations upon them. However, to date, the ECCC's work has not specifically involved the examination of crimes committed against children. Child soldiers and youthful cadres—often ideologically motivated—in turn perpetrated acts of atrocity throughout Cambodia (notably in Phnom Penh where, in the aftermath of the city's capture, they undertook many summary executions). The conduct of former child soldiers does not figure in the ECCC's work, which involves only senior leadership. When it comes to issues regarding age, the ECCC's concerns gravitate not toward youth, but to the other end of the life cycle. Its proceedings have led to poignantly visible, yet often unanticipated, trauma for elderly men who have testified either for the prosecution or independently as survivors.

(e) Summary

International criminal law as presently constituted does not prohibit the prosecution of persons under the age of eighteen, including child soldiers, at the time of commission of an alleged atrocity offense. Nonetheless, transnational advocacy efforts actively posit that "[b]ased on the Statute of the International Criminal Court, the Special Court for Sierra Leone and the practice of the *ad hoc* tribunals, there is an emerging standard that children under eighteen should not be prosecuted by international courts and tribunals."[102]

This emerging standard serves as a persuasive tool. Its growing force is apparent given the recourse to it to condemn contrarian national practices as unlawful. For example, in her censure of the prosecution of Omar Ahmed Khadr (a Canadian national associated with al-Qaeda as a child) by the United States through a military commission at Guantánamo Bay, Radhika Coomaraswamy—the UN Special

---

[100] Law on the Establishment of the Extraordinary Chambers, with inclusion of amendments as promulgated on 27 October 2004, NS/RKM/1004/006. The ECCC Internal Rules (revised on February 9, 2010) mention minority in the context of Rule 24(2)(f) (a witness under fourteen years old can make a statement without having taken an oath), Rule 25(4) (the statement of a child can be recorded in a manner to reduce traumatization), and Rule 112 (the child of a convicted person may apply for revision of judgment following the death of a convicted person).

[101] S.C. Res. 1757 (2007), U.N. Doc. S/RES/1757 (May 30, 2007).

[102] *Introduction*, *in* CHILDREN AND TRANSITIONAL JUSTICE, *supra* note 41, at xv, xxv–xxvi. Nor do transnational advocacy efforts rooted in interpretations of international law necessarily limit their exhortations only to the jurisdiction of international courts or tribunals. *See*, e.g., Nienke Grossman, *Rehabilitation or Revenge: Prosecuting Child Soldiers for Human Rights Violations*, 38 GEO. J. INT'L L. 323, 342 (2007) ("The Rome Statute and the Optional Protocol to the CRC arguably demonstrate an emerging consensus that children aged fifteen to eighteen should also be shielded from criminal liability."); CHILDREN AND JUSTICE, *supra* note 61, at 35 ("The coming into force of the [Optional Protocol to the CRC] in 2002, which sets the age of active participation in hostilities at 18, has led to a call for the age of criminal responsibility for international crimes to be set at 18.").

Representative for Children and Armed Conflict—noted that "[t]he U.N. position is that children should not be prosecuted for war crimes."[103] According to Michael Wessells, the Office of the Special Representative for Children and Armed Conflict had formerly argued that the SCSL's jurisdiction should include "the most feared young offenders," which contrasts with its current approach that no child, impliedly referencing the international definition of a child as a person under the age of eighteen, should be prosecuted for war crimes; in September 2011, moreover, the Office promulgated among its "key advocacy messages" to "[c]onsider excluding children under 18 from criminal responsibility for crimes committed when associated with armed forces or armed groups."[104] This contrast, further consolidated by recent policy developments, reflects a palpable evolution in legal thinking.

International criminal law's reluctance to exercise jurisdiction over minors is more than just a procedural technicality or admissibility criterion. It is more than just a gravity limitation or leadership requirement. It instrumentalizes, reflects, and contributes to the substantive notion within the international legal imagination that it is unimportant, embarrassing, and unhelpful for child soldiers to answer for their involvement in acts of atrocity in a courtroom. This substantive notion, which is consciously cultivated by much of global civil society, tethers to faultless passive victim imagery. Choices by the international legal imagination to abjure international trials before international institutions, in turn, constrict the range of policy options available to domestic institutions. The international, after all, socializes the domestic.[105]

States retain a diversity of ages of criminal responsibility in their various national legislative instruments. Those post-conflict societies whose atrocities have become subject to international judicialization efforts, however, are being pulled—in terms of policy, law, and practice—toward excluding children under the age of eighteen from assessments of penal responsibility for their alleged commission of acts of extraordinary international criminality. This pull, moreover, transcends courtrooms and jailhouses. In this latter regard, it excessively isolates child soldier returnees from the tough questions that societies must reckon with in order to come to terms with mass violence. For those child soldiers who engage in acts of

---

[103] Finn, *supra* note 68; *see also* Michael Isikoff, *Landmark Gitmo trial puts White House in tight spot*, NBC News (August 10, 2010) (on file with the author) (reporting Coomaraswamy as stating that "[s]ince World War II, no child has been prosecuted for a war crime" and also quoting David Crane, commenting on the Khadr prosecution, as stating that "[n]o child has the *mens rea*—the criminal mind—to commit war crimes" and impliedly referring to children under the age of eighteen); William Glaberson, *A Legal Debate in Guantánamo on Boy Fighters*, N.Y. TIMES (June 3, 2007) (noting that Khadr's defense lawyers argued that evolving legal concepts "require that countries treat child fighters as victims of warfare, rather than war criminals"). In October 2010, Khadr was convicted through a plea bargain on charges that included violation of the laws of war, thereby averting a formal trial. For more information on the *Khadr* case, *see supra* Chapter 1, note 44.

[104] Michael Wessells, CHILD SOLDIERS: FROM VIOLENCE TO PROTECTION 221 (2006, first paperback 2009); CHILDREN AND JUSTICE, *supra* note 61, at 36.

[105] For a sociological approach to compliance with international law that unpacks the notion of acculturation, *see* Ryan Goodman and Derek Jinks, *International Law and State Socialization: Conceptual, Empirical, and Normative Challenges*, 54 DUKE L. J. 983 (2005).

serial atrocity, their role as perpetrators is counterproductively unexplored. Looking ahead, and recognizing the delicacy of the task, this book argues that this aspect should be given greater attention.

(iii) Torsions and Distortions

Minors readily face prosecution and punishment in national legal systems for serious violations of ordinary criminal law. Their capacity, although diminished, is not existentially doubted. Certainly once in the teenage years, they are not presumptively viewed as faultless passive victims. A juxtaposition therefore arises between the treatment of children by the international legal imagination in cases of extraordinary international crimes, on the one hand, and the treatment of children by national jurisdictions in cases of ordinary common crimes, on the other. This juxtaposition does not align with international law's perception of extraordinary international crimes as being of greater gravity than ordinary common crimes.

In the West, retributive attitudes toward youth who commit ordinary common crimes have hardened over the past couple of decades. The delinquent youth has been balefully portrayed, especially in cases of serious violent crime. Correspondingly, restorative and rehabilitative justice initiatives have regressed. At the time of the James Bulger murder, British newspapers "sought to reflect the mood of the nation by labelling the killers variously as 'evil', 'beasts' and 'bastards'. . . . Mr. Justice Moreland said the boys . . . were guilty of an act of 'unparalleled evil and barbarity'."[106] Although in very recent years this regression may have abated somewhat—in part, because of increasing acceptance of neurobiological evidence of adolescent diminished culpability—the delinquent minor in the West still tends to be cast in a decidedly negative light. In the United Kingdom, the child prison population has noticeably declined following Parliament's passage of the 2008 Criminal Justice and Immigration Act, but "the number of children sentenced to long sentences has increased;" specifically, "[s]ince April 2008, there has been a continuous increase in the number of children in custody serving long term sentences as a percentage of the total population."[107] During the 2011 unrest in London, British Prime Minister Cameron, brushing aside structural explanations for youth violence and giving voice to considerable public opinion, admonished rioters (some of whom were teenagers) that: "[I]f you are old enough to commit these crimes, you are old enough to face the punishment."[108] Nor are *les racailles* in Paris viewed as vulnerable victims. The unconstitutionality of the juvenile death penalty in the United States hung on the narrowest of margins—a single vote of a Supreme Court judge in a five to four split. So, too, did the US Supreme Court's 2011 ruling (in a case involving a thirteen year-old special

---

[106] Haroon Siddique, *James Bulger killing: the case history of Jon Venables and Robert Thompson*, THE GUARDIAN (March 3, 2010).

[107] The Howard League for Penal Reform, *Children and long sentences: a briefing* (June 2010), *available at* <http://www.howardleague.org/fileadmin/howard_league/user/pdf/Briefings/Children_and_long_sentences_briefing.pdf>.

[108] *Parliament recalled to tackle riots—David Cameron*, BBC News (August 9, 2011).

education student), that a child's age properly informs the determination of whether a person questioned by police is in custody in the sense that a *Miranda* warning is to be issued.[109] Prosecutorial approaches to Lee Boyd Malvo (the seventeen year-old accomplice of the Washington D.C. sniper) were harsh in light of public outrage. These same publics, however, are steeped in compassion for the distant child soldier, whose crimes are constructed as entirely compelled by others.

This apparent paradox is rendered somewhat intelligible in light of the fact that many child soldiers are subject to extensive brutalities. To be sure, poverty, lack of opportunity, peer pressure, addiction, socialization into violence, and abuse mold the backgrounds of many youthful perpetrators of ordinary common crime. Acts of atrocity, however, typically occur in a context characterized by situational and structural forces that exceed those present in the context in which serious ordinary common crimes tend to occur. Nonetheless, this paradox also belies a deeper subtext. Political discourse may demonize violent children in Western societies because it is difficult for such discourse to fully pathologize their broader social environments insofar as those, too, are Western. Pathologizing those environments means that structural elements of society become responsible, whether directly or indirectly, for violent juvenile delinquency. On the other hand, it may be comparatively easy for Westerners to cling to the apparent faultlessness of far-away exoticized child soldiers insofar as the source of their violence can be apportioned to customary social structures that Westerners (and, in close connection thereto, transnational norm entrepreneurs) already tend to view with reserve and, as a result, readily can pathologize. In short, the distant child soldier is viewed as a faultless victim of a malignant broader social environment. The close-at-hand child criminal is viewed as an aberrant delinquent, or idiosyncratically particularized as the product of a blameworthy dysfunctional family, within an otherwise salutary broader social environment.

The traction of the faultlessness of the child soldier is inconsistent. It also depends upon who, exactly, constitutes the aggrieved community. A truly problematic double-standard emerges. Global civil society is not the source of this double-standard. States are. The faultless passive victim image inures much more robustly to the benefit of children implicated in extraordinary international crimes against interests or populations *outside* the centers of global politics than those who target interests or populations *within* those centers. Whereas powerful countries can better resist international pressures, weaker countries cannot, thereby leading to uneven norm internalization. Transnational conceptions of faultlessness do not fully reach those children who inflict atrocious acts, such as terrorist bombings, against Westerners. Whereas the child perpetrator targeting Africans in new wars tends to be cast as a mindless captive of purposeless violence, the child perpetrator targeting Westerners tends to be cast as an intentional author of purposeful violence.

[109] J.D.B. v. North Carolina (No. 09-11121, slip op. (June 16, 2011)).

In addition to the broadly publicized Khadr case, the conviction in the United States of Abduwali Abdukhadir Muse, a Somali minor and "pirate," presents as an example of this dichotomy. Muse was initially charged *inter alia* with piracy as defined by the law of nations in relation to the seizure of the *Maersk Alabama*, a United States-flagged ship, in April 2009 and the kidnapping of its captain.[110] Muse lacks birth records. His lawyers allege that he was about fifteen or sixteen years old at the time of the offense.[111] Muse entered a guilty plea in May 2010 to lesser charges (hijacking, hostage-taking, kidnapping, and conspiracy), thereby avoiding a piracy conviction which carries a mandatory life sentence. Still, Muse faced an agreed-upon sentencing range of twenty-seven to nearly thirty-four years. Although his lawyers argued that his youth justified sentencing him at the minimum of the specified range, prosecutors described Muse as extraordinarily depraved, violent, and an undisputed leader. As a result, they urged a sentence at the highest end. On the question of sentencing, Muse's lawyers evoked a similar narrative to that applicable to child soldiers: that is, "like other young Somalis, [Muse] had been driven into piracy by the abysmal conditions in his war-torn country."[112] Muse, they submitted, grew up "in desperate poverty and was almost always hungry," and became "caught up in the piracy networks" while a young teenager.[113] These submissions fell flat. Muse's youth proved irrelevant to questions of his culpability and inconsequential to his punishment. On February 16, 2011, Muse was sentenced to the very maximum of the stipulated range.

The intersection of international refugee law with child soldiers also is telling. The grant of protected refugee status hinges upon proof that an applicant has faced past persecution, or has a well-founded fear of future persecution, on account of race, religion, nationality, membership in a particular social group, or political opinion.[114] By virtue of Article 1F(a) of the Refugee Convention, however, any person in respect to whom there are serious reasons for considering has "committed a crime against peace, a war crime, or a crime against humanity" is excludable from eligibility for refugee status.[115] Article 1F(a) neither contains any minimum age requirement in its obligation to deny refugee status to persons who would otherwise satisfy the refugee definition, nor does it distinguish between adults and children.

---

[110] United States of America v. Abduwali Abdukhadir Muse, Complaint (April 21, 2009) (on file with the author).

[111] After hearing all the available evidence, Judge Peck declared Muse to be an adult and that he would be prosecuted as such. Benjamin Weiser, *Pirate Suspect Charged as Adult in New York*, N.Y. Times (April 22, 2009).

[112] Benjamin Weiser, *Leniency of Sentence for Somali Hijacker Is at Issue*, N.Y. Times (February 13, 2011).

[113] *Id.*

[114] Child soldiers may experience difficulty to fit in a specified protected class. *See, e.g.,* Lukwago v. Ashcroft, 329 F.3d 157 (3d Cir., 2003) (US federal appeals court opaquely declining to find that abducted child soldiers in Northern Uganda were a particular social group on account of their age, but finding that the class of former child soldiers who have escaped from the LRA fits within the remit of a particular social group with a well-founded fear of future persecution by the LRA (citing also the applicant's imputed anti-LRA political opinion)).

[115] Convention relating to the Status of Refugees, 189 U.N.T.S. 150 (July 28, 1951, entered into force April 22, 1954).

At the national level, contemporary exclusionary provisions—which, emulating the Convention, often include some sort of reasonable apprehension that an applicant has committed war crimes or crimes against humanity—overall do not mandate the exemption of persons under the age of eighteen at the time of the impugned act. No presumption ascribes faultless victim status to former child soldiers in this context; nor guarantees to liberate the child soldier from the consequences of prior acts. Depending on individual circumstances, and the specifics of the national legislative scheme in question, some former child soldiers reasonably believed to have been implicated in acts of atrocity may be granted refugee or other protected asylum status. But this outcome arises from careful individual balancing of a nexus of factors, in which age might figure.[116] No presumption arises to suspend Article 1F(a)—or comparable national analogs such as the "persecutor bar" in the United States[117]—singularly or determinatively because of age.

Former child soldiers implicated in crimes against humanity or war crimes have been excluded from refugee status.[118] Case-law in Canada, as succinctly summarized by Joseph Rikhof, is indicative.[119] An applicant who was a member of a terrorist organization in Turkey between the ages of eleven and thirteen could be denied asylum in Canada if the applicant's having "knowledge of some of the acts of violence"[120] were to be established. One minor from El Salvador was denied asylum in Canada because he had voluntarily enlisted in state fighting forces to avenge atrocities committed by insurgents against his family members;[121] another Salvadoran national, who had joined the army at the age of thirteen and rose to the level of sergeant, also was excluded;[122] and yet another Salvadoran applicant, forcibly recruited into the army (but who ultimately deserted after having served as an interrogator), also was excluded from refugee status.[123] In 2005, the Canadian Federal Court of Appeal affirmed the deportation of a minor who had distributed propaganda for a terrorist organization in Iran while between the ages of sixteen and

---

[116] United Nations High Commissioner for Refugees, *Advisory Opinion* (September 12, 2005) (referencing *inter alia* age, maturity, voluntariness and length of service, individual responsibility, duress, involuntary intoxication, promotion based on commission of crimes, education, trauma suffered, and treatment by military personnel). The US Board of Immigration Appeals has moved toward this approach in some nonprecedential, unpublished decisions involving child soldiers. Bryan Lonegan, *Sinners or Saints: Child Soldiers and the Persecutor Bar to Asylum after* Negusie v. Holder, 31 B.C. Third World L. J. 71, 81–82 (2011). France has pursued such an approach to a different subsection of Art. 1F (the serious non-political crime exclusion).

[117] The US Department of Homeland Security has turned to this bar, albeit not always successfully or consistently, to oppose refugee status for former child soldiers. For critique, *see* Lonegan, *supra* note 116, at 74 ("Barring child soldiers from asylum protection penalizes them for having been the victims of a crime and undercuts all of the United States' efforts to protect them.").

[118] Grover, *'Child Soldiers' as 'Non-Combatants', supra* note 17, at 61 ("[C]hildren suspected of having committed an international crime are often refused asylum.") (citation omitted).

[119] Joseph Rikhof, *Child soldiers: Should they be punished?*, Sword & Scale: Canadian Bar Association National Military Law Section Newsletter 5–6 (May 2009), *available at* <http://www.cba.org/CBA/newsletters-sections/pdf/05-09-military_2.pdf>.

[120] *Id.* at 5 (citing Saridag v. Canada (1994) 85 F.T.R. 307).

[121] *Id.* (citing Ramirez v. Canada [1992] 2 F.C. 306).

[122] *Id.* (citing Penate v. Canada [1994] 2 F.C. 79).

[123] *Id.* (citing Gracias-Luna v. Canada, IMM-1139-92 (May 25, 1995)).

eighteen.[124] The Canadian jurisprudence is not uniform, however. Rikhof notes a case in which a minor from El Salvador was granted asylum despite the exclusion clause "as a result of a number of factors, including but not exclusively age."[125] Factors included forcible conscription at the age of sixteen, brief service, and desertion as soon as it became feasible to do so. The court in that case opined that: "A person forcibly conscripted into the military and who on one occasion witnesse[d] the torture of a prisoner while on assigned guard duty cannot be considered at law to have committed a crime against humanity."[126]

Canadian authorities, nevertheless, even have exhibited reticence to admit former child soldiers into the country on short-term visas. For example, Kabba Williams, who had been abducted into the RUF in 1991, had been denied a visitor's visa to enter Canada for the benign purpose of speaking on a panel at the University of Alberta in 2008. The Canadian immigration officer reportedly denied the application on the basis that there were reasonable grounds to believe that Williams had committed a war crime, genocide, or crime against humanity during the Sierra Leonean conflict. The immigration officer's decision, initially supported by the executive, ultimately was reversed when a new Minister took over the portfolio. That said, the new Minister only issued Williams a special permit (granted to persons otherwise inadmissible to Canada) instead of a regular visitor's visa, thereby retaining the possibility that he might still be considered a war criminal. A media report faulted the immigration officer's failure to "take[] into account international law which stipulates that children under 18 cannot be held responsible for actions committed during wartime."[127] This media report also cited David Matas, a distinguished Canadian lawyer, as stating his "understanding of international law that a child can't commit a crime against humanity. Child soldiers are victims." The turn to "international law" thereby served as a persuasive tool to obtain a limited political exception in this one instance, but the architecture of the overall framework persists.

In sum, the passive faultless victimhood of child soldiers bumps up against definite limits when foreign states are called upon to admit former child soldiers, including those who seek refugee status. The fact that their victimhood only goes so far unveils a pernicious equivocation and a troubling duality in the application of transnational norms. Differential expectations arise as to how communities are to internalize the notion of the child soldier as faultless passive victim. Refugee and asylum law involves knotty relationships between powerful and wealthy states, on the one hand, and poorer, insecure, and war-torn states that tend to produce refugees and asylum-seekers, on the other. Powerful states who officially support the faultless passive victim image when blanketed upon weaker states may not fully

---

[124] *Id.* at 5–6 (citing Poshteh v. Canada [2005] 3 F.C. 487).

[125] *Id.* at 5 n. 35 (citing Moreno v. Canada (1992) 21 Imm. L. R. (2d), 225).

[126] Lonegan, *supra* note 116, at 99 (citing Moreno v. Canada).

[127] Jared Ferrie, *Former child soldier gets cold welcome from Canada*, THE NATIONAL (UAE) (November 13, 2008), *available at* <http://www.thenational.ae/news/worldwide/americas/former-child-soldier-gets-cold-welcome-from-canada> (visited on September 17, 2011). The information in the immediately preceding sentences of this paragraph comes from this source.

internalize this image themselves when it implicates their own national interests. Such unevenness may corrode the credibility of international regulatory and best practice efforts. Sadly, this unevenness also blocks a possible avenue of escape for mobilized child soldiers.

Teenage bombers targeting Western interests would, even if they had been resocialized comparably to an abducted child fighter in—for example—the DRC or Nepal, likely get far less mileage out of a claim that the attacks were not their fault. When Western societies are afflicted by child soldier violence, the protective narrative imagery disintegrates. An impression arises, then, that powerful states simply may not believe the circulated imagery; or that they may be unwilling to assume the risk that the imagery may be wrong, inordinately essentialized, or problematically fictionalized. Yet this imagery continues to be transplanted, with *in situ* contestation redirected, to postcolonial spaces affected by child soldiering.

(iv) Conclusion

No *opinio juris* establishes that prosecuting a person under the age of eighteen at the time of the impugned extraordinary international crime before an international criminal court or tribunal, or any national court, would be unlawful. Nonetheless, diverse, vocal, and influential actors firmly discourage such prosecutions. Notwithstanding some problematic political selectivity, law and practice overall are receptive to their exhortations. In the end, the "dominant view in international law," according to legal scholar Pacifique Manirakiza, "is that minors who have committed international crimes, such as genocide, crimes against humanity or war crimes, are victims of the adults who recruited them and are not legally culpable."[128]

The impulse to shield child soldiers suspected of committing international crimes from the atrocity trial is both laudable and appropriate. This impulse, however, extends well beyond criminal jurisdictions. It has come to hollow the rigor of transitional accountability mechanisms from outside the criminal law—such as truth commissions, welcoming ceremonies, cleansing rituals, or community service requirements—in their application to former child soldiers in post-conflict societies. This book counters by pursuing an equilibrium in which former child soldiers implicated in acts of atrocity are not subject to retributive criminal trials but, instead, participate in restorative, reintegrative, and rehabilitative justice mechanisms in a manner that dexterously investigates their multiple roles. In order to remain legitimate, these transitional justice mechanisms must not be contingent on the nationality of the targeted constituency. Arriving at this endgame, however, first requires recalibrating the prevailing mindset within the international legal imagination.

---

[128] Pacifique Manirakiza, *Les enfants face au système international de justice: à la recherche d'un modèle de justice pénale internationale pour les délinquants mineurs*, 34 QUEEN'S L. J. 719, 719 (2009) (English-language abstract). Manirakiza attributes this view to influential human rights discourse that posits child soldiers as coerced, and first and foremost as victims. *Id.* at 722. He questions the prudence of this view in terms of respecting the balance between the interests of the victim, the child, and society in general.

5

Unlawful Recruitment and Use of Children:
From Proscription to Prevention

What is the lawful age of recruitment into state armed forces? Into irregular armed groups distinct from the state? For active participation in hostilities? Which sanctions arise for adults who engage in prohibited practices? For states? As with its immediate predecessor, this Chapter considers international law (settled, emergent, and aspirational), best practices, and influential policy frameworks.

Under conventional and customary international humanitarian law and international human rights law it is, at the very least, unlawful to recruit or use anyone under the age of fifteen in armed forces or armed groups. That said, "[m]any humanitarian organizations and pressure groups consider[] fifteen years of age too young for military enrollment."[1] Global civil society, UN agencies, and transnational norm entrepreneurs—advancing the Straight 18 position—aim to replace fifteen with eighteen. Such was the goal of Olara Otunnu, the first UN Special Representative for Children and Armed Conflict, in the context of the recruitment of children in hostilities.[2] The strength of this conviction has since consolidated and expanded within the Office of the Special Representative.

On a broader note, David Rosen, writing in 2009, remarks that "[m]ost human rights groups...declare that there is now a universal ban on the recruitment of children under age eighteen."[3] Michael Wessells reports that the Coalition to Stop the Use of Child Soldiers has "spearheaded an international campaign to establish 18 years as the minimum age of recruitment."[4] The Integrated Disarmament, Demobilization and Reintegration Standards identify as the "UN's advocacy position" that "[n]o person under 18 shall be recruited into or used in

---

[1] Alcinda Honwana, CHILD SOLDIERS IN AFRICA 36 (2006).

[2] Olara Otunnu, *Keynote Address: The Convention and children in situations of armed conflict, in* CHILDREN IN EXTREME SITUATIONS, Working Paper Series No. 00-05, LSE Development Studies Institute 48, 56 (Lisa Carlson, Megan Mackeson-Sandbach, and Tim Allen eds, 2000), *available at* <http://www2.lse.ac.uk/internationalDevelopment//pdf/WP05.pdf> (remarking that he "support[s] very strongly the movement which is underway to seek to raise the age limit to 18, in part because that will conform with the age of majority as provided in the [CRC] and in many domestic legislation").

[3] David M. Rosen, *Who Is a Child? The Legal Conundrum of Child Soldiers*, 25 CONN. J. INT'L L. 81, 100 (2009).

[4] Michael Wessells, CHILD SOLDIERS: FROM VIOLENCE TO PROTECTION 234 (2006, first paperback 2009).

armed forces or groups."[5] Upping the chronological threshold reduces the pool of lawfully available fighters. In light of the demographics of many conflict societies, this reduction may be sizable.

The views of global civil society and child rights advocates do not constitute international law. Notwithstanding a few exceptions, neither do the views of intergovernmental organizations, including UN agencies. These actors, however, certainly shape the content of binding international law as traditionally made. Owing in large part to their activities and lobbying efforts, international law is moving, albeit somewhat unevenly, toward eighteen as the threshold age of permissible military service. Eighteen is becoming the new normal; it is naturalizing as *de lege ferenda*. The fact that widely accepted definitions of child soldiers, and children associated with armed forces or armed groups, cover all persons below the age of eighteen further contributes to this evolutive normalization.[6]

In armed conflict, international criminal law ascribes individual penal responsibility to adult conscriptors or enlisters when the implicated children are under the age of fifteen, regardless of the modality of recruitment. International criminal law also ascribes individual penal responsibility to adults who use children under the age of fifteen to participate actively in hostilities. These practices therefore have become illicit. Guilt can be assessed and punishment imposed by international criminal courts or tribunals. To date, however, only a handful of prosecutions have taken place. Elements of global civil society also push for this age cut-off to be raised to eighteen, notably but not exclusively in the case of armed groups.[7] The Straight 18 position endeavors to constellate all aspects of the legal architecture of the protective regime around the age of eighteen. International human rights law and international humanitarian law have proven more receptive than international criminal law to this advocacy push. This is understandable. It is one thing to prohibit something. It is quite another to cast the prohibited conduct as a war crime and then incarcerate wrongdoers. Conversely, however, this means that a gap emerges in the protective regime. Perhaps full attainment of the Straight 18 agenda would be facilitated were its pursuit to be paired with a less typified and more vivified portrayal of those persons intended for protective coverage? Such a discursive switch also would attenuate externalities that arise from excessive infantilization of fifteen, sixteen, and seventeen year-olds.

International criminal prosecutions of adult recruiters and users help condemn child soldiering. These prosecutions may go some modest way to draw down the incidence of this practice. The tendency of international lawyers and policymakers, however, is to exaggerate the deterrent value of these prosecutions. Exaggeration is

---

[5] *Integrated Disarmament, Demobilization and Reintegration Standards* §5.30, p. 24 (2006), *available at* <http://www.unddr.org/iddrs/05/download/IDDRS_530.pdf>.

[6] Jeff McMahan, *Child Soldiers: The Ethical Perspective* 12 (working paper, 2007) ("[I]n law the category of child soldiers includes all those below the age of 18.").

[7] REDRESS Trust, VICTIMS, PERPETRATORS OR HEROES? CHILD SOLDIERS BEFORE THE INTERNATIONAL CRIMINAL COURT 1 (2006); No Peace Without Justice and UNICEF Innocenti Research Centre, INTERNATIONAL CRIMINAL JUSTICE AND CHILDREN 26 (2002) [hereinafter INTERNATIONAL CRIMINAL JUSTICE AND CHILDREN].

imprudent. It distracts from the need to search beyond the architecture of the courtroom and jailhouse in order to meaningfully dissuade and, ultimately, end child soldiering. For example, state responsibility for unlawful recruitment of children, along with other forms of collective sanction, remains undertheorized and underdeveloped. This book hopes to encourage deeper reflection and more action along these lines. As part of their goal to accentuate the moral culpability of adult defendants, criminal prosecutions emphasize how former child soldiers are flattened by post-traumatic stress syndrome. When their emphasis on disability becomes excessive, criminal proceedings inadvertently hamper prospective rights-based approaches to assert juvenile civic and political participation. These prosecutions also may favor superficial explanations of mass atrocity that frustrate aggrieved communities and survivors by failing to reflect actual lived experiences.

(i) International Human Rights Law and Humanitarian Law

Although forward-moving and gaining considerable traction, the push to establish eighteen as the minimum age of permissible military service in international humanitarian law and international human rights law remains somewhat uneven. States display greater support for a requirement of eighteen as the minimum age for membership in armed groups (in practice, rebel groups that challenge state authority) than in their own national armed forces. Within the context of armed forces, moreover, states demonstrate greater support for eighteen as the minimum age for conscription or compulsory recruitment than for voluntary enlistment. Among states that still permit voluntary enrollment under the age of eighteen, a strong consensus is emerging that such enrollees should not be directly deployed in hostilities. That said, the trend-lines are for law to approach armed forces similarly to armed groups and to view voluntary recruitment as indistinguishable from forcible recruitment. Hence, the move is to collapse these residual vestiges of differential treatment. Remaining distinctions are not accreting; rather, they are eroding.

(a) Hard Law

Pursuant to the CRC, states "shall take all feasible measures to ensure that persons who have not attained the age of fifteen years do not take a direct part in hostilities."[8] CRC Article 38(3) provides that:

States Parties shall refrain from recruiting any person who has not attained the age of fifteen years into their armed forces. In recruiting among those persons who have attained the age of

---

[8] United Nations Convention on the Rights of the Child, G.A. Res. 44/25, Art. 38(2), Annex, U.N. Doc. A/RES/44/25 (November 20, 1989) (entered into force September 2, 1990) [hereinafter CRC].

fifteen years but who have not attained the age of eighteen years, States Parties shall endeavour to give priority to those who are oldest.

The Optional Protocol to the CRC on the Involvement of Children in Armed Conflict, which was adopted in 2000, entered into force in 2002.[9] As of May 2011, 141 states are parties thereto. The Office of the Special Representative for Children and Armed Conflict—in cooperation with the Special Representative on Violence against Children, UNICEF, the Office of the High Commissioner for Human Rights, and the Committee on the Rights of the Child—initiated the "Zero under 18" campaign in May 2010 to achieve universal ratification of the Optional Protocol.

The Optional Protocol aims to remedy some of the CRC's perceived inadequacies. It specifies that states "shall take all feasible measures to ensure that members of their armed forces who have not attained the age of 18 years do not take a direct part in hostilities."[10] On the one hand, the Optional Protocol reflects an incremental move, in that the language "all feasible measures" does not plainly read as imperative. On the other hand, the Optional Protocol has been interpreted as "elevating the minimum age for combat participation to 18."[11]

In any event, a firmer ban emerges in Article 2, which provides that states "shall ensure that persons who have not attained the age of 18 years are not compulsorily recruited into their armed forces." Optional Protocol Article 3(1) then somewhat nebulously adds:

States Parties shall raise the minimum age for the voluntary recruitment of persons into their national armed forces from that set out in Article 38, paragraph 3, of the [CRC], taking account of the principles contained in that article and recognizing that under the [CRC] persons under the age of 18 years are entitled to special protection.

Article 3(1) mandates states to increase the threshold age for the voluntary recruitment of persons into their national armed forces beyond fifteen—ostensibly, then, at the very least to sixteen.[12] The Optional Protocol *stricto sensu* permits recruitment of sixteen and seventeen year-olds into national armed forces. Their recruitment, however, is to be genuinely voluntary and carried out with the informed consent of the recruit's parents or legal guardians; in addition, such recruits are to be fully informed of the duties involved in service and must provide reliable proof of age.[13]

---

[9] Optional Protocol to the CRC on the involvement of children in armed conflict, G.A. Res. 54/263, U.N. Doc. A/RES/54/263 (May 25, 2000) (entered into force February 12, 2002) [hereinafter Optional Protocol]. The United States, which is not a party to the CRC, is a party to the Optional Protocol.

[10] *Id.* Art. 1.

[11] Wessells, CHILD SOLDIERS, *supra* note 4, at 234. For a more activist interpretation, *see* INTERNATIONAL CRIMINAL JUSTICE AND CHILDREN, *supra* note 7, at 15 ("The Protocol reflects an emerging international consensus that 18 years should be the minimum age for recruitment into armed forces and groups and for participation in hostilities.").

[12] REDRESS Trust, *supra* note 7, at 24.

[13] Optional Protocol, *supra* note 9, Art. 3(3); Rachel Brett and Irma Specht, YOUNG SOLDIERS: WHY THEY CHOOSE TO FIGHT 114 (2004).

The Optional Protocol requires each state party to deposit a binding declaration upon ratification or accession that sets forth its minimum age of voluntary recruitment as determined under national law. Well over two-thirds of all ratifying states have adopted eighteen as the minimum age in this regard (including Uganda, Sierra Leone, Colombia, and the DRC), thereby reflecting an increasingly generalized practice among states. To be clear, states that have filed a declaration of the age of eighteen do not in all instances have the capacity (or necessarily the intent) to vigorously police the age of new recruits. For other states—including a number of Western states—the declared age of voluntary recruitment is lower. A non-exhaustive list of examples include: seventeen years (Australia, Austria, Azerbaijan, Cape Verde, China, Cuba, France, Germany, Ireland (with a further exception to sixteen in the case of apprentices), Israel, Italy, Luxembourg, Netherlands, New Zealand, Poland, and United States); sixteen-and-a-half years (Singapore); and sixteen years (Bangladesh, Belize, Canada, Egypt, El Salvador, India, and the United Kingdom).

The Optional Protocol is more restrictive in cases of armed groups. These groups "should not, under any circumstances, recruit or use in hostilities persons under the age of 18 years."[14] What is more, pursuant to Article 4(2), states agree to take "all feasible measures" to criminalize such practices. The law is quite clear regarding eighteen as the minimum age for armed groups. Rosen chides this purported "double standard[],"which permits "sovereign states to recruit child soldiers but bars rebel groups from doing the same."[15] Perhaps this asymmetry does represent state political interests to restrict the activities of non-state actors. In any event, global civil society is not the culprit here. Its unequivocal aim is to eliminate this unevenness by promoting the universality of the Straight 18 position.

Other international instruments also address child recruitment. The International Labor Organization's Convention No. 182 on the Prohibition and Immediate Action for the Elimination of the Worst Forms of Child Labor defines a child as a person under the age of eighteen.[16] This convention explicitly links "forced or compulsory recruitment of children for use in armed conflict" to "slavery or practices similar to slavery" and obliges ratifying member states to "take immediate and effective measures to secure the prohibition and elimination" thereof.[17] The African Charter on the Rights and Welfare of the Child, which came into force in November 1999, is a regional instrument. It defines a child as "every human being below the age of 18 years" and requires parties to "take all necessary measures to ensure that no child shall take a direct part in hostilities and refrain, in particular, from recruiting any child."[18]

Article 38(1) of the CRC requires that states "undertake to respect and to ensure respect for rules of international humanitarian law applicable to them in armed conflicts which are relevant to the child." The Fourth Geneva Convention, which

---

[14] Optional Protocol, *supra* note 9, Art. 4(1).

[15] David M. Rosen, ARMIES OF THE YOUNG: CHILD SOLDIERS IN WAR AND TERRORISM 146 (2005).

[16] 38 I.L.M. 1207, Art. 2 (June 17, 1999). Recommendation 190 accompanying this Convention encourages the criminalization of forced/compulsory recruitment.

[17] *Id.* Arts 1, 3(a).

[18] OAU Doc. CAB/LEG/24.9/49 (1990), Arts 2, 22(2) (entered into force November 29, 1999).

concerns civilian persons, grants a number of special protections to children.[19] These protections, which may begin at different ages (twelve, fifteen, or eighteen), include barring the occupying power from compelling persons under the age of eighteen to work.

Article 77(1) of Additional Protocol I mandates for parties to a conflict that "[c]hildren shall be the object of special respect and shall be protected against any form of indecent assault."[20] Article 77(2) states that "Parties to the conflict shall take all feasible measures in order that children who have not attained the age of fifteen years do not take a direct part in hostilities and, in particular, they shall refrain from recruiting them into their armed forces," while also specifying that, "[i]n recruiting among those persons who have attained the age of fifteen years but who have not attained the age of eighteen years the Parties to the conflict shall endeavor to give priority to those who are oldest." Article 77(3) addresses what a party is to do when it captures enemy fighters who, despite the requirements of Article 77(2), are under the age of fifteen. In such situations, such captured persons "continue to benefit from the special protection accorded . . . , whether or not they are prisoners of war." Furthermore, pursuant to Article 77(4), "[i]f arrested, detained or interned for reasons related to the armed conflict, children shall be held in quarters separate from the quarters of adults, except where families are accommodated as family units." Additional Protocol I also accords children priority in the distribution of relief consignments and restricts the ability of a party to the conflict to evacuate children other than its nationals to a foreign country.[21]

Additional Protocol II, which relates to non-international armed conflict, asserts in Article 4(3)(c) that "children who have not attained the age of fifteen years shall neither be recruited in the armed forces or groups nor allowed to take part in hostilities."[22] This prohibition is firmer than its counterpart for international armed conflict in Additional Protocol I. Article 4(3) of Additional Protocol II, which generally requires that "children shall be provided with the care and aid they require," makes specific (though not exclusive) reference to education, family reunification, and the temporary removal of children from areas plagued by hostilities to safer areas. Similarly to Additional Protocol I, in Article 4(3)(d) Additional Protocol II extends special protection to children below the age of fifteen even "if they take a direct part in hostilities despite the provisions of subparagraph (c) and are captured."

---

[19] Geneva Convention (IV) relative to the Protection of Civilian Persons in Time of War, Arts 14, 17, 23, 24, 38, 50, 51, 68, 82, 89, 94, and 132, 75 U.N.T.S. 287 (August 12, 1949).

[20] Protocol Additional to the Geneva Conventions of 12 August 1949, and relating to the Protection of Victims of International Armed Conflicts (Protocol I), 1125 U.N.T.S. 3 (June 8, 1977).

[21] *Id.* Arts 70(1), 78.

[22] Protocol Additional to the Geneva Conventions of 12 August 1949, and relating to the Protection of Victims of Non-International Armed Conflicts (Protocol II), 1125 U.N.T.S. 609 (June 8, 1977). For interpretive details, *see* International Committee of the Red Cross (ICRC) Commentaries to Additional Protocol II, cmt 4557 ("Not only can a child not be recruited, or enlist himself, but furthermore he will not be 'allowed to take part in hostilities', i.e., to participate in military operations such as gathering information, transmitting orders, transporting ammunition and food-stuffs, or acts of sabotage.").

(b) Soft Law, Policy, and Best Practices

The Machel Report, Cape Town Principles, and Paris Commitments and Principles constitute the most influential among formally non-binding documents concerned with the legally permissible age of association with armed forces or armed groups. Other reports, instruments, and resolutions also touch upon this question, to be sure, as do a number of regional declarations.[23]

The Machel Report advocates for eighteen as the minimum age for involvement in armed forces or armed groups. Although recognizing that "[i]n addition to being forcibly recruited, youth also present themselves for service," the Machel Report argues that:

It is *misleading*, however, to consider this voluntary. While young people may appear to choose military service, the choice is not exercised freely. They may be driven by any of several forces, including cultural, social, economic or political pressures [emphasis mine].[24]

Assumptions regarding the inability to volunteer most directly relate to child soldiers under the age of fifteen, but also extend to—and animate—the drive to increase the minimum age of participation in armed forces and groups to eighteen. For example, the UNICEF Innocenti Research Centre maintains that "[w]hen it comes to children—especially children under 15—so-called 'voluntary recruitment' is always a misnomer."[25]

The Machel Report gives examples of children who appear to join armed forces in order to make the best of a bad situation or for whom the military experience may even have some positive aspects.[26] Owing to its overarching normative conclusion that voluntariness is impossible for children in these contexts, however, the Machel Report predetermines the kinds of inferences that can be extrapolated from this evidence. The Machel Report's invocation of the term "misleading" bears closer scrutiny. This term is a conversation-stopper. It embarrasses alternate or more nuanced interpretations that may suggest some residual element of volition, exercise of discretion, or capacity among recruits. Deployment of this term might even insinuate that such interpretations come with sinister motivations. Frankly, the Machel Report's effective equation of voluntariness with free choice renders the concept operationally meaningless within the context of conflict zones. It remains unclear whether the "cultural, social, economic or political pressures" that void the

---

[23] Wessells, CHILD SOLDIERS, *supra* note 4, at 234–235 (listing the following Declarations: Maputo (1999), Montevideo (1999), Berlin (1999), Kathmandu (2000), and Amman (2001)); The Secretary General, *Children and armed conflict*, delivered to the Security Council and the General Assembly, U.N. Doc. S/2005/72-A/59/695 (February 9, 2005); UN General Assembly Resolution S-27/2, *A world fit for children*, Annex (October 11, 2002) (also discussing children's rights generally).

[24] Report of the Expert of the Secretary-General, *Impact of Armed Conflict on Children*, U.N. Doc. A/51/306 ¶ 38 (August 26, 1996), *available at* <http://www.unicef.org/graca/a51-306_en.pdf> [hereinafter Machel Report].

[25] INTERNATIONAL CRIMINAL JUSTICE AND CHILDREN, *supra* note 7, at 73–74 (noting also that "[c]hild rights advocates maintain that children's participation in armed forces will always involve some form of pressure, be it cultural, political, or simply the need to ensure their safety or daily subsistence").

[26] Machel Report, *supra* note 24, at ¶¶ 39–43, 57.

ability of adolescents to volunteer suddenly cease for everyone over the chronological hump of eighteen. Taking the Machel Report's approach to voluntariness seriously may therefore mean liberating many adults in conflict zones from their choices to associate with armed forces or armed groups. Might this approach, however well-intended, simply come to foster collective non-responsibility or, even, impunity? Alternately, might the Machel Report's approach disproportionately penalize very young adults by unrealistically aggrandizing their autonomy? Pursuing a more liminal middle-ground might avoid either of these unattractive extremes.

The Cape Town Principles begin with the following: "A minimum age of 18 years should be established for any person participating in hostilities and for recruitment in all forms into any armed force or armed group."[27] The Cape Town Principles exhort governments to ratify the Optional Protocol, which they interpret as "raising the minimum age from 15 to 18 years."[28] The Cape Town Principles state that governments:

[S]hould adopt national legislation that sets a minimum age of 18 years for voluntary and compulsory recruitment and should establish proper recruitment procedures and the means to enforce them. Those persons responsible for illegally recruiting children should be brought to justice.[29]

The Cape Town Principles also emphasize the demobilization of all persons younger than eighteen from all armed forces and armed groups.

The Paris Commitments update the Cape Town Principles, while also lauding them for their helpfulness in guiding decisions and actions taken to prevent the unlawful recruitment of persons under the age of eighteen into armed forces or groups.[30] The Paris Commitments call upon parties to uphold international law, notably the Optional Protocol. In this regard, the Paris Commitments are about compliance with extant international law. At the same time, though, they also aspire to shift the content of international law and policy. They hope to nudge both closer to the Straight 18 position.

Paris Commitment 6 exhorts effective investigation and prosecution of "those persons who have unlawfully recruited children under 18 years of age into armed forces or groups, or used them to participate actively in hostilities." This Commitment also discourages the use of amnesties for perpetrators of such crimes. Paris Commitment 8 invokes collective action by calling for state cooperation "with the implementation of targeted measures taken by [the] Security Council against parties to an armed conflict which unlawfully recruit or use children, such as, but

---

[27] Cape Town Principles and Best Practices 1 (April 27–30, 1997), *available at* <http://www.unicef.org/emerg/files/Cape_Town_Principles(1).pdf>.

[28] *Id.*

[29] *Id.*; *cf. id.* at 2 ("Governments and communities that regard children as adults before the age of 18 can establish a dialogue about the importance of limiting the age of recruitment to persons 18 or older.").

[30] The Paris Commitments to Protect Children from Unlawful Recruitment or Use by Armed Forces or Armed Groups (February 2007), preamble, *available at* <http://www.child-soldiers.org/childsoldiers/Paris_ Commitments_March_2007.pdf> [hereinafter Paris Commitments].

not limited to, a ban on arms and equipment transfers or military assistance to these parties." Paris Commitment 10 provides that children who have been unlawfully recruited or used by armed forces are not to be considered as deserters under domestic law.[31]

The Paris Principles recognize that the age of unlawful recruitment or use is not yet universally eighteen as a matter of binding law. This age depends on which specific international treaty or national law is applicable in any given instance.[32] Ironically, France is among the states that permit seventeen year-old volunteers to be recruited into national military service. However, as with the Paris Commitments, the Paris Principles are hortatory. Although they recognize that states "have different obligations under international law," they also affirm that "a majority of child protection actors will continue advocating for States to strive to raise the minimum age of recruitment or use to 18 in all circumstances."[33] The Paris Principles aim to affect the behavior of a broad range of actors, including those with international legal personality. The Paris Principles also continue the push to collapse the distinctions among kinds of recruitment, such as compulsory, forced, and voluntary, by crisply defining recruitment in Principle 2.4 as comprising all three.

UN Security Council resolutions condemn and call for an end to the unlawful recruitment or use of children in hostilities.[34] Resolution 1612, adopted in 2005, established a Monitoring and Reporting Mechanism and a working group on children and armed conflict. The UN Secretary-General issues annual reports that explicitly name parties who recruit child soldiers or use children in situations of armed conflict. These parties are placed on what has been called a "list of shame."[35] Resolution 1882 (adopted in 2009) additionally requires to list parties to armed conflicts that engage in patterns of killing, maiming, or raping children or other forms of sexual violence against children. Special Representative Coomaraswamy has praised the Security Council's "focus on recruitment and use and the accompanying threat of targeted measures against persistent violators [for resulting

---

[31] Paris Commitment 5 adheres to the "principle that the release of all children recruited or used unlawfully by armed forces or groups shall be sought unconditionally at all times."

[32] The Paris Principles: Principles and Guidelines on Children Associated with Armed Forces or Armed Groups (February 2007), Prin. 6.4, *available at* <http://www.child-soldiers.org/childsoldiers/ Paris_ Principles_March_2007.pdf> [hereinafter Paris Principles] (calling upon states to "take necessary steps to ensure that all relevant international standards are ratified, respected and reflected in national law").

[33] *Id.*, Prin. 1.14. Regarding armed groups, *see id.* Prin. 7.11 ("[A]ctors working to promote and support the release of children should make contact with those armed groups who are recruiting or have recruited children and affiliated bodies where this can be done safely, in order to negotiate commitments to establish a minimum age of 18 years for recruitment or participation in armed conflict and to release children in their ranks.").

[34] Pertinent resolutions include 1261 (1999), 1314 (2000), 1379 (2001), 1460 (2003), 1539 (2004), 1612 (2005), and 1882 (2009). The UN General Assembly also is active on this subject. *See* Vesselin Popovski, *Children in Armed Conflict: Law and Practice of the United Nations*, in INTERNATIONAL CRIMINAL ACCOUNTABILITY AND THE RIGHTS OF CHILDREN 37, 40–42 (Karin Arts and Vesselin Popovski eds, 2006).

[35] United Nations Department of Public Information, Press Conference on Security Council Resolution on Children and Armed Conflict (August 4, 2009), *available at* <http://www.un.org/ News/briefings/docs//2009/090804_1882.doc.htm>.

in] the release of scores of children in conflicts around the world."[36] She also has noted that the "threat of Security Council sanction has moved many groups to enter into action plans with the UN system to release children," while specifically citing examples from Côte d'Ivoire, CAR, Nepal, Sri Lanka, and the Philippines.[37] Looking ahead, it would be desirable to have more of these sorts of collective measures and sanctions.

(c) Summary

In her expert report prepared for the ICC, Elisabeth Schauer observed that instruments that "state that the enlistment, recruitment, use and/or deployment of child soldiers under the age of 15 is a war crime" are "not in line . . . anymore" with the "'straight 18' approach to recruitment" as affirmed by other instruments.[38] In legal interpretive guidelines issued in 2009, the UN High Commissioner for Refugees highlighted the "growing consensus regarding the ban on the recruitment and use of children below 18 years in armed conflict," while additionally noting that, although not binding, the Paris Principles "reflect a strong trend for a complete ban on under-age recruitment."[39] Although the Straight 18 position is not (yet) settled international humanitarian or human rights law, it heralds the future of international humanitarian and human rights law. Might it be counterproductive, however, to chronologically expand the membership of the protected class while statically relying on uniform, atrophied, and infantilized assumptions of the capacities of class members? Collapsing the distinction between abduction/forced recruitment and voluntary recruitment, and flatly declaring the impossibility of volunteerism, may become more tenuous the older the child soldier and the larger the number of persons to whom the declaration applies.

(ii) International Criminal Law

Whether in international or non-international armed conflict, the conscription or enlistment of children under the age of fifteen, or their use to participate actively in hostilities, is a war crime to which individual criminal responsibility attaches. The stigma of the humanitarian prohibition thereby deepens. This proscription is both conventional and customary. A fundamental precept underpinning this war crime

---

[36] *Id.*

[37] Radhika Coomaraswamy, *Child Soldiers: Root Causes and UN Initiatives* 10 (February 2009) (lecture on file with the author).

[38] Elisabeth Schauer, *The Psychological Impact of Child Soldiering*, Prosecutor v. Lubanga, Case No. ICC-01/04-01/06, Public Document (ICC Trial Chamber I, February 25, 2009), p. 7.

[39] Guidelines on International Protection: Child Asylum Claims, HCR/GIP/09/08 (December 22, 2009) ¶ 19 and n. 42.

is that "[r]esponsibility is placed on the adult who permits participation and never on the child."[40]

This war crime is not directly incorporated into either the ICTY or ICTR statutes. Prosecution of the conscription, enlistment, or use of child soldiers, however, plays an integral part of the work of the SCSL and the ICC.

(a) Special Court for Sierra Leone

Among several other crimes, the SCSL Statute proscribes "[c]onscripting or enlisting children under the age of 15 years into armed forces or groups or using them to participate actively in hostilities."[41] The SCSL is the first internationalized institution to convict defendants (to date, five) on these specific charges, while acquitting three.

In May 2004, the SCSL Appeals Chamber issued an important decision on a preliminary motion that had been brought by defendant Sam Hinga Norman. Norman was the CDF's National Coordinator. He died in February 2007. The Appeals Chamber ruled that individual penal responsibility for the crime of recruiting child soldiers in either international or non-international armed conflict had crystallized as customary international law prior to November 1996 (the start of the SCSL's temporal mandate).[42] To reach this result, the Appeals Chamber drew from international human rights law, international humanitarian law, and national practices. The majority judgment was not without controversy, assuredly, including on grounds related to the principle of legality.[43] Justice Geoffrey Robertson, who dissented therefrom, concluded that, by 1996, customary international law had not yet attached individual penal responsibility to those adults who *enlist* volunteers under the age of fifteen.

The SCSL has concluded three cases. Two involved rebel groups (the *AFRC* and *RUF* cases). The third concerned pro-government militia (the *CDF* case). Each of

---

[40] Chen Reis, *Trying the Future, Avenging the Past: The Implications of Prosecuting Children for Participation in Internal Armed Conflict*, 28 COLUM. HUMAN RIGHTS L. REV. 629, 654 (1997).

[41] Statute of the Special Court for Sierra Leone, UN-Sierra Leone (January 16, 2002), Art. 4(c), 2178 U.N.T.S. 145 [hereinafter SCSL Statute] (Art. 4 is entitled "Other serious violations of international humanitarian law").

[42] Prosecutor v. Norman, Case No. SCSL-2004-14-AR72(E), Decision on Preliminary Motion Based on Lack of Jurisdiction (Child Recruitment) (SCSL Appeals Chamber, May 31, 2004); *see also* Prosecutor v. Brima, Kamara, and Kanu, Case No. SCSL-04-16-A, Appeals Judgment (SCSL Appeals Chamber, February 22, 2008) ¶ 295 [hereinafter AFRC Appeals Judgment]; Prosecutor v. Fofana and Kondewa, Case No. SCSL-04-14-A, Appeals Judgment (SCSL Appeals Chamber, May 28, 2008) ¶ 139 [hereinafter CDF Appeals Judgment] (the recruitment and use of children to participate actively in hostilities had crystallized as customary international law crimes prior to November 1996).

[43] *See*, e.g., Tim Kelsall, CULTURE UNDER CROSS-EXAMINATION: INTERNATIONAL JUSTICE AND THE SPECIAL COURT FOR SIERRA LEONE 148–151 (2009); *see also id.* at 158 (noting that the SCSL majority "gave no weight to the fact that in 1996, when reporting to the Committee on the Rights of the Child, even the Sierra Leonean government's legal expert referred only to the fact that, pursuant to the Geneva Convention, children may not be *conscripted* into the armed forces; nor to the fact that under a Sierra Leonean military forces act, recruitment was legal at any age with parental consent") (italics in original) (citation omitted).

these three cases implicated multiple defendants. The SCSL is currently in deliberations regarding a fourth case, against Charles Taylor (the former Liberian head-of-state) for his alleged support of atrocity in Sierra Leone.[44] Arguments ended in Taylor's trial on March 11, 2011. A verdict is shortly expected, which is likely to be followed by appeals. In each of these four cases, prosecutors charged multiple crimes, including the unlawful conscription, enlistment, or use of child soldiers.

In the *AFRC* case, three former militia leaders were convicted *inter alia* of charges related to child soldiering. These specific convictions were affirmed on appeal in 2008. So, too, were final sentences (encompassing the totality of the defendants' criminal conduct) of forty-five, fifty, and fifty years. The interface of the *AFRC* case with child soldiering centered on practices of abduction. In its 2007 judgment in *AFRC*, SCSL Trial Chamber II defined conscription as implying "compulsion" and as encompassing "acts of coercion, such as abductions and forced recruitment."[45] It defined enlistment as "accepting and enrolling individuals when they volunteer to join an armed force or group," which it immediately qualified by awkwardly adding: "Enlistment is a voluntary act, and the child's consent is therefore not a valid defence."[46] The bottom line is that enlistment of children under the age of fifteen is impermissible regardless of circumstances.

In May 2008, the SCSL Appeals Chamber released its judgment in the *CDF* case. The CDF militia primarily was comprised of traditional rural hunters known as the Kamajors (or Kamajohs), who formed a social institution. Historically in Sierra Leone, the Kamajors assisted rural chiefs in defending villages. In the 1990s, the Kamajors fought to repel RUF attacks.[47] They supported the democratically elected government of President Tejan Kabbah after a 1997 coup drove it from power. Many children presented themselves for enrollment in the CDF. The *CDF* case involved two defendants, one of whom, Allieu Kondewa, had been convicted (among other counts) by SCSL Trial Chamber I of enlistment of a child under the age of fifteen as a combatant.[48] Prior to the conflict, Kondewa had been "an illiterate herbalist and masked dancer."[49] He became the CDF's High Priest.

The *CDF* Trial Chamber[50] had heard considerable evidence about the CDF's use of child soldiers generally, but "very little testimony that connected the enlistment or use of those children to particular acts [of the defendants]."[51] TF2-021, a former child soldier, was the main witness proffered to link Kondewa to

---

[44] In addition, in a separate matter, in June 2011 the SCSL indicted five defendants for contempt over allegations of witness tampering.

[45] Prosecutor v. Brima, Kamara, and Kanu, Case No. SCSL-04-16-T, Trial Judgment (SCSL Trial Chamber, June 20, 2007) ¶ 734 [hereinafter AFRC Trial Judgment].

[46] *Id.* ¶ 735 (citing the ICC's *Lubanga* confirmation of charges decision).

[47] Prosecutor v. Sesay, Kallon, and Gbao, Case No. SCSL-04-15-T, Trial Judgment (SCSL Trial Chamber, March 2, 2009) ¶ 16 [hereinafter RUF Trial Judgment].

[48] The second defendant was Moinina Fofana. The third defendant was Sam Hinga Norman who, as previously mentioned, predeceased the verdict.

[49] Kelsall, *supra* note 43, at 158.

[50] Prosecutor v. Fofana and Kondewa, Case No. SCSL-04-14-T, Trial Judgment (SCSL Trial Chamber, August 2, 2007) [hereinafter CDF Trial Judgment].

[51] Nancy Amoury Combs, Fact-Finding without Facts: The Uncertain Evidentiary Foundations of International Criminal Convictions 216 (2010).

unlawful enlistment. Legal scholar Nancy Combs carefully reviewed TF2-021's testimony, only to find it "problematic in numerous regards":

[It was] sharply inconsistent with the assertions he [TF2-021] made in his previous statements.... In his statement, he said that no one was forced to join the Kamajors; at trial, he testified that he and others were forced to join.... TF2-021's testimony was also just plain wrong at times.[52]

Nonetheless, "[t]he Trial Chamber not only relied on TF2-021's testimony and not only relied on it as the exclusive evidence on which to base its conviction of Kondewa; the Trial Chamber did not even mention the foregoing problems."[53]

On appeal, this particular conviction was overturned. The SCSL Appeals Chamber found a lack of proof of the required nexus between Kondewa and the moment at which TF2-021 had actually been enlisted into the CDF. Enlistment did not manifest when Kondewa ritualistically initiated the child. Rather, it had occurred at an earlier point, that is, when the CDF had captured him and had forced him to carry looted property.[54] Put differently, TF2-021 had actually been recruited by others before Kondewa initiated him. The SCSL Appeals Chamber did not preclude the prospect that ritualistically initiating a child into the Kamajors could equate enlistment. Quite the contrary; it just did not find the initiation to have equated enlistment in the specific situation of Kondewa and TF2-021. Although it reversed some of Kondewa's convictions, the SCSL Appeals Chamber also entered new ones. It increased his overall sentence from eight to twenty years. The SCSL Appeals Chamber rejected political motives or fighting for a just cause as a possible mitigating factor in sentencing.

The *CDF* appeals judgment confirmed that conscription and enlistment constitute different modes of recruitment. Enlistment, for its part, was held to mean "any conduct accepting the child as part of the militia," though "there must be a nexus between the act of the accused and the child joining the armed force or group," "knowledge on the part of the accused that the child is under the age of 15," and knowledge that the child "may be trained for combat."[55] Justice Winter, in her partially dissenting judgment, held that enlistment could involve more than one act over time.

In the *RUF* case, two of the three accused—Sesay and Kallon—were convicted by SCSL Trial Chamber I of planning the use of children under the age of fifteen to actively participate in hostilities. The third accused, Gbao, was acquitted of this specific charge. Sesay had held a number of leadership positions in the RUF, Kallon had served as Sesay's deputy, and Gbao had been the RUF's security commander. Sentences for the three convicts on the totality of their criminal conduct were: fifty-two years (Sesay), forty years (Kallon), and twenty-five years (Gbao). Initially, two more defendants had been indicted; their indictments, however, were withdrawn

---

[52] *Id.* at 217–218.
[53] *Id.* at 218.
[54] CDF Appeals Judgment, *supra* note 42, at ¶¶ 142, 145.
[55] *Id.* ¶¶ 141, 144. If the child "is allowed to voluntarily join..., his or her consent is not a valid defence." *Id.* ¶ 140.

in 2003 following their deaths. In addition to consolidating the law regarding child soldiering, the *RUF* trial judgment broke new ground in terms of the war crime of attacking personnel involved with peacekeeping missions and the crime against humanity of forced marriage as an "other inhumane act."

The *RUF* trial judgment authenticated the organization's heavy reliance on abducted children—in some instances, as young as (or even younger) than ten years-old.[56] Owing to the prevalence of abduction, and consonant with the prosecutorial decision not to bring evidence of voluntary enlistment, SCSL Trial Chamber I limited its findings to conscription and active use in hostilities.[57] SCSL Trial Chamber I found that, once involved with the RUF, children were either selected for combat or not. Those selected for combat were trained in military tactics and ambushes and were grouped into Small Boys Units and Small Girls Units.[58] Some children between eight and seventeen years of age were used to commit terrible atrocities.[59] Other children who were not selected for combat instead fulfilled missions such as cooking, courier services, domestic labor, and finding food. SCSL Trial Chamber I found that active participation in hostilities included committing crimes against civilians, engaging in arson, guarding military objectives and mines, and serving as spies and bodyguards.[60]

On October 26, 2009, the SCSL Appeals Chamber largely affirmed Trial Chamber I's findings. It upheld the two child soldiering convictions, the one acquittal, and the overall sentences.[61] The Appeals Chamber underscored that adults are "under a duty to act with due diligence to ensure that children under the age of 15 are not recruited or used in combat."[62]

The SCSL also has addressed crimes against humanity that may disproportionately affect children. For example, Article 2(g) of the SCSL Statute proscribes—as crimes against humanity—rape, sexual slavery, enforced prostitution, forced pregnancy, and any other form of sexual violence. SCSL Statute Article 2(i) proscribes "other inhumane acts," which the *AFRC* appeals judgment interpreted as including acts of forced marriage perpetrated against girls.[63] This crime is not limited to forced marriage with minors, though minors are frequently the victims of such repugnant arrangements.[64] The *AFRC* appeals judgment conceptually differen-

---

[56] RUF Trial Judgment, *supra* note 47, at ¶¶ 1616–1617, 1625–1632, 1695, 1708, 1711, 1714.

[57] *Id.* ¶¶ 1694–1695.

[58] *Id.* ¶¶ 1619–1622, 1632, 1637.

[59] *Id.* ¶ 1649 ("Fighters were armed with sticks, knives, cutlasses, guns and RPGs, with which they would kill children, elderly men and women, and teenagers. They also engaged in beating people and raping children, and those children who were permitted to live were forced to join the movement.").

[60] *Id.* ¶¶ 1712–1731. Domestic chores, farm work, and conducting food finding missions were found not to constitute active participation in hostilities. *Id.* ¶¶ 1739, 1743.

[61] Prosecutor v. Sesay, Kallon, and Gbao, Case No. SCSL-04-15-A, Appeals Judgment (SCSL Appeals Chamber, October 26, 2009) [hereinafter RUF Appeals Judgment].

[62] *Id.* ¶ 923.

[63] Forced marriage is defined as "a situation in which the perpetrator through his words or conduct, or those of someone for whose actions he is responsible, compels a person by force, threat of force, or coercion to serve as a conjugal partner resulting in severe suffering, or physical, mental or psychological injury to the victim." AFRC Appeals Judgment, *supra* note 42, at ¶ 196.

[64] *Id.* ¶ 200.

tiated forced marriage from sexual slavery and the other crimes listed in Article 2(g) of the SCSL Statute, but declined to enter new convictions on this basis. Convictions for forced marriage (as "other inhumane acts") and for sexual slavery (under Article 2(g)) were rendered at trial in the *RUF* case and subsequently affirmed on appeal. SCSL Statute Article 5, which covers crimes under Sierra Leonean law, provides jurisdiction over specific offenses committed against girls.[65]

As a matter of law, the SCSL's jurisprudence on child soldiering is groundbreaking. The *RUF* case's exposition of the brutalities of abduction as a recruitment method has served important expressive and denunciatory goals. Notwithstanding the SCSL's many achievements, however, Tim Kelsall questions its approach to mediating international law with Sierra Leonean justice expectations. Kelsall argues that the SCSL "failed in crucial ways to adjust to the local culture in which it worked."[66] Among a variety of examples, he cites the prosecution of persons who enlisted child soldiers. He describes this charge as inappropriate and ethnocentric. Kelsall differentiates voluntary enlistment from "abducting a young person from their family and community, often after having killed their parents, and then forcing them to fight," which "clearly transgresse[s] a local norm."[67] He also critiques the SCSL judgments on child soldiering, notably in the *CDF* case, for portraying "childhood as a pristine state of psychological innocence and vulnerability," which he casts as "incongruent with local ideas."[68] Finally, Kelsall also laments that an influential *amicus curiae* brief characterized the children as "passive victims devoid of agency."[69]

A retributive imbalance arises when the adult abductor is undifferentiated from the adult who enlists a minor who comes forth to defend a village or pursue a livelihood. It may be that, in sentencing, international criminal law could punish those adults who forcibly abducted children more onerously than those who enlisted volunteers. Given the trend-line toward the legal equivalence of both modalities of recruitment (and the rejection of fighting for a just cause as a mitigating factor in sentencing), however, it increasingly seems untenable to justify heavier punishment for one modality in situations where other variables are held constant.

An alternate—and I argue preferable—approach would preserve the criminalization of all forms of child recruitment (whether voluntary enlistment, conscription, or abduction), but distinguish among forms when it comes to assessing the defendant's culpability, apportioning blame, and determining sentence. In parallel,

---

[65] Art. 5(a) of the SCSL Statute proscribes:
Offences relating to the abuse of girls under the Prevention of Cruelty to Children Act, 1926 (Cap. 31):
    i Abusing a girl under 13 years of age, contrary to section 6;
    ii Abusing a girl between 13 and 14 years of age, contrary to section 7;
    iii Abduction of a girl for immoral purposes, contrary to section 12.

[66] Kelsall, *supra* note 43, at 3.
[67] *Id.* at 231.
[68] *Id.* at 155.
[69] *Id.* at 155–156.

I recommend exploring how birth into armed forces or armed groups might be cognizable as a form of illicit recruitment.

(b) International Criminal Court

The ICC serves a punitive function. The Rome Statute also enables it to fulfill a participatory and reparative role for victims.[70] This is a notable innovation. The Rome Statute framework also envisages that other cognate institutional organs attend to the interests of victims. The discussion that follows examines both of these functions—prosecution of defendants and empowerment of victims—within the context of ICC cases that implicate the practice of child soldiering.

(1) Criminal Sanction

As a threshold matter, the ICC "shall have jurisdiction in respect of war crimes in particular when committed as part of a plan or policy or as part of a large-scale commission of such crimes."[71] Hence, before the ICC can assume jurisdiction, the impugned conduct must be of considerable magnitude. Rome Statute Article 8(2) (b)(xxvi) proscribes, within international armed conflict, the war crime of "[c]onscripting or enlisting children under the age of fifteen years into the national armed forces or using them to participate actively in hostilities." Within armed conflict not of an international nature, Article 8(2)(e)(vii) proscribes "[c]onscripting or enlisting children under the age of fifteen years into armed forces or groups or using them to participate actively in hostilities." Humanitarian organizations and child rights agencies played an instrumental role in the Rome Statute's incorporation of these two war crimes.[72]

In addition to these two pillars, several other Rome Statute proscriptions bear upon violence that may disproportionately, though certainly not exclusively, harm children. In terms of war crimes, one example is intentionally attacking schools and buildings dedicated to education; the crimes against humanity of enslavement, sexual slavery, and enforced prostitution also come to mind.[73] Furthermore, Rome

---

[70] The Extraordinary Chambers in the Courts of Cambodia (ECCC) also provide surviving victims the opportunity to participate. Such victims may do so formally in criminal processes as civil parties. In theory, but not evidently in practice, this opportunity surpasses the level of victim involvement contemplated by the Rome Statute. ECCC Internal Rule 23(1) allows victims to seek collective and moral reparations. Although the Khmer Rouge specifically used child soldiers and systematically inflicted human rights violations upon them, pursuing redress for the suffering of former child soldiers does not figure centrally in the ECCC's work.

[71] Rome Statute of the International Criminal Court, Art. 8(1), 2187 U.N.T.S. 90 (July 17, 1998, entered into force July 1, 2002) [hereinafter Rome Statute].

[72] Cécile Aptel, *International Criminal Justice and Child Protection, in* CHILDREN AND TRANSITIONAL JUSTICE: TRUTH-TELLING, ACCOUNTABILITY AND RECONCILIATION 67, 73 (UNICEF Innocenti Research Centre and Human Rights Program at Harvard Law School, Sharanjeet Parmar, Mindy Jane Roseman, Saudamini Siegrist, and Theo Sowa eds, 2010); *see also* Rosen, ARMIES OF THE YOUNG, *supra* note 15, at 9 ("Humanitarian groups have had an enormous influence in shaping the international treaties that seek to ban the use of child soldiers, especially the provisions of the Rome Statute.").

[73] Rome Statute, *supra* note 71, Arts 7(1)(c), 7(1)(g), 7(1)(k), 7(2)(c), 8(2)(b)(ix), and 8(2)(e)(iv).

Statute Article 6(e) includes within the definition of genocide the forcible transfer of children of one enumerated group to another enumerated group.

The elements of the child soldiering crime under Rome Statute Article 8(2)(b) (xxvi) are as follows:

1. The perpetrator conscripted or enlisted one or more persons into the national armed forces or used one or more persons to participate actively in hostilities.
2. Such person or persons were under the age of 15 years.
3. The perpetrator knew or should have known that such person or persons were under the age of 15 years.
4. The conduct took place in the context of and was associated with an international armed conflict.
5. The perpetrator was aware of factual circumstances that established the existence of an armed conflict.[74]

Elements of the crime under Article 8(2)(e)(vii) read identically, save for reference to the non-international nature of the armed conflict. In both cases, a negligence standard of failing to exercise due diligence applies.[75]

The architecture of the Rome Statute presents a disturbing gap. No sanction arises for commanders who have children aged fifteen or older serving in armed forces or groups. By virtue of Article 26, moreover, the Rome Statute excludes these children from the ICC's jurisdiction even when they abduct younger children, commit acts of atrocity, or order other children to undertake such acts.[76] Perversely, the ICC's statutory framework may incentivize adult soldiers (including low-level cadres) to see that heinous crimes, brutal abductions, and actual enlistments are performed by children aged fifteen, sixteen, or seventeen. The combined effect of Rome Statute Articles 8(2)(b)(xxvi), 8(2)(e)(vii), and 26 might rearrange the age of abductors from over eighteen to under eighteen—and decrease the number of fourteen year-old abductees while increasing the number of sixteen year-old abductees—instead of necessarily deterring the phenomenon of abduction overall. If adopted, the Straight 18 position would remedy some of these architectural externalities, assuredly, but so long as it relies on disabling fictions of victimhood and dependence it will, in turn, germinate its own set of problematic side-effects. Advocacy positions that only emphasize chronological bright-lines will

[74] Assembly of States Parties, Elements of Crimes, ICC-ASP/1/3 (part II-B), Art. 8(2)(b) (xxvi) (September 9, 2002).

[75] Prosecutor v. Katanga and Chui, Case No. ICC-01/04-01/07, Decision on the confirmation of charges (ICC Pre-trial Chamber I, September 30, 2008) ¶ 252 [hereinafter Katanga and Chui confirmation of charges decision]; *see also* Gerhard Werle, PRINCIPLES OF INTERNATIONAL CRIMINAL LAW 417 (2nd edn, 2009) ("[T]hose who purposely close their eyes to a child's age are also acting intentionally—for example, by failing to make inquiries about the child's age even though the child could, by his or her appearance, be younger than 15.") (citation omitted).

[76] *Cf.* Amnesty International, *Child Soldiers: Criminals or Victims?* 15 (AI Index: IOR 50/02/00 (2000)) (noting that "there may be examples of young commanders of units who committed mass atrocities, including murder and rapes, who were clearly willing and acted without coercion, and who may have forced other children to commit such acts").

at once protect one age group too much and the immediately adjacent age group too little. When the law draws bright-lines, it exposes outsiders to the very vicissitudes from which it aims to insulate insiders.

Turning to practice, at the ICC several of the individuals thus far publicly indicted have been charged with the war crime of unlawful conscription, enlistment, or use of children. Indictees include senior LRA officials, notably leader Joseph Kony. In the DRC situation, ICC Pre-trial Chamber I confirmed such charges against defendants Germain Katanga (allegedly commander of the rebel Force de résistance patriotique en Ituri (FRPI)) and Mathieu Ngudjolo Chui (allegedly former leader of the Front des nationalistes et intégrationnistes (FNI)).[77] Both of these defendants also are charged with other war crimes and crimes against humanity. An arrest warrant has been issued and unsealed against Bosco Ntaganda (alleged to be the Deputy Chief of the General Staff of the Forces patriotiques pour la libération du Congo (FPLC)). Ntaganda, charged *inter alia* with child soldiering crimes, remains at large. He apparently is being protected by the DRC government and has been integrated at a high level into its national army.

Some jurisdictions currently being monitored by the ICC—for example, Colombia and Afghanistan—involve conflicts that have seen the use of child soldiers. Child soldiers also have been used in Libya and Côte d'Ivoire, which present as recently active ICC situations, although there is no indication that child soldiering crimes specifically are under investigation.

The ICC's first trial—that of DRC rebel leader Thomas Lubanga Dyilo—is proceeding exclusively on counts of the charge of conscripting or enlisting children under the age of fifteen or using them to participate actively in hostilities in the Ituri region of eastern DRC. Lubanga allegedly founded (and was President of) the Union des patriotes congolais (UPC) and served as commander of the FPLC. In accordance with the Rome Statute, many persons have been granted victim status and can thusly participate in the criminal proceedings against Lubanga.

Lubanga had been arrested in 2006. His trial only began in January 2009. Its evidentiary phase concluded in April 2011. Closing statements wrapped up in September 2011. At the time of writing, a verdict has not yet been delivered by Trial Chamber I, though one is anticipated in early 2012. At that juncture, Lubanga could appeal a guilty verdict and the Office of the Prosecutor (OTP) could appeal an acquittal. Cross-appeals are possible, as are sentence appeals. This case, therefore, will in all likelihood live on for several more years.

The proceedings against Lubanga have proven to be a staccato process fraught with and frayed by due process challenges. The start date of the trial had been delayed because of the OTP's reticence to disclose potentially exculpatory evidence. Insofar as the OTP based cross-examinations upon undisclosed information, this reticence continued to stymie the trial even after it had commenced. In October

---

[77] Katanga and Chui confirmation of charges decision, *supra* note 75. In this case, Pre-trial Chamber I noted child soldiers to have participated directly in attacks, including by "killing civilians, destroying properties, and pillaging goods." *Id.* ¶ 257. It also noted children to have been used as bodyguards. *Id.* ¶ 386.

2010, the ICC Appeals Chamber ruled that the proceedings could continue. It thereby reversed an earlier decision by trial judges to stay the proceedings and release Lubanga.[78] Trial judges had been concerned with this disclosure issue. In November 2010, new controversies arose with the defense claiming that OTP intermediaries coached witnesses to fabricate evidence. Judges eventually ruled that the proceedings ought to continue despite these allegations of misconduct and abuse of process. A final ruling on the defense claim apparently will appear in the eventual trial judgment.

In 2007, ICC Pre-trial Chamber I confirmed the criminal charges against Lubanga, who was reputed to have had about 3,000 child soldiers under the age of fifteen within his militia.[79] The confirmation of charges decision, which unpacks important substantive aspects of the child soldiering war crime, was informed by, and in turn informs, the SCSL case-law, thereby suggesting the interactive nature of the jurisprudence of these two institutions.[80] In what should, by now, be apparent as a pattern, ICC Pre-trial Chamber I found that, whereas conscription is forcible recruitment, enlistment "pertains more to voluntary recruitment."[81] Pre-trial Chamber I rejected the consent of the children as a valid defense.[82] Trial Chamber I will have to independently interpret each of these key terms, but likely will hew to the approaches taken by Pre-trial Chamber I.

Pre-trial Chamber I also considered the scope of the Rome Statute's prohibition on using children to participate actively in hostilities. It ruled that this language was broader than antecedent phraseology, that is, "take a direct part in hostilities" found in Article 77(2) of Additional Protocol I. Pre-trial Chamber I interpreted the Rome Statute's language to cover activities such as combat, as well as cognate activities such as reconnaissance, spying, transportation, sabotage, courier services, being dispatched as a decoy, and guarding military objects, quarters, or personnel.[83] Pre-trial Chamber I did note that this language was not limitless. It excluded from its purview conduct such as food delivery to an airbase or domestic help in married officers' quarters. Its treatment of this language, however, meshes with broader legal and policy trends to include a broad array of activities within the rubric of child soldiering.

ICC Chief Prosecutor Luis Moreno-Ocampo argued in his opening statement in the *Lubanga* trial that no "distinction as to gravity" arises between conscripting children, enlisting them, or using them to participate actively in hostilities.[84]

---

[78] The Appeals Chamber ruled it was error to immediately stay the proceedings without first imposing sanctions.

[79] Prosecutor v. Lubanga, Case No. ICC-01/04-01/06, Decision on the confirmation of charges (ICC Pre-trial Chamber I, January 29, 2007) [hereinafter Lubanga confirmation of charges decision]. Pre-trial Chamber I confirmed charges under both Arts 8(2)(b)(xxvi) and 8(2)(e)(vii).

[80] To date, some differences have arisen between the SCSL and ICC approaches to this war crime. Although of interest to experts, these differences remain for the most part technical.

[81] Lubanga confirmation of charges decision, *supra* note 79, at ¶ 246.

[82] *Id.* ¶ 247.

[83] *Id.* ¶¶ 261–263.

[84] Luis Moreno-Ocampo, *Opening Statement*, The Case of the Prosecutor v. Lubanga, ICC-01/04-01/06, pp. 9–10 (The Hague, January 26, 2009).

Establishing an adult's culpability for conscription, enlistment, or use does not formally hinge on any proof of the child soldier's absence of free will. According to Moreno-Ocampo: "The Rome Statute renders irrelevant that children joined 'voluntarily', or that parents entrusted them 'voluntarily' to the [*sic*] Lubanga's militia.... '[V]oluntariness' or so called 'consent' is not a valid defence...."[85] Schauer, in her expert report, later recursively chimed in by submitting that "children's choices to join armed groups cannot be considered 'voluntary' from a psychological point of view."[86] For now, international criminal law formally assumes only that children under the age of fifteen are incapable of exercising any consent in volunteering. Extant international criminal prosecutions, however, are not incompatible with the broader notion that no one under the age of eighteen can ever consensually volunteer. These prosecutions, in fact, give considerable currency to this broader notion. Schauer in no way limited her report or testimony only to the subgroup of child soldiers under the age of fifteen. In conformity with general international legal norms, her understanding of child soldiers and of children involved the under-eighteen age group.

The assumptive erasure, as a matter of law, of the forcible abduction/voluntary enlistment distinction does not, however, self-evidently compute as commonsensical in light of the varied motivations of militarized youth, including children implicated in the commission of acts of atrocity. Unsurprisingly, then, when it comes to prosecutorial strategy, proof of involuntariness—regarding the issue of joining, as well as the purposes for which the children were used—still seems to help build a more persuasive case against the accused. Proof of involuntariness may encourage the buy-in of local populations regarding the value of the criminal proceedings against the adult recruiter. It matters, after all, to establish that what the accused did was both unlawful and unjust. Although there was no strictly legal reason for him to do so, Moreno-Ocampo in his opening statement in *Lubanga* followed suit by emphasizing that there:

> [W]as no free will for those children and their parents in the violent context of Ituri. Power belonged not to the law but to those bearing weapons.[87]

Notwithstanding testimony regarding the existence of forcible kidnapping, a number of OTP witnesses in *Lubanga* also stated that they had joined voluntarily.[88] Their testimony was more hued than Moreno-Ocampo's bold introductory foreshadowing. The international legal imagination's expectations of what the child soldiers would say contrasted with what they actually said, thereby causing

---

[85] *Id.* at 10–11.

[86] Schauer, *supra* note 38, at 7. Schauer testified that children lack access to information, do not comprehend the structures or interests involved, are unaware of indoctrination rituals, and do not have full understanding of the consequences of their actions or of the moral aspects of warfare. ICC Case No. 01/04-01/06, English language Transcript (April 7, 2009) lines 24–25 on p. 12 and lines 1–19 on p. 13.

[87] Moreno-Ocampo, *supra* note 84, at 10.

[88] Jennifer Easterday, *Expert Reports on the Psychological Impact of Child Soldiering* (May 15, 2009), *available at* <http://www.lubangatrial.org>; Rosen, *Who Is a Child?*, *supra* note 3, at 101–102.

unnecessary embarrassment.[89] Another learning lesson concerns the need for protective measures for child soldiers who testify. The first witness in *Lubanga*, a child soldier who recanted his initial testimony after returning from lunch, apparently did so out of fear, anger, and inadequate trial preparation (two weeks later, under protective mechanisms, this witness repeated his initial testimony). Child soldiers who have testified at the ICC as witnesses in criminal proceedings (for example, for the OTP) have received benefits, including health care and security. These benefits are to be provided, but it is wise to do so in a manner that empathizes with the perceptions and feelings of home communities grappling with poverty and insecurity.[90] Failing to do so might prompt resentment.

The credibility of child soldiers as witnesses may be weakened by their typification as faultless passive victims whose conduct is reductively attributed to coercion and who lack the capacity to make decisions.[91] These portrayals, after all, may jaundice external perceptions of the veracity of their recollections when they testify against others or claim reparations.

According to Michael Wessells, depicting former child soldiers as "emotionally crippled and damaged for life" risks emphasizing "deficits," while overlooking the reality that they "exhibit considerable resilience."[92] Such depictions may garner sympathy, but they also enfeeble. Yet Moreno-Ocampo portrayed the former child soldiers as ineffaceably wounded. In his opening statement, he froze them as prisoners of their past:

They cannot forget the beatings they suffered; they cannot forget the terror they felt and the terror they inflicted; they cannot forget the sounds of their machine guns; they cannot forget that they killed; they cannot forget that they raped and that they were raped.[93]

It is one thing to recognize the painful personal histories of child soldiers in Ituri who had initially been recruited while under the age of fifteen. It is quite another, however, to immobilize them statically in relation to the harms they had suffered. These harms then become indelible. Moreno-Ocampo's tactic to highlight those former child soldiers who have since turned to drugs to cope, who have become prostitutes, and who are orphaned and jobless—also part of his opening statement—ultimately collectivizes frailty. Drawing attention to those who suffer the most may, in turn, desolately define the group as asphyxiated by suffering and hamstrung by despondency.

Nuance stands at cross-purposes with the prosecutorial imperative to convict. No different than any other prosecutor, Moreno-Ocampo's goal is to convict Lubanga of the stated charges. Casting the child soldiers—in law and in rhetoric—

---

[89] Coming forward to present for service was not self-evidently uncommon in the DRC, even among the subgroup of child soldiers under the age of fifteen.

[90] I thank Cynthia Chamberlain for this observation.

[91] Moreno-Ocampo argued that Lubanga "stole the childhood of the victims by forcing them to kill and rape. [He] victimised children before they ever had the chance to grow up into full human beings who could make their own decisions." Moreno-Ocampo, *supra* note 84, at 29.

[92] Wessells, CHILD SOLDIERS, *supra* note 4, at x, 4.

[93] Moreno-Ocampo, *supra* note 84, at 2.

generically as inept and damaged arguably facilitates the attainment of this goal. The deployment of this strategy, however, may trigger unforeseen social costs. Should convicting perpetrators become inextricably intertwined with tropes of youth helplessness, prosecutions may well incarcerate a few adults while perpetuating gerontocracy.

In an *amicus curiae* brief submitted in the *Lubanga* case, Special Representative Coomaraswamy contended that "[t]he line between voluntary and forced recruitment is therefore not only legally irrelevant but practically superficial . . . "[94] Relatedly, it has been posited that it "would be better to consider" enlistment and conscription as one crime "for recruiting child soldiers."[95] Although this approach is economical, treating enlistment as interchangeable with forcible conscription does some injustice to those child soldiers who were forcibly conscripted, in particular abductees. Their situation is simply not the same as those who exercised some initiative in their enlistment. Abductees tend to be younger than those who present themselves for service. Commanders may treat abductees more harshly than they treat volunteers.[96] A study from Nepal found that children who were forcibly conscripted into service (or joined because of pressure) were much more likely than children who volunteered to experience psychosocial problems following their return to the community.[97] Other reports also indicate that "[i]t would appear that [children] who enlisted voluntarily are less prone to long-term post traumatic stress disorder" than children who were "brutally abducted."[98] Conversely, volunteers may experience different kinds of obstacles and impediments upon returning home after conflict. Much depends on the nature of the armed faction and the perceived legitimacy of its cause. In this vein, volunteers may face greater hurdles in terms of reinsertion, communal integration, and overcoming public suspicion and anger, especially following atrocity-producing conflicts. Accordingly, transitional justice measures might prove more salient to children who had exercised initiative in coming forward and were enlisted. The bottom line, as Chapter 6 unpacks more robustly, is that it is quite debatable whether the deployment of uniform methods to reintegrate former child soldiers (predicated upon the commonality of group members) is operationally preferable to more flexible methods keyed to individual characteristics (such as gender, conduct during the conflict, materiality of combat experience, the kind of armed faction, or initial path to recruitment).

Disconnects have appeared between the *Lubanga* proceedings and local justice expectations. Chronic delays have tainted the trial's legitimacy. The exclusive focus

---

[94] *Written Submissions of the United Nations Special Representative of the Secretary-General on Children and Armed Conflict*, Prosecutor v. Lubanga, Document ICC-01/04-01/06-1229-AnxA ¶ 14 (March 18, 2008).

[95] Aptel, *supra* note 72, at 80.

[96] Alice Schmidt, *Volunteer* Child *Soldiers as Reality: A Development Issue for Africa*, 2(1) NEW SCHOOL ECONOMIC REVIEW 49, 63 (2007).

[97] Theresa Betancourt, Ivelina Borisova, Julia Rubin-Smith, Tara Gingerich, Timothy Williams, and Jessica Agnew-Blais, PSYCHOSOCIAL ADJUSTMENT AND SOCIAL REINTEGRATION OF CHILDREN ASSOCIATED WITH ARMED FORCES AND ARMED GROUPS: THE STATE OF THE FIELD AND FUTURE DIRECTIONS 22–23 (2008) (reporting study results).

[98] REDRESS Trust, *supra* note 7, at 13.

of the charges on the conscription, enlistment, or use of child soldiers, while "highlight[ing] the plight of the thousands of child soldiers in Congo," has, according to political scientist Phil Clark, led "many Congolese [to be] angry that the ICC has not charged Lubanga with more serious crimes, including the mass murder, rape, mutilation, and torture for which the UPC is notorious."[99] Moreover, as highlighted by the REDRESS Trust:

> In eastern DRC it is not generally known that the recruitment of children into armed groups is a war crime. Sensitisation about the criminal aspect of recruitment of children has been met with a considerable degree of surprise.[100]

On the one hand, sensitization may help edify a norm against the recruitment or use of child soldiers. The currency of this norm is to be desired, insofar as it would diminish the marketability of "ignorance of the law" excuses peddled by commanders. On the other hand, public surprise in the afflicted regions regarding the institutional choices made by the OTP corrosively exposes the OTP to suggestions that it is apathetic about the most foul of Lubanga's conduct and that of militia members. For example, investigators have unearthed evidence of widespread sexual violence, but their focus—encouraged by prosecutorial priorities—remained fixed on the unlawful recruitment or use of child soldiers. Eastern DRC was, and still is, among the most dangerous places in the world for women. Electing not to prosecute rampant sexual violence in such a high-profile inaugural trial certainly sent a callous message. In turn, this message prompted an ultimately unsuccessful attempt by victims to add more charges after the trial already had begun. Various motivations fuelled this attempt. One was the pressing need for gender justice. Another was the sentiment that prosecuting Lubanga only for conscription, enlistment, or use failed to reflect the full array of indignities that the child soldiers had suffered. The narrowness of the stated charges, moreover, also purged the conduct of the child soldiers from the discursive realm. Lubanga's forces, including child soldiers, mostly were members of his Hema ethnic group, but the violence they inflicted largely was directed against persons outside the Hema group, notably the Lendu people. The single-mindedness of the child soldiering charges neglects this element to the violence. Illegally recruited Hema children are specified as victims in the ICC indictment, while those Lendu (regardless of their age) attacked by adults and children in Lubanga's militia remain unrecognized. Other arrest warrants and cases before the ICC—including in the DRC situation—are not as parsimonious in

---

[99] Phil Clark, *In the Shadow of the Volcano: Democracy and Justice in Congo*, DISSENT 29, 34 (Winter 2007); *see also* Mariana Goetz, *The International Criminal Court and its Relevance to Affected Communities*, *in* COURTING CONFLICT? JUSTICE, PEACE, AND THE ICC IN AFRICA 65, 69 (Nicolas Waddell and Phil Clark eds, 2008) ("Lubanga's rebel movement committed widespread murder, rape, torture and pillaging. The population considers these crimes, rather than child recruitment (which is often seen as a necessary 'service' during conflict), as representative of the violence inflicted by Lubanga.").

[100] REDRESS Trust, *supra* note 7, at 18 (citation omitted). *See also* Cécile Aptel and Virginie Ladisch, THROUGH A NEW LENS: A CHILD-SENSITIVE APPROACH TO TRANSITIONAL JUSTICE 3 (ICTJ, August 2011) (concluding that "the focus on the crime of illegal recruitment and use . . . may not be fully understood by local communities, in places such as the DRC, and may not necessarily have positively affected the release of the children concerned, both in the DRC and in Colombia").

that they charge some defendants with recruitment or use of child soldiers along with several other crimes. In this regard, these prosecutions may avoid some of the disappointments of the inaugural *Lubanga* case.

Foreign states, such as Uganda and Rwanda, backed regional militia leaders in the DRC's Ituri district. The individualization of responsibility upon Lubanga, and a handful of other rebel leaders, skirts these statal contributions to the violence and may, even, divert attention away from them. Furthermore, the ICC's focus on rebel activity in the DRC situation triggers the specter of partiality. A very similar dynamic arises in the Uganda situation. For largely political reasons, the ICC has failed to investigate the DRC and Ugandan governments, even though both have perpetrated serious crimes, including the conscription, enlistment, or active use of child soldiers.[101]

Ron Atkinson argues that the brutality of the LRA toward children, which has become the defining transnational iconicity of the Northern Ugandan conflict, redirects attention from the Ugandan government's policy—just recently winding down—of having forcibly relocated nearly two million Acholi from their homes to squalid internally displaced persons' camps. In these camps, residents faced systematic human rights abuses, illness, and, ironically, enhanced susceptibility to LRA violence and abduction.[102] The popularized association of the LRA with lurid incidents of child abduction artificially inflates the legitimacy of the Ugandan government and offers it cover for its own wide-scale human rights abuses. The practice of child abduction by the LRA plays into the hands of those who benefit from a characterization of the Northern Ugandan conflict as an epic confrontation between the uncivilized Northerners and the civilized state. This narrative bleaches uncivilized acts by the civilized, in this case structural violence by the Ugandan government. Such asymmetries are not lost on local populations. Holistic approaches to transitional justice in Northern Uganda would have to include governmental accountability and also aim to redress feelings among the Acholi population of their perceived alienation from the Ugandan state. Furthermore, in an observation that bears directly on the credibility of transnational actors in local political life in Northern Uganda, Atkinson notes that "because ... humanitarian organisations necessarily had to work with the government to provide assistance, they became increasingly suspect in the eyes of many people."[103]

---

[101] Nicholas Waddell and Phil Clark, *Introduction, in* COURTING CONFLICT? JUSTICE, PEACE, AND THE ICC IN AFRICA 7, 10 (Nicholas Waddell and Phil Clark eds, 2008) (explaining the absence of prosecution of state actors on the basis of the ICC's concern "to avoid jeopardising relationships upon which it relies for its daily operations"). The Ugandan government had "recruited recent LRA escapees into government armed forces to take part in operations against the LRA." Angela Veale and Aki Stavrou, *Former Lord's Resistance Army Child Soldier Abductees: Explorations of Identity in Reintegration and Reconciliation,* 13(3) PEACE AND CONFLICT: JOURNAL OF PEACE PSYCHOLOGY 273, 275 (2007) (citation omitted).

[102] Ronald R. Atkinson, THE ROOTS OF ETHNICITY: THE ORIGINS OF THE ACHOLI OF UGANDA 283 (2nd edn, 2010); *see also id.* at 305 (noting that "the structural violence of camp life produced a far greater number of deaths than those caused by the LRA, just more quietly and unobtrusively").

[103] *Id.* at 307.

(2) Victim Reparations and Trial Participation

The Rome Statute permits reparations to victims, including children under the age of eighteen. The ICC may make a reparative order directly against a convicted person (as of the time of writing, it has not convicted anyone); it also can order the reparative award to be made through the separate Trust Fund for victims.[104] How is the Trust Fund capitalized? Through fines, forfeitures, and orders to freeze the assets of convicts; funds also may be independently offered by states or private parties. Awards to victims may be individual or collective.

To date, the Trust Fund has allocated funds, derived from voluntary grants, *inter alia* to a number of projects in Uganda and the DRC. Beneficiary projects include programs for child soldiers and abductees as well as programs geared to communities, war victims, victims of sexual violence, teenage mothers, orphans, and also to support services, agricultural initiatives, and communications. The Trust Fund has done well to disburse funds widely among war-afflicted constituencies. A resource focus excessively tilted toward child soldier returnees may elicit tensions within the community. A delicate situation remains for the ICC reparative framework, however, even in cases where funds assist communities as a whole. In such instances, former child soldiers effectively receive support from the same body of funds that is intended for all victim-survivors. These child soldiers thereby come to stand equivalently alongside survivors in whose harms they may have played a part.

Where their personal interests are affected, the Rome Statute also enables victims to participate in the criminal proceedings against the accused.[105] On this latter aspect, the definition of who, exactly, counts as a victim has proven nettlesome. In 2009, Trial Chamber I blocked individuals victimized by unlawfully recruited child soldiers from participating in the criminal proceedings against Lubanga.[106]

By way of background, within the context of the ICC framework and in the case of natural persons, victims are defined as those "who have suffered harm as a result of the commission of any crime within the [ICC's] jurisdiction."[107] Natural persons, it has been ruled, "can be the direct or indirect victims of a crime."[108] Whereas a direct victim is one "whose harm is the 'result of the commission of a crime within the jurisdiction of the Court'," an indirect victim is one "who suffer[s] harm as a result of the harm suffered by direct victims."[109]

---

[104] Rome Statute, *supra* note 71, Art. 75(2).

[105] *See generally id.* Art. 68(3).

[106] Prosecutor v. Lubanga, Case No. ICC-01/04-01/06, Decision on "indirect victims" (ICC Trial Chamber I, April 8, 2009) [hereinafter Decision on "indirect victims"].

[107] ICC Rules of Procedure and Evidence, U.N. Doc. PCNICC/2000/1/Add.1 (2000), Rule 85(a). Victims also may include "organizations or institutions that have sustained direct harm to any of their property which is dedicated to religion, education, art or science or charitable purposes, and to their historic monuments, hospitals and other places and objects for humanitarian purposes." *Id.* Rule 85(b).

[108] Decision on "indirect victims", *supra* note 106, at ¶ 41 (quoting Prosecutor v. Lubanga, Case No. ICC-01/04-01/06, Decision on victims' participation (ICC Trial Chamber I, January 18, 2008) ¶ 91).

[109] *Id.* ¶ 44.

Trial Chamber I's 2009 decision in *Lubanga* was prompted by a request for guidance from the ICC Registry. In November 2008, approximately 200 applications had been brought by persons seeking to participate in the proceedings. These applicants claimed they had suffered harm as a result of harms committed by the UPC, including in some instances by individual child soldiers.[110] The Registry queried whether applicants could be considered indirect victims if they were victims of crimes committed by children under the age of fifteen who were unlawfully involved in the UPC. Trial Chamber I took up the question. The OTP supported these applications and their understanding of the scope of indirect victims. So, too, did the Office for Public Counsel for Victims. The defense resisted, submitting *inter alia* that "the commission of war crimes, crimes against humanity or acts of genocide cannot be considered to be the normal or natural consequence of participation in hostilities, whether or not the combatants are children below the age of fifteen."[111]

Trial Chamber I, referencing Additional Protocol I and the CRC, noted that the offenses charged against Lubanga "were clearly framed to protect the interests of children in this age group."[112] The former child soldiers were held to be the direct victims. If under the age of fifteen at the relevant time (namely, the initial moment of alleged unlawful conscription, enlistment, or active use), then they would be eligible to participate in the proceedings.

Indirect victims "must establish that, as a result of their relationship with the direct victim, the loss, injury, or damage suffered by the latter gives rise to harm to them."[113] Hence, "the harm suffered by indirect victims must arise out of the harm suffered by direct victims, brought about by the commission of the crimes charged."[114] Indirect victims are those with "close personal relationships" to the direct victims: parents, for example, and also possibly an individual who intervenes to prevent a child from being unlawfully recruited.[115] With regard to the specific applicants in question, Trial Chamber I ruled that:

Excluded from the category of 'indirect victims', however, are those who suffered harm as a result of the (later) **conduct** of direct victims.... Indirect victims ... are restricted to those whose harm is linked to the *harm* of the affected children when the confirmed offenses were committed, not those whose harm is linked to any subsequent conduct by the children, criminal or otherwise.... [T]he person attacked by a child soldier is not an indirect victim for these purposes because his or her loss is not linked to the *harm* inflicted on the child when the offence was committed.[116]

---

[110] *Id.* ¶ 2. One applicant (a/0107/06) claimed "to have seen many children among the UPC who returned once the Lendu forces had left. The children allegedly participated in the military operations like adults. Indeed, he maintains they were the most active among the group: using arms, killing, torturing and pillaging." *Id.* ¶ 15.
[111] *Id.* ¶ 9.
[112] *Id.* ¶ 48.
[113] *Id.* ¶ 49.
[114] *Id.*
[115] *Id.* ¶¶ 50–51.
[116] *Id.* ¶ 52 (emphases in original).

Hence, "applicants who are alleged to be the victims of crimes committed by children who had been conscripted or enlisted whilst under the age of fifteen or used to participate actively in hostilities do not qualify as (indirect) victims of the crimes...."[117]

Within the *Lubanga* case, a hierarchy of victims has emerged on matters of participation. The child soldiers unequivocally are able to claim victim status. Persons harmed by the child soldiers fall outside the legal definition of victim and, hence, have no participatory status in proceedings on charges of unlawful enlistment, conscription, or use. Participation in criminal proceedings has important expressive value. One of the reasons states included participatory avenues in the Rome Statute was to render ICC justice more meaningful to afflicted communities. Curial interpretation in *Lubanga*, however, has ignited an insider/outsider dynamic among victims which, in turn, may yield tension and disappointment. This interpretation has rendered the harmful conduct of the child soldiers uncognizable and, even, invisible.

Looking ahead, charging an adult accused with a different crime requiring—as among its elements—proof of the underlying acts (including possibly the acts of child soldiers following recruitment) would foreseeably permit a broader array of victims to participate in the proceedings. International criminal law has developed a variety of doctrines that can assign culpability in situations of connived collective crime. These doctrines may be clumsy and controversial, but they exist. They can be deployed with a view to criminalizing much more than just the act of conscription, enlistment, or use of children to participate actively in hostilities. Command responsibility, for example, permits a superior to be held accountable for the acts of subordinates.[118] Liability theories such as "perpetrator behind the perpetrator" may implicate higher-level defendants, regardless of whether the direct perpetrator also is personally responsible for acts of atrocity.[119] The perpetrator behind the perpetrator theory consequently may be of particular interest in the context of the acts of child soldiers. Both of these approaches more accurately reflect the complexity of the impugned violence than the very reserved criminalization only of the act of conscripting, enlisting, or use. In both cases, in terms of penology, why not consider ordering child recruits to commit atrocities or failing to prevent them from so doing as an aggravating factor in sentencing?

In another decision in the *Lubanga* case, Trial Chamber I considered the preconditions for the participation of child victims in the criminal proceedings.

---

[117] *Id.* ¶ 54. For critical assessment of this decision, *see* Valentina Spiga, *Indirect Victims' Participation in the* Lubanga *Trial*, 8 J. INT'L CRIM. JUST. 183 (2010) (arguing in favor of an interpretation of indirect victims that would include those persons affected by crimes committed by child soldiers).

[118] Rome Statute, *supra* note 71, Art. 28.

[119] *See*, e.g., Katanaga and Chui confirmation of charges decision, *supra* note 75, at ¶ 496 ("A concept has developed in legal doctrine that acknowledges the possibility that a person who acts through another may be individually criminally responsible, regardless of whether the executor (the direct perpetrator) is also responsible. This doctrine is based on the early works of Claus Roxin and is identified by the term: 'perpetrator behind the perpetrator' (*Täter hinter dem Täter*).") (footnote omitted).

Interpreting the ICC Rules of Procedure and Evidence, Trial Chamber I unanimously held that applicants who are under the age of eighteen and who request to participate in the proceedings as victims do not require a person to act on their behalf.[120] This result is by no means objectionable. It is to be praised. However, the reasoning by which Trial Chamber I justified this entitlement to children within international criminal procedure contrasts with the conventional wisdom of the international legal imagination regarding the allocation of obligations to children. Trial Chamber I deliberately took a nuanced and progressive approach to assessing the capacity of the applicants. It noted that "although the applicants are still children, they are all over the age of 15. Indeed, they are relatively close to adulthood (18 years of age)."[121] Emphasizing the "idea that the views of a child shall be given due weight in accordance with his or her maturity," and underscoring the compatibility of that idea with internationally recognized human rights, Trial Chamber I held that:

There is no evidence to suggest the applicants in this group are particularly immature or that they do not understand the application they are individually making. Although the Chamber would normally expect a person to act on behalf of a minor, the fact that the applicants are very close to the age of legal maturity at the moment when the trial is to commence, creates a strong case for the Chamber to admit these applications.[122]

Trial Chamber I laudably pursued an individuated, careful, and considered approach to assessing the capacity of these children. It ruled that the "absence of a person acting on their behalf does not act as a bar to their participation."[123] This approach, I would add, should inform determinations regarding the obligations that children, in particular older adolescents, owe to others for their conduct. Such even-handedness would impartially instantiate a robust human rights paradigm of personhood and evolving capacities.

(c) Summary

In armed conflict, international criminal law proscribes the conscription or enlistment of children under the age of fifteen or their use to participate actively in hostilities. This crime also is entering national jurisdictions.[124] In Colombia, FARC officials have been prosecuted and convicted by national courts on charges of illegal military recruitment of minors. In the DRC, the recruitment of children under the age of eighteen apparently is a war crime.[125] In this vein, the IDDRS reports that

---

[120] Prosecutor v. Lubanga, Case No. ICC-01/04-01/06, Decision on the applications by victims to participate in the proceedings (ICC Trial Chamber I, December 15, 2008).

[121] *Id.* ¶ 92.

[122] *Id.* ¶¶ 95–96.

[123] *Id.* ¶ 97.

[124] *See,* e.g., Aptel, *supra* note 72, at 73 n. 17 (noting Germany). The Child Soldiers Accountability Act (United States, 2008) criminalizes this conduct and also renders aliens who have recruited or used child soldiers removable from the US.

[125] REDRESS Trust, *supra* note 7, at 28 (citing Art. 173 of Law No. 023/2002 of the Military Justice Code (November 18, 2002) and reporting military convictions of three local commanders for

"[m]any states have criminalized the recruitment of children below the age of 18."[126] Some movement, moreover, is afoot within global civil society to increase the restricted age under international criminal law from fifteen to eighteen. The push to expand the scope of the international war crime garners more traction in cases of armed groups recruiting children, along with forced recruitment or active use of children in hostilities by either armed forces or groups.

Referencing ICC prosecutions for conscripting, enlisting, or using children in armed conflict, Special Representative Coomaraswamy contends that "[t]he deterrence effect of even one conviction should be substantial."[127] Chief Prosecutor Moreno-Ocampo is, as expected, bullishly optimistic in this regard.[128] Paris Principle 8.1 also generally posits the "powerful deterrent" value of holding individuals accountable for this crime. It seems worthwhile, then, to explore these deterrence claims somewhat more closely, all the more given the domestication of the proscription into national penal jurisdictions.

(iii) Whither Deterrence?

By deterrence, international criminal law largely contemplates general deterrence. In a nutshell, general deterrence posits that potential perpetrators are dissuaded from committing acts of atrocity because their predecessors or contemporaries (whether in the same region or elsewhere) face or have faced penal sanction. *Arguendo*, potential perpetrators are aware, pay attention, and are presumed to act somewhat rationally. They fear prosecution and punishment. Their fears grow when others are seen to have been prosecuted and punished. Potential perpetrators respond by refraining from undertaking the proscribed conduct. Specific deterrence differs from general deterrence. It posits that punishment of a perpetrator deters that specific perpetrator from reoffending in the future. Although the sentencing judgments of international criminal tribunals do mention specific deterrence, the penological focus of international criminal law lies much more with general deterrence.

Ideally, when potential or actual adult recruiters or users of children in armed conflict are deterred, the illicit practice of child soldiering diminishes. Reducing the incidence of this practice helps scrub an odious stain from humanity, while also immediately assisting children under threat of recruitment. Criminalization may

---

child abduction in the DRC in 2006); *cf. Report of the Special Representative of the Secretary-General for Children and Armed Conflict*, delivered to the UN General Assembly, U.N. Doc. A/62/228, Part two, ¶ 46 (August 13, 2007) (noting that "[i]n March 2007, a local tribunal in the [DRC] prosecuted and sentenced a military commander for the recruitment and use of children").

[126] IDDRS, *supra* note 5, at §6.20, p. 15, *available at* <http://www.unddr.org/iddrs/06/20.php>. The IDDRS describes the criminalization of the recruitment of children under eighteen "as reflected in the Optional Protocol." *Id.* at §6.20, p. 16.

[127] Coomaraswamy, *supra* note 37, at 9.

[128] Moreno-Ocampo, *supra* note 84, at 30 ("If convicted, Thomas Lubanga's sentence will send a clear message: The era of impunity is ending.").

prompt those commanders who have already recruited protected children to release them. Deterring recruiters arguably would cause the brutalities committed against child soldiers to abate and the entanglement of children with militarized life to unfurl. Violence that child soldiers commit against civilian or combatant populations presumably would also decline.

By deterring the recruitment and active use of child soldiers, criminalization also inures to the benefit of adults in armies or peace enforcement forces who may have to fight children as enemies and, even, kill them in combat or self-defense. Although theoretically general in application, this interest may be disproportionately couched in terms of protecting the welfare and sensibilities of Westerners. For example, Singer counsels how difficult it is for American soldiers to have to contend with child foes, who have "the capacity to fight with a terrible ferocity and commit horrifying acts of violence... [and] they may be even more effective combatants than their adult counterparts."[129] He also reports that British soldiers who had faced child combatants in West Africa in 2001 developed clinical depression and PTSD. Dallaire notes how adults, including Western soldiers or police, may hesitate to counterattack (even in self-defense) when confronted with child soldiers, thereby generating a tactical advantage for commanders who insidiously deploy children in conflict.[130]

In any event, the debate over the deterrent function of international criminal law remains ongoing and largely unresolved.[131] Insufficient data exist to conclude whether the threat of individual prosecution or punishment actually deters the commission of atrocity crimes. We all can hope. But, for the moment, international criminal law has not yet discharged the burden of proof regarding the deterrent value of its interventions.

A number of structural factors vex international criminal law's ability to attain its deterrent aspirations.[132] One such factor is the reality that only a tiny number of potential suspects ever are indicted, let alone apprehended. Criminologists long have shown that it is the likelihood of getting caught that best deters potential offenders from offending. Moreover, deterrence assumes that some sort of rational cost-benefit calculus occurs within the minds of potential perpetrators. The bare rudiments of this calculus involve comparing the "pros" of criminal conduct to the "cons" of getting caught and punished. Whether such a calculus transpires in the mind of an individual before he or she commits a serious ordinary common crime in times of peace remains a subject of ongoing debate. The ability of potential perpetrators meaningfully to engage in this calculus within the context of extraordinary international crime in times of conflict, however, seems somewhat fantastic. This is not to say that group members fail to exercise some volition, discretion, or

[129] P.W. Singer, CHILDREN AT WAR 168–170 (2006) (also referring *en passant* to Indian and Colombian forces).

[130] Roméo Dallaire, THEY FIGHT LIKE SOLDIERS, THEY DIE LIKE CHILDREN 119 (2010).

[131] Beth Van Schaack, *Crimen Sine Lege: Judicial Lawmaking at the Intersection of Law and Morals*, 97 GEO. L. J. 119, 146 (2008).

[132] *See generally* Mark A. Drumbl, ATROCITY, PUNISHMENT, AND INTERNATIONAL LAW 169–173 (2007) (citing many other observers); Julian Ku and Jide Nzelibe, *Do International Criminal Tribunals Deter or Exacerbate Humanitarian Atrocities?*, 84 WASH. U. L. Q. 777 (2006).

forethought in committing extraordinary international crimes. Rather, it is to say that it seems implausible that, on the whole, they would resist doing so merely out of fear of eventual criminal prosecution or carceral punishment in The Hague or some other juridical setting.

Commanders intoxicated by genocidal furor and inflated by narcissism may believe they are doing "good" by eliminating the evil "other." Their attachment to the normative value of atrocity warps whatever cost-benefit analysis they may undertake. Even if commanders were to take the prospect of international incarceration seriously, however, disavowing child soldier recruitment or use is not the only available behavioral option. Other conceivable options are to continue to recruit child soldiers and, then, to simply conceal that behavior; to refuse to surrender; to refuse to hand over child soldiers as part of the official demobilization process and, instead, dismiss them surreptitiously such that they remain unable to access training and reinsertion programs; or perhaps even to abuse them further such that far fewer survive conflict. Ironically, the more transnational norm entrepreneurs disseminate imagery of child soldiers as easily programmable automatons, the more recruiters may simply come to believe it and, as a result, may more hungrily pursue children's membership in fighting forces.

The rub of my argument is that preventative and deterrent goals would more robustly be attained were diverse accountability mechanisms to address the multiple roots of child soldiering. These roots include: adult commanders, enlisters, conscriptors, and users of children; the children themselves, at times acting dispositionally, tactically, and volitionally; families who encourage children to fight or who abandon them to warlords; local officials who feel a need to supply a certain number of soldiers to warring powers in order to preserve their credibility; the state that fails to protect; national politicians addled by corruption and self-interest; decaying infrastructure and dismantled institutions; legacies of the slave trade, colonialism, and mercantilism; poverty, spurious occupational opportunities, and dim educational options; foreign financiers who arm; the lucrative small-arms trade; international commercial markets in which looted natural resources are traded (along with those foreigners who purchase them); international peacekeepers who are ineffective or, even, themselves abuse residents of war-stricken societies; and powerful foreign governments who gaze elsewhere or support hateful regimes while atrocity rages. Instead of contenting itself with a handful of expensive trials, perhaps the international legal imagination might do more to effectively fund counterpropaganda and counterabduction training in areas susceptible to child recruitment.[133] Why not better protect refugee and internally displaced persons' camps?[134] Invest more

---

[133]   *See*, e.g., Bernd Beber and Christopher Blattman, *The Logic of Child Soldiering and Coercion* 28 (February 2011, cited with permission) ("Just as Western school-children perform fire drills, or learn not to speak to strangers, so should children in war zones be drilled in escape and resistance to misinformation.").

[134]   Simon Reich and Vera Achvarina, *Why Do Children 'Fight'? Explaining Child Soldier Ratios in African Intrastate Conflicts* (University of Pittsburgh, Ford Institute for Human Security: Policy Brief 04-3 (2005)).

rigorously in education?[135] Why not do more to augment quality of life for all children in conflict zones, including on essentials such as health care and food?

Notwithstanding international criminal law's current operational focus, the fact remains that it is not just non-state actors or rebel groups that recruit or use child soldiers. In Burma, for example, children constitute a substantial part of state armed forces. The Somali government, which is armed and financed by the United States, conscripts and enlists child soldiers. Would internationally-conducted prosecutions of leaders of rebel groups realistically deter these states (and their officials) from turning to child soldiers, especially when no international criminal court or tribunal exercises jurisdiction over them? Anomalies arise even where international jurisdiction exists, for example in the DRC and Uganda, whose state officials self-referred internal situations to the ICC in the hopes of sparking greater international oversight of rebel groups. These states can count on the ICC's need for their cooperation, in turn, to shield their own human rights practices from thorough scrutiny.

Paradoxically, indicting a handful of rebel leaders and detaining an even smaller subset thereof for prosecution might expiate the pressure for truly meaningful action by incubating a false perception that enough already is being done. International criminal law may coddle the illusion of preventing human rights abuses through the prosecution of a handful of human rights abusers. It may dull the resolve to do more by presenting the palliative allure of premature closure.

A polycentric vision of justice—in which international criminal prosecutions constitute *a* practice, not *the* iconic practice—instead might activate state responsibility and, thereby, contribute an additional tool to efforts to curb child soldiering.[136] To date, state responsibility for child soldiers has attracted only modest attention beyond the activities of the Security Council in preparing its "list of shame." Although supposedly dual, the relationship between state responsibility and individual penal culpability is actually hierarchical, with the latter coming at the expense of the former.[137]

[135] Theresa S. Betancourt, Stephanie Simmons, Ivelina Borisova, Stephanie E. Brewer, Uzo Iweala, and Marie de la Soudière, *High Hopes, Grim Reality: Reintegration and the Education of Former Child Soldiers in Sierra Leone*, 52(4) COMP. EDUC. REV. 565, 584 (2008) (noting in the context of Sierra Leone that "[t]o date, the international community has failed to provide sufficient, sustained resources for educational opportunities").

[136] *Cf.* Stephan Parmentier, Kris Vanspauwen, and Elmar Weitekamp, *Dealing with the Legacy of Mass Violence: Changing Lenses to Restorative Justice, in* SUPRANATIONAL CRIMINOLOGY: TOWARDS A CRIMINOLOGY OF INTERNATIONAL CRIMES 335, 337 (Alette Smeulers and Roelof Haveman eds, 2008) (observing "the dominant approach to dealing with international crimes, namely through retributive justice and specifically through criminal prosecutions"); Mark Freeman, TRUTH COMMISSIONS AND PROCEDURAL FAIRNESS 10 (2006) (noting "the importance of criminal trials remains unrivaled").

[137] On purported duality in the case of genocide, *see Case Concerning the Application of the Convention on the Prevention and Punishment of the Crime of Genocide* (BiH v. Serbia and Montenegro), Judgment (International Court of Justice, February 26, 2007) ¶ 178. On the reality of subalternity in the context of genocide, *see* Amabelle C. Asuncion, *Pulling the Stops on Genocide: The State or the Individual?*, 20 EUR. J. INT'L L. 1195, 1196 (2009) ("The legal architecture for genocide prosecution, however, is designed for individual convictions and state acquittal.").

These proposals for reform, in turn, prompt new questions. Could muscular instantiations of state responsibility permit individual recruiters or users to avoid findings of criminal wrongdoing? Could such persons come to obscure their culpability by drowning it within the murk of structural connivance? If international criminal prosecutions of adult recruiters carry value independent of the weak promise of deterrence—for example, expressive or incapacitative—then something might be lost by the prospect that such prosecutions would become existentially threatened, in this case by stripping their singularity as tools of justice. Might presenting child soldiers as operating along a continuum of circumscribed action hinder the ascription of responsibility for child soldiering to adult recruiters or users? What about to the state or to other institutional actors? If youth exhibit some initiative in joining, *arguendo*, why should state officials be held responsible?

These concerns, however instructive, are predicated on a zero-sum view of the interaction among justice mechanisms. The game, however, need not be zero-sum. I do not believe it is inexorable that increasing the number of justice mechanisms would lead to a mutually exclusive competition. Nor do I see how a circumscribed action model would trigger a race-to-the-bottom to blame only the child soldier while threatening the state responsibility that I hope to enliven. Engaging a cooperative array of diverse justice mechanisms to pursue responsibility for child soldiering would shift the legal landscape in the direction of making it more difficult for any one actor to evade accountability. The current framework, which narrowly pins responsibility upon the small constituency of adult recruiters or users, requires rethinking. This constituency, assuredly, is ugly and blameworthy. But the fact remains that it is a conveniently easy target to blame. Squarely striking this target yields only a partial, expedient, and largely symbolic print of justice. Wessells' guidance is apposite:

At the grassroots level, children's disaffection with the political system and their inability to meet basic needs, access education, or obtain paying jobs creates conditions that are ripe for child soldiering. Even if the criminalization strategy helps stop recruiters and commanders from enlisting and using children as soldiers, it does not accomplish the parallel task of reducing children's motivation to become soldiers.[138]

In the earlier discussion of Sierra Leone, I suggested ways in which the war crime of conscripting, enlisting, or using children in hostilities might be fine-tuned while also becoming more comprehensive. My ambitions are neither for this conduct to become ignored by international criminal courts or tribunals nor, in turn, for these institutions to be overlooked, shuttered, or dismissed. Instead, my goal is simply to emphasize that much more needs to be done to deter child soldiering. Just because required preventative activity transcends courtrooms and jailhouses does not mean that it abandons them.

---

[138] Wessells, CHILD SOLDIERS, *supra* note 4, at 240.

(iv) Conclusion

Whether keyed to the increasingly dated *lex lata* prohibition related to persons under the age of fifteen or the powerful *lex ferenda* pull toward persons under the age of eighteen, influential advocates construct the voluntary recruitment of child soldiers as "always a misnomer."[139] This construction obviates the need to theorize the behavior and conduct of juveniles during armed conflict. The adult is all that matters. The adult is at the center and, once again, the child is relegated to the periphery. Yet, for Jo Boyden, a nagging question persists, namely, "whether conceptualising child soldiering solely in terms of adult culpability and adult infractions is adequate."[140] Can the international legal imagination realistically halt child soldiering based on partial or anodyne understandings of the problem at hand?

The practice of child soldiering is simply not reducible to the deviance of sociopathic adult recruiters or conflict entrepreneurs. It is not epiphenomenal to their malevolence. Nor is children's involvement in fighting forces entirely aleatory, to wit, a case of being in the wrong place at the wrong time. The child soldier is not foundationally hapless. Effective deterrence of child soldiering hinges upon ferreting out its many contributory variables. International criminal law, after all, can only do so much.

However immediately destabilizing, it is only by revisiting orthodoxies regarding how children join fighting forces and why some children become implicated in the serial commission of acts of atrocity that rehabilitation and reinsertion initiatives undertaken on their behalf actually can be improved. This revitalization would further the goals of the Optional Protocol which, in Article 6(3), provides that, when necessary, states parties shall accord demobilized or released children all appropriate assistance for their physical and psychological recovery and social reintegration. A need therefore arises to consider the dispositional acts that some minors—in particular, older adolescents—undertake to enter fighting forces and, once they are there, that inform their involvement in the commission of atrocity crimes. It is to this delicate task that this book now turns in Chapter 6.

---

[139] See discussion *supra* note 25.
[140] Jo Boyden, *Children, War and World Disorder in the 21st Century: A Review of the Theories and the Literature on Children's Contributions to Armed Violence* 8 (Queen Elizabeth House, University of Oxford, Working Paper No. 138, 2006).

6

Rights, Wrongs, and Transitional Reconstruction

How to approach child soldiers as and after they exit conflict? Faultless passive victim imagery shapes the place designated for child soldiers within the architecture of *inter* and *post bellum* peace and justice settlements. The influence of this imagery is both salutary and perplexing. It is salutary when it curtails the application of national penal law to child soldiers in cases of their alleged implication in extraordinary atrocity crimes. It perplexes when it emaciates transitional justice mechanisms that operate away from courtrooms and jailhouses, to wit, truth and reconciliation commissions, traditional ceremonies, and restorative measures. This Chapter additionally will show that other externalities arise from current policy preferences and tendencies.

(i) Disarmament, Demobilization, and Reintegration

Ideally, disarmament, demobilization, and reintegration (DDR) programming intends to redirect all persons associated with armed forces or armed groups— adults as well as children—away from militarized life. In some jurisdictions, DDR explicitly adds rehabilitation as a fourth goal and becomes identified as DDRR. This was the case in Liberia.

DDR programming can occur during conflict, but it mainly takes place after conflict. Disarmament, DDR's first step, means the collection, disposal, or destruction of weapons. In some instances, members of armed forces or armed groups receive inducements (financial or otherwise) to surrender their weapons. Demobilization, the second step, refers to the disbanding of armed forces or armed groups and the discharge of individual members. In the specific case of child soldiers, the term "release" may be preferred in that it adverts to the unlawful nature of the underlying military service.

Reintegration, the trickiest step, then follows. Reintegration is an ongoing process. It centers upon reuniting demobilized persons with their families and communities. Its aim is to reinsert returnees into civilian life and sustainable employment. Reintegration initiatives generally incorporate rehabilitation programming and counseling. Following atrocity-producing conflicts, the fact that "many perpetrators of . . . crimes are returning to the community poses immense psychological and social challenges."[1] For the preponderant number of child soldiers, reintegration must come at home. Hardly any child soldiers end up living Ishmael Beah's transnational life of authorship and advocacy, of television and radio, and of New York and Geneva. Home, however, is often the same space in which the children initially had been drawn into conflict, suffered abuses, and where some then assailed others. Reintegration, therefore, is not an arm's-length or abstract exercise. Reintegration occurs face-to-face; and must have the mettle to manage the strains and stresses of day-to-day encounters between the aggrieved and those who had caused them harm. The quotidian nature of these encounters in no way dulls their poignancy. In some situations, children from opposing factions return to the same community. This adds an additional layer of complexity to the reintegration matrix.

Disarmament and demobilization offer quickly identifiable results that are compatible with short-term feedback loops. Reintegration involves longitudinal assessment and is more difficult to ascertain, let alone define. Agencies and donors, therefore, tend to focus on the first two steps. Fortunately, as this Chapter synthesizes, academic research is emerging on the topic of the reintegration of persons formerly associated with armed forces or groups, including children. This research, in turn, can help guide future policy development.

Should DDR programming centrally focus on former combatants (in practice, often haphazardly determined by persons who carry guns or can produce a gun)? Or should it cover all persons formerly associated with fighting factions? Happily, the push is toward the latter approach, which is more holistic. The eligibility of a broad array of persons formerly associated with armed forces or groups for DDR programming does not—and should not—preordain the monochrome nature of the content of such programming.

DDR aspires to be a structured and predictable process. In this vein, best practices and policy manuals are emerging as to what DDR programming ideally ought to look like. UN agencies or NGOs often become involved in the preparation of such documents. One comprehensive and innovative compendium is called the Integrated Disarmament, Demobilization and Reintegration Standards.[2]

In practice, however, DDR is not always structured, nor integrated, nor predictable. While conflict is ongoing, significant numbers of mobilized persons (including children) may exit militarized life on their own through escape or abandonment. In Uganda, for example, spontaneous demobilization happened with "great regularity" and "young people...abducted by the L.R.A. often

---

[1] Prudence Acirokop, *The Potential and Limits of* Mato Oput *as a Tool for Reconciliation and Justice, in* Children and Transitional Justice: Truth-Telling, Accountability and Reconciliation 267, 276 (UNICEF Innocenti Research Centre and Human Rights Program at Harvard Law School, Sharanjeet Parmar, Mindy Jane Roseman, Saudamini Siegrist, and Theo Sowa eds, 2010) [hereinafter Children and Transitional Justice].

[2] *Integrated Disarmament, Demobilization and Reintegration Standards* (2006), *available at* <http://www.unddr.org/iddrs> [hereinafter IDDRS].

escape[d] and [found] their way home."[3] They trickled back in uncoordinated fashion. Uganda lacked a formal national DDR program.[4] Global civil society and UN agencies interceded to help provide programming for returnees. It has been estimated that half of LRA abductees from the northern Acholi districts passed through a formal reintegration process.[5] In Colombia, many child recruits were informally discharged, meaning that relatively few ended up in official DDR programs.

Furthermore, on a general note, sometimes DDR programming includes only adults. Upon release, children are summarily dispatched home. In yet other situations, programming may be chaotic, entropic, and unmonitored. Significant regional or local variation may arise within the same jurisdiction. Bottom-up efforts may plug gaps—or they may not—therefore creating an *ad hoc* patchwork. The fact that DDR may not be nationally standardized is not necessarily a problem if effective local mechanisms become established. However, a situation where some localities remain bereft of programming is not desirable.

Some recent DDR initiatives (Liberia and Sierra Leone) have enjoyed successes, particularly when it comes to disarmament and demobilization.

DDR began in Sierra Leone in July 1998.[6] It involved soldiers of all ages from all armed forces and groups. DDR proceeded through phases. The DDR process worked at full strength as of 2002. Overall, 72,490 combatants of all ages were registered.[7] 6,774 children (all but 513 of whom were male) proceeded through the DDR process: 3,710 were RUF, 2,026 CDF, and 427 AFRC (the remainder was non-affiliated or from other factions, including the SLA).[8] Following disarmament, former child soldiers were demobilized. Children under the age of fifteen typically were sent to interim care centers under the auspices of UNICEF and partnered child protection agencies. Fifteen, sixteen, and seventeen year-olds tended to be placed in group homes or allowed to live independently.[9] Reintegration then ensued. In Sierra Leone, this third step focused on family and community reunification. Not all returnees, however, have family to come back to.

---

[3] Michael Wessells, *Psychosocial Issues in Reintegrating Child Soldiers*, 37 CORNELL INT'L L.J. 513, 514 (2004); *cf.* IDDRS, *supra* note 2, at §5.30, p. 20, *available at* <http://www.unddr.org/iddrs/05/download/IDDRS_530.pdf> (noting that "[a]n estimated 30 percent of child combatants never enter formal DDR").

[4] Michael Wessells, CHILD SOLDIERS: FROM VIOLENCE TO PROTECTION 174 (2006, first paperback 2009).

[5] Jeannie Annan, Moriah Brier, and Filder Aryemo, *From "Rebel" to "Returnee": Daily Life and Reintegration for Young Soldiers in Northern Uganda*, 24 JOURNAL OF ADOLESCENT RESEARCH 639, 642 (2009).

[6] WITNESS TO TRUTH: REPORT OF THE SIERRA LEONE TRUTH & RECONCILIATION COMMISSION, Volume 3B, Chapter 4 ¶ 393 (Children and the Armed Conflict in Sierra Leone) (2004), *available at* <http://www.sierra-leone.org/Other-Conflict/TRCVolume3B.pdf> [hereinafter SLTRC, VOL. 3B, CH. 4].

[7] TRUTH AND RECONCILIATION COMMISSION REPORT FOR THE CHILDREN OF SIERRA LEONE 24 (Child-Friendly Version, 2004) [hereinafter SLTRC CHILDREN'S REPORT].

[8] SLTRC, VOL. 3B, CH. 4, *supra* note 6, ¶ 394.

[9] *Id.* ¶ 395–396.

In terms of training, DDR in Sierra Leone presented former child soldiers with a number of programmatic options.[10] Some pursued the option to serve in the newly constituted national armed forces. Those who chose to enroll in school were relieved of the need to pay school fees and could participate in special rapid education programs. Slightly over half of the former child soldiers chose skills-training as an option (for example, carpentry, hairdressing, tailoring, auto mechanic work, or weaving). Individuals who elected skills-training received a basic monthly allowance and, following completion, a start-up kit. Some child soldiers opted for agricultural training (similar to skills-training) and enlistment in public works projects. DDR programming in Sierra Leone also included scar removal and drug addiction counseling.

In Liberia, child soldiers went through the same disarmament procedures as adults, but did not have to hand in weapons in order to be eligible.[11] In Liberia, 11,870 children were officially demobilized (this figure represented slightly over one-tenth of the total number of demobilized fighters).[12] Approximately 9,000 were boys. Overall, the process in Liberia was similar to Sierra Leone's.

Notwithstanding these overall successes, in both Sierra Leone and Liberia—and elsewhere—DDR programs also have encountered particularized difficulties in cases of adults as well as children.

Doubts have been raised, for example, regarding the value-added that DDR programming actually brought to the reintegration of adult ex-combatants in Sierra Leone.[13] DDR has been faulted for low participation of girl soldiers and for unresponsiveness to their needs.[14] DDR also has been criticized for disregarding the interests of victims of gender-based violence generally; for falling short in encouraging affected communities and individual participants to exercise input in and ownership over the process; for failing to actuate meaningful employment prospects or pedagogical opportunities; and for neglecting to build sustainable local capacity. Programs have been chided both for overlooking child soldiers and for excessively prioritizing them.[15] After conflict, and following unsuccessful

---

[10] For details regarding these options, *see* Myriam Denov, CHILD SOLDIERS: SIERRA LEONE'S REVOLUTIONARY UNITED FRONT 158 (2010).

[11] Save the Children, WHEN CHILDREN AFFECTED BY WAR GO HOME: LESSONS LEARNED FROM LIBERIA 20 (2003).

[12] Republic of Liberia, Truth and Reconciliation Commission, VOLUME II: CONSOLIDATED FINAL REPORT 316 (June 30, 2009), *available at* <http://trcofliberia.org/resources/reports/final/volume-two_layout-1.pdf> [hereinafter LIBERIA TRC FINAL REPORT].

[13] Macartan Humphreys and Jeremy M. Weinstein, *Demobilization and Reintegration*, 51(4) JOURNAL OF CONFLICT RESOLUTION 531, 533, 549 (2007) ("Evidence from Sierra Leone does not support the hypothesis that participation in a DDR program increases the degree to which combatants are accepted by their families and communities.").

[14] Coalition to Stop the Use of Child Soldiers, CHILD SOLDIERS GLOBAL REPORT 2008 16 (2008). Denov highlights the reluctance of girl soldiers to participate in DDR programs in Sierra Leone owing to fears of public acknowledgement of their role in conflict and the impact thereof on their marriageability. Denov, *supra* note 10, at 163. For these girls, "the risks of participating in DDR, and exposing their former roles as fighters, far outweighed the potential benefits." *Id.*

[15] For discussion of overlooking children, *see* Lydia Polgreen, *Fewer Conflicts Involve Child Soldiers, Report Finds*, N.Y. TIMES (May 22, 2008) A18 (reporting that, although "[i]nternational donors have spent millions to ease fighters back into civilian life, ... children are often left out. In the [CAR] ...

experiences with DDR programs, some former child soldiers turn to crime, while others drift into prostitution, menial labor, or dangerous work. In the DRC, despite the existence of an official DDR program since 2004, re-recruitment of demobilized children chronically persists.[16] DDR initiatives may disproportionately focus on urban youth instead of rural youth, thereby failing to redress the pre-existing marginalization of rural constituencies.

Ah-Jung Lee, moreover, worries that DDR may disempower former child soldiers by exposing them to the machinations of military commanders and influential adults tasked with identifying who, exactly, qualifies as a child soldier and, hence, who becomes eligible to receive benefits from internationally supported programs.[17] She pungently adds:

[R]eintegration benefits for 'child soldiers' often went to those who were already better off and most connected to the local power networks . . . [H]umanitarian assistance ended up strengthening these very patronage systems and brought the young ex-combatants back to the bottom of their social hierarchy.[18]

DDR programs routinely award assistance to demobilized persons, including child soldiers. By local standards, this assistance may be quite generous. It includes cash payments, resettlement packages, waived school fees, household items, training, benefits, and jobs. Although well-intended, this aspect of DDR programming can prove tricky to manage. The allocation of assistance to former child soldiers has aggravated their stigmatization by sparking resentment within their families and communities.[19] Benefits may flow to children who committed atrocities in the community, which raises the ominous specter of "blood money" that rewards violence.[20] Disparities emerge between programs for returnees supported by DDR and external funds, on the one hand, and inadequately resourced reparative programs for conflict victims (including children) who had never associated with armed forces or groups, on the other hand.[21] These disparities exacerbate social tensions, which bubble up even when formerly abducted child soldiers are the

---

about 7,500 fighters were demobilized and given cash and training to start new lives. Only 26 children participated even though children were believed to make up a large portion of the fighters.").

[16] Inna Lazareva, *Many DRC Children Volunteer to Fight*, IWPR ICC-Africa Update (No. 291, March 10, 2011).

[17] Ah-Jung Lee, *Understanding and Addressing the Phenomenon of 'Child Soldiers'* 27 (Refugee Studies Center, Working Paper Series No. 52, Oxford University, 2009) (Master's Thesis).

[18] *Id.* at 28.

[19] Neil Boothby, Jennifer Crawford, and Jason Halperin, *Mozambique child soldier life outcome study: Lessons learned in rehabilitation and reintegration efforts*, 1(1) GLOBAL PUBLIC HEALTH 87, 99 (2006) (education stipends awarded to former child soldiers induced tensions within families because they "singled out" the former child soldier for support "over the family's other children").

[20] Wessells, CHILD SOLDIERS, *supra* note 4, at 169.

[21] REPORTING TRANSITIONAL JUSTICE: A HANDBOOK FOR JOURNALISTS 69 (2007), *available at* <http://www.communicatingjustice.org/en/handbook> (noting that it is "not uncommon" for the "benefits of a DDR program to dwarf the benefits offered to victims as part of a reparations program, if one exists" and that "[t]his kind of perceived 'special treatment' for ex-combatants often creates resentment within the community").

programmatic beneficiaries.[22] Perversely, the availability of cash benefits may "giv[e] very poor children who see their peers receiving cash at demobilization an incentive to join the armed group in the hope of obtaining the same reward."[23] Either on their own or acting at the behest of others, children may exit and then rejoin armed groups multiple times in order to receive several rounds of payments. Myriam Denov reports that demobilized RUF child soldiers who "did not receive their financial benefits on time" ended up organizing "a violent attack against the DDR programmers."[24]

Having recently been chastened by each of the Special Representatives of the Secretary-General for Children and Armed Conflict, the IDDRS, and Paris Principle 7.35, the practice of uncritically awarding benefits, in particular cash payments at the point of demobilization, is steadily waning. Paris Principle 7.30 buttresses this trend by noting that "[i]nclusive programming which supports children who have been recruited or used as well as other vulnerable children benefits the wider community." A move to substitute the conceptual baseline from faultless passive victimhood to circumscribed action would provide an even firmer footing for all future DDR benefits to be distributed incrementally during reintegration and within a *quid pro quo* system of mutual and reciprocal obligation. Requiring conditionality, incrementalism, and exchange within a multivalent nexus would help dissipate tensions while still preserving the necessary flow of support to all war-affected children, including children formerly associated with armed forces or groups.

A web of obligation also would help stanch potential corruption on the part of the community in positioning itself vis-à-vis international aid. Susan Shepler reports that Sierra Leonean communities created "a list of child soldiers, so as to be ready in case an NGO with ready funds for reintegration programs came around."[25] Village leaders compiled the information. Shepler observes:

The lists they came up with generally did not match what I knew about the actual participation of children in fighting. The chief's son, the imam's son, and those who were currently attending school appeared on the list—youth who were not former combatants. Inclusion on the list was based on connections or on who could best use the aid, not necessarily on who had actually participated in fighting.[26]

Gerontocracy and hierarchy may inequitably distort the flow of funds and resources. Similar to Lee's observations, then, the already worst-off fall even further

---

[22] REDRESS Trust, Victims, Perpetrators or Heroes? Child Soldiers Before the International Criminal Court 12 (2006); Jeannie Annan, Christopher Blattman, and Roger Horton, The State of Youth and Youth Protection in Northern Uganda: Findings from The Survey for War Affected Youth 77, 80 (September 2006) [hereinafter SWAY]; Susan Shepler, *The Rites of the Child: Global Discourses of Youth and Reintegrating Child Soldiers in Sierra Leone*, 4 J. Hum. Rts. 197, 201–202 (2005).

[23] Wessells, *Psychosocial Issues*, *supra* note 3, at 523.

[24] Denov, *supra* note 10, at 152.

[25] Shepler, *supra* note 22, at 206 (footnote omitted).

[26] *Id.* (footnote omitted).

behind. Transnational interventions must remain mindful not to inadvertently provide scaffolding for patrimonialism.

Traditionally, as a matter of both policy and practice, DDR tends to unfold separately from transitional justice. This means that DDR proceeds without addressing the potential responsibility of demobilized persons for systematic human rights abuses. The gulf between transitional justice and DDR arises for both adults and children, but is particularly wide in the case of children.

Why this gulf? One reason lies with DDR's immediate prioritization of military and security objectives, namely, cessation of hostilities, discarding of weapons, and sustaining a ceasefire. Sequencing is a challenge. Complex situations arise when demobilization is secured for combatants in atrocity-producing conflicts through collective guarantees of amnesty that, in turn, become formalized in peace agreements. Kimberly Theidon rues how, to the extent that DDR programs are reduced to "'dismantling the machinery of war,' [they] fail[] to adequately consider how to move beyond demobilizing combatants to facilitating social reconstruction and coexistence."[27] In response, drawing from her work in Colombia and Peru, Theidon sees potential in local transitional justice initiatives.[28]

The routine telegraphing of discourses of faultless passive victimhood and non-responsibility additionally helps account for the weak deployment of transitional justice in DDR processes specific to child soldiers. For example, reception centers in Northern Uganda:

[P]romote the innocence of the returned youth, stressing to both young people and families that any perpetration of violence was forced upon [returnees] and therefore not their choice. Community sensitizations have been carried out to instill this message in families and community members, and consequently the innocence discourse is prevalent throughout the area.[29]

At a policy level, attempts have been undertaken to refresh DDR so as to narrow its current distance from transitional justice processes. The IDDRS, for instance, urges conjunction. It rebukes the present landscape in which "formal institutional connections between DDR and transitional justice are rarely considered," noting also that "[t]he lack of coordination between transitional justice and DDR may lead to unbalanced outcomes and missed opportunities."[30] Depending on the

---

[27] Kimberly Theidon, *Transitional Subjects: The Disarmament, Demobilization and Reintegration of Former Combatants in Colombia*, 1 INT'L J. TRANSITIONAL J. 66, 67 (2007) (footnote omitted).

[28] *Id.*; Kimberly Theidon, *Justice in Transition: The Micropolitics of Reconciliation in Postwar Peru*, 50(3) JOURNAL OF CONFLICT RESOLUTION 433 (2006).

[29] Annan, Brier, and Aryemo, *supra* note 5, at 643 (citation omitted). Community sensitizations play an important role generally in DDR programs for former child soldiers. *See*, e.g., Theresa Betancourt, Ivelina Borisova, Julia Rubin-Smith, Tara Gingerich, Timothy Williams, and Jessica Agnew-Blais, PSYCHOSOCIAL ADJUSTMENT AND SOCIAL REINTEGRATION OF CHILDREN ASSOCIATED WITH ARMED FORCES AND ARMED GROUPS: THE STATE OF THE FIELD AND FUTURE DIRECTIONS 12 (2008) (noting that the reintegration phase usually contains *inter alia* "[s]ensitization of communities via open community discussions regarding the return of ex-[children associated with fighting forces] (to promote forgiveness and acceptance)").

[30] IDDRS, *supra* note 2, at §6.20, pp. 3–4, *available at* <http://www.unddr.org/iddrs/06/20.php>.

circumstances, the IDDRS supports transitional justice processes as part of DDR programming for children.[31]

Would the reorientation proffered by the IDDRS affect actual practice when it comes to child soldiers implicated in acts of atrocity? Perhaps, but unless the international legal imagination revisits the intensity of victimhood imagery and replaces it with something more subtle—such as a model of circumscribed action— recourse to transitional justice in child DDR programming will likely remain sporadic and superficial.

(ii) National Penal Law

Many jurisdictions retain national law that permits the prosecution of persons under the age of eighteen on charges of extraordinary international crime. Some national jurisdictions have, in fact, initiated such prosecutions. These prosecutions tend, however, to be very infrequent. Looking ahead, the directional movement in post-conflict societies increasingly will trend—*de jure* or *de facto*—even further away from the criminal prosecution of former child soldiers within national courts, whether civilian or military, in cases of extraordinary international crime. This movement likely will be more pronounced in post-conflict societies whose atrocities have become subject to international judicialization or rule of law efforts.

Three factors energize this movement. The first factor involves amnesties that immunize their recipients from criminal prosecution and/or civil lawsuit. Amnesties may be collectively negotiated for combatants of all ages, including child soldiers, as part of peace talks. Amnesties may comport with local justice values—or they may not—but, regardless, international criminal lawyers denounce them in cases of mass atrocity crimes.[32] Paradoxically, however, a second factor that imperils national criminal prosecutions specifically of child soldiers is international criminal law itself, which, as Chapter 4 discussed, remains skittish about prosecuting persons under the age of eighteen at the time of the alleged atrocity crime. Transnationalized best practices, soft law documents, model guidelines, and policy blueprints evincing *inter alia* the Straight 18 position constitute a third factor that discourages domestic criminal prosecutions of child soldiers for atrocity crimes. For example, although not condemning criminal prosecutions of child soldiers as unlawful, the IDDRS firmly cautions against them, advising in no uncertain terms that "children shall not be prosecuted or detained ... for criminal acts committed while associated with armed forces or groups;" what is more, also as discussed earlier in Chapter 4, the Office of the Special Representative of the UN Secretary-General for Children and Armed Conflict encourages states to consider "excluding children below 18 from criminal responsibility for crimes committed

---

[31] *Id.* at §5.30, pp. 9 and §6.20, pp. 15–18.

[32] For its part, Paris Principle 3.5 admonishes: "No amnesty for crimes under international law, including those committed against children, should be granted in any peace or cease-fire agreement."

while associated with an armed force or an armed group, by virtue of their age, the chain of command and the forced nature of their recruitment."[33]

Developments in a number of jurisdictions attest to this legal movement.

Although Liberia's Truth and Reconciliation Commission recommended domestic criminal prosecutions for atrocity perpetrators, it simultaneously proposed excluding minors from the national juridical framework under which such prosecutions would occur. International law explicitly was referenced to buttress this recommendation.

In Colombia, although child soldiers are characterized as victims, they are not automatically deemed to be non-responsible as a matter of law. Nevertheless, not a single criminal case has been brought against a child soldier even within the juvenile justice system. In fact, "the recognition of their victim status by the [Colombian] Constitutional Court has translated into a lower court determining that there is no criminal jurisdiction under the Justice and Peace law for crimes committed by child combatants."[34] The Justice and Peace law is a fulcrum of the architecture of transitional justice in Colombia.

Rwandan authorities prosecuted persons fourteen years of age and older for involvement in the 1994 genocide. These prosecutions were organized under national enabling legislation for neo-traditional *gacaca* jurisdictions and antecedent specialized chambers of national courts. Although a convict's minor status shortened the period of imprisonment, incarceration consistently was imposed as a sentence in these cases. The Rwandan President, however, has since released individuals who had been minors at the time of their detention on genocide-related charges.

In the DRC, child soldiers have been prosecuted under national and military law and, in select instances, harshly sentenced. These prosecutions, however, seem to have ceased. Legislation enacted in the DRC in 2002 prohibits children under the age of eighteen from the jurisdiction of military courts.[35]

Following an attack on Sudanese government forces in May 2008, ninety-nine children aged between eleven and seventeen were among those arrested. UNICEF subsequently intervened, offering "legal advice to the Government of Sudan," that, among other factors, led to "a Presidential decree issued fewer than three months later that pardoned all the children."[36] Sarah Nouwen has identified a proposed increase in the age of criminal responsibility in Sudan to eighteen. Notwithstanding

---

[33] IDDRS, *supra* note 2, at §5.30, p. 9; Office of the Special Representative of the Secretary-General for Children and Armed Conflict, CHILDREN AND JUSTICE DURING AND IN THE AFTERMATH OF ARMED CONFLICT 50 (Working Paper No. 3, September 2011) [hereinafter CHILDREN AND JUSTICE].

[34] Cécile Aptel and Virginie Ladisch, THROUGH A NEW LENS: A CHILD-SENSITIVE APPROACH TO TRANSITIONAL JUSTICE 24 (ICTJ, August 2011) (noting also that, according to a Colombian prosecutor, this means that children associated with armed forces or armed groups can "take part in the proceedings as victims, with assurances that they will not be prosecuted").

[35] REDRESS Trust, *supra* note 22, at 28 (citing Law No. 023/2002 of the Military Justice Code (November 18, 2002)).

[36] UNICEF Innocenti Research Centre in cooperation with the International Center for Transitional Justice, CHILDREN AND TRUTH COMMISSIONS 14 (2010) [hereinafter CHILDREN AND TRUTH COMMISSIONS] (footnote omitted).

the Sudanese government's hostility toward the ICC, Nouwen reports that "[a]n official in the legislative drafting department of the [Sudanese] Ministry of Justice explains the proposed increase in the age of criminal responsibility from puberty to 18 years with reference to not only the Convention on the Rights of the Child, but also the Rome Statute."[37] The Doha Document for Peace in Darfur, completed in 2011, stipulates that children implicated in the conflict who may have been involved in the commission of crimes under international law shall be considered primarily as victims, not as alleged perpetrators. This document prohibits the recruitment and use of boys and girls under the age of eighteen by armed forces and by armed groups.

Global civil society has lobbied to discourage national criminal prosecutions of child soldiers in Uganda. In 2002, for example, Ugandan authorities charged two ex-LRA members aged fourteen and sixteen with treason. Referencing this incident, Rikhof reports that "[a]s a result of a letter by Human Rights Watch to the Ugandan government, the charges were withdrawn and the boys were allowed to apply for amnesties in 2003."[38]

Notwithstanding their inoperative status, peace agreements conducted between the LRA and the Ugandan government—in whose negotiation internationals had a hand—also gesture toward the place of child soldiers within national penal law. These negotiations—held in Juba, South Sudan—unfolded under the ICC's shadow. Negotiating parties felt that domestic criminal trials were more likely than traditional justice modalities to satisfy the complementarity principle.[39] These negotiations led to a number of instruments, notably an Agreement on Accountability and Reconciliation (2007 Juba Agreement) and a subsequent Annexure (2008) thereto.[40] Although clause 12 of the 2007 Juba Agreement excludes children from formal criminal law adjudication, neither the 2007 Juba Agreement nor the Annexure define the term child. Under Ugandan national penal law, twelve is the age of criminal responsibility. If this understanding were adopted for the purpose of the 2007 Juba Agreement and Annexure, then the clear majority of child soldier returnees theoretically would be prosecutable. Another inoperative Juba Agreement concluded in February 2008 specifically on the topic of DDR for LRA fighters (2008 Juba DDR Agreement), however, defines a child as any person below the age of eighteen.[41] If the definitional gap in the 2007 Juba Agreement

---

[37] E-Mail from Sarah Nouwen to Mark Drumbl (March 3, 2009) (on file with the author).

[38] Joseph Rikhof, *Child soldiers: Should they be punished?*, SWORD & SCALE: CANADIAN BAR ASSOCIATION NATIONAL MILITARY LAW SECTION NEWSLETTER 4 (May 2009), *available at* <http://www.cba.org/CBA/newsletters-sections/pdf/05-09-military_2.pdf> (also recording interventions by Human Rights Watch regarding child soldiers who had been sentenced to death in the DRC) (footnote omitted).

[39] Michael Otim and Marieke Wierda, International Center for Transitional Justice, *Briefing: Uganda: Impact of the Rome Statute and the International Criminal Court* 1, 3 (2010) (noting also that, in Uganda, "other transitional justice options such as truth-seeking and reparations are increasingly being neglected, despite the expressed desires of affected populations for these forms of justice").

[40] Agreement on Accountability and Reconciliation between the Government of the Republic of Uganda and the Lord's Resistance Army/Movement and Annexure, Juba, Sudan (June 29, 2007, Annexure from February 19, 2008).

[41] Juba Agreement concluded in February 2008 specifically on the topic of disarmament, demobilisation, and reintegration for LRA fighters, Art. 1 (on file with the author).

were filled with language from the 2008 Juba DDR Agreement then, indeed, all LRA members below the age of eighteen would be excluded.[42] This latter interpretation is reasonable. After all, the 2008 Juba DDR Agreement is of a specialized nature and bears explicit connections to the 2007 Juba Agreement.

The Ugandan situation also pivots to a discussion of amnesty arrangements. Amnesties were initialized in Uganda in 2000 by the Amnesty Act.[43] This legislation provided unqualified amnesty for any rebels active against the government. By October 2008, over 10,000 former LRA members had been amnestied.[44] The categorical nature of the amnesties has somewhat muddied in the case of senior LRA commanders in light of subsequent national legislative developments. Amnesties also were negotiated in Sierra Leone pursuant to the 1999 Lomé Peace Agreement. The SCSL Statute does not recognize the amnesty provisions of the Lomé Agreement in cases of the prosecution of persons falling within SCSL jurisdiction. Amnesty frameworks in both Northern Uganda and Sierra Leone included child combatants.

As a general matter, amnesties may be qualified or unqualified. Qualified amnesties imply a degree of individuation and invoke some element of exchange—that is, telling the truth, making amends, or apologizing—prior to vesting. In other words, the applicant must earn the amnesty. Unqualified amnesties vest automatically once combatants lay down arms and exit the armed faction. No further condition subsequent arises. A model of circumscribed action would incline toward qualified amnesties. This model, however, also would support gentler conditionality for child returnees than for their adult counterparts. The grant of amnesty, for instance, could hinge upon individual participation in truth and reconciliation commissions and traditional reintegration ceremonies.

Child soldiers should not be criminally prosecuted internationally, nationally, or locally for alleged implication in acts of atrocity. I remain skeptical of the ability of the atrocity trial and sequestered incarceration to attain declared penological goals, regardless of the age of the defendant, with the exception of the very highest-level leaders.[45] My skepticism is especially pronounced when trials are held in international courts. It also extends, however, to criminal proceedings conducted in national or local courts pursuant to liberal legalist procedures.

The retributive ambitions of international criminal law are vexed by the widespread, grievous, and systematic nature of extraordinary international criminality.

[42] *But see* Acirokop, *supra* note 1, at 275 ("It remains to be seen if substantive legislation for prosecution of serious crimes will include children above age twelve or exclude all children.")

[43] *Id.* at 275 n. 105 (recording that amnesties also provided child ex-combatants with a resettlement package, reportedly the sum of $US 150, a blanket, a mattress, and other household and agricultural items). For public views on amnesties in Northern Uganda, *see* Phuong Pham, Patrick Vinck, Marieke Wierda, Eric Stover, and Adrian di Giovanni, Forgotten Voices: A Population-Based Survey of Attitudes About Peace and Justice in Northern Uganda 5 (2005) (noting that although 65% of respondents support the amnesty process for LRA members, only 4% said the amnesties "should be granted unconditionally").

[44] Ronald R. Atkinson, The Roots of Ethnicity: The Origins of the Acholi of Uganda 300 (2nd edn, 2010).

[45] Mark A. Drumbl, Atrocity, Punishment, and International Law (2007).

These characteristics tend to be more pronounced in the context of extraordinary international crimes than in the context of ordinary common crimes. Mass atrocity is so grave that it may become impossible to award a perpetrator his or her just deserts while still respecting a minimally agreed upon core of human rights. Paradoxically, and unlike common criminals, atrocity perpetrators operate within situations of collective connivance. Especially in cases of discrimination-based violence, perpetrators are often besieged, if not besotten, by communal pressures and disorienting propaganda. They arguably have less autonomy and agency than the typical common criminal, yet their offenses typically are more serious. Assessment of their individual blameworthiness (a key element of the proportionality calculus central to retributive justice) accordingly becomes problematic. The fact that the scope of discretion exercised by many child soldiers, although not evanescent, typically is narrower than that of adults renders the determination of retributive punishment even more tenuous for them. This determination basically becomes pointless.

Are adults primed to undertake acts of atrocity deterred by the prospect that they might eventually be hauled before an international criminal tribunal or a national court? I remain unconvinced. My doubts derive from multiple sources: the low likelihood of getting caught, the evidentiary difficulties in securing criminal convictions, the sheer distance of international institutions and the dilapidation of their national counterparts, and endemic selectivity. Most foundationally, however, potential perpetrators of extraordinary international crimes may not engage in the kind of cost-benefit analysis that encourages them to stay acts of violence today owing to fears of eventual carceral punishment. Once again, the narrower, albeit still tangible, scope of discretion typically available to child soldiers suggests that they would be even less deterrable than adults. So, too, does their typically more impetuous cognitive state; not to mention the effects of narcotics in certain cases.

Although the futuristic prospect of individual punishment by international or national criminal courts would likely not deter a child soldier from committing a crime in the here and now of collective violence, ironically, the prospect of criminal prosecution and punishment may inhibit the child soldier from the very different decision to exit armed factions. Duthie and Specht, in fact, report testimony from former child soldiers that they would not leave armed forces or groups were they to face the prospect of criminal trials.[46] Although the probative value of this evidence on the question of exit is far from dispositive, it does adumbrate a more independently thinking child soldier than that offered by prevailing discourse. Explicitly filling the justice gap with modalities *other than* retributive criminal trials and imprisonment, however, may pacify anxieties voiced by child soldiers. Mainstreaming endogenous reintegration ceremonies, restorative community service, and truth

---

[46] Roger Duthie and Irma Specht, *DDR, Transitional Justice, and the Reintegration of Former Child Combatants*, *in* Disarming The Past: Transitional Justice And Ex-Combatants 190, 213 (International Center for Transitional Justice, Ana Cutter Patel, Pablo de Greiff, and Lars Waldorf eds, 2009); *see also* Wessells, Child Soldiers, *supra* note 4, at 220 (reporting that "former child soldiers see their prosecution and punishment not as brakes on cycles of violence but as warrants for additional fighting").

and reconciliation commissions could offer a sense of predictability about what the passage into civilian life would entail. In this regard, the justice reforms foreshadowed by this book could *encourage* disarmament and demobilization.

The third major penological aspiration of international criminal law is expressivism. This aspiration involves authenticating an historical record and consolidating the value of law. In the case of child soldiers, the dramaturgical aspect of the criminal trial—geared as it is to polarities of guilt or innocence and victim or perpetrator—is of modest value. Criminal trials for child soldiers yield superficial explanations of the etiology of mass atrocity. This especially is the case when trials are inspired by demon and bandit imagery that overplays the responsibility of the child.

Penological goals of rehabilitation, restoration, and reintegration do not centrally figure among international criminal law's aspirations. These goals, nonetheless, are very pertinent to juveniles (and low-level adult cadres, as well). Child soldiers who commit grievous atrocity crimes can become productive and functional community members. That said, incarceration fosters neither reinsertion nor reunification. Nor does it readily permit the making of amends or the ritualistic cleansing of the militarized youth or the affected community. Assessments of duress, coercion, impairment, and the psychological effects of captivity (i.e. the "Stockholm Syndrome") upon moral culpability are necessary in order for retributive punishment to be fair and proportionate. These assessments, however, are of greatly reduced salience when the goal of the justice intervention is reintegrative, rehabilitative, or restorative. In these latter instances, the proportionality between the offender's blameworthiness and the just deserts that he or she deserves is not of central concern.

Finally, the logistics of atrocity trials also inform my circumspection regarding their suitability. Technical procedures, complex evidentiary rules, and the role of counsel constitute key elements upon which the legitimacy of the atrocity trial rests. These elements, however, can alienate trial participants, including witnesses and defendants. Victims may find the atrocity trial frustrating in that they exert little to no control over its direction.

(iii) Truth and Reconciliation Commissions

Truth commissions endeavor to clarify the past. They promote transitional justice by investigating systematic human rights abuses. Truth commissions tend to be headed by a panel of distinguished individuals. In some instances, the commission gathers testimony and statements from human rights abusers, bystanders, victims, and the public at large. Truth commissions generally issue a public report. The report may limit itself to an abstract description of what had happened or, depending on the mandate, may identify individual perpetrators, specify victims, assign institutional responsibility, and recommend reforms. Some truth commissions also have a reconciliation mandate. Reconciliation may be achieved simply through publication of the commission's report or, more assertively, by engaging the commission directly in matters of accountability and reparations.

To varying degrees, a number of truth and reconciliation commissions have included children in their work. This section takes up three examples: South Africa, Sierra Leone, and Liberia. The final reports of truth commissions in Peru, Guatemala, and Timor-Leste each also considered the situation of children. In the specific case of Timor-Leste, the final day of commission hearings was dedicated to children. *Nunca Más*, the report of Argentina's truth commission, publicized crimes against children perpetrated under the aegis of the military dictatorship. These crimes included the kidnapping of children from their parents, forced adoptions by state officials, torture, disappearance, and murder.

To date, on the whole, reparations for children from national truth and reconciliation commissions have been slight.

(a) South Africa

The South African Truth and Reconciliation Commission (South Africa TRC) adopted a policy "not to take testimony from children under the age of eighteen, reflecting advice given by child specialists."[47] Nor did the South Africa TRC provide an option for children to give statements.[48] The South Africa TRC did hold special unofficial children's hearings. It also obtained general information on violations committed against children. Adults could speak of their experiences as children.[49] Piers Pigou observes that, over time, the South Africa TRC came to some regret that its own processes did not allow "for a more rounded assessment of how children and young people had engaged with and responded to violence."[50] Pigou notes that "young people's positive experiences of survival and resistance" remained unexplored, along with "their involvement as perpetrators of violence and the complex relationship between victimhood and perpetration."[51] He chides the South Africa TRC's special hearings for children and youth for not:

[E]xamin[ing] in great detail the involvement of children in militarized structures linked to the liberation movements. It could be argued that significant opportunities were missed to develop an understanding of children and youth as agents and perpetrators. This aspect is crucial in terms of developing recommendations to rehabilitate and reintegrate those affected back into communities and in establishing a more nuanced understanding of the violence and contributing factors.[52]

---

[47] Piers Pigou, *Children and the South African Truth and Reconciliation Commission, in* CHILDREN AND TRANSITIONAL JUSTICE, *supra* note 1, at 115, 118.

[48] *Id.* at 156; *Introduction, in* CHILDREN AND TRANSITIONAL JUSTICE, *supra* note 1, at xv, xxii. *See also* CHILDREN AND TRUTH COMMISSIONS, *supra* note 36, at 10 ("[A]dults from non-governmental organizations . . . and other professionals working with children were asked to testify on their behalf . . . ").

[49] Nienke Grossman, *Rehabilitation or Revenge: Prosecuting Child Soldiers for Human Rights Violations*, 38 GEO. J. INT'L L. 323, 352 (2007).

[50] Pigou, *supra* note 47, at 130.

[51] *Id.*

[52] *Id.* at 135.

(b) Sierra Leone

From its inception, the Sierra Leone Truth and Reconciliation Commission (Sierra Leone TRC) strove to incorporate children into its work. It was "the first truth commission to involve children in statement-taking and in closed and thematic hearings."[53] Over three hundred children came forward to give statements; some of these children then were invited to testify in closed and confidential hearings. Victims of crimes committed by children also shared their testimonies and experiences. Child representatives and protection agencies addressed the Sierra Leone TRC directly in thematic hearings and came to play an important role in its activities.

The Sierra Leone TRC produced a detailed official Report, one part of which specifically addressed children and the armed conflict. In addition, as a complement, the Sierra Leone TRC prepared an abridged version for children to read (known as the Child-Friendly Version).

The Sierra Leone TRC Report authenticated the innumerable acts of violence perpetrated against children during the armed conflict. The Report touched upon the multiple roles of children, including their commission of gross human rights abuses against the civilian population. It noted that the conflict in Sierra Leone "forced children into assuming 'dual identities' of both victim and perpetrator."[54]

Although the Sierra Leone TRC did not hide violence perpetrated by children, it immersed it within the prevailing discourse of incapacity and victimization. In support of this narrative, the Sierra Leone TRC Commissioners interpreted international and comparative criminal law in accordance with the aspirations of the Straight 18 position:

> In most countries, children under the age of 18 are not regarded as having the legal capacity to be responsible for their actions (*doli capax*). The Rome Statute of the ICC uses 18 as the age of legal capacity and children's rights advocates argue that most national jurisdictions should be adjusted accordingly.[55]

The Sierra Leone TRC's account remains an authoritative one that overlaps with, but also departs from, ethnographic accounts of the relationship between children, militarization, and conflict in Sierra Leone. The Sierra Leone TRC Report mentioned the atrocities committed by child soldiers, but with limited exception underscored their compelled nature.[56] It concluded that "armed groups deliberately

---

[53] Philip Cook and Cheryl Heykoop, *Child Participation in the Sierra Leonean Truth and Reconciliation Commission*, in CHILDREN AND TRANSITIONAL JUSTICE, *supra* note 1, at 159, 161. The Sierra Leone TRC supported traditional rituals and viewed them as harmonious with goals of reconciliation. That said, although "[s]ome civil society members further recommended children's participation in traditional ceremonies . . . the child participation working group advised against incorporating traditional practices and ceremonies for healing and reconciliation into the proceedings of the [Sierra Leone] TRC." *Id.* at 181 (footnote omitted).

[54] SLTRC, VOL. 3B, CH. 4, *supra* note 6, ¶ 225.

[55] *Id.* ¶ 200.

[56] *See, e.g., id.* ¶ 7 ("They were also forced to become perpetrators and carry out aberrations violating the rights of other civilians."). For more subtlety, *see id.* ¶ 227 (children "[i]nitially . . . had to

engineered children into becoming perpetrators, forcing them to commit atrocities or themselves be killed."[57] According to the Sierra Leone TRC, in the case of child soldiers, "[r]efusal to carry out an order was simply not countenanced" and "[d]eath or other violent reprisal for refusal to carry out the order was almost instantaneous."[58] The Child-Friendly Version of the Report framed the narrative as follows:

> We are the children of Sierra Leone. The war was targeted against us, our families and our communities. It was a brutal conflict, which we did nothing to cause, but we suffered terribly because of it. . . . Children of this country were forced to fight for a cause we could not understand. . . . Our hands, which were meant to be used freely for play and schoolwork, were used instead, by force, to burn, kill and destroy.[59]

The Sierra Leone TRC Report emphasized the children's immaturity, malleability, and vulnerability; their susceptibility to manipulation; as well as their desire to "please their elders."[60] Ultimately, and invoking psychological and environmental pressures, the Sierra Leone TRC Report doubted that the children had capacity. The Report maintained that, whereas "[a]dults usually have the maturity to think through survival mechanisms in difficult situations,"[61] children impliedly by omission do not.

The Sierra Leone TRC Report underscored drug and alcohol use among all members of armed factions and traced the commission of atrocities thereto. The Report linked drug and alcohol use to capacity in the case of children.[62] The Report noted that "[i]t can be argued that many child combatants still committed violations without having to be drugged," but quickly added that the "heat and tension of the conflict, the group violence already present in the conflict and peer pressure could also act as powerful narcotics."[63] According to the Sierra Leone TRC, "[t]he conflict was responsible for producing child perpetrators."[64] Inferentially, then, child perpetrators did not tactically wend their way through the conflict. They were, rather, the unwitting products of the noxious environment.

As to the question of enlistment, the Report admonished that:

> [T]he notion of children 'volunteering' to join the armed groups . . . [is] completely unacceptable as children . . . do not have the ability or the capacity to 'volunteer'. Simply put 'they have no choice'.[65]

---

be coerced into committing abuses but soon many of them began to initiate heinous atrocities without having to be compelled to do so").

[57] *Id.* ¶ 207.

[58] *Id.* ¶ 229. "Their physical size and their incredible vulnerability made them succumb quite easily." *Id.*

[59] SLTRC CHILDREN'S REPORT, *supra* note 7, at 3.

[60] SLTRC, VOL. 3B, CH. 4, *supra* note 6, ¶ 209.

[61] *Id.* ¶ 215.

[62] *Id.* ¶¶ 195–197. "Most of the testimonies made to the Commission confirmed that children carried out the most atrocious violations while under the influence of these drugs. The capacity of children to take responsibility for their acts remains an issue open for debate." *Id.* ¶ 197.

[63] *Id.* ¶ 199.

[64] *Id.* ¶ 121.

[65] *Id.* ¶ 234.

The Sierra Leone TRC Report acknowledged that "youth who took up arms testified . . . that their dissatisfaction with their social and economic conditions led them to join the RUF."[66] It elsewhere noted that factors such as employment and patriotism helped account for recruitment of children into the SLA.[67] However, these elements tended to get lost in the overall Report. As is commonplace in discussion of child soldiering, the Report can be read to understate the prevalence or relevance of volunteerism.

The dominant discourse, then, boils down to somewhat of a contradiction. Incapacity renders children unable to volunteer for military life. But these very children have the capacity to volunteer to participate in a national truth and reconciliation commission that redresses the effects of militarization on the social landscape. The only way for children, in fact, to participate in the truth and reconciliation commission is through volunteerism, thereby implying that their capacity to do so is far from ephemeral.

The goal of the Sierra Leone TRC was to include children's experiences in its findings, but also to ensure that no individual child soldier's conduct became subject to assessment, evaluation, or critique. The Sierra Leone TRC attained this goal through the drafting of the Report. It also turned to procedural mechanisms that had *a priori* been put in place to cull evidence from former child soldiers. Assuredly, the mandate of the Sierra Leone TRC was not to judge or impose punishment on anyone. In its relationship with child soldiers, however, the Sierra Leone TRC likely exceeded what was minimally needed to satisfy this institutional mandate. Procedurally, all children were treated equally and "neutrally as witnesses" regardless of "whether they had perpetrated violations."[68] To ensure this outcome, "the statement-taking forms for children omitted the section designated for perpetrators."[69] Furthermore, child participation was entirely voluntary, confidential, and anonymous; with the informed consent of the child and the child's parent or guardian; children could withdraw at any point; children could give their statement in the presence of a trusted social worker; and, finally, "there would be no sharing of information outside the Truth Commission and . . . all children would be considered only as victims of the war."[70]

Children who testified as victims helped edify an historical record. Included among this group were children who had inflicted terrible indignities on third-party civilians. The controlled nature of the interaction of former child soldiers with the Sierra Leone TRC, however, inhibited the injection of texture into the Report's overall narrative and crimped the range of inferences to be drawn from dispassionate examination of youth perpetration of violence. Children—accompanied by social workers—presented their own expectations to an expert meeting in Freetown

---

[66] *Id.* ¶ 44.
[67] *Id.* ¶ 283.
[68] *Id.* ¶¶ 17, 198.
[69] Cook and Heykoop, *supra* note 53, at 171.
[70] Saudamini Siegrist, *Child Participation in International Criminal Accountability Mechanisms: The Case of the Sierra Leone Truth and Reconciliation Commission, in* INTERNATIONAL CRIMINAL ACCOUNTABILITY AND THE RIGHTS OF CHILDREN 53, 62 (Karin Arts and Vesselin Popovski eds, 2006).

regarding what the Sierra Leone TRC should deliver. They took the position that "all children involved in the TRC should be recognised primarily as victims of the war that targeted them and exploited their vulnerability."[71] Legal scholar Matthew Happold skillfully deracinates the underlying paradox:

On the one hand, children are said to have the capacity to do good things, such as participating meaningfully in drafting a child-friendly version of the report of the [Sierra Leone TRC].... On the other hand, it is argued that they are too immature to be held responsible for the bad things they do, such as committing atrocities in the civil war in that country.[72]

In the end, the Sierra Leone TRC brought children into reconstructive conversations. This outcome should be applauded. Yet, the Sierra Leone TRC did so in a strategically targeted manner. Owing to a variety of pressures, ideologies, and agendas, the potentially three-dimensional status of child soldiers as perpetrators, witnesses, and victims eased into a two-dimensional portrayal of child soldiers as victims and witnesses alone.

(c) Liberia

The Truth and Reconciliation Commission of Liberia (Liberia TRC) delivered a detailed and authoritative account of armed violence in the country between 1979 and 2003. The Liberia TRC found that among all of the multiple warring factions, the NPFL (National Patriotic Front of Liberia) alone accounted for approximately 40% of all human rights violations.

Much like the Sierra Leone TRC, the Liberia TRC endeavored to ensure that children fulfilled a significant role in its work.[73] Children's participation in the Liberia TRC could only be voluntary on the basis of the informed consent of the child and parent/guardian; the Liberia TRC lacked the power of subpoena over children.[74] The Liberia TRC collected confidential statements from children. Children also testified. The Liberia TRC held several regional hearings and panel discussions with children. Similarly to the Sierra Leone TRC, it also convened thematic hearings on children with children's rights experts. UNICEF was one of the Liberia TRC's key partners. So, too, were other child protection agencies.

All parties to the Liberian conflict recruited children, including by force. Males in the fifteen to nineteen age cohort were the main targets.[75] The Liberia TRC found that children constituted "approximately 10 to 20 percent of members of

---

[71] *Id.* at 59.

[72] Matthew Happold, *The Age of Criminal Responsibility for International Crimes under International Law, in* INTERNATIONAL CRIMINAL ACCOUNTABILITY AND THE RIGHTS OF CHILDREN 69, 84 (Karin Arts and Vesselin Popovski eds, 2006).

[73] *See generally* Theo Sowa, *Children and the Liberian Truth and Reconciliation Commission, in* CHILDREN AND TRANSITIONAL JUSTICE, *supra* note 1, at 193 (providing extensive details on the interface between children and the Liberia TRC). For the Liberia TRC, determination of childhood hinged upon a person's age at the time of the TRC's activities, not age at the time of the armed conflict.

[74] *Id.* at 203.

[75] LIBERIA TRC FINAL REPORT, *supra* note 12, at 275.

armed groups" and were "central to . . . logistics and combat efforts in that [armed groups] relied heavily on children to be porters, cleaners, cooks, scouts, domestic and sexual slaves, as well as active combatants."[76] In its Final Report, the Liberia TRC recognized the multiple roles played by children during the conflict.[77] It noted that "[t]hus abused, children found themselves both victims and perpetrators during the war."[78] However, the perpetrator designation largely dissipated insofar as the Liberia TRC emphasized the diminished capacity of children and the forcible nature of their recruitment. Characteristically turning to the passive voice, and constructing the children's tragic experiences as epiphenomena to adult malevolence, the Liberia TRC concluded:

Children were routinely coerced and manipulated by commanders to commit brutal acts in violation of international law against the civilian population, including their family members and other children. These acts included abductions, killings, torture, rape and other forms of sexual violence, pillage and the destruction of property. Children were exploited and manipulated through repeated physical and psychological acts and frequently drugged for them to be able to commit these crimes. They were socialized into committing abuse, the routine use of violence, and the power of the gun as the central norms that ruled their lives.[79]

Unlike the Sierra Leone TRC, the Liberia TRC expressly pursued a prosecutorial agenda. It recommended legislation for an Extraordinary Criminal Court in Liberia to prosecute atrocity perpetrators. As a general matter, the Liberia TRC repudiated the concept of amnesties for heinous crimes, which it derided as "unacceptable, immoral and promot[ing] impunity."[80] The Liberia TRC did, however, determine "that all individuals who cooperated with the TRC and admitted their wrongs and spoke truthfully before or to the TRC as an expression of remorse will not be recommended for prosecution."[81]

That said, the Liberia TRC categorically approached alleged perpetrators under the age of eighteen in a different fashion. It determined:

[T]hat children are neither culpable nor responsible for acts of violations of human rights laws, humanitarian rights law violations, war crimes or egregious violation of domestic criminal law.[82]

---

[76] *Id.* at 315.

[77] In addition, the Liberia TRC prepared a supplemental document that dealt only with children. Republic of Liberia, Truth and Reconciliation Commission, REPORT, VOLUME THREE: APPENDICES, TITLE II: CHILDREN, THE CONFLICT AND THE TRC CHILDREN AGENDA (2009) [hereinafter LIBERIA TRC REPORT, VOLUME THREE], *available at* <http://trcofliberia.org/resources/reports/final/volume-three-2_layout-1.pdf>. This document catalogued the abuses suffered by children. It detailed the prevalence of abduction of children into armed forces or armed groups. This document can be read as viewing the incidence of abduction as more widespread than the perspective offered by the ethnographic literature concerning Liberia (discussed in Chapter 3 *supra*). That said, this document also noted the many motivations exhibited by children who had presented themselves for military service. *Id.* at 53–60.

[78] LIBERIA TRC FINAL REPORT, *supra* note 12, at 315.

[79] *Id.*

[80] *Id.* at 403.

[81] *Id.* at 20 (Determinations).

[82] *Id.* at 338.

"[B]ecause children are neither culpable nor held responsible for their actions during time of war," the Liberia TRC recommended that "all children who participated in the armed conflict be protected without limitation from all forms of sanctions including criminal prosecution, civil liability, or public sanctions."[83]

The Liberia TRC's Final Report evidenced some ambiguity whether children were to receive an unqualified amnesty or whether they fell outside the scope of responsibility entirely. The Liberia TRC noted that "children expect [to] be excluded from any form of criminal prosecution and they do not expect to be amnestied, since amnesty would imply that children were guilty of the commission of crimes."[84] In one part, the Liberia TRC Final Report adhered to this view, which overall appears to be textually preponderant.[85] In another part—the consolidated determinations section—the Final Report, however, availed itself of amnesty language.[86] The national legislation recommended by the Liberia TRC for atrocity prosecutions excluded all children from the Extraordinary Criminal Court's jurisdiction.[87] In support of this approach, the Liberia TRC's separate Appendix on children explicitly referred to the "common practice of international criminal tribunals to exclude children under the age of 18 from prosecution for grave human rights violations," while also noting that "[t]he Rome Statute ... explicitly sets the age of legal accountability at 18."[88]

(d) Summary

When it comes to addressing the situation of children in conflict, the work of the Sierra Leone TRC and the Liberia TRC was more sublime than that of the South Africa TRC. The Sierra Leone TRC and the Liberia TRC broke new ground in constructively engaging the delicate topic of children and systemic armed violence. That said, both of these TRCs still approached this topic in a way that occasioned opportunity costs. Their methodologies, however praiseworthy, thinned the completeness of the truths they authenticated, the wholeness of the reconciliation they encouraged, and the robustness of the juvenile rights they fostered. The approaches

---

[83] *Id.* at 387.

[84] *Id.* at 317 (but also noting: "Children also expressed a desire for some form of local reconciliation and processes of forgiveness for the wrongs they know they committed during the war. Many children expressed regret and remorse and would like to have their feelings acknowledged by families and wider communities.").

[85] *Id.* at 403; *see also* LIBERIA TRC REPORT, VOLUME THREE, *supra* note 77, at 105 ("Therefore, children under the age of 18 do not have any criminal responsibility for their actions and they cannot be held accountable for crimes committed under international human rights or international humanitarian law. Since children are not considered to be responsible for gross human rights violations and serious violations of humanitarian law, there can be no amnesty extended to children.").

[86] LIBERIA TRC FINAL REPORT, *supra* note 12, at 19 (Determinations) ("Children are entitled to general amnesty for crimes committed during their minority.").

[87] *Id.* at 447 (listing Draft Statute: Extraordinary Criminal Court, Art. 16 ("The Court shall have no jurisdiction over any person classified as a child or that was under the age of 18 when the alleged crime was committed. The Court shall have jurisdiction over any person that was 18 years of age or older when the alleged crime was committed.")).

[88] LIBERIA TRC REPORT, VOLUME THREE, *supra* note 77, at 67.

of these two TRCs, nonetheless, have since become naturalized within best practices as elaborated in influential documents such as the Paris Principles.

(iv) Endogenous Restoration and Reintegration Mechanisms

Endogenous—that is, customary and traditional—ceremonies and rituals are culturally specific.[89] Along with their rich diversity, however, they also tend to share some points in common.

One such point is the notion that combatants, including children and adolescents, become polluted or contaminated by war and, hence, would gain from purification or cleansing in their return journey to civilian life.[90] Endogenous ceremonies and rituals may be undertaken to pacify the spirits of people who died in conflict, including people killed by the returning combatant. These mechanisms may also fulfill a welcoming function, which is particularly germane to returnees who served for many years in fighting forces or who associated with units known to have serially committed acts of violence against civilian populations. In some instances, rituals and ceremonies are revivalist insofar as the returnee sheds the past and is reborn.

According to Alcinda Honwana, rituals and ceremonies provide "[a]n acknowledgement of the atrocities [child soldiers] committed or witnessed."[91] Endogenous mechanisms commonly evoke restorative aspects. Compensation may be paid or community service fulfilled, following which normal social relationships resume. Some rituals and ceremonies pursue collective forgiveness through atonement, service, or assertion of responsibility; others do not involve such aspects at all or emphasize them to lesser degrees; while others are purely symbolic. In fact, many traditional ceremonies neither require nor even contemplate confession or discussion. They are future-oriented and actualize justice through the making of amends or completion of works. Regardless of methodology, once the ritual or ceremony concludes, the matter typically closes. The past is sealed away and is no longer prologue.

Endogenous mechanisms protect not only the returnee, but also parents and family members.[92] In addition, they help shield communities from "ancestral rebuke that may be brought on because of what the child had done."[93] In an obverse sense, these mechanisms also provide the family and community with an opportunity to ask for the child's forgiveness for having enabled, encouraged, or

---

[89] For clarification of use of the term endogenous, *see supra* Chapter 1 note 43.

[90] *Cf.* Alcinda Honwana, CHILD SOLDIERS IN AFRICA 6 (2006) ("War pollution is considered a threat to society, so young women and men who served and fought in militias must undergo a process of cleansing as they make the transition from the state of war back into normal society. This reintegration is accomplished with local practices, which differ profoundly from Western psychotherapeutic approaches.").

[91] *Id.* at 110. Honwana comments favorably about purification rituals in Angola and Mozambique.

[92] *See* Save the Children, *supra* note 11, at 96 (noting that "if a child had committed atrocities, this was not only a stigma for the children themselves but also for their parents").

[93] Boothby, Crawford, and Halperin, *supra* note 19, at 96.

obliged him or her to associate with fighting factions. The former child soldier may thereby receive some explanation for why adults abetted the violence that engulfed the community. Restorative initiatives recognize the collective nature of war wounds—rather than construct trauma as an individual malady—and may, thereby, facilitate collective healing.[94]

Endogenous ceremonies and rituals are no panacea. Romanticizing them is unhelpful. Their success is by no means assured. In Northern Uganda, for example, "[m]any returnees report ongoing stigma, even after undergoing such rituals, and live in fear of reprisal from the offended family."[95] Insofar as bottom-up restorative initiatives may threaten the state's grip on authoritative decision-making, state officials may meddle with and manipulate the operation thereof. Endogenous mechanisms may be undermined by corruption and bias among decision-makers, alcoholism among elders, and inability among families to pay compensation. It is not a given that younger generations have any interest in tradition. The magnitude and gravity of atrocity crimes juxtaposes brusquely with the informality of restorative processes. Traditional mechanisms may lack the capacity or elasticity to deal with mass violence. Ceremonies may perpetuate patriarchy. They may be ill-equipped to respond to sexual violence and forced marriage. Moreover, the composition of the communities into which returnees are to be reinserted may have dramatically changed over the course of the conflict, with disruption, displacement, and security concerns roiling the social order. If returnees committed crimes in diverse and distant locations, restoration cannot logistically be satisfied in only one place. Narrative distortions arise if the same "big men" who had encouraged the recruitment of children into armed service come to control endogenous ceremonies and rituals. Control by "big men" would warp the rituals and ceremonies such that they would consolidate the same oppressive gerontocracy for whose overthrow children initially may have fought. Although endogenous ceremonies are not generally punitive, neither are they inoculated from the risks of issuing onerous sanction and inflicting human rights violations on participants.

The point of cataloguing these concerns is not to discredit endogenous mechanisms. Rather, it is to present an even-handed picture of their potentials and limitations. Many of these concerns could be constructively mediated.[96] On balance, these mechanisms can go some way to foster reintegration, reconciliation, and restoration in the context of children formerly associated with armed forces or groups.

Endogenous ceremonies and rituals indeed have been deployed, to varying degrees, in a number of post-conflict societies in the specific case of youth returnees, including child soldiers implicated in the commission of acts of atrocity.

---

[94] Wessells, CHILD SOLDIERS, *supra* note 4, at 151–152.

[95] Acirokop, *supra* note 1, at 283. For incisive critique of traditional justice in Northern Uganda, *see* Tim Allen, *Ritual (Ab)use? Problems with Traditional Justice in Northern Uganda*, in COURTING CONFLICT? JUSTICE, PEACE AND THE ICC IN AFRICA 47 (Nicholas Waddell and Phil Clark eds, 2008).

[96] For example, through adoption of a qualified deference test as set out in Chapter 7 *infra*.

There is evidence that local communities favor these interventions.[97] Deployment of traditional mechanisms has elicited supportive commentary on the part of a diverse set of researchers.[98] Although not unabashedly positive in their assessments, these researchers cite the contributions of these mechanisms to reparation, social reinsertion, reintegration (notably for children at high risk of marginalization or re-recruitment), and collective reconciliation.

Traditional ceremonies and rituals form part of the fabric of legal systems worldwide. At this juncture, it might be helpful to briefly turn to some illustrative country-specific discussion from Africa.

Denov reports that her RUF respondents noted that "community-cleansing rituals" helped them to begin "afresh" and also provided them "a feeling of acceptance and importance."[99] Williamson concludes that traditional cleansing ceremonies in Sierra Leone "appear to have increased community acceptance of the children as well as enable the children to feel acceptable."[100]

Among the Acholi community of Northern Uganda, child soldier returnees have participated in *nyouo tong gweno* and *mato oput*. *Nyouo tong gweno* is a cleansing and welcoming ceremony for community members who have been away from home for long periods of time. *Mato oput* "aims at reestablishing relationships suspended between two clans in response to a killing, whether deliberate or accidental."[101] Prudence Acirokop, who conditionally supports the participation of children in traditional justice methods, concludes that *mato oput*, "[w]ith its core principles of apology, compensation and forgiveness, . . . can serve as a form of accountability and a tool for generating acknowledgement and long-term reconciliation."[102]

In Mozambique, the value of endogenous ceremonies in fostering community acceptance, trust, and cohesion has been underscored. So, too, has the ability of these ceremonies to alleviate feelings of guilt and shame on the part of former child soldiers.[103] The most efficacious activities in Mozambique included those that *inter*

---

[97] Office of the Special Representative of the Secretary-General for Children and Armed Conflict, *Disarmament, demobilization and reintegration programmes for children*, available at <http://www.un. org/children/conflict/english/ddrforchildren.html> (stating that in Sierra Leone traditional approaches were cited as providing the most positive reconciliation experiences); Phuong Pham, Patrick Vinck, Eric Stover, Andrew Moss, Marieke Wierda, and Richard Bailey, WHEN THE WAR ENDS: A POPULA-TION-BASED SURVEY ON ATTITUDES ABOUT PEACE, JUSTICE, AND SOCIAL RECONSTRUCTION IN NORTHERN UGANDA 5 (2007) (finding that 49% of respondents "said local customs and rituals are useful to deal with the LRA" and that 57% "said those LRA who return to their communities should participate in traditional ceremonies").

[98] Theresa S. Betancourt, Stephanie Simmons, Ivelina Borisova, Stephanie E. Brewer, Uzo Iweala, and Marie de la Soudière, *High Hopes, Grim Reality: Reintegration and the Education of Former Child Soldiers in Sierra Leone*, 52(4) COMP. EDUC. REV. 565, 574–575 (2008); Joanne N. Corbin, *Returning home: resettlement of formerly abducted children in Northern Uganda*, 32(2) DISASTERS 316, 325 (2008); Duthie and Specht, *supra* note 46, at 218; Angela Veale and Aki Stavrou, *Former Lord's Resistance Army Child Soldier Abductees: Explorations of Identity in Reintegration and Reconciliation*, 13(3) PEACE AND CONFLICT: JOURNAL OF PEACE PSYCHOLOGY 273, 273, 290 (2007).

[99] Denov, *supra* note 10, at 169.

[100] John Williamson, *The disarmament, demobilization and reintegration of child soldiers: social and psychological transformation in Sierra Leone*, 4(3) INTERVENTION 185, 196 (2006).

[101] Acirokop, *supra* note 1, at 277 (footnote omitted).

[102] *Id.* at 268.

[103] Boothby, Crawford, and Halperin, *supra* note 19, at 95–97.

alia "instilled a sense of social responsibility" and promoted self-regulatory be-havior.[104] Viriato Castelo-Branco delivers a positive report regarding the role of traditional healers and religious leaders in Mozambique. He specifically cites the *khufemba* method, through which "a former child soldier who wants to return to a community where he committed offences during the war can speak with the spirits of those whom he killed, and seek counsel on how to atone for his sins."[105] Following the healer's entering into a trance to act as a medium for the spirits of the dead, the child "can be integrated back to the community by performing tasks requested by the spirits."[106]

The international legal imagination, nevertheless, has mixed feelings about endogenous ceremonies and rituals.

Many international actors, including UNICEF, support these mechanisms.[107] More and more, the "how to" of DDR—notably, the IDDRS—gestures toward the salutary reintegration potential of endogenous ceremonies in the case of child soldiers and even places these mechanisms within a justice framework.[108] Innova-tive references in the IDDRS to endogenous mechanisms may well come to update the traditionally reserved posture of DDR practitioners toward transitional justice generally. Notwithstanding welcome conceptual improvements, the actual integra-tion of traditional mechanisms into DDR programming still remains embryonic.

In this vein, international actors also tend to be jittery about—and some are often downright uncomfortable with—traditional mechanisms. International crim-inal lawyers may become especially anxious when traditional mechanisms contem-plate a transitional justice orientation. For the international criminal lawyer, justice fundamentally reposes upon the formal tenets of liberal legalism. Insofar as endog-enous justice practices often depart from these tenets, they come to be viewed with suspicion. International criminal lawyers may exhort the amendment, moderniza-tion, or ouster of customary justice mechanisms. They may turn to transnational persuasive authority as a justificatory template in this regard. On the topic of child soldiers, the content of transnational persuasive authority includes the additional ingredient of faultless passive victimhood.

In addition, Acirokop reports that, in the case of Northern Uganda, faith-based NGOs told child soldiers that "cultural rituals are satanic and ungodly and that they should not participate in them" and, instead, advised them "to pray and to forgive and forget what happened in the bush."[109] In some instances, participants in more elaborate traditional ceremonies (which are locally perceived as more

---

[104] *Id.* at 87.

[105] Viriato Castelo-Branco, *Child Soldiers: The Experience of the Mozambican Association for Public Health (AMOSAPU)*, 7(4) DEVELOPMENT IN PRACTICE 494, 495 (1997).

[106] *Id.*

[107] No Peace Without Justice and UNICEF Innocenti Research Centre, INTERNATIONAL CRIMINAL JUSTICE AND CHILDREN 135 (2002); CHILDREN AND JUSTICE, *supra* note 33, at 45, 47.

[108] IDDRS, *supra* note 2, at §6.20, p. 26; *see also id.* §5.30, p. 26. For discussion of the Cape Town Principles and Paris Principles on this aspect, *see supra* Chapter 4(i)(b).

[109] Acirokop, *supra* note 1, at 287 (footnote omitted).

effective) incur personal financial costs.[110] Accordingly, Acirokop encourages donors and aid agencies to support these ceremonies given that there are "children who wish to take part but cannot afford to participate because of financial constraints."[111]

In sum, ceremonies and rituals happen, but they do not happen enough.[112] Moreover, when they do happen, their operation is overly filtered through transnational norms. Justice aspects—as understood locally—wither. The vitality of endogenous mechanisms thereby becomes less than what it could be. To be sure, it is imprudent to approach traditional mechanisms recklessly. Buoyed as it is by the tendentiousness of prevailing imagery of faultless passive victimhood, however, the international legal imagination has come to err too much on the side of caution.

(v) A Need to Inquire and for Further Inquiry

The good news is that, whether within DDR programs or outside of them, large numbers of combatants—including children—return to and are accepted by their communities of origin. In its findings, for example, the Liberia TRC referenced "[a] survey among 600 former combatants, children and adults combined [that] found that 94% of those former fighters who went through the DDRR process said they had no problems being re-accepted to their communities."[113] In Sierra Leone, one study records 93% of adult ex-combatants as reporting no problems on the measure of acceptance (its sample includes a substantial proportion of individuals who had joined fighting factions as children and were over eighteen when the war ended); this study does note "much higher" nonacceptance rates among former RUF members than former CDF members.[114] Another observer exalts the successful reintegration of children formerly associated with armed forces or armed groups in

---

[110] *Id.* at 285 (noting the prevalence of this financial problem and delivering the following individual example from a seventeen year-old boy: "I don't have money to buy a goat and chicken for the ceremony and my mother does not have the money, so I continue to suffer" (quoting Bob, an interviewee)).

[111] *Id.*

[112] According to one estimate, in Northern Uganda "only 19 per cent of formerly abducted individuals were found to have experienced any ritual upon return to their communities." Corbin, *supra* note 98, at 325 (citation omitted). Annan, Brier, and Aryemo, however, report that "[o]ver half of male youth who returned had a ceremony or ritual performed to cleanse them from their past." Annan, Brier, and Aryemo, *supra* note 5, at 660 (citation omitted). The inoperative 2007 Juba Agreement and Annexure contemplated a truth commission/historical inquiry and alternate justice mechanisms (including traditional rituals), but exhibited reserve in terms of including children therein other than as voluntary witnesses or victims.

[113] LIBERIA TRC REPORT, VOLUME THREE, *supra* note 77, at 72 (identifying the researcher as J. Pugel).

[114] Humphreys and Weinstein, *supra* note 13, at 542–543 (cautioning, however, that "the difficulties faced by 7 percent of respondents should not be under-emphasized" and that the survey "plausibly underestimates the number of nonreintegrated fighters"). This survey was conducted between June and August 2003, about a year after the end of the conflict. *Id.* at 540. Owing to human subjects' concerns, Humphreys and Weinstein did not interview soldiers who were children at the end of the fighting. *Id.* at 565 n. 6. In any event, they found that "[t]wo characteristics thought to be major factors in the reintegration process, age and gender, exhibit weak effects across dimensions,"

Sierra Leone, noting that "community members spoke eloquently about their forgiveness for the[] children because they understood that they had been forced to do what they did."[115] Notwithstanding that reintegration is difficult to measure and the actual meaning of the term remains fuzzy, these overall reports are encouraging.

One persistent challenge, however, lies in the fact that a small but important subgroup of child soldiers—to wit, returnees suspected of implication in acts of atrocity—experience significant difficulties in reintegrating.[116] Members of this subgroup, who have the potential to become spoilers, constitute an at-risk constituency. Their salience exceeds their numbers. The generally good news, moreover, may belie longer-term hardships that are often privately internalized by returnees and community members. After all, "acceptance and physical reintegration are not necessarily synonymous with reconciliation."[117] Furthermore, many child soldiers who were not implicated in acts of atrocity face poor occupational, civic, and educational prospects. Girl soldiers continue to carry an enormous burden of stigma. Children born into armed forces or armed groups also face impediments to social inclusion (which differs from initial social acceptance), as do their mothers, many of whom are girls themselves.

Once conflict ends, a significant number of persons initially recruited or used as child soldiers will have aged into adulthood. By the time that post-conflict programming begins, that number will be even higher. The person entering the armed group may be a child, but the person exiting it and coming home to the community may be an adult—both chronologically as well as experientially. That person, moreover, may head a household.

The initial phase of SWAY in Northern Uganda brings into sharper relief key subtleties overlooked by breezy descriptions of the successful reintegration of former child soldiers. On the one hand, the SWAY report affirms LRA escapees as having received a generally strong and positive reception when they returned home.[118] Family members were overwhelmingly receptive, communities less so (although community acceptance increased over time).[119] Community members invoked the coercive nature of LRA captivity as a basis to welcome escapees. On the other hand, the SWAY report also locates some unevenness in the reintegration experience. It identifies specific subgroups of formerly abducted youth who experienced difficulties upon

---

although they also emphasized the conditionality of these specific results and the need to interpret them with caution. *Id.* at 546, 565 n. 6.

[115] Williamson, *supra* note 100, at 189 (based on a 2002 visit). Williamson credits "sensitization work" in achieving this attitudinal transformation, along with a variety of initiatives including traditional cleansing ceremonies and family reunification programs. *Id.* at 189, 195–196.

[116] *See generally* Duthie and Specht, *supra* note 46, at 192 ("[T]here is evidence to suggest that some former child combatants experience a great deal of difficulty adjusting to normal life and being accepted by their communities, at least in part because of the past crimes they or other child combatants committed.").

[117] Veale and Stavrou, *supra* note 98, at 289.

[118] SWAY, *supra* note 22, at vii, 63, 66–67.

[119] Annan, Brier, and Aryemo, *supra* note 5, at 651–652 (referencing initial SWAY findings).

reintegration, including community persecution, targeting, and insults. It includes among these subgroups particular youth who "the community knows or suspects ... were involved in raids or killings."[120]

Other research involving Northern Uganda raises similar themes and presents them much more firmly. Angela Veale and Aki Stavrou report that "[r]eturnees such as those who have been members of the LRA for a long time, or who have been implicated in the commission of major human rights violations, appear to be at higher risk of rejection on return."[121] The longer a person's stay with the armed force or group, the more that communities may infer some exercise of dispositional volition. Communities might hesitate to ascribe as much weight to the age-driven binary of purposeless minor/purposeful adult as the international legal imagination does.[122] Welcome has its limits. Even though many communities in Northern Uganda simply wanted their abducted children back home, it does not inexorably follow that reintegration is a placid exercise, especially initially. Nor does it follow that reintegration premised upon excuse offers a strong foundation for durable social reconciliation.

Jeannie Annan, Moriah Brier, and Filder Aryemo undertook in-depth qualitative interviews with twenty-three male returnees (sixteen of whom were under the age of eighteen at the time of abduction and, hence, are former child soldiers) among the broader SWAY sample. These interviews evoked various themes, including concern regarding educational and economic opportunities, as well as fear between returnees and community members. Annan, Brier, and Aryemo found that, instead of being aggressive upon return, interviewed youth tended to be passive.[123] Why? In part, their passivity traced to fear of reprisal, concern about physical weakness, and trepidation regarding the prospect of being branded a rebel. Many of the interviewees felt "unable to assert themselves in interpersonal conflicts."[124] The prospect that former child soldiers might slide into an enfeebled social posture clearly is disconcerting from a human rights perspective. This prospect portends poorly for their eventual civic engagement. That said, it remains unclear whether programming

[120] SWAY, *supra* note 22, at 66; Christopher Blattman and Jeannie Annan, *Child combatants in northern Uganda: Reintegration myths and realities*, in SECURITY AND POST-CONFLICT RECONSTRUCTION: DEALING WITH FIGHTERS IN THE AFTERMATH OF WAR 103, 115 (Robert Muggah ed., 2009) (noting that, upon return, "particular youth are targeted and insulted when the community knows or suspects they were involved in raids or killings" and referencing SWAY).
[121] Veale and Stavrou, *supra* note 98, at 273, 287–288 (citing research of Rodriguez, Smith-Derksen, and Akera); *see also* Angela Veale, *The Criminal Responsibility of Former Child Soldiers: Contributions from Psychology*, in INTERNATIONAL CRIMINAL ACCOUNTABILITY AND THE RIGHTS OF CHILDREN 97, 104–105 (Karin Arts and Vesselin Popovski eds, 2006) (reporting that, in Northern Uganda, although children abducted for short periods of time tended to feel welcome upon return, those abducted for long periods of time tended to feel unwelcome upon return and had subsequent bad experiences).
[122] Veale identifies false categories of "the misled" and "adult guilty" that "ignore[] local social perceptions that individuals have engaged in similar acts of violence and are similarly accountable." Veale, *The Criminal Responsibility of Former Child Soldiers*, supra note 121, at 104.
[123] Annan, Brier, and Aryemo, *supra* note 5, at 653–655, 664.
[124] *Id.* at 664.

interventions as presently conceptualized could decelerate, let alone reverse, this potential slide.

Veale and Stavrou similarly found that many returnees, even when accepted back, experienced a silencing and disenfranchisement.[125] Returnees who became angry or aggressive no longer were identified as a peer but, instead, as a rebel. After reporting that "[i]n spite of public discourses on peace, forgiveness, and reconciliation in Acholiland, we found evidence of real tensions in reintegration," Veale and Stavrou further observe:

Reintegration based solely on discourses of peace and forgiveness, without a mechanism for acknowledging identity transitions of returnees, especially for those who were members of the LRA for a long time, may leave them vulnerable to rejection and rerecruitment by armed groups.[126]

According to Veale and Stavrou, prevailing reintegration methodologies hampered returnees from feeling entitled to play an active role in peace-building. A gap emerged between accepting returnees back and offering them "full, legitimate participation."[127] Veale and Stavrou also draw attention to a critically important subtext, that is, in public "people rarely admitted to wanting revenge or recompense," but in private "they admitted that forgiveness with impunity was difficult."[128] Observing that "[j]ustice is not being addressed as an issue in the reintegration of formerly abducted children," Veale and Stavrou support culturally grounded justice and traditional reconciliation approaches to fill this space, so long as these approaches incorporate international child rights and protection safeguards.[129]

In an ethnographic study, Grace Akello, Annemiek Richters, and Ria Reis trenchantly question the effectiveness of reintegration processes for formerly abducted children in Northern Uganda.[130] These authors begin by emphasizing the centrality of "issues of vulnerability, innocence and victim hood" to extant programming, and then note that these issues are "closely related to core western ideas [about] children."[131] Their observations parallel Shepler's in the Sierra Leonean context, thus adverting to the portability of the preferred discourse. Akello, Richters, and Reis report that in Northern Uganda former child soldiers were presented as "innocent victims" and that their violent acts automatically were "explained by

---

[125] Veale and Stavrou, *supra* note 98, at 288. These authors undertook a qualitative study that involved exploratory interviews with ten formerly abducted youth, each of whom had been under the age of eighteen (ranging from twelve to seventeen) at the time of abduction into the LRA.

[126] *Id.* at 287–288.

[127] *Id.* at 289.

[128] *Id.* at 288 (reporting research by Tim Allen).

[129] *Id.* at 289–290.

[130] Grace Akello, Annemiek Richters, and Ria Reis, *Reintegration of former child soldiers in northern Uganda: coming to terms with children's agency and accountability*, 4(3) INTERVENTION 229, 233 (2006) (also taking note that that the rehabilitation and reintegration process of former child soldiers "is based on a view in which Christian values are blended with psychotherapeutic concepts").

[131] *Id.* (also remarking on the centrality of trauma).

emphasizing that they have been forced to do such horrendous things."[132] Yet, these authors remark that communities did not readily accept this (re)categorization of the child soldiers or of their actions:

In spite of the counsellors' insistence on former child soldiers' innocence regarding the atrocities they have been involved in, experience of such children point to widespread community resistance to their reintegration.... The unwillingness of communities to welcome formerly abducted child soldiers, is based on the refusal to accept the idea that such children are not accountable for the crimes they have committed.... The communities' difficulties in forgiving perpetrators of violence and their distrust of children whose violent past they know, led to rejection and open discrimination.[133]

Akello, Richters, and Reis uproot a "problematic discrepancy between the well-meant efforts of NGOs to reintegrate child soldiers with their communities, and the compelling need of these children and their communities to come to terms with accountability, and feelings of guilt and revenge."[134] They offer the following anecdote:

[I]n one group a boy mentioned how one ex-combatant had disclosed in his narratives that he had killed people of 'his own initiative'. Sometimes he would order the newly abducted people to kill, or he would do it himself. How then can people then consistently tell him that his problem of *cen* exists because he was 'just ordered to do such crimes'?[135]

According to Akello, Richters, and Reis, "[t]he NGO strategy of presenting an innocent victim to the community is effectively being challenged through gossip and slander about the supposedly innocent victims."[136] Moreover, these authors not-so-subtly imply that the neglect of traditional cleansing ceremonies by an influential NGO may account for why a substantial proportion of supposedly rehabilitated ex-combatants became juvenile prisoners.[137] Ultimately, Akello, Richters, and Reis contend that, "for successful reintegration to take place, children and their communities have to come to terms with the unavoidable change in the status of such children, and to deal with issues of accountability in a way that answers the needs of both the community and the anxieties of the children involved."[138] They identify as a particular challenge ex-combatants who had fought for a long time, returned as adults, and then "register[ed] as a former child soldier" because doing so is a "safe option."[139] Akello, Richters, and Reis also underscore

---

[132] *Id.*; *see also id.* at 234 ("By stressing the fact that the children were abducted, and thus forced to commit their horrendous acts, their essential innocence is emphasized throughout the reintegration process.").

[133] *Id.* at 234, 235, 239–240.

[134] *Id.* at 230.

[135] *Id.* at 241.

[136] *Id.*

[137] *Id.* at 240; *cf. id.* at 229 (remarking that "over 70% of prisoners in the juvenile crime unit in the Gulu District, Uganda are former child soldiers, incarcerated on charges of rape, assault and theft;" also noting an instance where none of 300 rescued children "were found residing in the community in which they were supposed to have been reintegrated").

[138] *Id.* at 229–230.

[139] *Id.* at 240.

the importance of listening to what the former child soldiers themselves have to say, and note with some irony that this may not always be as straightforward as it would otherwise seem:

Children themselves acknowledge that they are not free from responsibility for war crimes in the past, either explicitly when they talk about it amongst themselves, with the researcher or during counseling.... Surely key project planners and district officials would find it problematic if former child soldiers would tell the[m] that they 'do not feel traumatized', and do not 'see themselves as innocent victims' but as perpetrators of war crimes.[140]

To sum up: in Northern Uganda communities were sensitized into discourses of the child soldier's vulnerability and, hence, became tutored about the imperative of unconditional forgiveness. This approach dovetails with more broadly standardized methodologies, such as those posited in Paris Principles 7.42 and 7.44. This pedagogy, however, effected only halting progress in furthering the reintegration of former child soldiers believed to have been implicated in acts of atrocity. These discourses derive from and comport with the international legal imagination's pursuit of faultless passive victim imagery. This imagery homogenizes the role played by youth in atrocity in a manner that dissembles individual deportment. Communities riven by war, however, may perceive the child soldier in a considerably more idiosyncratic fashion. A disjuncture therefore emerges between transnational memorialization and local recollection. Sensitization efforts notwithstanding, twin histories emerge: the official transnational one, on the one hand, and the subaltern local one, on the other. The official version *simplifies* history, to be sure, but this is not the same as *clarifying* it.

An ambiguous situation therefore emerges. At the *macro* level, there may be cause to believe that these discourses, which match certain layers of community sentiment, do in fact facilitate acceptance and reintegration. Hence, it may be that—whatever its occlusions and omissions—the faultless passive victim image conveys tangible operational value. Conversely, however, more particularized research suggests that these discourses are unhelpful to certain subgroups of child soldiers whose individual members are at-risk. These discourses thereby fail to promote their best interests. The irascibility faced by these at-risk returnees would not ostensibly be surmounted should transnational efforts return to the same well-worn discourses and replay them more forcefully. For example, experts Christopher Blattman and Jeannie Annan report that "[f]or those youth who continue to be stigmatized by the community, it is not clear that the current approach—broad based community-sensitization meetings and public messages—will address the causes of the stigmatization."[141] Stigma is often personal and grievance-specific. Hence, more intensive, targeted, and culturally grounded interventions may be required.[142] Conflict resolution is needed. In short, transnational discourse under-

---

[140] *Id.*

[141] Blattman and Annan, *Child combatants in northern Uganda, supra* note 120, at 118.

[142] Annan, Brier, and Aryemo, *supra* note 5, at 663 (recommending "more intensive interventions" for those youth who persist with family or community problems, possibly including "rituals and ceremonies or other forums for justice and reconciliation").

estimates the complex and equivocal nature of community sentiment. The present operational landscape also restricts the opportunity for the community, including parents, to lance feelings of guilt with regard to their inability to protect children during times of conflict or, in some instances, their having encouraged (or even required) the child to participate in fighting forces.[143]

Turning to Sierra Leone, a number of former child soldiers have been rejected by their families and communities owing to wartime activities, with some ending up "enmeshed in a self-destructive lifestyle" or "living rough" on the streets.[144] Communities feared children they equated with acts of violence.[145] Child soldier returnees, as well, were anxious.[146] Some survivors in the community desired revenge and engaged in acts of vigilantism. Denov reports that all of her former RUF interviewees publicly hid their RUF affiliation owing to concerns about the prospect of discrimination or retaliation.[147]

Based on a survey of 1,043 former combatants in Sierra Leone (all adults at the time of the survey, but a substantial proportion of whom had joined fighting forces as children), Macartan Humphreys and Jeremy Weinstein conclude that "[p]ast participation in an abusive military faction is the strongest predictor of difficulty in achieving social reintegration."[148] Affiliation with units that were highly abusive toward civilian populations "strongly and negatively associated with an individual's reported ease in gaining acceptance."[149] Humphreys and Weinstein note that their research implies "that aspects of a combatant's wartime history should be taken into account more prominently in the design of DDR programs."[150] Although this path-breaking research is not on point for persons younger than eighteen at the end of the fighting, I do not believe it to be inapposite to discussions about policy options for this subgroup of returnees.

Some child soldier returnees face considerable community antagonism. This reality should not be blithely understated. This antagonism may manifest itself openly. Or it may simmer below the surface. Not all child soldiers were abducted or drugged. The poignancy of coming home appears as a thread in child soldier experiences across various regions.[151] The fact that community members

---

[143] Castelo-Branco, *supra* note 105, at 494 (reporting such guilt feelings).

[144] SLTRC, VOL. 3B, CH. 4, *supra* note 6, ¶¶ 380–381.

[145] Carrie E. Kimmel and Jini L. Roby, *Institutionalized Child Abuse: The Use of Child Soldiers*, 50(6) INTERNATIONAL SOCIAL WORK 740, 744 (2007) ("Communities may . . . fear ex-soldiers due to the acts of violence [they] committed . . . , as was experienced by some former Sierra Leone child soldiers who were not allowed to attend school, making reintegration difficult.").

[146] Jo Boyden, *The Moral Development of Child Soldiers: What Do Adults Have to Fear?*, 9 PEACE AND CONFLICT: JOURNAL OF PEACE PSYCHOLOGY 343, 346 (2003) (reporting that in Sierra Leone ex-combatants fear becoming scapegoats and being blamed for things that go wrong in the communities).

[147] Denov, *supra* note 10, at 203.

[148] Humphreys and Weinstein, *supra* note 13, at 533.

[149] *Id.* at 547.

[150] *Id.* at 563.

[151] *See*, e.g, International Labour Office, WOUNDED CHILDHOOD: THE USE OF CHILDREN IN ARMED CONFLICT IN CENTRAL AFRICA ix (2003) (reporting from Burundi, Congo-Brazzaville, the DRC, and Rwanda that "[c]ommunities are not always willing to receive former child soldiers" and noting "strong prejudices against them" and perceptions that "former child soldiers represent a danger for the population"); Wessells, CHILD SOLDIERS, *supra* note 4, at 78 ("[A] significant barrier to children's

demonstrate variable and volatile sentiments, ranging from joy to cordiality to antipathy, is understandable. In fact, it should be obvious. Regardless of who perpetrated it and why, mass atrocity invariably engenders a broad gamut of raw emotions among survivors and targeted populations. To pretend otherwise is foolhardy; to base policy on such pretension is quixotic. It is unwise to be too sanguine about the ability of community sensitization by international actors and activists to purge these emotions. The community may need to contend with past atrocity, not be talked out of contending with it.[152]

Mats Utas notes that youth in Liberia who "have committed crimes and atrocities in their communities... fear the way they would be received," and hence stay away from those communities that may represent "home" for them.[153] Although former child soldiers may wish to renew their lives by moving away from home, anticipatorily absconding to distant urban areas because of fear is not the most auspicious way to begin that journey. In Liberia, as in Sierra Leone and Uganda, experts sensitized discordant local communities about the need to welcome back child soldiers. In cases where families resisted reintegration, it was reported that communities "had their ways to let these children contribute to the community to ease the reconciliation process, for example via low paid labour."[154] Although community service may be an effective restorative and reparative device,[155] when communities turn to it privately and haphazardly to plug a perceived justice gap that persists despite ardent top-down sensitization efforts, a risk emerges for abuse of the former child soldiers and, in the least, for unregulated child labor.

Conduct during conflict—namely, why and how did the child join fighting factions and, once there, what did he or she do?—appears to matter to communities. In eastern DRC, for example, local perceptions regarding former child soldiers "are influenced by the political/ethnic relationship that the community had with the particular armed group the child was associated with and also with the nature of the circumstances surrounding the recruitment itself."[156] It appears to matter to communities how much—or how little—independence, cognizance, and discernment the youth had exercised. By implication, then, determining where an

---

reintegration is the searing memory of the children's attacks, destruction of homes, and theft of villagers' food and property.").

[152] For discussion in Cambodia, *see* Jo Boyden, *Anthropology Under Fire: Ethics, Researchers and Children in War, in* CHILDREN AND YOUTH ON THE FRONT LINE: ETHNOGRAPHY, ARMED CONFLICT AND DISPLACEMENT 237, 242 (Jo Boyden and Joanna de Berry eds, 2004) [hereinafter CHILDREN AND YOUTH ON THE FRONT LINE].

[153] Mats Utas, *Fluid Research Fields: Studying Excombatant Youth in the Aftermath of the Liberian Civil War, in* CHILDREN AND YOUTH ON THE FRONT LINE, *id.* at 209, 220.

[154] Save the Children, *supra* note 11, at 96 (quoting a family tracing and reunification advisor).

[155] *See*, e.g., *id.* at 97 ("For those young people who were serious about their reintegration, these projects offered a good opportunity to earn some respect from their communities.").

[156] REDRESS Trust, *supra* note 22, at 18; *see also* Eugène Kwibuka, *Born of War*, THE GLOBE AND MAIL (February 29, 2008) (reporting on reintegration challenges facing former child soldiers in the DRC and noting community resistance); Erick Kenzo, *Ex-Child Soldiers in DRC Drawn Back Into Military Ranks*, Institute for War & Peace Reporting (February 8, 2011) (noting a lack of community support and persistent discrimination in eastern DRC).

individual child soldier situates on a spectrum of circumscribed action should become germane to post-conflict programming.

The Northern Uganda, Sierra Leone, and Liberia experiences therefore offer valuable lessons for the future. Evidence suggests that former child soldiers suspected of implication in extraordinary international crimes, or of long-term affiliation with units known to have serially perpetrated such crimes, are inadequately served by programming animated by the iconicity of faultless passive victimhood. The *status quo*, therefore, falls short in promoting the best interests of this subgroup. Nor does responding to this shortfall by doing more of what the international community and local partners already are doing appear to be a fruitful course of action.

What then? One answer is to say that the interests of the many, which prevailing discourse appears to adequately serve, trump the needs of the few whom it ill-serves. Another answer, decidedly more fecund, is to reform the *status quo*, while also reimagining the conceptual discourse that envelops it. I do not believe policymakers should content themselves with programmatic architecture that fails to protect a definable subgroup of children formerly associated with armed forces or groups from suffering reprisals, stigmatization, or ostracism. I do not believe policymakers should minimize the estrangement that some former child soldiers face. This estrangement renders these returnees susceptible to re-recruitment or re-criminalization. It also stunts the development of a robust civic and public life for them. I do not think it wise to gloss over the need among victims of mass atrocity crimes to redress their harms. Nor do I believe that reform would disturb the interests of child soldier returnees who were not implicated in acts of atrocity or those who are integrating well.

Among possible reforms, I advance the normative claim that augmenting the robustness of transitional justice measures, other than criminal trials and imprisonment, could enhance the reintegration experience for this ill-served constituency of former child soldiers. Retributive goals do not propel this reform. Rather, reform is motivated by concerns that this subgroup is at-risk. In response, might nimbly designed transitional justice interventions allay the likelihood of recrudescence, recidivism, or marginalization? Might such interventions also help deliver a sense of restoration to aggrieved parties?

Although prompted by the documented shortcomings of the *status quo*, my claim reposes upon the conjectural premise that transitional justice processes outside of courtrooms and jailhouses can enhance reintegration, reconciliation, restoration, and social repair even in the very toughest cases—such as with child soldiers—where artificial victim/perpetrator polarities crumble. I am not renegade in accepting this premise. Others do so, as well.[157] However, this premise remains

---

[157] Duthie and Specht, for example, argue that transitional justice measures "may positively affect the reintegration of former child combatants... [by] ... minimizing social exclusion through the reduction of community members' and victims' feelings of injustice." Duthie and Specht, *supra* note 46, at 191. *See also* CHILDREN AND TRUTH COMMISSIONS, *supra* note 36, at x–xi, 65 (noting that "[g]reater understanding of the complex circumstances surrounding the participation of children committing serious offences can help foster a willingness to accept children back into society ... [and] ... there

conjectural. No evidence conclusively establishes positive causation between transitional justice, on the one hand, and reintegration of child soldiers (or other goals, such as restoration and reconciliation), on the other. In fact, there is cause to suspect that criminal trials, which represent one subset of transitional justice mechanisms, fall short of their self-avowed aspirations (retribution, deterrence, and expressivism) in cases of all mid- to low-level cadres and—were they ever to assume them—would be structurally compromised to deliver on goals of reintegration, reconciliation, and restoration. It is, however, somewhat facile to rely on the absence of hard evidence about the relationship between transitional justice (outside of courtrooms and jailhouses) and child soldiers to discourage such mechanisms for child soldiers. After all, no additional knowledge will be accumulated on this subject in the absence of actually undertaking concrete initiatives. Anecdotal evidence arises from credible sources that endogenous mechanisms might be helpful in this regard. But recourse to them has not yet routinely been cast as a justice process.

I draw these caveats to emphasize that this book does not herein make an empirical or evidentiary case. It does not arrive at a scientific conclusion. It forwards a hypothesis, which it urges be taken seriously. Yet this hypothesis is not random. It roots in a series of normative arguments. The remainder of this discussion postulates what benefits transitional justice might bring for child soldiers, only then to bookend itself by foreshadowing—once again, theoretically—risks that transitional justice might pose when applied to child soldiers. Examination of these risks, in turn, opens up an avenue to rekindle a discussion of the benefits that adroitly designed transitional justice initiatives like truth and reconciliation commissions, endogenous ceremonies, and community service might yield.

For Duthie and Specht, the major contribution of transitional justice in the case of child soldiers accrues to the receiving community.[158] Transitional justice, in this sense, would help redress community pain, expiate resentment, and restore a center of gravity. Child soldier returnees would become the indirect beneficiaries of this renewal of community health. A healthy community, after all, would not only accept these youths, but actively buy into their development. A healthy community would support them, invest in them, and entwine their individual futures with its collective ethos.

Might transitional justice, however, also offer direct benefits to former child soldiers implicated in acts of atrocity? Even to former child soldiers not implicated in such acts? For example, transitional justice measures might relieve the child soldier's own personal sense of injustice, including possibly toward the community that trifled while the specter of forcible recruitment loomed. Exploring the violent acts of child soldiers might more lucidly expose crimes committed against child

---

are strong indications that truth-telling and other transitional justice processes can help facilitate reintegration;" and that "children who may have participated in violations or crimes have the best prospects of dealing with their past if they are given the opportunity to account for their experiences through non-judicial processes").

[158] Duthie and Specht, *supra* note 46, at 197.

soldiers. Transitional justice processes might enable the child soldier to identify who in the community may have abetted unscrupulous warlords and shed light on whose omissions exacerbated threats of militarization. Transitional justice processes keyed to a model of circumscribed action could permit those members of notoriously abusive units who were abducted, tortured, and cruelly forced into killings to dissipate lingering associative stigma.

Transitional justice processes could open a venue to discuss much more than just responsibility and acknowledgement. Creative policymakers could seize upon this opportunity to help officialize stories of resistance to atrocity and authenticate histories of contestation to cruel orders. The participation of children in transitional conversations "can serve as an entry point for a larger social discourse on children and citizenship,"[159] one plausible outcome of which is to enervate gerontocracy.

Modifying the *status quo* to enliven the presence of transitional justice in the mix of *inter* and *post bellum* settlements assuredly triggers a cascade of new questions and concerns.

One knotty challenge involves how to encourage child soldiers implicated in acts of atrocity to participate in transitional justice initiatives. Some child soldiers may welcome an opportunity to come forward. Approaches that are purely voluntary, however, will not suffice. Nor is coerced or compelled participation by child soldiers in transitional justice initiatives desirable. Instead, might policymakers entertain conditioning the receipt of benefits and services (whether within or outside of child DDR programs) upon the child soldier's participation in these initiatives? At first blush, this proposal may seem harsh. It departs from Paris Principle 8.16, which stipulates that "[n]o provision of services or support should be dependent upon [children's] participation in [truth-seeking and reconciliation] mechanisms." Yet, the predicate that child soldiers only can participate voluntarily as victims or witnesses—however syntonic it may be with transnational sensibilities—falls short operationally. A need arises to develop a more affirmative participatory regimen through the use of both carrots and sticks. Developing such a regimen might flow more naturally were the controlling imagery dispelled and, instead, substituted with a more well-rounded approach rooted in a continuum of circumscribed action. Relatedly, the grant of benefits and services to post-conflict communities also might incorporate a conditionality of *a priori* or contemporaneous community participation in transitional justice processes.

Some child soldiers may prefer to hide their experiences instead of revisiting them. In response, it could be argued that, by constructively channeling community sentiment, transitional justice would weaken the impulse some former child soldiers feel to conceal their past. On the other hand, however, perhaps these child soldiers would not feel any differently even if a transitional justice process were established. They may not have faith in the process. Their fears may run deep. Or perhaps their reasons for concealment have nothing to do with community reaction. Perhaps they would simply like to forget the past and preoccupy themselves

---

[159] Cook and Heykoop, *supra* note 53, at 191.

with the future. If former child soldiers implicated in acts of atrocity prefer to hide that fact or avoid discussing it, should post-conflict programming not respect this choice?[160] Such respect would appreciate the autonomy of the former child soldier and, in this regard, shore up a human rights paradigm. That said, respecting this choice may prove deleterious to the interests of victims, many of whom also are children. It would be wrongheaded for the best interests of the child imperative to conflate only with children formerly associated with armed forces or armed groups. Instead, it ought to cover all children in post-conflict spaces—the preponderant majority of whom did not associate with armed forces or armed groups—especially since some among this majority may have suffered great indignities at the hands of children who did so associate. Tensions between the interests of child soldiers and those of the persons they harmed need not always be wholly resolved in favor of the child soldiers or structured as an either/or dynamic.

Transitional justice interventions discourage not thinking or talking about the past. But what if communities heal through silence and avoidance? Joanne Corbin reports from an internally displaced persons' camp in Northern Uganda that formerly abducted children were better accepted by the community when they "avoided discussion of their experiences of abduction or captivity."[161] Corbin observes that this approach contradicted Western practices to deal with trauma by talking about it. Western therapeutic focus lies with the individual's construction of the trauma experience, rather than the community's. "Non-[W]estern approaches," which, conversely, are more communally oriented, restore "well-being by addressing the disruption in the social and spiritual domains of life caused by the atrocities of war."[162]

Corbin's findings provide a timely reminder to underscore that transitional justice is not limited to Western justice. Instead, transitional justice should be about local justice. Hence, its modalities need not preoccupy themselves only with the child soldier's experiences, but could encompass the experiences and perceptions of the entire community. In this vein, Corbin learned from her interviews that formerly abducted children reconnected well with their communities when they engaged in productive and valued work.[163] Might this finding suggest the value of a

---

[160] Some child soldiers who favor concealment may do so ambivalently. Others may favor concealment because they fear criminal trials and imprisonment. Their fears may not extend to other transitional justice mechanisms.

[161] Corbin, *supra* note 98, at 327. Corbin's exploratory qualitative study involved interviews with eleven former child combatants (between twelve and nineteen years old at the time of abduction) and eleven adult community members. Corbin's respondents reported some harassment of formerly abducted children by community members who feared their behavior. *Id.* at 328–329.

[162] *Id.* at 328 (citations omitted).

[163] *Id.* at 327–328. Corbin generally welcomes traditional processes. In any event, Corbin's findings are richly textured. She comments that most formerly abducted children "spoke to us about experiences during abduction, in captivity and during escape." *Id.* at 328. Ultimately, Corbin maintains that "the advice . . . not to talk about the past may need to be balanced with a need to voice these experiences . . . in a culturally and communally responsive manner." *Id. See also generally* CHILDREN AND JUSTICE, *supra* note 33, at 28 ("Some form of accountability—based on restorative approaches—can contribute strongly to a child's reconciliation with his community, with the victim and with him or herself.").

...orative facet to the transitional justice process in which former child soldiers participate in rebuilding community infrastructure and construct healthy social relationships? Such restorative paths may, on the surface, appear to be silent about the past, but what they really offer is a different kind of conversation and a different kind of remembering.

Would mainstreaming transitional justice oust the benefits of *ad hoc* approaches by which some child soldiers seek forgiveness and acceptance through private conversations and methods? Invariably, any process of officialization may siphon off flexibility and informality. One of the weaknesses of *ad hoc* arrangements, however, is that the community owes the child no reciprocal, verifiable, or regulated obligation to forgive. Spontaneous confessions and repentance by child soldiers may well occasion their further estrangement from the community.[164] By structuring mutual and correlative obligations of acknowledgement, remedy, forgiveness, and closure as applicable to all stakeholders, transitional justice measures could mitigate the potential for abuse, taunting, or exploitation. On the other hand, official transitional justice might produce a public record that taints the child soldier with acts of atrocity. Some reports, however, suggest that such taint already unofficially befalls former child soldiers suspected of involvement in atrocity, manifesting itself through slander, gossip, calumny, marginalization, unemployment, and antipathy. Invocation of transitional justice initiatives—notably, endogenous mechanisms—could provide an opportunity to transcend this unofficial stigma.

The most complex set of challenges involves the relationships among girls formerly associated with armed forces or armed groups, transitional justice, and DDR programs. These intersectionalities are especially sensitive. Their effective mediation requires skill, care, and discretion. A move away from extant discourse that tends to homogenize the child soldier experience might assist girl soldiers in terms of the development of programmatic interventions that respond to their specific experiences, track their needs, and address the stigma they face. When the international legal imagination views all child soldiers equally and interchangeably as faultless victims, it may unintentionally disadvantage those child soldiers who actually suffered the most and harmed others the least, such as girls and children born into armed forces or groups. Insofar as many girl soldiers give birth while associated with armed factions, these two subgroups of child soldiers overlap.

Although a few girl soldiers do serially commit acts of atrocity,[165] the subgroup of child soldiers implicated in such acts predominantly is male in its composition. Girls do not serve as frequently as boys as front-line combatants. Girls associated with armed forces or groups suffer from alarmingly high rates of sexual violence and torture inflicted by boys and men, as well as forced marriage and sexual slavery. Not

---

[164] *See* Akello, Richters, and Reis, *supra* note 130, at 231 (discussing Apiyo, a fourteen year-old girl in Northern Uganda who had confessed to killing various people in her village, including close kin).

[165] Mats Utas, *Victimcy, Girlfriending, Soldiering: Tactic Agency in a Young Woman's Social Navigation of the Liberian War Zone*, 78(2) ANTHROPOLOGICAL QUARTERLY 403, 405 (2005) (reporting that "men and women alike committed atrocities," but also that from two to four percent of the fighters in the Liberian civil war were female).

all girl soldiers are victims of sexual violence, to be clear, and some armed groups crack down on sexual violence. The LTTE in Sri Lanka and armed opposition groups in the Philippines prohibited sexual exploitation or sexual violation of girl and women volunteers.[166] Nor are boy soldiers exempt from sexual violence.[167] Girl soldiers may sexually assault other girls.[168] However, sexual violence during armed conflict is widespread and largely presents as gender-based. Girl soldiers are targeted, as are women soldiers, along with girls and women outside of armed forces or groups.[169] Boy soldiers are among the perpetrators of this heinous violence—at times coerced by adults, at times not.

Although redress for sexual violence remains woefully inadequate, girls may feel uncertain about participating in transitional justice processes that implicate their abusers, whether boys or men. The international legal imagination has expended great effort in contemplating ways to render international trial processes gender-sensitive, to encourage girls and women to come forward to testify at international criminal prosecutions, and to offer resources and expertise for them in this regard. The international legal imagination believes that impunity for gender-based violence is utterly unacceptable. But actualizing this belief through only a handful of international criminal prosecutions yields a faint print of justice. The pressing need arises to thwart impunity through local initiatives and for creativity, commitment, and industriousness to be brought to bear in this regard. This means thinking hard about developing methodologies and measures to encourage the participation of girls formerly associated with armed forces or groups as witnesses within transitional justice processes aimed at redressing sexual violence, including acts perpetrated by boys. The international legal imagination can do more to engage with local communities to forge options that deliver a sense of justice, but whose operation neither shames nor adds to the burden of stigma already borne by victims of sexual violence.

The need for local justice efforts is all the more urgent in light of the possibility that assigning faultless victimhood status to returning male adolescents may divert attention from addressing the effects of masculinity norms upon them and, in turn, examining how, as returnees, they reproduce and reenact such norms.[170] Masculinities suffuse extraordinary and public violence against girls and women during conflict. But these norms do not simply disappear once conflict ends. Following

---

[166] Wessells, CHILD SOLDIERS, *supra* note 4, at 96.

[167] *See id.* at 97 ("In Afghanistan, where the overwhelming majority of child soldiers have been 14- to 18-year-old males, boys are at great risk of sexual exploitation. The practice of older Afghan men taking younger boys as sexual partners antedated the arrival of Islam and now exists alongside it.").

[168] Denov, *supra* note 10, at 124–125.

[169] *Cf.* Siobhán Wills, PROTECTING CIVILIANS: THE OBLIGATIONS OF PEACEKEEPERS 273–274 (2009) (reporting that "90% of all females above the age of 3 in parts of Liberia have been raped" and that "[u]p to 50% of women and girls in Sierra Leone have suffered some form or threat of sexual violence during the conflict").

[170] For general discussion of these norms and child soldiering *see* Dina Francesca Hayes, Fionnuala D. Ní Aoláin, and Naomi Cahn, *Masculinities and Child Soldiers in Post-Conflict Societies, in* MASCULINITIES AND LAW: A MULTIDIMENSIONAL APPROACH (Frank Cooper and Ann C. McGinley, eds, forthcoming 2011), *available at* <http://papers.ssrn.com/sol3/papers.cfm?abstract_id=1804564>.

conflict, I would argue, they come to shape ordinary and private violence against girls and women.

Transitional justice mechanisms also might bring out stories of resistance by girl soldiers, thereby projecting girls as more than victims and attesting to their resilience even in the most catastrophic of circumstances. Denov notes that some girls in the RUF reported using violent forms of resistance, including killing their rapists, to retaliate and protect themselves.[171] But mostly, resistance involves acts of omission, subterfuge, transgression, and escape.

Up and until the baseline imagery surpasses the tendentiousness of faultless passive victimhood or irreparable lost generations, incorporation of transitional justice into the *post bellum* operational framework for child soldiers likely will remain trivial. At the other extreme, baseline imagery of the child soldier as demon or bandit invokes inappropriate punitive and retributive modalities of sanction. Something less judgmental and more measured—such as the model of circumscribed action—may offer promise.

(vi) Conclusion

Michael Wessells emphasizes that "[o]ne of the greatest challenges in discussing child soldiers is to avoid implying that what is true of one subgroup of child soldiers is also true of other subgroups."[172] Generic remedial and reintegration programs have a propensity to neglect subgroups and their specific needs (e.g. girls, children born into armed groups, returnees who age into adulthood during conflict, and child soldiers implicated in acts of atrocity). In response, switching the discursive baseline from immediate protection of the incapable to incremental empowerment for the capable might encourage heterogeneous approaches and differential treatment. Each of the IDDRS, Paris Principles, and Cape Town Principles exhorts the need for fine-grained methodologies. Adoption of a circumscribed action model would provide a further impetus to craft particularized initiatives not only at the *meso* level for these subgroups, but also at the *micro* level for especially at-risk individuals within them.

This proposed reform prompts pragmatic questions regarding time allocation and resource investment. Can the international community and local partners afford to distinguish among child soldiers as individuals and, accordingly, tailor reintegrative programming? Would such tailoring exacerbate stigma? Lead to perceptions that former child soldiers are gobbling up a disproportionate share of scarce resources? On this note, it is crucial to recall the advantages of allocating support to war-afflicted constituencies as a whole. When the distribution of benefits to returnees anchors within conditionality frameworks of mutual

---

[171] Denov, *supra* note 10, at 134.
[172] Wessells, Child Soldiers, *supra* note 4, at 141. *Cf.* Honwana, *supra* note 90, at 161 ("Rather than placing them together in a single category, recognizing their particular situations and needs is more important.").

obligation, residual antagonism plausibly would dissipate. The community's own responsibilities would also become profiled. The fact that transitional justice processes deliver a nexus of mutual obligation adverts to yet another reason why they might develop into lynch-pins of a reformulated policy approach.

From a resource perspective, however, is it workable to bring child soldiers into transitional justice frameworks?

International courts and tribunals dominate the architecture of international justice as it now stands. These institutions deliver a method of justice that is most expensive. The combined budgets of the two *ad hoc* tribunals have totaled between $US 2 and 3 billion since their inception—in some years comprising 10% to 15% of the total UN budget.[173] Combined, these two tribunals have concluded proceedings against fewer than 200 persons. Their price tag *per* individual defendant is high, to say the least, hovering around some tens of millions of dollars. The Special Court for Sierra Leone also has been reprimanded for the girth of its budget.[174]

In contrast, the justice modalities I encourage—endogenous ceremonies, reinsertion rites, reparative mechanisms, and community service—do not consume a prohibitive level of resources. Helena Cobban reports that it had cost $US 1,075 to demobilize/reintegrate each former fighter in Mozambique and $US 1,066 *per* fighter in South Africa; and $US 4,290 for each amnesty application at the South Africa TRC.[175] The recommendation that truth and reconciliation commissions explore children's relationships with atrocity three-dimensionally (perpetrator, witness, and victim) instead of two-dimensionally (victim and perpetrator alone) would likely not trigger significant resource costs either. If a case successfully were made that transitional justice initiatives might assist those former child soldiers most susceptible to reintegrative impediments, then—other than being held up by their own preconceptions—would it not follow that donors and global civil society would redirect funding efforts to invest in such initiatives?[176]

Conceptualizing juveniles as non-responsible for systemic breaches of the rights of others during conflict does not augur well for their proactive status as rights-holders—and as stakeholders in a shared *civis*—following conflict. A group's ability to claim rights is emboldened when individual members of that group implicated in gross denials of the rights of others answer for their conduct. Unless paired with responsibilities, rights quickly become flimsy.

---

[173] Adam M. Smith, AFTER GENOCIDE: BRINGING THE DEVIL TO JUSTICE 182–183 (2009).

[174] Craig Timberg, *Sierra Leone Special Court's Narrow Focus*, WASH. POST (March 26, 2008) at A11 (noting that "resentment has arisen over the millions of dollars in donor money spent on the [SCSL]. Some Sierra Leoneans say these funds could be better spent on education, health care and other pressing daily needs, or to develop a functioning national justice system that would last beyond the [SCSL's] scheduled closure . . . "). By 2008, the SCSL had spent more than $US 150 million—certainly, "a massive sum for a country that the United Nations ranks as the least developed in the world." *Id.*

[175] Helena Cobban, AMNESTY AFTER ATROCITY? HEALING NATIONS AFTER GENOCIDE AND WAR CRIMES 209, table 6.1 (2007).

[176] Might the ICC Trust Fund for victims extend its support to local restorative justice efforts?

Many provisions of the Convention on the Rights of the Child "signal . . . a growing willingness to see children, at least in some circumstances, as partially autonomous agents often able to make decisions and choices on their own."[177] Faultless passive victim imagery, however, invokes several tenets that contradict international human rights law's struggle to advance children and juveniles as empowered members of society. One of these tenets is the purportedly apolitical nature of youth. Might accenting the apolitical nature of juveniles inadvertently pour a weak foundation for them to be taken seriously in peace-building, societal reconstruction, and community governance? To be respected? Might it render youth susceptible to dismissal as vapid or pre-logical? Vibrant engagement in public life invariably means acting politically. One of the costs of depoliticizing juveniles is that they may become seen as incapable of such engagement. If so, then, their opportunities to do so may become wan or, even, stultified. Fulsome protectionism can silence.

Children are more than just persons in a state of becoming. They are persons in a state of being. Their potentiality must not deplete their actuality.[178] They are about the future, to be sure, but they also are here, right now, in the present.

---

[177] Beth A. Simmons, MOBILIZING FOR HUMAN RIGHTS: INTERNATIONAL LAW IN DOMESTIC POLITICS 314 (2009).
[178] Shepler, *supra* note 22, at 206.

7

Reinvigorating the International Legal Imagination

Were this book to be persuasive, it would prompt the international legal imagination to shift gears. Instead of assuming child soldiers to be forlorn passive victims of a lost generation, the international legal imagination would come to better appreciate them as circumscribed actors.

To where would this shift nudge international law and policy? Not toward retributive criminal trials but, rather, toward restorative forms of justice to facilitate social repair in afflicted communities. Toward bringing into sharper relief how the expectations and experiences of individual child soldiers vary considerably. Toward a rigorous framework of juvenile rights that bases itself on mutual respect and reciprocal obligation. And toward a more finessed understanding of child soldiering, without which the practice cannot be ended. The international legal imagination would come to engage with, instead of wish away, the nettlesome reality that significant numbers of children exercise initiative in joining armed forces or armed groups. Notwithstanding their permeability, it is preferable to conceptually differentiate—rather than splice—the three basic paths to youth militarization, to wit, enlistment/presenting for service, abduction/forcible recruitment through serious threats, and birth into fighting forces. The current preference to criminally prosecute a handful of adult commanders for unlawful recruitment of children yields only a faint print of justice. In response, the reimaginative exercise contemplated by this book would allocate responsibility for the practice of child soldiering among the many individual, state, commercial, and organizational elements that have a hand in its nagging persistence. In short, rather than artificially shroud child soldier experiences through conceptual and doctrinal parsimony, this new approach would embrace the complexities of those experiences through conceptual and doctrinal suppleness.

Another implication of the arguments presented in this book would be for law and policy to invest less in categorical age demarcations. For example, why not situate all lower-level cadres enmeshed in atrocity—regardless of their age—along a continuum of circumscribed action with a view to enhancing the quality of restorative justice processes? Age could certainly be a factor in determining the extent to which an individual actor is deemed susceptible to conniving social forces, pressures, abuse, and coercion. But it does not have to be singularly determinative. Discussing Mozambique's civil war, during which serial human rights violations ravaged the social landscape, Jessica Schafer, for example, notes that "[a] high proportion of the soldiers were under eighteen but their experiences within this moral space did not differ substantially from those over eighteen."[1] A circumscribed actor spectrum would more adroitly articulate the continuities of these experiences. It would thus dissuade the infantilization of older children and the placing of exigent burdens on young adults.

The reimaginative exercise contemplated by this book would neither impose a new blueprint nor predetermine the content thereof. Rather, it would diversify programmatic initiatives undertaken on behalf of former child soldiers. This book aims to create more options, not preordain unitary legal reform, consolidated policy practices, or top-down operational imperatives. Its intention is to develop a less didactic approach that would energize the local and spark bottom-up engagement.

(i) Fears of Retributive Creep

Might stripping the prevailing legal fiction generate a risk that former child soldiers become subject to harsh punishment? Summarily prosecuted in show trials? Might authorities pretextually turn to models of circumscribed action to impose vindictive, humiliating, and punitive sanctions that masquerade as transitional justice measures? These concerns are not conjectural. Some readers justifiably may worry about the replication of situations such as child soldier Omar Khadr's detention and ultimate conviction by a US military commission on terrorism-related charges.

Reliance on faultless passive victimhood is not the only way to parry these frightful outcomes. Better gate-keeping mechanisms can be developed. I have elsewhere proposed the introduction of *qualified deference* as a standard to invigilate national and local transitional justice mechanisms in post-conflict spaces.[2] This approach accords national or local mechanisms a presumption of deference, but qualifies this presumption through a heuristic of six interpretive guidelines:

(1) good faith, as understood from the perspective of virtue ethics;
(2) the democratic and social legitimacy of the deployed mechanisms;
(3) the specific characteristics of the violence and of the current political context;
(4) the avoidance of gratuitous or iterated punishment;
(5) the effect of the procedure on the universal substance, such that procedural methods do not void the substantive content of the shared universal value; and
(6) the preclusion of the infliction of great evils upon anyone.

Although the deference presumption would weigh in favor of national and local initiatives, it remains contingent upon respecting these interpretive guidelines.

---

[1] Jessica Schafer, *The Use of Patriarchal Imagery in the Civil War in Mozambique and its Implications for the Reintegration of Child Soldiers*, in CHILDREN AND YOUTH ON THE FRONT LINE: ETHNOGRAPHY, ARMED CONFLICT AND DISPLACEMENT 87, 93–94 (Jo Boyden and Joanna de Berry eds, 2004).

[2] Mark A. Drumbl, ATROCITY, PUNISHMENT, AND INTERNATIONAL LAW 187–194 (2007) (entwining this standard with a cosmopolitan pluralist vision of international justice). The next several paragraphs of this section are adapted from the cited pages of this work.

The construction of *good faith* envisioned by qualified deference tracks that of virtue ethics. For the virtue ethicist, the just nature of laws generally depends on their expression of good motives on the part of their enactors.[3]

Democratic legitimacy is neither assured by legislative vote nor by executive decision-making. Centralized state institutions (even putatively representative ones) may not reflect on-the-ground priorities in afflicted constituencies. Accordingly, by democratic legitimacy I intend not a formal positivist process but, rather, a substantive form of social legitimacy.[4] Conversely, as this book's discussion of endogenous practices reveals, putatively local customs may in fact be promulgated by elites unrepresentative of local populations or religious leaders unrepresentative of the rank-and-file of spiritual communities. By channeling public participation in the construction of local norms, instead of binarily opposing extant local norms to transnational templates and then imposing those templates top-down, international intercessions can help overcome democratic deficits.

The *specific characteristics of the violence* and of the *current political context* consider the degree to which the violence was popular, whether it has ended, and whether the society has transitioned into peace and relative security. The extent to which a transitional justice mechanism was deliberately constructed to respond to the specifics of the atrocity in question also would weigh in favor of its retaining qualified deference. Considerations also include the effects of retrospective accountability on prospective stability; the capacity of national and local socio-legal institutions; corruption, venality, politicization, and complicity in violence on the part of institutional officials; and whether, post-conflict, the society is transitioning toward democracy or drifting toward a new totalitarianism.

The *avoidance of gratuitous iterated punishment* basically refers to *ne bis in idem* and to speedy resolution of an accusation. The requirement that the *procedural methods not void the substantive content* of the shared universal value excludes transitional justice initiatives that directly or indirectly redefine the content of universal substantive prohibitions (e.g. that denounce crimes against humanity) so as to trivialize them or render them inordinately elastic.

The final element of qualified deference is that the local or national justice modalities *not inflict great evils on any other individuals*, whether perpetrators, victims, witnesses, or members of the public. This guideline sets parameters to the kind of processes to be followed and the types of sanction to be imposed. Neither process nor sanction can take the form of what cosmopolitan values would condemn as a great evil. This guideline also is contextual. It would proactively

---

[3] Anthony Ellis, *Introduction*, in WAR CRIMES AND COLLECTIVE WRONGDOING 1, 14 (Aleksandar Jokić ed., 2001). *Cf.* Michael Slote, *War Crimes and Virtue Ethics*, *in id.* at 77, 81 (noting that a morality of war crimes based on sentimentalist virtue ethics will, in determining what is just, "look to what people (notably but not exclusively legislators) are trying to do with a nation's future") (emphasis omitted).

[4] Harvey M. Weinstein and Eric Stover, *Introduction: conflict, justice, and reclamation, in* MY NEIGHBOR, MY ENEMY: JUSTICE AND COMMUNITY IN THE AFTERMATH OF MASS ATROCITY 1, 18 (Eric Stover and Harvey M. Weinstein eds, 2004) ("[A] basic tenet of social reconstruction or reclamation is the need for post-war communities to define and take ownership of the processes of justice and reconciliation.").

assume a more robust form when juveniles become implicated in the justice process.[5]

The Khadr prosecution would not have passed muster under the qualified deference test. It ran afoul of good faith, given the dilatory nature of the process. Military commission procedural rules fell short of appropriate due process standards. Khadr's prosecution inflicted gratuitous punishment, namely lengthy pretrial detention. It also subjected him to great evils, notably, distressing custodial treatment and extraction of confessions through threats of gang rape.[6]

To sum up: qualified deference would oust transitional justice measures that imposed harsh modalities or vindictive methods on former child soldiers.

What if, as a result of the shift to the circumscribed action spectrum, a post-conflict society comes to believe, in good faith, that national criminal trials are appropriate for former child soldiers where there is well-founded evidence of their independent participation in acts of atrocity? It is one thing to say that an unfair trial cedes the presumption of qualified deference. But what about the post-conflict society that introduces criminal trials which are competently undertaken, impartial, well-intended, and respectful of all participants? This permutation reflects tension between two normative positions I advance: the unsuitability of criminal trials for acts of atrocity in the case of minors, on the one hand, and support for local autonomy and input in designing post-conflict reconstructive policies, on the other. Given the problematic experiences of some children with national penal systems, a need arises for strict scrutiny and an effects-based analysis in the application of the six interpretive guidelines to this permutation. Yet, I do not believe that a criminal trial ineluctably would offend the interpretive guidelines and, hence, would *ipso facto* be ousted by application of the qualified deference standard. This does not mean that such trials should be pursued. It just means that they would not be *per se* impermissible in all cases. Turning to punishment, sequestered penitentiary imprisonment of a child soldier would in overwhelming probability, be incompatible with a qualified deference standard. Hence, trials that inexorably lead to such sanction upon conviction would not pass muster.

(ii) Endnote: Broader Implications

Might this book's reimaginative journey gesture toward a wider horizon? This final section preliminarily explores reconceived approaches to ordinary common crimes, transnational crimes that presently fall outside international criminal jurisdiction, and the etiology of mass atrocity generally.

---

[5] *Cf.* United Nations Convention on the Rights of the Child, G.A. Res. 44/25, Art. 19, Annex, U.N. Doc. A/RES/44/25 (November 20, 1989) (entered into force September 2, 1990) (requiring state parties to protect children from all forms of physical or mental violence, injury or abuse, neglect or negligent treatment, and maltreatment or exploitation).

[6] *See supra* Chapter 1, note 44 and Chapter 4, note 103.

Extraordinary international crimes committed in periods of armed conflict differ from ordinary common crimes committed within national jurisdictions in peacetime. The model of circumscribed action addresses extraordinary international criminality. It may, nevertheless, also offer a prism for revisiting how national jurisdictions engage juvenile perpetrators of ordinary common crime. At present, national criminal jurisdictions tend to be dogged by the undertheorization of juvenile crime. If transposed into national jurisdictions, the circumscribed action model could enliven restorative, reintegrative, risk-based, and rehabilitative penological options and, thus, advance an alternate remedial ethos. Nor is there any reason why the circumscribed action spectrum could not apply to adults, as well.

The second possible linkage ties to the involvement of minors in transnational crimes that presently lie outside the formal parameters of international criminal law as enforced by international institutions. Might the international community's experiences with former child soldiers be instructive in terms of ameliorating responsive policies for minors implicated in transnational criminality? More grounded portrayals of children enmeshed in sex work, the drug trade, or dangerous child labor might augment preventative efforts. Criminal prosecutions of adult traffickers, abductors, or employers of minors are imperative. No differently than in the case of child soldiering, however, these prosecutions likely fulfill only a limited deterrent function: hence, relying inordinately on them may underwhelm. Recognizing that some children become entangled in transnational crime through push and pull dynamics of social navigation and circumscribed action may offer a more realistic vision of the nature of the problem. As with child soldiering, it is simply easier for internationalists to view the problem as one of abduction or unstoppable coercion, instead of one that involves a mix of compelled participants and participants who exercise some—and perhaps a fair bit of—initiative. Another lesson learned from experiences with former child soldiers is the importance of paying attention to, instead of disregarding, how the children actually see themselves. Dianne Otto, for example, concludes that young women (including older children) who engage in "survival sex" with UN peacekeeping personnel "are unlikely to view themselves as victims of exploitation or abuse."[7] Hence, policies that reductively and presumptively treat them as such may not be particularly effective.

Third, this reimaginative exercise prompts new ways to undertake philosophical and jurisprudential inquiries regarding the etiology of mass atrocity. It thereby squares with my prior scholarship, which examines the influence of situational and ecological factors on the role of the individual in episodes of collective violence.[8] The relevance of these structural factors is underappreciated in the case of adult perpetrators. International criminal law exaggerates the levels of personal control and autonomy exercised by adults within the cauldron of communal violence,

---

[7] Dianne Otto, *The Sexual Tensions of UN Peace Support Operations: A Plea for 'Sexual Positivity'*, XVIII Finnish Yearbook of International Law 33, 50 (2007).

[8] Drumbl, Atrocity, Punishment, and International Law, *supra* note 2, at 23–45.

particularly discrimination-based violence.[9] When adults commit acts of atrocity within such contexts, they tend not to conduct themselves deviantly. Their acts are deeply shaped by group pressure, official imploration, and pervasive propaganda. Atrocity perpetrators exhibit conformist tendencies and may come to believe that they are doing "good" by eliminating the "other." Acknowledging how structural factors inform mass violence does not drain responsibility from atrocity perpetrators for their actions. That said, serious questions do arise regarding the appropriateness of the criminal law, predicated as it is on ferreting out individual culpability, as an accountability mechanism.

International criminal law nevertheless persists in emphasizing the dispositional delinquency of the adult atrocity perpetrator while downplaying the ecological and collective factors that animate mass violence. International criminal law does so strategically. After all, constructing atrocity crime as the product of individual disposition—itself a legal fiction—justifies the measurement of guilt within liberal legalist processes, in particular retributive criminal trials.

In the case of perpetrators under the age of eighteen, however, international criminal law lurches to the opposite extreme. As this book has demonstrated, international criminal law underestimates dispositional factors while overestimating situational factors. Acts of atrocity by juveniles are reduced to epiphenomena of environment, socialization, narcotics, orders, or commands. The juvenile has neither motivation nor volition. Agency is absent.

International criminal law fails to engage with the variable interplay between disposition and situation for *all* persons implicated in the perpetration of acts of atrocity. Rather, it hugs two artificial bimodalities, each rooted in the categorism of age. As a result, adults who commit atrocity become typified in a way that obscures the reality that many may be child-like in their motivations. On the other hand, juveniles who commit atrocity become typified in a way that obscures the reality that many may share adult-like motivations, behavior, and expectations.

International criminal law derives its energy from, and in turn disseminates, polarities of guilt/or innocence, capacity/or incapacity, adult/or child, and victim/ or perpetrator. These rigid dyads, however, interface awkwardly with how, exactly, atrocity normalizes and metastasizes into a mass event. The criminal law's simplistic binary reductionisms mask how the aggrieved can aggrieve and victims can victim-ize. A captive can also be a captor. International criminal law, frankly, is uncom-fortable with these ambiguities.

Accordingly, although international criminal law remains the dominant account-ability mechanism for episodes of mass atrocity, it offers a clumsy fit with the etiology of collective violence and organizational massacre. The need, therefore, arises for international *criminal law* to recede and for international *post-conflict*

---

[9] Alette Smeulers and Barbora Holá, *Attributing guilt to and sentencing of various types of perpetrators* (2009 manuscript on file with the author), at p. 3 (critiquing international criminal law for its "fundamental attribution error"—namely, that it overestimates dispositional factors, such as blaming or crediting individuals, and it underestimates situational factors, such as blaming or crediting the environments in which these individuals operate—and closely incorporating language from Richard J. Gerrig and Philip G. Zimbardo, Psychology and Life 519 (18th edn, 2008)).

justice—a broader paradigm that includes diverse accountability modalities, a more sublime lexicon, and greater sensitivity to context—to step up.

The way forward, then, is not to have criminal trials nationally or locally for child soldiers and to incarcerate whoever may be found guilty. Nor is it for the ICC or other international criminal tribunals to expand their jurisdiction to include minors. Nor is it for more adults to be criminally prosecuted. Rather, the future lies in looking well beyond trials and imprisonment to encourage more fine-grained modalities of restoration, conflict resolution, and justice. So long as the atrocity trial shimmers as the ideal-type of justice, however, this path forward will remain illusory.

Bibliography

Abdullah, I. (1998), *Bush path to destruction: the origin and character of the Revolutionary United Front/Sierra Leone*, 36(2) JOURNAL OF MODERN AFRICAN STUDIES 203.

Abrams, K. (1995), *Sex Wars Redux: Agency and Coercion in Feminist Legal Theory*, 95 COLUMBIA LAW REVIEW 304.

Acirokop, P. (2010), *The Potential and Limits of* Mato Oput *as a Tool for Reconciliation and Justice*, *in* CHILDREN AND TRANSITIONAL JUSTICE: TRUTH-TELLING, ACCOUNTABILITY AND RECONCILIATION 267 (UNICEF Innocenti Research Centre and Human Rights Program at Harvard Law School, Sharanjeet Parmar, Mindy Jane Roseman, Saudamini Siegrist, and Theo Sowa eds) (Cambridge: Harvard University Press).

African Charter on the Rights and Welfare of the Child, OAU Doc. CAB/LEG/24.9/49 (1990) (entered into force November 29, 1999).

Agreement on Accountability and Reconciliation between the Government of the Republic of Uganda and the Lord's Resistance Army/Movement and Annexure, Juba, Sudan (June 29, 2007, Annexure from February 19, 2008), Annexure *available at* <http://www.iccnow.org/documents/Annexure_to_agreement_on_Accountability_signed_today.pdf> (visited on September 17, 2011).

Akakpo, K. (2012), *Procureur c. X: les leçons à tirer de la poursuite d'un enfant soldat pour crimes contre l'humanité* (manuscript on file with the author, with permission, forthcoming REVUE GÉNÉRALE DE DROIT).

Akello, G., Richters, A., and Reis, R. (2006), *Reintegration of former child soldiers in northern Uganda: coming to terms with children's agency and accountability*, 4(3) INTERVENTION 229.

Allen, T. (2008), *Ritual (Ab)use? Problems with Traditional Justice in Northern Uganda*, *in* COURTING CONFLICT? JUSTICE, PEACE AND THE ICC IN AFRICA 47 (Nicholas Waddell and Phil Clark eds) (London: Royal African Society).

Amann, D. M. (2001), *Calling Children to Account: The Proposal for a Juvenile Chamber in the Special Court for Sierra Leone*, 29 PEPPERDINE LAW REVIEW 167.

The American Non Governmental Organizations Coalition for the International Criminal Court (2002), *The International Criminal Court and Children's Rights*, available at <http://www.iccnow.org/documents/FS-AMICC-ICCnChildRights.pdf> (visited on September 3, 2011).

Amnesty International (2000), *Child Soldiers: Criminals or Victims?* (AI Index IOR 50/02/00), *available at* <http://www.amnesty.org/en/library/info/IOR50/002/2000> (visited on September 3, 2011).

Annan, J., Blattman, C., and Horton, R. (2006), THE STATE OF YOUTH AND YOUTH PROTECTION IN NORTHERN UGANDA: FINDINGS FROM THE SURVEY FOR WAR AFFECTED YOUTH (report prepared for UNICEF Uganda).

Annan, J., Brier, M., and Aryemo, F. (2009), *From "Rebel" to "Returnee": Daily Life and Reintegration for Young Soldiers in Northern Uganda*, 24(6) JOURNAL OF ADOLESCENT RESEARCH 639.

Aptel, C. (2010), *International Criminal Justice and Child Protection*, *in* CHILDREN AND TRANSITIONAL JUSTICE: TRUTH-TELLING, ACCOUNTABILITY AND RECONCILIATION 67 (UNICEF Innocenti Research Centre and Human Rights Program at Harvard Law

School, Sharanjeet Parmar, Mindy Jane Roseman, Saudamini Siegrist, and Theo Sowa eds) (Cambridge: Harvard University Press).

——and Ladisch, V. (2011), THROUGH A NEW LENS: A CHILD-SENSITIVE APPROACH TO TRANSITIONAL JUSTICE (New York and Brussels: International Center for Transitional Justice).

Arendt, H. (1977), EICHMANN IN JERUSALEM: A REPORT ON THE BANALITY OF EVIL (orig. 1963) (New York: Penguin Books).

Ariès, P. (1962), CENTURIES OF CHILDHOOD: A SOCIAL HISTORY OF FAMILY LIFE (Robert Baldick trans.) (New York: Vintage Books).

Armatta, J. (2010), TWILIGHT OF IMPUNITY (Durham: Duke University Press).

Arnett, J. (2004), EMERGING ADULTHOOD: THE WINDING ROAD FROM THE LATE TEENS THROUGH THE TWENTIES (New York: Oxford University Press).

Arzoumanian, N. and Pizzutelli, F. (2003), *Victimes et bourreaux: questions de responsabilité liées à la problématique des enfants-soldats en Afrique*, 85 REVUE INTERNATIONALE DE LA CROIX-ROUGE 827.

Assembly of States Parties, Elements of Crimes, ICC-ASP/1/3 (part II-B) (September 9, 2002), *available at* <http://www.icc-cpi.int/NR/rdonlyres/336923D8-A6AD-40EC-AD7B-45BF9DE73D56/0/ElementsOfCrimesEng.pdf> (visited on August 24, 2011).

Asuncion, A. C. (2009), *Pulling the Stops on Genocide: The State or the Individual?*, 20 EUROPEAN JOURNAL OF INTERNATIONAL LAW 1195.

Atkinson, R. R. (1994), THE ROOTS OF ETHNICITY: THE ORIGINS OF THE ACHOLI OF UGANDA (2nd edn, 2010) (Kampala: Fountain Publishers).

Baines, E. (2009), *Complex political perpetrators: reflections on Dominic Ongwen*, 47(2) JOURNAL OF MODERN AFRICAN STUDIES 163.

Bassiouni, M. C. (2010), *Mixed Models of International Criminal Justice, in* THE PURSUIT OF INTERNATIONAL CRIMINAL JUSTICE: A WORLD STUDY ON CONFLICTS, VICTIMIZATION, AND POST-CONFLICT JUSTICE, Volume I, 423 (M. Cherif Bassiouni ed.) (Antwerp: Intersentia).

Bauer, Y. (2001), RETHINKING THE HOLOCAUST (New Haven: Yale University Press).

Bayer, C., Klasen, F., and Adam, H. (2007), *Association of Trauma and PTSD Symptoms With Openness to Reconciliation and Feelings of Revenge Among Former Ugandan and Congolese Child Soldiers*, 298(5) JOURNAL OF THE AMERICAN MEDICAL ASSOCIATION 555.

BBC News (September 2, 2007), *Thousands of crimes by under-10s*, available at <http://news.bbc.co.uk/2/hi/uk_news/6974587.stm> (visited on September 17, 2011).

Beah, I. (2007), A LONG WAY GONE: MEMOIRS OF A BOY SOLDIER (New York: Sarah Crichton Books).

Beber, B. and Blattman, C. (2011), *The Logic of Child Soldiering and Coercion* (manuscript on file with the author).

Ben-Ari, E. (2009), *Facing Child Soldiers, Moral Issues, and "Real Soldiering": Anthropological Perspectives on Professional Armed Forces*, 37(1) SCIENTIA MILITARIA: SOUTH AFRICAN JOURNAL OF MILITARY STUDIES 1.

Bernal, V. (2000), *Equality to Die For?: Women Guerrilla Fighters and Eritrea's Cultural Revolution*, 23(2) POLITICAL AND LEGAL ANTHROPOLOGY REVIEW 61.

Betancourt, T., Borisova, I., Rubin-Smith, J., Gingerich, T., Williams, T., and Agnew-Blais, J. (2008), PSYCHOSOCIAL ADJUSTMENT AND SOCIAL REINTEGRATION OF CHILDREN ASSOCIATED WITH ARMED FORCES AND ARMED GROUPS: THE STATE OF THE FIELD AND FUTURE DIRECTIONS (Austin: Psychology Beyond Borders).

Betancourt, T., Simmons, S., Borisova, I., Brewer, S., Iweala, U., and de la Soudière, M. (2008), *High Hopes, Grim Reality: Reintegration and the Education of Former Child Soldiers in Sierra Leone*, 52(4) COMPARATIVE EDUCATION REVIEW 565.

Blattman, C. and Annan, J. (2009), *Child combatants in northern Uganda: reintegration myths and realities, in* Security and Post-Conflict Reconstruction: Dealing with Fighters in the Aftermath of War 103 (Robert Muggah ed.) (Abingdon: Routledge).

—— ——(2010a), *On the nature and causes of LRA abduction: what the abductees say, in* The Lord's Resistance Army: Myth and Reality 132, (Tim Allen and Koen Vlassenroot eds) (London: Zed Books).

—— ——(2010b), *The Consequences of Child Soldiering*, 92(4) Review of Economics and Statistics 882.

Boothby, N. (1992), *Displaced Children: Psychological Theory and Practice from the Field*, 5(2) Journal of Refugee Studies 106.

——, Crawford, J., and Halperin, J. (2006), *Mozambique child soldier life outcome study: Lessons learned in rehabilitation and reintegration efforts*, 1(1) Global Public Health 87.

Bouris, E. (2007), Complex Political Victims (Bloomfield, CT: Kumarian Press).

Boyden, J. (2000), *Children and Social Healing, in* Children in Extreme Situations, Working Paper Series No. 00-05, LSE Development Studies Institute 58 (Lisa Carlson, Megan Mackeson-Sandbach, and Tim Allen eds) (London: Development Studies Institute, London School of Economics and Political Science), *available at* <http://www2.lse.ac.uk/internationalDevelopment//pdf/WP05.pdf> (visited on September 17, 2011).

——(2003), *Children under Fire: Challenging Assumptions about Children's Resilience*, 13(1) Children, Youth and Environments, *available at* <http://www.colorado.edu/journals/cye/13_1/Vol13_1Articles/CYE_CurrentIssue_Article_ChildrenUnderFire_Boyden.htm> (visited on September 17, 2011).

——(2004), *Anthropology Under Fire: Ethics, Researchers and Children in War, in* Children and Youth on the Front Line: Ethnography, Armed Conflict and Displacement 237 (Jo Boyden and Joanna de Berry eds) (New York: Berghahn Books).

——(2006), *Children, War and World Disorder in the 21st Century: A Review of the Theories and the Literature on Children's Contributions to Armed Violence* (Queen Elizabeth House, University of Oxford, Working Paper No. 138).

——and de Berry, J. (2010), *Introduction, in* Children and Youth on the Front Line: Ethnography, Armed Conflict and Displacement (Jo Boyden and Joanna de Berry eds) (New York: Berghahn Books).

——, de Berry, J., Feeny, T., and Hart, J. (2002), *Children Affected by Armed Conflict in South Asia: A review of trends and issues identified through secondary research* (Refugee Studies Centre, Oxford University, Working Paper No. 7).

Brett, R. (2003), *Adolescents volunteering for armed forces or armed groups*, 85 International Review of the Red Cross 857.

——and Specht, I. (2004), Young Soldiers: Why They Choose to Fight (Boulder: Lynne Rienner Publishers).

Briggs, J. (2005), Innocents Lost: When Child Soldiers Go to War (New York: Basic Books).

Bringing the wicked to the dock, The Economist (March 9, 2006), *available at* <http://www.economist.com/node/5601334> (visited on August 24, 2011).

Brocklehurst, H. (2009), *Childhood in Conflict: Can the Real Child Soldier Please Stand Up?*, *in* Ethics, Law and Society, Volume iv, 259 (Jennifer Gunning, Søren Holm, and Ian Kenway, eds) (Farnham: Ashgate).

Brooks, R. E. (2003), *Law in the Heart of Darkness: Atrocity & Duress*, 43 Virginia Journal of International Law 861.

Brown v. Entertainment Merchants Association, US Supreme Court, 564 U.S. __ (2011).

Buss, E. (2000), *The Adolescent's Stake in the Allocation of Educational Control Between Parent and the State*, 67 University of Chicago Law Review 1233.

Cape Town Principles and Best Practices (April 27–30, 1997), *available at* <http://www.unicef.org/emerg/files/Cape_Town_Principles(1).pdf> (visited on September 17, 2011).

Caramés, A., Fisas, V., and Luz, D. (2006), Analysis of Disarmament, Demobilisation and Reintegration (DDR) programmes existing in the World during 2005 (Barcelona: Escola de cultura de Pau).

Carlson, K. and Mazurana, D. (2010), *Accountability for Sexual and Gender-Based Crimes by the Lord's Resistance Army*, in Children and Transitional Justice: Truth-Telling, Accountability and Reconciliation 235 (UNICEF Innocenti Research Centre and Human Rights Program at Harvard Law School, Sharanjeet Parmar, Mindy Jane Roseman, Saudamini Siegrist, and Theo Sowa eds) (Cambridge: Harvard University Press).

Carpenter, R. C. (2005), *"Women, Children and Other Vulnerable Groups": Gender, Strategic Frames and the Protection of Civilians as a Transnational Issue*, 49 International Studies Quarterly 295.

Case Concerning the Application of the Convention on the Prevention and Punishment of the Crime of Genocide (BiH v. Serbia and Montenegro), Judgment (International Court of Justice, February 26, 2007), *available at* <http://www.icj-cij.org/docket/files/91/13685.pdf?PHPSESSID=97a462daaea58d864fecadb976af5af0> (visited on August 24, 2011).

Castelo-Branco, V. (1997), *Child Soldiers: The Experience of the Mozambican Association for Public Health (AMOSAPU)*, 7(4) Development in Practice 494.

de Certeau, M. (1980), The Practice of Everyday Life (Steven Rendall trans., 1984) (Berkeley: University of California Press).

Charbonneau, L. (June 2, 2009), *Interview—ICC looking at child soldier issue in Darfur*, Reuters, *available at* <http://reliefweb.int/node/311888> (visited on August 24, 2011).

Clark, P. (2007), *In the Shadow of the Volcano: Democracy and Justice in Congo*, Dissent 29, *available at* <http://www.dissentmagazine.org/article/?article=724> (visited on August 24, 2011).

Clark, R. S. and Triffterer, O. (2008), *Article 26: Exclusion of jurisdiction over persons under eighteen*, in Commentary on the Rome Statute of the International Criminal Court: Observers' Notes, Article by Article (Otto Triffterer ed., 2nd edn) (Oxford: Beck/Hart).

Coalition to Stop the Use of Child Soldiers (2008), Child Soldiers Global Report 2008, *available at* <http://www.childsoldiersglobalreport.org/> (visited on September 3, 2011).

——, *Frequently Asked Questions*, *available at* <http://www.child-soldiers.org/childsoldiers/questions-and-answers> (visited on June 23, 2011).

Cobban, H. (2007), Amnesty After Atrocity? Healing Nations after Genocide and War Crimes (Boulder: Paradigm Publishers).

Cole, A. M. (2007), The Cult of True Victimhood: From the War on Welfare to the War on Terror (Stanford: Stanford University Press).

Combs, N. A. (2010), Fact-Finding Without Facts: The Uncertain Evidentiary Foundations of International Criminal Convictions (New York: Cambridge University Press).

Convention Concerning the Prohibition and Immediate Action for the Elimination of the Worst Forms of Child Labor, 38 I.L.M. 1207 (June 17, 1999).

Convention relating to the Status of Refugees, 189 U.N.T.S. 150 (July 28, 1951, entered into force April 22, 1954).

Cook, P. and Heykoop, C. (2007), *Child Participation in the Sierra Leonean Truth and Reconciliation Commission, in* CHILDREN AND TRANSITIONAL JUSTICE: TRUTH-TELLING, ACCOUNTABILITY AND RECONCILIATION 159 (UNICEF Innocenti Research Centre and Human Rights Program at Harvard Law School, Sharanjeet Parmar, Mindy Jane Roseman, Saudamini Siegrist, and Theo Sowa eds) (Cambridge: Harvard University Press).

Coomaraswamy, R. (2009), *Child Soldiers: Root Causes and UN Initiatives, available at* <http://www.casablanca-dream.net/literature/Views_on_Crisis/10_02_09_SRSG_at_University_of_Michigan.pdf> (visited on September 17, 2011).

Corbin, J. N. (2008), *Returning home: resettlement of formerly abducted children in northern Uganda*, 32(2) DISASTERS 316.

Coulter, C. (2009), BUSH WIVES AND GIRL SOLDIERS: WOMEN'S LIVES THROUGH WAR AND PEACE IN SIERRA LEONE (Ithaca: Cornell University Press).

Crossette, B. (October 6, 2000), *Sierra Leone to Try Juveniles Separately in U.N. Tribunal Plan*, N.Y. TIMES, *available at* <http://www.nytimes.com/2000/10/06/world/sierra-leone-to-try-juveniles-separately-in-un-tribunal-plan.html> (visited on August 24, 2011).

CRY FREETOWN (Insight News TV 2000, dir./prod. Ron McCullagh, narrated by Sorious Samura).

Dallaire, R. (2010), THEY FIGHT LIKE SOLDIERS, THEY DIE LIKE CHILDREN (London: Hutchison).

Denov, M. (2010), CHILD SOLDIERS: SIERRA LEONE'S REVOLUTIONARY UNITED FRONT (Cambridge: Cambridge University Press).

THE DILEMMA OF THE WHITE ANT (Television Trust for the Environment 2008, dir. Caroline Pare).

Drumbl, M. A. (2007), ATROCITY, PUNISHMENT, AND INTERNATIONAL LAW (New York: Cambridge University Press).

——(forthcoming 2012), *Policy through Complementarity: The Atrocity Trial as Justice, in* THE INTERNATIONAL CRIMINAL COURT AND COMPLEMENTARITY, Volume I, 197 (Carsten Stahn and Mohamed M. El Zeidy eds) (Cambridge: Cambridge University Press).

Dugger, C. W. (April 30, 2011), *Separating Free Speech From Hate in South Africa*, N.Y. TIMES, *available at* <http://www.nytimes.com/2011/05/01/world/africa/01southafrica.html?pagewanted=all> (visited on August 24, 2011).

Du Plessis, M. (2004), *Children under International Criminal Law*, 13(2) AFRICAN SECURITY REVIEW 103.

Dupuy, P. (1991), *Soft Law and the International Law of the Environment*, 12 MICHIGAN JOURNAL OF INTERNATIONAL LAW 420.

Duthie, R. and Specht, I. (2009), *DDR, Transitional Justice, and the Reintegration of Former Child Combatants, in* DISARMING THE PAST: TRANSITIONAL JUSTICE AND EX-COMBATANTS 190 (International Center for Transitional Justice, Ana Cutter Patel, Pablo de Greiff, and Lars Waldorf eds) (New York: Social Science Research Council).

Easterday, J. (May 15, 2009), *Expert Reports on the Psychological Impact of Child Soldiering*, *available at* <http://www.lubangatrial.org> (visited on September 17, 2011).

Economic and Social Council Res. No. 2005/20: Guidelines on Justice in Matters Involving Child Victims and Witnesses of Crime (July 22, 2005), *available at* <http://www.unhcr.org/refworld/docid/468922c92.html> (visited on August 24, 2011).

Eggers, D. (2006), WHAT IS THE WHAT: THE AUTOBIOGRAPHY OF VALENTINO ACHAK DENG (San Francisco: McSweeney's).

Ellis, A. (2001), *Introduction, in* WAR CRIMES AND COLLECTIVE WRONGDOING 1 (Aleksandar Jokić ed.) (Malden: Blackwell Publishers).

Ellis, S. (2003), *Young Soldiers and the Significance of Initiation: Some Notes from Liberia, available at* <http://www.ascleiden.nl/pdf/conference24042003-ellis.pdf> (visited on September 17, 2011).

Engle, K. (2005), *Feminism and Its (Dis)contents: Criminalizing Wartime Rape in Bosnia and Herzegovina*, 99(4) AMERICAN JOURNAL OF INTERNATIONAL LAW 778.

Fahim, K. (March 11, 2011), *In Libya Revolt, Youth Will Serve, or at Least Try*, N.Y. TIMES, *available at* <http://www.nytimes.com/2011/03/12/world/africa/12youth.html?pagewanted=all> (visited on August 24, 2011).

Feld, B. C. (1998), *Juvenile and Criminal Justice Systems' Responses to Youth Violence*, 24 CRIME & JUSTICE 189.

Ferreira, N. (2008), *Putting the Age of Criminal and Tort Liability into Context: A Dialogue Between Law and Psychology*, 16 INTERNATIONAL JOURNAL OF CHILDREN'S RIGHTS 29.

Ferrie, J. (November 13, 2008), *Former child soldier gets cold welcome from Canada*, THE NATIONAL (UAE), *available at* <http://www.thenational.ae/news/worldwide/americas/former-child-soldier-gets-cold-welcome-from-canada> (visited on September 17, 2011).

Fichtelberg, A. (2008), *Liberal Values in International Criminal Law*, 6 JOURNAL OF INTERNATIONAL CRIMINAL JUSTICE 3.

Finn, P. (February 10, 2010), *The boy from the battlefield: Youngest Guantanamo detainee awaits military trial on war crimes charges*, WASHINGTON POST at A01.

Finnström, S. (2008), LIVING WITH BAD SURROUNDINGS: WAR, HISTORY, AND EVERYDAY MOMENTS IN NORTHERN UGANDA (Durham: Duke University Press).

Flint, J. and de Waal, A. (2005), DARFUR: A SHORT HISTORY OF A LONG WAR (London: Zed Books).

Fontana, B. (1997), *Child Soldiers and International Law*, 6(3) AFRICAN SECURITY REVIEW 51, *available at* <http://www.iss.co.za/pubs/asr/6No3/Fontana.html> (visited on September 17, 2011).

Francis, D. J. (2007), *'Paper protection' mechanisms: child soldiers and the international protection of children in Africa's conflict zones*, 45(2) JOURNAL OF MODERN AFRICAN STUDIES 207.

——(2008), *International Conventions and the Limitations for Protecting Child Soldiers in Post-conflict Societies in Africa, in* CHILDREN AND WAR: IMPACT, PROTECTION AND REHABILITATION, PHASE II: PROTECTION 8, *available at* <http://www.arts.ualberta.ca/childrenandwar/papers/Children_and_War_Phase_II_Report.pdf> (visited on September 17, 2011).

Freeland, S. (2008), *Mere Children or Weapons of War—Child Soldiers and International Law*, 29 UNIVERSITY OF LA VERNE LAW REVIEW 19.

——(February 15, 2010), *Innocence Lost as Recruitment of Child Soldiers Continues*, SYDNEY MORNING HERALD, *available at* <http://www.smh.com.au/opinion/society-and-culture/innocence-lost-as-recruitment-of-children-continues-20100214-nzb7.html> (visited on August 24, 2011).

Freeman, M. (2006), TRUTH COMMISSIONS AND PROCEDURAL FAIRNESS (Cambridge: Cambridge University Press).

Fuller, L. L. (1967), LEGAL FICTIONS (Stanford: Stanford University Press).

Geertz, C. (2001), AVAILABLE LIGHT: ANTHROPOLOGICAL REFLECTIONS ON PHILOSOPHICAL TOPICS (Princeton: Princeton University Press).

Geneva Convention (IV) relative to the Protection of Civilian Persons in Time of War, 75 U.N.T.S. 287 (August 12, 1949).

Gettleman, J. (June 13, 2010), *Children Carry Guns for a U.S. Ally, Somalia*, N.Y. TIMES, *available at* <http://www.nytimes.com/2010/06/14/world/africa/14somalia.html> (visited on August 24, 2011).

Glaberson, W. (June 3, 2007), *A Legal Debate in Guantánamo on Boy Fighters*, N.Y. TIMES, *available at* <http://www.nytimes.com/2007/06/03/us/03gitmo.html> (visited on August 24, 2011).

Glazer, I. M. (2006), *Book Review*, 79(2) ANTHROPOLOGICAL QUARTERLY 373.

Goetz, M. (2008), *The International Criminal Court and its Relevance to Affected Communities, in* COURTING CONFLICT? JUSTICE, PEACE, AND THE ICC IN AFRICA 65 (Nicolas Waddell and Phil Clark eds) (London: Royal African Society).

Goodman, R. and Jinks, D. (2005), *International Law and State Socialization: Conceptual, Empirical, and Normative Challenges*, 54 DUKE LAW JOURNAL 983.

Goodwin, J. (February 14, 1999), *Sierra Leone is No Place to be Young*, N.Y. TIMES MAGAZINE 48, *available at* <http://www.nytimes.com/1999/02/14/magazine/sierra-leone-is-no-place-to-be-young.html> (visited on August 24, 2011).

Goodwin-Gill, G. and Cohn, I. (1994), CHILD SOLDIERS: THE ROLE OF CHILDREN IN ARMED CONFLICTS (New York: Oxford University Press).

Graham v. Florida, US Supreme Court, 560 U.S. ___ (2010) (slip op.).

Greene, A. L. (1986), *Future-time Perspective in Adolescence: The Present of Things Future Revisited*, 15(2) JOURNAL OF YOUTH AND ADOLESCENCE 99.

Grossman, N. (2007), *Rehabilitation or Revenge: Prosecuting Child Soldiers for Human Rights Violations*, 38 GEORGETOWN JOURNAL OF INTERNATIONAL LAW 323.

Grover, L. (2005), *Trial of the Child Soldier: Protecting the Rights of the Accused, in* 65 ZEITSCHRIFT FÜR AUSLÄNDISCHES ÖFFENTLICHES RECHT UND VÖLKERRECHT 217.

Grover, S. (2008), *'Child Soldiers' as 'Non-Combatants': The Inapplicability of the Refugee Convention Exclusion Clause*, 12(1) INTERNATIONAL JOURNAL OF HUMAN RIGHTS 53.

Guidelines on International Protection: Child Asylum Claims under Articles 1(A)2 and 1(F) of the 1951 Convention and/or 1967 Protocol relating to the Status of Refugees, HCR/GIP/09/08 (December 22, 2009), *available at* <http://www.unhcr.org/refworld/docid/4b2f4f6d2.html> (visited on August 24, 2011).

Hague Convention on the Civil Aspects of International Child Abduction (October 25, 1980), T.I.A.S. No. 11670.

Hannan, L. (June 27, 2007), *Uganda's boy soldier turned rebel chief is a victim, not a criminal, says his family*, THE INDEPENDENT, *available at* <http://www.independent.co.uk/news/world/africa/ugandas-boy-soldier-turned-rebel-chief-is-a-victim-not-a-criminal-says-his-family-454833.html> (visited on August 24, 2011).

Happold, M. (2006), *The Age of Criminal Responsibility for International Crimes under International Law, in* INTERNATIONAL CRIMINAL ACCOUNTABILITY AND THE RIGHTS OF CHILDREN 69 (Karin Arts and Vesselin Popovski eds) (The Hague: Hague Academic Press).

Hart, J. (2006a), *Saving children: What role for anthropology?*, 22(1) ANTHROPOLOGY TODAY 5 (2006).

——(2006b), *The Politics of "Child Soldiers"*, XIII(1) BROWN JOURNAL OF WORLD AFFAIRS 217.

Hayes, D. F., Ní Aoláin, F. D., and Cahn, N. (forthcoming 2011), *Masculinities and Child Soldiers in Post-Conflict Societies, in* MASCULINITIES AND LAW: A MULTIDIMENSIONAL APPROACH (Frank Cooper and Ann C. McGinley, eds) (New York: New York University

Press), *available at* <http://papers.ssrn.com/sol3/papers.cfm?abstract_id=1684156> (visited on September 17, 2011).

Henig, R. M. (August 22, 2010), *What is it About 20-Somethings?*, N.Y. TIMES MAGAZINE at MM28, *available at* <http://www.nytimes.com/2010/08/22/magazine/22Adulthood-t.html> (visited on August 24, 2011).

Hick, S. (2001), *The Political Economy of War-Affected Children*, 575 ANNALS OF THE AMERICAN ACADEMY OF POLITICAL AND SOCIAL SCIENCE 106.

Hoffman, D. (2006), *Disagreement: Dissent Politics and the War in Sierra Leone*, 52(3) AFRICA TODAY 3.

Honwana, A. (2005), *Innocent & Guilty: Child-Soldiers as Interstitial & Tactical Agents, in* MAKERS & BREAKERS: CHILDREN & YOUTH IN POSTCOLONIAL AFRICA 31 (Alcinda Honwana and Filip de Boeck eds) (Trenton, NJ: Africa World Press).

——(2006), CHILD SOLDIERS IN AFRICA (Philadelphia: University of Pennsylvania Press).

The Howard League for Penal Reform (June 2010), *Children and long sentences: a briefing*, *available at* <http://www.howardleague.org/fileadmin/howard_league/user/pdf/Briefings/Children_and_long_sentences_briefing.pdf> (visited on September 17, 2011).

Hughes, M. (March 16, 2010), *The Big Question: Should 12, rather than 10, be the age of criminal responsibility?*, THE INDEPENDENT, *available at* <http://www.independent.co.uk/extras/big-question/the-big-question-should-12-rather-than-10-be-the-age-of-criminal-responsibility-1921857.html> (visited on August 24, 2011).

Human Rights Watch (2003), "YOU'LL LEARN NOT TO CRY": CHILD COMBATANTS IN COLOMBIA.

——(2007), SOLD TO BE SOLDIERS: THE RECRUITMENT AND USE OF CHILD SOLDIERS IN BURMA.

——(2008), COERCION AND INTIMIDATION OF CHILD SOLDIERS TO PARTICIPATE IN VIOLENCE.

Humphreys, M. and Weinstein, J. M. (2007), *Demobilization and Reintegration*, 51(4) JOURNAL OF CONFLICT RESOLUTION 531.

ICC Elements of the Crimes, U.N. Doc. PCNICC/2000/1/Add.2 (2000).

ICC Rules of Procedure and Evidence, U.N. Doc. PCNICC/2000/1/Add.1 (2000).

Instructions to the Court's expert on child soldiers and trauma, *Prosecutor v. Thomas Lubanga Dyilo*, ICC Case No. 01/04-01/06 (February 6, 2009).

Integrated Disarmament, Demobilization and Reintegration Standards (2006, and ongoing), *available at* <http://www.unddr.org/iddrs> (visited on September 17, 2011).

Internal Rules, Extraordinary Chambers in the Courts of Cambodia (June 12, 2007), *available at* <http://www.eccc.gov.kh/en/document/legal/internal-rules> (visited on September 3, 2011).

International Center for Transitional Justice (2007), REPORTING TRANSITIONAL JUSTICE: A HANDBOOK FOR JOURNALISTS, *available at* <http://www.communicatingjustice.org/en/handbook> (visited on September 17, 2011).

International Committee of the Red Cross (ICRC) Commentaries to Additional Protocol II, *available at* <http://www.icrc.org/ihl.nsf/FULL/475?OpenDocument> (visited on August 24, 2011).

International Covenant on Civil and Political Rights, U.N. Doc. A/6316 (1966), 999 U.N.T.S. 171 (entered into force March 23, 1976).

International Institute for Educational Planning, GUIDEBOOK FOR PLANNING EDUCATION IN EMERGENCIES AND RECONSTRUCTION, Chapter 2.5, *available at* <http://unesdoc.unesco.org/images/0019/001902/190223e.pdf> (visited on September 17, 2011).

International Labour Office (2003), WOUNDED CHILDHOOD: THE USE OF CHILDREN IN ARMED CONFLICT IN CENTRAL AFRICA.

Isikoff, M. (August 10, 2010), *Landmark Gitmo trial puts White House in tight spot*, NBC News (on file with the author).

Iweala, U. (2005), Beasts of No Nation: A Novel (New York: HarperCollins Publishers).

Jaffe, G. (March 2, 2011), *Lt. Gen. John Kelly, who lost son to war, says U.S. largely unaware of sacrifice*, Washington Post, *available at* <http://www.washingtonpost.com/wp-dyn/content/article/2011/03/01/AR2011030106938.html?nav=emailpage> (visited on August 24, 2011).

J.D.B. v. North Carolina, US Supreme Court, No. 09-11121, slip op. (June 16, 2011).

Johnson, S. (2009), *Hard Target: The Hunt for Africa's Last Warlord*, Newsweek, *available at* <http://www.thedailybeast.com/newsweek/2009/05/15/hard-target.html> (visited on August 24, 2011).

Juba Agreement concluded in February 2008 specifically on the topic of disarmament, demobilisation, and reintegration for LRA fighters, *available at* <http://www.beyondjuba.org/peace_agreements.php> (visited on September 17, 2011).

Judicial System Monitoring Programme (2005), *The Case of X: A Child Prosecuted for Crimes against Humanity* (Dili, Timor-Leste: JSMP), *available at* <http://www.jsmp.minihub.org/Reports/jsmpreports/The%20Case%20of%20X/case_of_x_final_e.pdf> (visited on August 24, 2011).

Kaldor, M. (1999), New & Old Wars: Organized Violence in a Global Era (Cambridge: Polity Press).

Kamara, M. and McClelland, S. (2008), The Bite of the Mango (Toronto/Vancouver: Annick Press).

Kaplan, R. D. (2000), The Coming Anarchy (New York: Random House).

Keitetsi, C. (2002), Child Soldier: Fighting for My Life (Johannesburg/Cape Town: Jacana Media).

Kelsall, T. (2009), Culture under Cross-Examination: International Justice and the Special Court for Sierra Leone (New York: Cambridge University Press).

Kennedy, D. (2004), The Dark Sides of Virtue: Reassessing International Humanitarianism (Princeton: Princeton University Press).

Kenzo, E. (February 8, 2011), *Ex-Child Soldiers in DRC Drawn Back Into Military Ranks*, Institute for War & Peace Reporting, *available at* <http://reliefweb.int/node/388146> (visited on August 24, 2011).

Kiesling, E. C. (2006), *Let the Children Kill!* H-War Book Review, *available at* <http://www.h-net.org/reviews/showrev.php?id=11321> (visited on August 24, 2011).

Kimmel, C. E. and Roby, J. L. (2007), *Institutionalized Child Abuse: The Use of Child Soldiers*, 50(6) International Social Work 740.

Kohrt, B. A., Jordans, M., Tol, W. A., Speckman, R. A., Maharjan, S. M., Worthman, C. M., and Komproe, I. H. (2008), *Comparison of Mental Health Between Former Child Soldiers and Children Never Conscripted by Armed Groups in Nepal*, 300(6) Journal of the American Medical Association 691.

Kohrt, B. A., Tol, W. A., Pettigrew, J., and Karki, R. (2010), *Children and Revolution: Mental Health and Psychosocial Well-Being of Child Soldiers in Nepal*, in The War Machine and Global Health 89, 91 (Merrill Singer and G. Derrick Hodge eds) (Plymouth: AltaMira Press).

Kourouma, A. (2000), Allah n'est pas obligé (Paris: Editions du Seuil).

Ku, J. and Nzelibe, J. (2006), *Do International Criminal Tribunals Deter or Exacerbate Humanitarian Atrocities?*, 84 Washington University Law Quarterly 777.

Kwibuka, E. (February 29, 2008), *Born of War*, THE GLOBE AND MAIL, *available at* <http://www.theglobeandmail.com/archives/born-of-war/article669911/email/> (visited on August 24, 2011).

Law on the Establishment of the Extraordinary Chambers, with inclusion of amendments as promulgated on 27 October 2004, NS/RKM/1004/006.

Lazareva, I. (March 10, 2011), *Many DRC Children Volunteer to Fight*, IWPR ICC-Africa Update (No. 291), *available at* <http://reliefweb.int/node/391408> (visited on August 24, 2011).

Lee, A. (2009), *Understanding and Addressing the Phenomenon of 'Child Soldiers': The Gap Between the Global Humanitarian Discourse and the Local Understandings and Experiences of Young People's Military Recruitment* (Refugee Studies Center, Working Paper Series No. 52, Oxford University) (Master's Thesis).

Leebaw, B. (2011), JUDGING STATE-SPONSORED VIOLENCE, IMAGINING POLITICAL CHANGE (Cambridge: Cambridge University Press).

Letter to Prime Minister Sheikh Hasina Re: International Crimes (Tribunals) Act (July 8, 2009), *available at* <http://www.hrw.org/en/news/2009/07/08/letter-prime-minister-sheikh-hasina-re-international-crimes-tribunals-act> (visited on September 17, 2011).

Lonegan, B. (2011), *Sinners or Saints: Child Soldiers and the Persecutor Bar to Asylum after Negusie v. Holder*, 31 BOSTON COLLEGE THIRD WORLD LAW JOURNAL 71.

Machel, G. (2010), *Foreword, in* CHILDREN AND TRANSITIONAL JUSTICE: TRUTH-TELLING, ACCOUNTABILITY AND RECONCILIATION (UNICEF Innocenti Research Centre and Human Rights Program at Harvard Law School, Sharanjeet Parmar, Mindy Jane Roseman, Saudamini Siegrist, and Theo Sowa eds) (Cambridge: Harvard University Press).

Macmillan, L. (2009), *The Child Soldier in North-South Relations*, 3 INTERNATIONAL POLITICAL SOCIOLOGY 36.

Mæland, B. (2010), *Constrained but not Choiceless: On Moral Agency among Child Soldiers, in* CULTURE, RELIGION, AND THE REINTEGRATION OF FEMALE CHILD SOLDIERS IN NORTHERN UGANDA 57 (Bård Mæland ed.) (New York: Peter Lang).

Manirakiza, P. (2009), *Les enfants face au système international de justice: à la recherche d'un modèle de justice pénale internationale pour les délinquants mineurs*, 34(2) QUEEN'S LAW JOURNAL 719.

Maroney, T. (2009), *The False Promise of Adolescent Brain Science in Juvenile Justice*, 85 NOTRE DAME LAW REVIEW 89.

Marten, J. (2009), *Book Review*, 2(1) JOURNAL OF THE HISTORY OF CHILDHOOD AND YOUTH 142.

Masland, T. (May 13, 2002), *Voices of the Children*, NEWSWEEK 24, 28 *available at* <http://www.thedailybeast.com/newsweek/2002/05/12/voices-of-the-children-quot-we-beat-and-killed.html> (visited on September 3, 2011).

Mattioli, G. and van Woudenberg, A. (2008), *Global Catalyst for National Prosecutions? The ICC in the Democratic Republic of Congo, in* COURTING CONFLICT? JUSTICE, PEACE AND THE ICC IN AFRICA 55 (Nicholas Waddell and Phil Clark eds) (London: Royal African Society).

Mawson, A. (2004), *Children, Impunity and Justice: Some Dilemmas from Northern Uganda*, in CHILDREN AND YOUTH ON THE FRONT LINE: ETHNOGRAPHY, ARMED CONFLICT AND DISPLACEMENT 130 (Jo Boyden and Joanna de Berry eds) (New York: Berghahn Books).

McDonnell, F. J. H. and Akallo, G. (2007), GIRL SOLDIER: A STORY OF HOPE FOR NORTHERN UGANDA'S CHILDREN (Grand Rapids: Chosen Books).

McIntyre, A., Aning, E. K., and Addo, P. N. N. (2002), *Politics, War and Youth Culture in Sierra Leone: An Alternative Interpretation*, 11(3) AFRICAN SECURITY REVIEW 7, *available at*

<http://www.iss.co.za/Pubs/ASR/11No3/McIntyre.html> (visited on September 17, 2011).

McMahan, J. (2007), *Child Soldiers: The Ethical Perspective* (working paper).

——(2009), KILLING IN WAR (Oxford: Clarendon Press).

Mcmillan, N. (2011), *Crimes Against Humanity: A Critical Reflection on the Internationalisation of Personalised Suffering* (unpublished manuscript).

Meierhenrich, J. (2012), LAWFARE (draft monograph).

Mergelsberg, B. (2010), *Between two worlds: former LRA soldiers in northern Uganda, in* THE LORD'S RESISTANCE ARMY: MYTH AND REALITY 156 (Tim Allen and Koen Vlassenroot eds) (London: Zed Books).

Millard, A. S. (2001), *Children in Armed Conflicts: Transcending Legal Responses,* 32(2) SECURITY DIALOGUE 187.

Miller, D. (1997), CAPITALISM: AN ETHNOGRAPHIC APPROACH (Oxford: Berg).

Moreno-Ocampo, L., *Opening Statement, The Case of the Prosecutor v. Thomas Lubanga Dyilo,* ICC-01/04-01/06 (The Hague, January 26, 2009), *available at* <http://www.icc-cpi.int/NR/rdonlyres/82809488-9418-4AA9-BCF4-5FE3D609CBA7/279630/ICCOTPSTLMO20090126ENG2.pdf> (visited on September 17, 2011).

Murphy, W. P. (2003), *Military Patrimonialism and Child Soldier Clientalism in the Liberian and Sierra Leonean Civil Wars,* 46(2) AFRICAN STUDIES REVIEW 61.

Mutua, M. (2001), *Savages, Victims, and Saviors: The Metaphor of Human Rights,* 42 HARVARD INTERNATIONAL LAW JOURNAL 201.

No Peace Without Justice and UNICEF Innocenti Research Centre (2002), INTERNATIONAL CRIMINAL JUSTICE AND CHILDREN.

Nutt, S. (November 5, 2010), *Arms and the Child* (review of R. Dallaire, THEY FIGHT LIKE SOLDIERS, THEY DIE LIKE CHILDREN), THE GLOBE AND MAIL, *available at* <http://www.theglobeandmail.com/news/arts/books/they-fight-like-soldiers-they-die-like-children-by-romo-dallaire/article1787085/> (visited on August 24, 2011).

Ocowun, C. (June 4, 2009), *LRA's Kwoyelo charged with kidnap,* NEW VISION (on file with author).

Office of the Special Representative of the Secretary-General for Children and Armed Conflict, *Disarmament, demobilization and reintegration programmes for children, available at* <http://www.un.org/children/conflict/english/ddrforchildren.html> (visited on September 17, 2011).

——(2011), CHILDREN AND JUSTICE DURING AND IN THE AFTERMATH OF ARMED CONFLICT (Working Paper No. 3) (New York: United Nations).

Olusanya, O. (2006), *Granting Immunity to Child Combatants Supranationally, in* SENTENCING AND SANCTIONING IN SUPRANATIONAL CRIMINAL LAW 87 (Roelof Haveman and Olaoluwa Olusanya eds) (Antwerp: Intersentia).

Optional Protocol to the CRC on the involvement of children in armed conflict, G.A. Res. 54/263, U.N. Doc. A/RES/54/263 (May 25, 2000) (entered into force February 12, 2002).

Otim, M. and Wierda, M. (2010), International Center for Transitional Justice, *Briefing: Uganda: Impact of the Rome Statute and the International Criminal Court, available at* <http://ictj.org/sites/default/files/ICTJ-Uganda-Impact-ICC-2010-English.pdf> (visited on August 24, 2011).

Ottenhof, R. (2001), *Criminal responsibility of minors in national and international legal order,* 72 REVUE INTERNATIONALE DE DROIT PÉNAL 669.

Otto, D. (2007), *The Sexual Tensions of UN Peace Support Operations: A Plea for 'Sexual Positivity,'* XVIII FINNISH YEARBOOK OF INTERNATIONAL LAW 33.

Otunnu, O. (2000), *Keynote Address: The Convention and Children in Situations of Armed Conflict*, in CHILDREN IN EXTREME SITUATIONS, Working Paper Series No. 00-05, LSE Development Studies Institute 48 (Lisa Carlson, Megan Mackeson-Sandbach, and Tim Allen eds) (London: Development Studies Institute, London School of Economics and Political Science), *available at* <http://www2.lse.ac.uk/internationalDevelopment//pdf/WP05.pdf> (visited on September 17, 2011).

The Paris Commitments to Protect Children from Unlawful Recruitment or Use by Armed Forces or Armed Groups (February 2007), *available at* <http://www.child-soldiers.org/childsoldiers/Paris_Commitments_March_2007.pdf> (visited on September 17, 2011).

The Paris Principles: Principles and Guidelines on Children Associated with Armed Forces or Armed Groups (February 2007), *available at* <http://www.child-soldiers.org/childsoldiers/Paris_Principles_March_2007.pdf> (visited on September 17, 2011).

Parliament recalled to tackle riots—David Cameron (August 9, 2011), BBC News (on file with the author).

Parmar, S. (2010), *Realizing Economic Justice for Children: The Role of Transitional Justice in Post-Conflict Societies*, in CHILDREN AND TRANSITIONAL JUSTICE: TRUTH-TELLING, ACCOUNTABILITY AND RECONCILIATION 365 (UNICEF Innocenti Research Centre and Human Rights Program at Harvard Law School, Sharanjeet Parmar, Mindy Jane Roseman, Saudamini Siegrist, and Theo Sowa eds) (Cambridge: Harvard University Press).

Parmentier, S., Vanspauwen, K., and Weitekamp, E. (2008), *Dealing with the Legacy of Mass Violence: Changing Lenses to Restorative Justice*, in SUPRANATIONAL CRIMINOLOGY: TOWARDS A CRIMINOLOGY OF INTERNATIONAL CRIMES 335 (Alette Smeulers and Roelof Haveman eds) (Antwerp: Intersentia).

Peters, K. and Richards, P. (1998a), *Fighting with Open Eyes: Youth Combatants Talking About War in Sierra Leone*, in RETHINKING THE TRAUMA OF WAR 76 (Patrick J. Bracken and Celia Petty eds) (London: Free Association Books).

——(1998b), *'Why We Fight': Voices of Youth Combatants in Sierra Leone*, 68(2) AFRICA 183.

Pham, P., Vinck, P., and Stover, E. (2008), *The Lord's Resistance Army and Forced Conscription in Northern Uganda*, 30(2) HUMAN RIGHTS QUARTERLY 404.

Pham, P., Vinck, P., Stover, E., Moss, A., Wierda, M., and Bailey, R. (2007), WHEN THE WAR ENDS: A POPULATION-BASED SURVEY ON ATTITUDES ABOUT PEACE, JUSTICE, AND SOCIAL RECONSTRUCTION IN NORTHERN UGANDA, *available at* <http://reliefweb.int/sites/reliefweb.int/files/resources/79A8E1ABA07F5799852573B500752BEC-Full_Report.pdf> (visited on September 3, 2011).

Pham, P., Vinck, P., Wierda, M., Stover, E., and di Giovanni, A. (2005), FORGOTTEN VOICES: A POPULATION-BASED SURVEY OF ATTITUDES ABOUT PEACE AND JUSTICE IN NORTHERN UGANDA, *available at* <http://reliefweb.int/sites/reliefweb.int/files/resources/A1AABC919BF22E384925704A0022B98D-hrc-uga-25jul.pdf> (visited on September 3, 2011).

Piaget, J. (1947), LA PSYCHOLOGIE DE L'INTELLIGENCE (Paris: Armand Colin).

Pierson, P. (2000), *Not Just What, but* When: *Timing and Sequence in Political Processes*, 14(1) STUDIES IN AMERICAN POLITICAL DEVELOPMENT 72.

Pigou, P. (2010), *Children and the South African Truth and Reconciliation Commission*, in CHILDREN AND TRANSITIONAL JUSTICE: TRUTH-TELLING, ACCOUNTABILITY AND RECONCILIATION 215 (UNICEF Innocenti Research Centre and Human Rights Program at Harvard Law School, Sharanjeet Parmar, Mindy Jane Roseman, Saudamini Siegrist, and Theo Sowa eds) (Cambridge: Harvard University Press).

Polgreen, L. (May 22, 2008), *Fewer Conflicts Involve Child Soldiers, Report Finds*, N.Y. TIMES A18, *available at* <http://www.nytimes.com/2008/05/22/world/africa/22child .html> (visited on August 24, 2011).

Popovski, V. (2006), *Children in Armed Conflict: Law and Practice of the United Nations, in* INTERNATIONAL CRIMINAL ACCOUNTABILITY AND THE RIGHTS OF CHILDREN 37 (Karin Arts and Vesselin Popovski eds) (The Hague: Hague Academic Press).

Press Release, Special Court for Sierra Leone, Public Affairs Office, *Special Court Prosecutor Says He Will Not Prosecute Children* (November 2, 2002), *available at* <http://www.sc-sl .org/LinkClick.aspx?fileticket=XRwCUe%2BaVhw%3D&tabid=196> (visited on August 24, 2011).

Prosecutor v. Brima, Kamara, and Kanu, Case No. SCSL-04-16-A, Appeals Judgment (SCSL Appeals Chamber, February 22, 2008).

Prosecutor v. Brima, Kamara, and Kanu, Case No. SCSL-04-16-T, Trial Judgment (SCSL Trial Chamber, June 20, 2007).

Prosecutor v. Erdemović, Case No. IT-96-22-A, Appeals Judgment (ICTY Appeals Chamber, October 7, 1997).

Prosecutor v. Fofana and Kondewa, Case No. SCSL-04-14-A, Appeals Judgment (SCSL Appeals Chamber, May 28, 2008).

Prosecutor v. Fofana and Kondewa, Case No. SCSL-04-14-T, Trial Judgment (SCSL Trial Chamber, August 2, 2007).

Prosecutor v. Katanga and Chui, Case No. ICC-01/04-01/07, Decision on the confirmation of charges (ICC Pre-trial Chamber I, September 30, 2008).

Prosecutor v. Lubanga, Case No. ICC-01/04-01/06, English language Transcript (April 7, 2009).

Prosecutor v. Lubanga, Case No. ICC-01/04-01/06, Decision on "indirect victims" (ICC Trial Chamber I, April 8, 2009).

Prosecutor v. Lubanga, Case No. ICC-01/04-01/06, Decision on the confirmation of charges (ICC Pre-trial Chamber I, January 29, 2007).

Prosecutor v. Lubanga, Case No. ICC-01/04-01/06, Decision on the applications by victims to participate in the proceedings (ICC Trial Chamber I, December 15, 2008).

Prosecutor v. Norman, Case No. SCSL-2004-14-AR72(E), Decision on Preliminary Motion Based on Lack of Jurisdiction (Child Recruitment) (SCSL Appeals Chamber, May 31, 2004).

Prosecutor v. Orić, Case No. IT-03-68-A, Appeals Judgment (ICTY Appeals Chamber, July 3, 2008).

Prosecutor v. Orić, Case No. IT-03-68-T, Trial Judgment (ICTY Trial Chamber, June 30, 2006).

Prosecutor v. Sesay, Kallon, and Gbao, Case No. SCSL-04-15-A, Appeals Judgment (SCSL Appeals Chamber, October 26, 2009).

Prosecutor v. Sesay, Kallon, and Gbao, Case No. SCSL-04-15-T, Trial Judgment (SCSL Trial Chamber, March 2, 2009).

Protocol Additional to the Geneva Conventions of 12 August 1949, and relating to the Protection of Victims of International Armed Conflicts (Protocol I), 1125 U.N.T.S. 3 (June 8, 1977).

Protocol Additional to the Geneva Conventions of 12 August 1949, and relating to the Protection of Victims of Non-International Armed Conflicts (Protocol II), 1125 U.N.T.S. 609 (June 8, 1977).

Rayman, G. (March 18, 2008), *Boy Soldier of Fortune: A celebrated memoir threatens to blow into a million little pieces*, VILLAGE VOICE, *available at* <http://www.villagevoice.com/ 2008-03-18/news/boy-soldier/full> (visited on September 17, 2011).

REDRESS Trust (2006), VICTIMS, PERPETRATORS OR HEROES? CHILD SOLDIERS BEFORE THE INTERNATIONAL CRIMINAL COURT, *available at* <http://www.redress.org/downloads/ publications/childsoldiers.pdf> (visited on September 3, 2011).

Reich, S. F. and Achvarina, V. (2005), *Why Do Children 'Fight'? Explaining Child Soldier Ratios in African Intrastate Conflicts* (Pittsburgh: University of Pittsburgh, Ford Institute for Human Security: Policy Brief 04-3).

Reis, C. (1997), *Trying the Future, Avenging the Past: The Implications of Prosecuting Children for Participation in Internal Armed Conflict*, 28 COLUMBIA HUMAN RIGHTS LAW REVIEW 629.

Report of the Expert of the Secretary-General, *Impact of Armed Conflict on Children*, U.N. Doc. A/51/306 (August 26, 1996), *available at* <http://www.unicef.org/graca/a51-306_en.pdf> (visited on September 17, 2011).

Report of the Special Representative of the Secretary-General for Children and Armed Conflict (August 13, 2007), delivered to the United Nations General Assembly, U.N. Doc. A/62/ 228.

Republic of Liberia, Truth and Reconciliation Commission (2009a), REPORT, VOLUME THREE: APPENDICES, TITLE II: CHILDREN, THE CONFLICT AND THE TRC CHILDREN AGENDA, *available at* <http://trcofliberia.org/resources/reports/final/volume-three-2_layout-1.pdf> (visited on September 17, 2011).

——(2009b), VOLUME II: CONSOLIDATED FINAL REPORT, *available at* <http://trcofliberia .org/reports/final-report> (visited on September 17, 2011).

Retraining Tiger Cubs, (July 16, 2009) THE ECONOMIST, *available at* <http://www .economist.com/node/14052240> (visited on September 17, 2011).

Richards, P. (1996), FIGHTING FOR THE RAINFOREST: WAR, YOUTH & RESOURCES IN SIERRA LEONE (Oxford: James Currey).

Richman, N. (1993), *Annotation: Children in Situations of Political Violence*, 34(8) JOURNAL OF CHILD PSYCHOLOGY AND PSYCHIATRY 1286.

Rikhof, J. (2009), *Child soldiers: Should they be punished?*, SWORD & SCALE: CANADIAN BAR ASSOCIATION NATIONAL MILITARY LAW SECTION NEWSLETTER 4, *available at* <http://www .cba.org/CBA/newsletters-sections/pdf/05-09-military_2.pdf> (visited on September 17, 2011).

Rome Statute of the International Criminal Court, July 17, 1998, 2187 U.N.T.S. 90 (entered into force July 1, 2002).

Roper v. Simmons, US Supreme Court, 543 U.S. 551 (2005).

Rosen, D. M. (2005), ARMIES OF THE YOUNG: CHILD SOLDIERS IN WAR AND TERRORISM (New Brunswick: Rutgers University Press).

——(2007), *Child Soldiers, International Humanitarian Law, and the Globalization of Childhood*, 109(2) AMERICAN ANTHROPOLOGIST 296.

——(2009), *Who Is a Child? The Legal Conundrum of Child Soldiers*, 25 CONNECTICUT JOURNAL OF INTERNATIONAL LAW 81.

Rosenbloom, S. R. (2007), *Transgressive Questions about Child Soldiers*, 30(1) QUALITATIVE SOCIOLOGY 109.

Sarfaty, G. A. (2009), *Why Culture Matters in International Institutions: The Marginality of Human Rights at the World Bank*, 103 AMERICAN JOURNAL OF INTERNATIONAL LAW 647.

Saunders, D. (July 10, 2011), *Ill-equipped teenagers members of the Libyan anti-Gadhafi rebels*, THE GLOBE AND MAIL UPDATE, *available at* <http://www.theglobeandmail.com/news/

world/ill-equipped-teenagers-members-of-the-libyan-anti-gadhafi-rebels/article2092964/>
(visited on August 24, 2011).

Savage, C. (August 27, 2010), *U.S. Wary of Example Set by Tribunal Case*, N.Y. Times, *available at* <http://www.nytimes.com/2010/08/28/us/28gitmo.html?_r=1&ref=todayspaper> (visited on August 24, 2011).

——(October 25, 2010), *Deal Averts Trial in Disputed Guantanamo Case*, N.Y. Times, *available at* <http://www.nytimes.com/2010/10/26/us/26gitmo.html?scp=1&sq=Deal%20Averts%20Trial%20in%20Disputed%20Guantanamo%20Case&st=cse> (visited on August 24, 2011).

Save the Children (2003), When Children Affected by War Go Home: Lessons learned from Liberia, *available at* <http://www.savethechildren.org.uk/en/docs/when_children_affected_by_war_go_home.pdf> (visited on September 17, 2011).

S. C. Res. 1757 (2007), U.N. Doc. S/RES/1757 (May 30, 2007).

Schabas, W. A. (2007), An Introduction to the International Criminal Court (3rd edn) (Cambridge: Cambridge University Press).

Schafer, J. (2004), *The Use of Patriarchal Imagery in the Civil War in Mozambique and its Implications for the Reintegration of Child Soldiers, in* Children and Youth on the Front Line: Ethnography, Armed Conflict and Displacement 87 (Jo Boyden and Joanna de Berry eds) (New York: Berghahn Books).

Schauer, E. (2009), *The Psychological Impact of Child Soldiering, Prosecutor v. Lubanga,* Case No. ICC-01/04-01/06, Public Document (ICC Trial Chamber I).

Schmidt, A. (2007), *Volunteer Child Soldiers as Reality: A Development Issue for Africa,* 2(1) New School Economic Review 49.

Secret, M. (March 5, 2011), *States Prosecute Fewer Teenagers in Adult Courts,* N.Y. Times, *available at* <http://www.nytimes.com/2011/03/06/nyregion/06juvenile.html?pagewanted=all> (visited on August 24, 2011).

The Secretary General, *Children and Armed Conflict,* delivered to the Security Council and the General Assembly, U.N. Doc. A/59/695- S/2005/72 (February 9, 2005).

Shadid, A. (March 12, 2011), *Veering From Peaceful Models, Libya's Youth Revolt Turns Toward Chaos,* N.Y. Times, *available at* <http://www.nytimes.com/2011/03/13/world/africa/13opposition.html?pagewanted=all> (visited on August 24, 2011).

Shaffer, G. C. and Pollack, M. A. (2010), *Hard vs. Soft Law: Alternatives, Complements, and Antagonists in International Governance,* 94 Minnesota Law Review 706.

Shepler, S. (2004), *The Social and Cultural Context of Child Soldiering in Sierra Leone* (unpublished manuscript).

——(2005), *The Rites of the Child: Global Discourses of Youth and Reintegrating Child Soldiers in Sierra Leone,* 4(2) Journal of Human Rights 197.

——(2007), *Book Review: Armies of the Young: Child Soldiers in War and Terrorism,* 17(3) Children, Youth and Environments, *available at* <http://cye.colorado.edu/cye_journal/review.pl?n=236> (visited on August 24, 2011).

Shulman, L. R. (2006), *The Role of Early Childhood Development Programs in Conflict and Post-Conflict Settings,* in Children and War: Impact, Protection and Rehabilitation, Phase II: Protection 24, *available at* <http://www.arts.ualberta.ca/childrenandwar/papers/Children_and_War_Phase_II_Report.pdf> (visited on September 17, 2011).

Siddique, H. (March 3, 2010), *James Bulger killing: the case history of Jon Venables and Robert Thompson,* The Guardian, *available at* <http://www.guardian.co.uk/uk/2010/mar/03/james-bulger-case-venables-thompson> (visited on August 24, 2011).

Sieff, K. (September 15, 2011), *Young Afghan fighters eager to rejoin Taliban,* Washington Post (on file with the author).

Siegrist, S. (2006), *Child Participation in International Criminal Accountability Mechanisms: The Case of the Sierra Leone Truth and Reconciliation Commission, in* INTERNATIONAL CRIMINAL ACCOUNTABILITY AND THE RIGHTS OF CHILDREN 53 (Karin Arts and Vesselin Popovski eds) (The Hague: Hague Academic Press).

——(2010), *Child Rights and Transitional Justice, in* CHILDREN AND TRANSITIONAL JUSTICE: TRUTH-TELLING, ACCOUNTABILITY AND RECONCILIATION 1 (UNICEF Innocenti Research Centre and Human Rights Program at Harvard Law School, Sharanjeet Parmar, Mindy Jane Roseman, Saudamini Siegrist, and Theo Sowa eds) (Cambridge: Harvard University Press).

Sierra Leone Child Rights Act 2007 (September 3, 2007), Supplement to the Sierra Leone Gazette Extraordinary Vol. CXXXVIII, No. 43.

Simmons, B. A. (2009), MOBILIZING FOR HUMAN RIGHTS: INTERNATIONAL LAW IN DOMESTIC POLITICS (New York: Cambridge University Press).

Singer, P. W. (2004), *Talk Is Cheap: Getting Serious About Preventing Child Soldiers*, 37 CORNELL INTERNATIONAL LAW JOURNAL 561.

——(2006), CHILDREN AT WAR (Berkeley: University of California Press).

Slobogin, C. and Fondacaro, M. R. (2009), *Juvenile Justice: The Fourth Option*, 95 IOWA LAW REVIEW 1.

Slote, M. (2001), *War Crimes and Virtue Ethics, in* WAR CRIMES AND COLLECTIVE WRONGDOING 77 (Aleksandar Jokić ed.) (Malden: Blackwell Publishers).

Smeulers, A. (2008), *Perpetrators of International Crimes: Towards a Typology, in* SUPRANATIONAL CRIMINOLOGY: TOWARDS A CRIMINOLOGY OF INTERNATIONAL CRIMES 233 (Alette Smeulers and Roelof Haveman eds) (Antwerp: Intersentia).

——and Holá, B. (2009), *Attributing guilt to and sentencing of various types of perpetrators* (manuscript on file with the author).

Smith, A.M. (2009), AFTER GENOCIDE: BRINGING THE DEVIL TO JUSTICE (Amherst NY: Prometheus Books).

Sowa, T. (2010), *Children and the Liberian Truth and Reconciliation Commission, in* CHILDREN AND TRANSITIONAL JUSTICE: TRUTH-TELLING, ACCOUNTABILITY AND RECONCILIATION 193 (UNICEF Innocenti Research Centre and Human Rights Program at Harvard Law School, Sharanjeet Parmar, Mindy Jane Roseman, Saudamini Siegrist, and Theo Sowa eds) (Cambridge: Harvard University Press).

Spiga, V. (2010), *Indirect Victims' Participation in the* Lubanga *Trial*, 8 JOURNAL OF INTERNATIONAL CRIMINAL JUSTICE 183.

Statute of the Special Court for Sierra Leone, U.N-Sierra Leone (January 16, 2002), 2178 U.N.T.S. 145.

Steinberg, L. and Scott, E. S. (2003), *Less Guilty by Reason of Adolescence: Developmental Immaturity, Diminished Responsibility, and the Juvenile Death Penalty*, 58 AMERICAN PSYCHOLOGIST 1009.

Strange, H. (June 16, 2008), *Inside the RUF: at last the child soldiers of Sierra Leone have their say*, LONDON TIMES, *available at* <http://www.timesonline.co.uk/tol/news/world/africa/article4129610.ece> (visited on August 24, 2011).

Summerfield, D. (2000), *Childhood, War, Refugeedom and 'Trauma': Three Core Questions for Mental Health Professionals*, 37(3) TRANSCULTURAL PSYCHIATRY 417.

T v. UK; V. v. UK, 30 EHRR 121 (2000).

Theidon, K. (2006), *Justice in Transition: The Micropolitics of Reconciliation in Postwar Peru*, 50(3) JOURNAL OF CONFLICT RESOLUTION 433.

Theidon, K. (2007), *Transitional Subjects: The Disarmament, Demobilization and Reintegration of Former Combatants in Colombia*, 1 INTERNATIONAL JOURNAL OF TRANSITIONAL JUSTICE 66.

Timberg, C. (March 26, 2008), *Sierra Leone Special Court's Narrow Focus*, WASHINGTON POST at A11, *available at* <http://www.washingtonpost.com/wp-dyn/content/article/2008/03/25/AR2008032503156.html> (visited on August 24, 2011).

Tokar, C. (2006), *Indigenous Protections of Children in Armed Conflict: Observations from Sierra Leone and Liberia, in* CHILDREN AND WAR: IMPACT, PROTECTION AND REHABILITATION, PHASE II: PROTECTION 19, *available at* <http://www.arts.ualberta.ca/childrenandwar/papers/Children_and_War_Phase_II_Report.pdf> (visited on September 17, 2011).

Truth & Reconciliation Commission, Sierra Leone (2004a), TRUTH AND RECONCILIATION COMMISSION REPORT FOR THE CHILDREN OF SIERRA LEONE (Child-Friendly Version), *available at* <http://www.unicef.org/infobycountry/files/TRCCF9SeptFINAL.pdf> (visited on September 3, 2011).

——(2004b), WITNESS TO TRUTH: REPORT OF THE SIERRA LEONE TRUTH & RECONCILIATION COMMISSION, Volume 3B, Chapter 4 (Children and the Armed Conflict in Sierra Leone), *available at* <http://www.sierra-leone.org/Other-Conflict/TRCVolume3B.pdf> (visited on September 3, 2011).

UN General Assembly Resolution S-27/2, *A world fit for children*, Annex (October 11, 2002).

UNICEF (2002), ADULT WARS, CHILD SOLDIERS: VOICES OF CHILDREN INVOLVED IN ARMED CONFLICT IN THE EAST ASIA AND PACIFIC REGION, *available at* <http://www.unicef.org/sowc06/pdfs/pub_adultwars_en.pdf> (visited on September 3, 2011).

UNICEF Innocenti Research Centre in cooperation with the International Center for Transitional Justice (2010), CHILDREN AND TRUTH COMMISSIONS (Florence: UNICEF).

United Nations Convention on the Rights of the Child, G.A. Res. 44/25, Annex, U.N. Doc. A/RES/44/25 (November 20, 1989) (entered into force September 2, 1990).

United Nations Department of Public Information, Press Conference on Security Council Resolution on Children and Armed Conflict (August 4, 2009), *available at* <http://www.un.org/News/briefings/docs//2009/090804_1882.doc.htm> (visited on September 17, 2011).

United Nations Guidelines for the Prevention of Juvenile Delinquency (The Riyadh Guidelines), G.A. Res. 45/112, Annex, U.N. Doc. A/RES/45/112 (December 14, 1990).

United Nations Rules for the Protection of Juveniles Deprived of their Liberty (Havana Rules), G.A. Res. 45/113, Annex, U.N. Doc. A/RES/45/113 (December 14, 1990).

United Nations Standard Minimum Rules for the Administration of Juvenile Justice, G.A. Res. 40/33, U.N. Doc. A/RES/40/33 (November 29, 1985).

United Nations Transitional Administration in East Timor (UNTAET) Regulation No. 2000/30 on Transitional Rules of Criminal Procedure (September 25, 2000), *available at* <http://www.eastimorlawjournal.org/UNTAETLaw/Regulations/Reg2000-30.pdf> (visited on September 17, 2011).

United Nations War Crimes Commission, LAW REPORTS OF TRIALS OF WAR CRIMINALS, Vol. I (1947).

United Nations War Crimes Commission, LAW REPORTS OF TRIALS OF WAR CRIMINALS, Vol. IX (1949).

United States of America v. Abduwali Abdukhadir Muse, Complaint (April 21, 2009).

Utas, M. (2003), SWEET BATTLEFIELDS: YOUTH AND THE LIBERIAN CIVIL WAR (Stockholm: Lindblom & Co.).

——(2004), *Fluid Research Fields: Studying Excombatant Youth in the Aftermath of the Liberian Civil War*, in CHILDREN AND YOUTH ON THE FRONT LINE: ETHNOGRAPHY, ARMED CONFLICT AND DISPLACEMENT 209 (Jo Boyden and Joanna de Berry eds) (New York: Berghahn Books).

——(2005a), *Agency of Victims: Young Women in the Liberian Civil War*, in MAKERS & BREAKERS: CHILDREN & YOUTH IN POSTCOLONIAL AFRICA 53 (Alcinda Honwana and Filip de Boeck eds) (Trenton: Africa World Press).

——(2005b), *Victimcy, Girlfriending, Soldiering: Tactic Agency in a Young Woman's Social Navigation of the Liberian War Zone*, 78(2) ANTHROPOLOGICAL QUARTERLY 403.

Van Schaack, B. (2008), *Crimen Sine Lege: Judicial Lawmaking at the Intersection of Law and Morals*, 97 GEORGETOWN LAW JOURNAL 119.

Veale, A. (2003), FROM CHILD SOLDIER TO EX-FIGHTER: FEMALE FIGHTERS, DEMOBILISATION AND REINTEGRATION IN ETHIOPIA (Pretoria: Institute for Security Studies, Monograph 85).

——(2006), *The Criminal Responsibility of Former Child Soldiers: Contributions from Psychology*, in INTERNATIONAL CRIMINAL ACCOUNTABILITY AND THE RIGHTS OF CHILDREN 97 (Karin Arts and Vesselin Popovski eds) (The Hague: Hague Academic Press).

——and Stavrou, A. (2007), *Former Lord's Resistance Army Child Soldier Abductees: Explorations of Identity in Reintegration and Reconciliation*, 13(3) PEACE AND CONFLICT: JOURNAL OF PEACE PSYCHOLOGY 273.

Vilmer, J. (2009), RÉPARER L'IRRÉPARABLE: LES RÉPARATIONS AUX VICTIMES DEVANT LA COUR PÉNALE INTERATIONALE (Paris: PUF).

Waddell, N. and Clark, P. (2008), *Introduction*, in COURTING CONFLICT? JUSTICE, PEACE, AND THE ICC IN AFRICA 7 (Nicholas Waddell and Phil Clark eds) (London: Royal African Society).

WAR CHILD (2008) (documentary film, dir./prod. Karim Chrobog).

Weinstein, H. M. and Stover, E. (2004), *Introduction: conflict, justice, and reclamation*, in MY NEIGHBOR, MY ENEMY: JUSTICE AND COMMUNITY IN THE AFTERMATH OF MASS ATROCITY 1 (Eric Stover and Harvey M. Weinstein eds) (Cambridge: Cambridge University Press).

Weiser, B. (February 13, 2011), *Leniency of Sentence for Somali Hijacker Is at Issue*, N.Y. TIMES, *available at* <http://www.nytimes.com/2011/02/14/nyregion/14pirate.html> (visited on August 24, 2011).

——(April 21, 2009), *Pirate Suspect Charged as Adult in New York*, N.Y. TIMES, *available at* <http://www.nytimes.com/2009/04/22/nyregion/22pirate.html?pagewanted=all> (visited on August 24, 2011).

Werle, G. (2009), PRINCIPLES OF INTERNATIONAL CRIMINAL LAW (2nd edn) (The Hague: TMC Asser Press).

Wessells, M. (2004), *Psychosocial Issues in Reintegrating Child Soldiers*, 37 CORNELL INTERNATIONAL LAW JOURNAL 513.

——(2006), CHILD SOLDIERS: FROM VIOLENCE TO PROTECTION (first paperback 2009) (Cambridge: Harvard University Press).

West, H. G. (2004), *Girls with Guns: Narrating the Experience of War of FRELIMO's 'Female Detachment'*, in CHILDREN AND YOUTH ON THE FRONT LINE: ETHNOGRAPHY, ARMED CONFLICT AND DISPLACEMENT 105 (Jo Boyden and Joanna de Berry eds) (New York: Berghahn Books).

Wierda, M., STOCKTAKING: COMPLEMENTARITY, ICTJ Briefing, The Rome Statute Review Conference (June 2010, Kampala), *available at* <http://ictj.org/sites/default/files/ICTJ-RSRC-Global-Complementarity-Briefing-2010-English.pdf> (visited on August 24, 2011).

Williamson, J. (2006), *The disarmament, demobilization and reintegration of child soldiers: social and psychological transformation in Sierra Leone*, 4(3) INTERVENTION 185.

Wills, S. (2009), PROTECTING CIVILIANS: THE OBLIGATIONS OF PEACEKEEPERS (Oxford: Oxford University Press).

Wilson, R. A. (2001), *Children and War in Sierra Leone: A West African Diary*, 17(5) ANTHROPOLOGY TODAY 20.

WIT LICHT (2008, recut as THE SILENT ARMY, dir. Jean van de Velde).

Written Submissions of the United Nations Special Representative of the Secretary-General on Children and Armed Conflict, Prosecutor v. Lubanga, Case No. ICC-01/04-01/06, Annex A (March 18, 2008).

Index